KRISHNA
POCKET GUIDE

Conceived and Compiled
by
Bhakta Vijai
Assisted by Isvara Dasa

Project Consultant and Publisher: Isvara Dasa

Touchstone Media

Krishna Pocket Guide
Conceived and Compiled by Bhakta Vijai
Assisted by Isvara dasa

Consultant and Publisher: Isvara dasa
Edited by Isodyana dasi

1st Edition (March 2001) 2000 copies
2nd Edition (June 2001)   2000 copies
3rd Edition (April 2003) 3000 copies

ISBN 81-87897-12-0

Printed in India

Acknowledgements

I thank His Divine Grace A.C. Bhaktivedanta Swami Prabhupada for his inspiring and authoritative books on Vedic knowledge which he presented to the English-speaking world. His books, in turn, catalysed me to take up the task of writing this book as part of the wider preaching program that he always wanted. I used his books as references and extensively quoted from them.

I thank Isvara Dasa and his team for their generous help in getting the book to its final shape and destination in spite of their busy schedule. They helped in the process of typing, editing, proofreading, advising, necessary additions, copywriting, advertising, printing and distribution.

Dedication

This book is dedicated to His Divine Grace A.C. Bhaktivedanta Swami Prabhupada, who single-handedly planted the seed of Krishna's love in the hearts of millions in the Western world. His name will be heard far and wide for many thousands of years to come.

Hare Krishna!

Contents

KRISHNA'S QUALITIES

In the Bible, Jesus Christ prayed to the father who is in heaven, hallowed (holy) is His name. In the immortal Bhagavad-gita, Lord Krishna made the declaration that He is the seed-giving father of all that be. He is the basis of everything. Everything rests on Him as pearls are strung on tread. The same Lord Krishna is known, all over the world in varieties of different cultures and in varieties of different languages as Jehovah, Allah, Adonai, Dieu, Vishnu, Rama, Olorun, etc. Lord Krishna Himself says, "There is no one equal to or above Me, I am in everything and everything is in Me, I am the cause of all causes."

Who is Krishna?

- Krishna is the Supreme God, *param brahma*.
- Krishna is the source of all that exists.
- Krishna is the beginning, middle, and the end.

1

- Krishna is unborn, *ajam*.
- Krishna is the cause of all that is, that was, or that will ever be.
- Krishna is complete, *purnam*.

Why is Krishna Attractive?

Because Krishna possesses all the six opulence in unlimited degree.

- All wealth
- All power
- All fame
- All beauty
- All wisdom
- All renunciation

Where does Krishna Live?

- Krishna lives in Goloka Vrindavana, in the unlimited spiritual cosmos, as Krishna Himself.
- Krishna as the four-handed Narayana, lives in the Vaikuntha planets, in the unlimited spiritual cosmos, which surrounds Goloka Vrindavana.

- Krishna expands Himself as Maha-Vishnu and creates the limited material cosmos.
- Krishna enters each and every universe as Garbhodakasayi Vishnu and maintains them.
- Krishna enters each and every living and non-living, moving or non-moving body as Ksirodakasayi Vishnu and maintains them.

When does Krishna Incarnate?

Krishna incarnates whenever and wherever there is a decline in religious principles and a predominant rise in irreligion. At that times He incarnates to protect the devotees and annihilate the miscreants, millennium after millennium.

Krishna descends to Earth, once in a day of Brahma, or every 8.6 billion years.

Krishna's Various Names and Their Meanings

- Krishna - The Supreme all-attractive form of Godhead.
- Parthasarathi – The charioteer of Arjuna.

- Vasudeva – The son of Vasudeva.
- Devakinandana - The son of Mother Devaki.
- Nandanandana - The son of Nanda Maharaja.
- Yashodanandana - The son of Mother Yashoda.
- Madhusudhana - The of the demon Madhu.
- Narayana - The shelter of all human beings.
- Govinda – The giver of pleasure to cows and senses.
- Keshava - The killer of Kesi demon.
- Madhava - The husband of the Goddess of Fortune.
- Ranchor - The one who fled from fighting .
- Janardhana - The maintainer of all living entities.
- Lakshmipathi - The husband of Goddess Lakshmi
- Hrishikesa - The owner of all senses.
- Mukunda - The giver of liberation.
- Damodara - One who was bound by ropes through His belly.
- Hari - He takes away all distress .
- Acyuta - One who never falls down.
- Ajita – The unconquerable.
- Yogeshwara - master of mystic powers.
- Jagatpati - The master of the cosmic manifestation.
- Yadunandana - The son of the Yadu dynasty.

- Brahmanya-deva - He is worshipped by all brahmins .
- Jananivasa - He is present in everyone's heart.
- Vamana – The drawf-incarnation, who taught a lesson to King Bali.
- Trinayana – The seer of the three worlds.
- Shripati –The husband of the Goddess of Fortune Laksmi.
- Sankarshan – The Supreme shelter and attractor of all living entities.

What are Krishna's Transcendental Qualities?

- Never pollutes.
- Never dies.
- Never ages.
- Never laments.
- Never becomes hungry or thirsty.
- Never unlawful. All His actions are correct.
- Never changes. He is firm in His decisions.

Who are the Ten Major Incarnations of Krishna?

- The fish protected all species of life by navigating their ship to safety during universal cyclone.
- The tortoise helped in the churning of the universal ocean by carrying and balancing Mount Meru on its back, as the demigods and demons pulled the celestial serpent Vasuki.
- The boar saved planet earth by repositioning it back into its original orbit after it was displaced by the demon Hiranyaksha.
- The half lion and half human form saved His dear devotee Prahlada from the clutches of his demonic father Hiranyakashipu.
- The dwarf taught lesson to King Bali, by occupying all the universal space in three steps.
- Parasurama, killed demonic kings of the world twenty-one times.
- Lord Rama killed King Ravana, the kidnapper of His wife.
- Krishna Himself, in His original form, conducted His pastimes and rid the earth of bad people.

- Lord Buddha saved Vedic religion from contamination of human and animal killing.
- Kalki, yet to come at the end of Kaliyuga, to destroy all demoniac people.

What did Krishna Teach and to Whom?

Krishna taught the science of Bhagavad-gita:
- To the sun-god Vivasvan, hundreds of millions of years ago. The sun-god taught it to Manu, the father of mankind two millions years ago. Manu taught it to Iksvaku, the emperor of Earth, at that time.
- To His friend Arjuna, 5100 years ago.

Krishna Taught the Science of the Vedas:
- To Brahma, during the time of creation, 151 trillion years ago.
- To Vyasadeva, 5000 years ago.

Who is Krishna's Immediate Expansion?

Krishna's immediate expansion is Baladeva.

The quadruple expansions of Baladeva are:
- Vasudeva (Soul).
- Sankarshan (Ego).
- Pradyumna (Mind).
- Aniruddha (Intelligence).

Sankarshan expanded into Narayana.

The quadruple expansions of Narayana are:
- Vasudeva (Soul).
- Sankarshan (Ego).
- Pradyumna (Mind).
- Aniruddha (Intelligence).

SANKARSHAN
↓
KARANODAKASAYI VISHNU
↓
GARBHODAKASAYI VISHNU
↓
BRAHMA
↓ ↓
NARADA FOUR KUMARAS MARICI SHIVA

Krishna is the Reservoir Of:

- Truth - *sac*.
- Knowledge - *cid*.
- Bliss - *ananda*.
- Personality - *vigraha*.

Krishna in His Vishnu Form Carries:

- *Sankha* - conchshell.
- *Gada* - club.
- *Kamala* - lotus flower.
- *Chakra* - blazing disk.

KRISHNA ON EARTH

Krishna's Age-Wise Acts

- At 1 month old, He killed Putana.
- At 3 months old, He killed Sakatasura.
- At 1 year old, He killed Trinavarta.
- At 2 years old He killed Vatsasura.
- At 4 years old, He killed Bakasura.
- At 5 years old, Aghasura.
- At 6 years old, He killed Dhenukasura.
- At 7 years old, He lifted Govardhana hill.
- At 8 years old, He performed the rasa dance.
- At 12 years old, He killed Kamsa.

When did Krishna Last Come to Earth and His Activities?

- Krishna appeared 5000 years ago.
- Krishna appeared into the Yadu dynasty.
- Krishna appeared as the son of Devaki and Vasudeva.
- Krishna appeared in Mathura.
- Krishna was raised by Yashoda Mata and Nanda Maharaja.
- Krishna spent His childhood in Vrindavana.
- Krishna spent His adulthood in Mathura.
- Krishna accepted 16,108 wives.
- Krishna begot 161,080 sons.
- Krishna ruled over the Bhoja, Vrishni, and Andhaka dynasties.
- Krishna helped the Pandavas in regaining their kingdom, which was deceitfully usurped in a game of dice, by the Kauravas.
- Krishna lived on Earth for 125 years.

How to Identify Krishna?

- Krishna possesses nineteen auspicious markings on His lotus feet.

- Krishna plays His celestial flute.
- Krishna balances His body on His left leg and rests His right leg in front.
- Krishna's eyes are like rose petals.
- Krishna is ever youthful.
- Krishna's bodily complexion is that of the color of the new rain-cloud - bluish and blackish.
- Krishna has a peacock feather in His crown.
- Krishna has the *Shrivatsa* (white tuft of hair) symbol on His chest.
- Krishna wears the *Kaustubha* jewel around His neck.
- Krishna wears the *Vaijayanti* garland which extends from His neck to His knees.
- Krishna wears yellow garments.

Krishna Killed Demons Like:

- Putana - came under the pretext of breast-feeding Krishna to poison Him.
- Trinavarta - came as a whirlwind to steal Krishna.
- Vatsasura - came as a calf to kill Krishna.
- Bakasura - came as a gigantic bird to punch Krishna.

- Aghasura - came as a huge snake to devour Krishna
- Dhenukasura - came as a donkey to kick Krishna.
- Sakatasura - came as a food cart to rundown Krishna.
- Sankhasura - came as a rich man to kidnap the *gopis*.
- Aristasura - came as a big bull and charged at Krishna.
- Kesi - came as a horse to kick Krishna.
- Vyomasura - came as sky demon to kidnap the cowherd boys.
- Kuvalayapida - came as an elephant to trample Krishna and Balarama.
- Canura, Mustika, Sala, Kuta, Tosala - tried to strangle Krishna and Balarama in a wrestling match, but were all killed by Krishna and Balarama.
- Kamsa –Krishna's maternal uncle, tried to kill Krishna and Balarama, in various ways.
- Pancajana - had the body of a conchshell and killed Sandipani Muni's son by swallowing him.
- Kamsa's Washerman - insulted and spoke ill of Krishna and His cowherd boys and relatives.
- Satadhanava - stole the Syamantaka-mani (jewel) and killed King Satrajit.

- Mura - the five-headed demon, who tried to charge at Krishna with his trident.
- Narakasura - kidnapped 16,000 maiden princesses.
- Banasura - the thousand-handed demon, who captured Aniruddha, was defeated and 996 of his arms were cut off.
- Paundraka - the impostor of Vasudeva.
- Kasiraja - Paundraka's friend, and attacked Krishna.
- Sudaksina - created the demon Daksinagi to kill Krishna, but was himself killed by the demon due to Krishna's tactics.
- Sisupala - insulted Krishna during the Rajasuya-yajna, and after the hundredth insult, was beheaded by Krishna with His Sudarshan chakra.
- Salva - King of Sauba attacked Dwarka for twenty-seven days with his flying spaceship.
- Dantavakra - King of Karusa.
- Viduratha - was also beheaded by Krishna by His Sudharshana chakra.
- Vrkasura (Bhasmasura) - tried to kill Lord Shiva, Krishna indirectly got him killed by acting as an intelligent young and beautiful brahmin boy.

What Miracles did Krishna Perform?

- Lifted Govardhana hill for seven days.
- Replaced all the cowherd boys and calf's when Brahma stole them.
- Delivered Nalakuvara & Manigriva who were cursed to be born in the form of trees.
- Subdued the giant Kaliya snake.
- Swallowed the forest fire.
- Got His father released from the clutches of Varunadeva.
- Liberated Vidyadhara, who came as a snake and tried to swallow Nanda Maharaja.
- Showed Vishnuloka within the River Yamuna to His uncle Akrura.
- Gave benediction of *sarupya mukti* to a tailor for his services.
- Gave benediction of eternal devotional service to a florist for his two flower garlands.
- Transformed a hunchback woman into a most beautiful woman in return for her sandalwood pulp.
- Broke the huge bow of Kamsa into two pieces at the Dhanur-*yajna*, when He pulled and tied the string to the bow.
- Brought His spiritual master's son back to life,

- by ordering the superintendent of death, Yamaraja, to reverse the death process.
- Defeated Jarasandha and his army seventeen times.
- Indirectly killed Kalayavana, during a war.
- Jumped along with Balarama eighty-eight miles from the top of a mountain to avoid a forest fire.
- Mucukunda was delivered from his eternal sleep and was benedicted with devotional service.
- Protected His ten-day old son, Pradyumna, when he was kidnapped and thrown into the river by Sambara who wanted to kill him.
- Defeated the gorilla king Jambavan after continuously fighting for twenty-eight days without getting tired.
- Married 16,108 girls and bestows upon them economical, moral, and spiritual strengths.
- Spent His time and energy with each one, by expanding into 16,108 Krishnas.
- Defeated King Indra and brought the flowering *parijata* tree from heaven to earth to please His wife Satyabhama.
- Liberated King Nrga from the form of a lizard by touching him.
- Brought the assembly hall of the demigods, called Sudharma, to Dwaraka.

- Saved Pariksit in the womb of his mother, Uttara, when she was struck by Aswatthama.
- Brought back to life the six dead children of mother Devaki, from the Sutala planetary system ruled by Maharaja Bali.
- Krishna helped Arjuna bring back the dead children of a Brahmin from Maha-Vishnu, to save Arjuna from suicide for failing to protect the life of the Brahmin's son.

The Names of Krishna's Horses and Charioteer

Commander-in-chief of the Yadu army:
- Yuyudhana or Satyaki.

Charioteer's name:
- Daruka.

Four horses names and colors:
- Saibya - greenish.
- Sugriva - greyish.
- Meghapuspa - bluish.
- Balahaka - ash shade.

What Is Krishna's Paraphernalia Called?

- Krishna's conchshell - Panchajanya.
- Krishna's bow - Sarnga.
- Krishna's club - Kamodaki.

Krishna's Mercy!

- Played flute for Radharani and the *gopis*.
- Ate the food offered by the brahmins' wives.
- Got the residents of Vrindavan to worship Govardhana hill.
- Conducted the *rasa* dance when He was eight years old.
- Gave respect and material opulence to His poor friend Sudama.
- Krishna instigated His friend Arjuna in kidnapping His sister Subhadra, knowing their love for each other.
- Krishna gave liberation to King Bahulasva, the King of Mithila and to Srutadeva, a Brahmin, at the same time, after they served Him with love and affection.

SRIMATI RADHARANI

Who is Krishna's Internal Potency and Constant Companion?

Srimati Radharani is Krishna's internal potency. Krishna enjoys Himself only through His special expansion in the form of Srimati Radharani.

What are Srimati Radharani's Special Attributes?

- The glories of Lord Krishna's name, fame and qualities are always inundating Her speech.
- Srimati Radharani induces Krishna to drink the honey of the conjugal relationship.
- She is engaged in satisfying all the transcendental lusty desires of Krishna.
- Srimati Radharani is a mine filled with valuable jewels of love for Krishna.
- Her transcendental body is complete with unparalleled spiritual qualities.
- Srimati Radharani's hair is very curly.

- Her two eyes are always moving to and fro.
- All transcendental qualities are manifested only in Srimati Radharani.
- She alone is able to fulfill all the desires of Krishna.
- Satyabhama, one of the queens of Lord Krishna, desires the fortunate position and excellent qualities of Srimati Radharani.
- All the *gopis* learn the art of dressing from Srimati Radharani.
- The goddess of fortune, Laksmi, and the wife of Lord Siva, Parvati, desire Her beauty and qualities.
- Arundhati, the celebrated chaste wife of Vasistha, also wants to imitate the chastity and religious principles of Srimati Radharani.
- If even Lord Krishna Himself cannot reach the limit of the transcendental qualities of Srimati Radharani, what to talk of any insignificant living entity?
- Srimati Radharani is the goddess of devotion.
- Srimati Radharani is the origin of love of Krishna.
- Srimati Radharani is the most dear friend of Krishna

**Supreme Lord Krishna and
His Pleasure Potency, Srimati Radharani**

How Many Times did Krishna Expand Himself?

- First, when Lord Brahma stole the cowherd boys and their calves for one year.
- Second, when He married 16,000 wives at the same time, to satisfy their love, affection, and attention.
- Third, when Krishna and the sages met both King Bahulasva and the Brahmin, Srutadeva, at the same time.

Krishna's Contradictions!

- Stealing the *gopis* dresses - giving unlimited saris to Draupadi.
- Stealing butter - giving unlimited food to the devotees.
- Lifting Govardhana hill - even though He was a child.
- Attracting the fair complexioned *gopis* - even though He has a darkish hue.
- Indirectly killing all the opposing armies - even though He was a charioteer.

Krishna's Sublime Teachings

- Milk should first be given to the calves and then to humans.
- Butter and yogurt should first be given to children, then to adults, and then for sale.
- Worship only Him and not demigods.
- Women should be protected. He upheld the dignity of the 16,000 kidnapped damsels by freeing them and then marrying them.
- He reciprocates with His devotees. He honoured the love of Rukmini by escorting her to safety and then marrying her.

What Did Narada See in the Various Palaces of Dwarka, When Krishna Expanded Himself?

- Krishna was resting on a bed, fanned by Rukmini.
- Krishna was playing chess with Satyabhama.
- Krishna was petting His small children.
- Krishna was participating in a sacrifice.
- Krishna was feeding brahmins and the poor.

- Krishna was practicing sword fighting.
- Krishna was riding horses.
- Krishna was in a meeting with His ministers.
- Krishna was giving spiritual advice to devotees.
- Krishna was swimming in a pool.
- Krishna was joking and laughing with friends.
- Krishna was meditating.
- Krishna was conducting welfare activities.
- Krishna was supervising the construction of temples and monastries.
- Krishna was reciting the Vedas and *Puranas*.
- Krishna was serving the elderly and old people.

What did Krishna Steal?

- Krishna stole milk.
- Krishna stole butter.
- Krishna stole yogurt.
- Krishna stole the *gopis'* dresses.
- Krishna stole the *gopis'* heart.

KRISHNA'S FAMILY AND FRIENDS

Krishna's Family Trees

KRISHNA & RUKMINI
↓
PRADYUMNA & RUKMAVATI
↓
ANIRUDDHA & USA
↓
VAJRA
↓
PRATIBAHU → SUBALA → SANTASENA → SATASENA

Arjuna's Family Trees

ARJUNA & SUBADRA
↓
ABHIMANYU & UTTARA
↓
PARIKSIT

Who is More Dear to Krishna Among the Thousands of Gopis?

- There are 16,108 predominant gopis.
- Of these, 108 are more prominent ones.
- Of these, eight are special.
- Of these, Lalita, Vishaka, Candravali and Radharani are close to Krishna.
- And the topmost is Radharani, who is the pleasure potency of the Supreme God Krishna.

Who are the Six Dead Children of Mother Devaki?

In the millennium of Svayambhuva Manu, Prajapati Marici begot six sons in the womb of his wife Urna. The six sons became demigods. Later they were cursed to be born to the demon King Hiranyakasipu. And in this millennium of Vaivasvata Manu, they were born to mother Devaki, and after being killed by Kamsa, they were born in the Sutala planetary system ruled by Bali Maharaja. After being brought back to life by Krishna to please His mother, the six sons went back to the higher planetary system to become demigods again.

The six sons were:

- Smara
- Udgitha
- Parisvanga
- Patanga
- Ksudrabhri
- Ghrini

Who were Krishna's Eight Most Prominent Wives?

- Rukmini, Krishna's first wife, was the daughter of Bishmaka, the King of Vidarbha.

- Jambavati was His second wife, and the daughter of Jambavan, the gorilla king.
- Satyabhama, His third wife, was the daughter of Satrajit.
- Kalindi was the Yamuna River personified.
- Mitravinda was the sister of Vindya and Anuvindya.
- Nagnajiti was the daughter of Nagnajit, the King of Kosala.
- Bhadra was the daughter of Krishna's aunt, Srutakriti.
- Laksmana was the daughter of the King of Madra.

How did Krishna Marry His Eight Prominent Wives?

- Rukmini was kidnapped, at the time of her marriage.
- Jambavati was given in charity by Jambavan.
- Satyabhama was given in charity by Satrajit.
- Kalindi was favoured due to her austerities.
- Mitravinda was kidnapped from the *svayamvara*.
- Nagnajiti was won when Krishna tamed the bulls of King Nagnajit.

- Bhadra was given to Krishna by her brothers.
- Laksmana was taken by Krishna at her *svayamvara*.

How Many Sons of Krishna were Maharathis?

They were sixteen and their names were as follows:
- Pradyumna • Diptiman • Bhanu • Samba
- Madhu • Brhadbhanu • Citrabhanu • Vrka
- Aruna • Puskara • Vedabalu • Srutadeva
- Sunandana • Citrabalu • Virupa • Kavi.

What did Arjuna see at the Place of Maha-Vishnu?

- Laksmi - the goddess of fortune, on His chest.
- Ananta - the celestial snake bedrest of Maha-Vishnu, who carries the material cosmos on His billion hoods.
- Chakra - the celestial weapon of Maha-Vishnu.
- Pusti - the energy of nourishment.
- Sri - the energy of beauty.
- Kirti - the energy of reputation.
- Aja - the energy of material creation.

What is a Rajasuya Yajna?

When the world was under one government, in order to establish the supremacy of the world, the ruling emperor would send out his commanders to every corner of the earth challenging all other lesser kings. If the lesser king challenged any of the emperor's commander, then a war would take place. If no one challenged the emperor, then the emperor would proceed to perform the sacrifice establishing his supremacy on the planet.

During the Rajasuya Yajna Who Conquered Who?

- Sahadeva - with the help of the Srinjaya tribe reconquered the south of Bharat (India), including Sri Lanka.
- Nakula - with the help of Matsyadesa reconquered the West of Bharat (India), including Middle-east and Mediterranean countries.
- Arjuna - with the help of Kekayadesa reconquered the north of Bharat (India), including Central Asia and Siberia.

- Bhimasena - with the help of Madradesa reconquered the east of Bharat (India), including China and Southeast Asian countries.

Who were the Great Brahmins and Sages Invited for the Rajasuya Yajna?

Vyasadeva, Bharadvaja, Gautama, Vasistha, Kanva, Kavasa, Visvamitra, Sumati, Paila, Parasara, Garga, Kratu, Jaimini, Vitihotra, Madhucchanda, Virasena, and Akrtavrana, Vanadeva, Trita, Maitreya, Cyavana, Asita, Sumantu, Vaisampayana, Atharva, Kasyapa, Dhaumya, Parasurama, Sukracarya, and Asuri.

During the Rajasuya Yajna Who Was In Charge?

- Bhimasena - kitchen and cooking.
- Duryodhana - treasury.
- Sahadeva - reception.
- Nakula - store.
- Arjuna - comforts of the elderly people.
- Krishna - washing the feet of all the guests.
- Draupadi - catering and food distribution.
- Karna - charity.

Places Chronologically Visited by Lord Balarama

- Forest of Naimisaranya.
- River Kausiki.
- River Sarayu.
- Place Prayaga (Sarasvati, Ganga, Yamuna).
- Place Gandaki.
- River Gomati.
- River Vipasa.
- River Sona.
- Place Gaya (Vishnu temple).
- Delta of Ganga (Ganga sagara).
- Mahendra parvata (met Parasurama).
- River Godavari.
- River Veni (Krishna).
- River Pampa.
- River Bhimarathi (Kartikeya temple).
- Place Sailapura.
- Place Venkatachala.
- Place Vishnukanchi.
- Place Shivakanchi.
- River Kaveri.
- Place Rangaksetra (Vishnu temple).
- Place Madura-Madurai.
- Place Setubandhu(Rameshwaram).

- River Kritamala.
- River Tamraparni.
- Hills of Malaya (met Agastya).
- Kanyakumari.
- Phalgunatirtha (Padmanabha).
- Pancapsara Lake.
- Gokarnatirtha (Shiva temple).
- Island Aryadevi.
- Place Surparaka.
- River Tapi (Tapti).
- River Payosni.
- River Nirvindhya.
- Forest Dandakaranya.
- River Narmada.
- Place Mahismati Puri.
- Place Prabhasatirtha.

MATERIAL LIFE AND OTHER RELATED TOPICS

What is Krishna's Material Energy Made Of?

The gross body and the subtle body are material, not spiritual.

The gross body consists of:
- Earth - *Bhumi*.
- Water - *Varuna*.
- Air - *Vayu*.
- Fire - *Agni*.
- Ether - *Akasha*.

The subtle body consist of:
- Mind - *Manasa*.
- Intelligence - *Buddhi*.
- Ego - *Ahankar*.

What are the Modes of Material Nature?

- The mode of goodness - *sattva guna*.
  Vishnu is in charge of this mode and He maintains the universe.
- The mode of passion - *rajo guna*.
  Brahma is in charge of this mode and he creates the universe.
- The mode of ignorance - *tamo guna*.
  Siva is in charge of this mode and he destroys the universe.

What are the Three Divisions of the Vedas?

- *Karma kanda* - fruitive activities.
- *Jnana kand*a – philosophical speculation.
- *Upasana kanda* - worship.

Which Activities are in the Mode of Goodness?

- Eating foods which increase the duration of one's life, purify one's existence, and give strength, health, happiness and satisfaction. Such foods are juicy, fatty, wholesome, and pleasing to the heart.
- Performing sacrifices according to the direction of the scriptures, as a matter of duty, and without desiring any reward.
- Performing austerities of the body to worship the Supreme Lord, the *brahmins*, the spiritual master, and superiors like the father and mother. And performing austerities of cleanliness, simplicity, celibacy and non-violence. These should be performed in transcendental faith, without expecting material benefits, for the pleasure of the Supreme Lord.
- Performing austerities of speech by speaking words that are truthful, pleasing, beneficial, and not agitating to others, and also by regularly reciting Vedic literature.
- Performing austerities of the mind which result in satisfaction, simplicity, gravity, self-control,

and purification of one's existence.

- Giving in charity, out of duty, without expectation of return, at the proper time and place, and to a worthy person.

- Having knowledge by which the one undivided spiritual nature is seen in all living entities, though they are divided into innumerable forms.

- Doing actions which are regulated and are performed without attachment, without love or hatred, and without desire for fruitive results.

- Performing one's duty without false ego, with great determination and enthusiasm, and without wavering in success or failure.

- Understanding what ought to be done and what ought not to be done, what is to be feared and what is not to be feared, what is binding and what is liberating.

- Having determination which is unbreakable, which is sustained with steadfastness by yoga practice, and which thus controls the activities of the mind, life, and senses.

- Becoming happy even though in the beginning it may be just like poison, but at the end, it is just like nectar, and which awakens one to self-realization.

Which Activities are in
the Mode of Passion?

- Eating foods that are too bitter, too sour, too salty, very hot, pungent, dry, and burning. Such foods cause distress, misery, and disease.
- Performing sacrifices for some material benefit or for the sake of pride.
- Performing austerities out of pride and for the sake of gaining respect, honor, and worship.
- Giving in charity with the expectation of some return, or with a desire for fruitive results, or in a grudging mood.
- Having knowledge by which one sees that in every different body there is a different type of living entity.
- Doing actions which require great effort in order to gratify one's desires.
- Performing one's duty, being attached to work and the fruits of work, desiring to enjoy those fruits, and being greedy, always envious, impure, and moved by joy and sorrow.
- Having determination by which one holds fast to fruitive results in religion, economic development, and sense gratification.
- Enjoying happiness which is derived from

contact of the senses with their objects and which appears like nectar at first but poison at the end.

Which Activities are in the Mode of Ignorance?

- Eating foods which were prepared a long time back, and which are tasteless, decomposed, and putrid.
- Performing sacrifices without regard for the direction of scriptures, without distribution of *prasadam* (spiritual food), without chanting of Vedic hymns or remuneration to the priests, and without faith.
- Performing austerities out of foolishness, with self-torture, or to destroy or injure others.
- Giving in charity in an impure place, at an improper time, to unworthy persons, or without proper attention and respect.
- Having knowledge, by which one is attached to one kind of work as the all in all, without knowledge of the truth, and which is very meager.
- Doing action which is performed in illusion,

in disregard to scriptural injunctions, and concern for future bondage, or which cause violence or distress to others.

- Performing one's duty which is always against the injunctions of the scriptures, by one who is materialistic, obstinate, cheating and expert in insulting others, and who is lazy, always morose, and procrastinating.

- Under the spell of illusion, considering irreligion to be religion and religion to be irreligion, and striving always in the wrong direction.

- Having determination which cannot go beyond dreaming, fearfulness, lamentation, moroseness, and illusion.

- Enjoying happiness which is blind to self-realization, which is delusion from beginning to end, and which arises from sleep, laziness, and illusion.

What are the Four Types of Vedic Marriages?

- Arranged marriage - by the will of the parents and relatives.

- Royal marriage - by the king for his daughter, in which either a contest or choice, or both are involve.
- Gandharva marriage - by mutual selection of the couple.
- Raksasa or demonic marriage - done by either force or intimidation.

What Types of Material Assets does one Desires?

- To have a very good family.
- To be very beautiful.
- To have many riches.
- To be very learned.
- To be in good health.

What are the Five Stages of Realization of the Living Being?

- Annamaya - food, air and water.
- Pranamaya - safety and security.
- Manomaya - mental speculation.
- Vijnanamaya - knowledge acquisition.
- Anandamaya - bliss through devotion.

Which are the
Eight Sense Organs?

Gross sense organs:
- Sense of sight.
- Sense of smell.
- Sense of taste.
- Sense of hearing.
- Sense of touch.

Subtle sense organs:
- Mind.
- Intelligence.
- Ego.

What are the Six Sensory Whips?

- Lamentation.
- Illusion.
- Hunger.
- Infirmity.
- Death.
- Thirst.

What are the Seven Layers of the Body?

- Skin.
- Flesh.
- Bone.
- Muscles.
- Marrow.
- Fat.
- Semen.

What are the Nine Gates of the Body?

- Two eyes.
- Two ears.
- One genital.
- Two nostrils.
- One mouth.
- One rectum.

What are the Airs Existing in the Body?

- Prana.
- Vyana.
- Udana.
- Apana.
- Samana.

What are the Three Gates to Hell?

- Lust.
- Anger.
- Greed.

What are the Four Aspirations of Material life?

- Dharma - righteousness and religion.
- Kama - desires and sense gratification.
- Artha - wealth for self and society.
- Moksha - liberation from birth and death.

What is the Celestial Water Known As?

- Mandakini - in the upper planetary system.
- Ganga - in the middle planetary system.
- Bhogavati - in the lower planetary system.

What are the Twenty-three Fields of Activities?

Five great elements called *mahabutas*:
- Earth.
- Water.
- Fire.
- Air.
- Ether.

Three subtle elements:
- False ego.
- Intelligence.
- Independent mind.

Five acquiring senses:
- Eyes.
- Ears.
- Nose.

- Tongue.
- Skin.

Five working senses:
- Voice.
- Legs.
- Hands.
- Anus.
- Genitals.

Five objects of senses:
- Smell.
- Taste.
- Form.
- Touch.
- Sound.

What are the Six Interactions?

- Consciousness.
- Desire.
- Happiness.
- Convictions.
- Hatred.
- Distress.

What are the Different Worlds Known As?

- Gandharva loka.
- Siddha loka.
- Jana loka.
- Tapa loka.
- Naga loka.
- Yaksa loka.
- Raksasa loka.
- Paksi loka.
- Carana loka.

What are Fourfold Material Miseries of Life?

- *Janma* - birth.
- *Mruthyu* - death.
- *Jara* - old age.
- *Vyadhi* – disease.

What are the Four Defects of Mundane Persons?

- Is sure to commit mistakes.
- Is invariably illusioned.
- Has a natural tendency to cheat.
- Is limited by imperfect senses.

What are the Six Kinds of Aggressors?

- One who gives poison.
- One who sets fire to the house.
- One who attacks with deadly weapons.
- One who plunders riches.
- One who occupies another's land.
- One who kidnaps another's wife.

What are the Six Kinds of Bodily Transformations?

- The body takes its birth.
- The body grows.
- The body produces some effects.

- The body remains for some time.
- The body gradually dwindles.
- The body at last vanishes, death.

What are the Four Acts of Conditioned Life?

- Eating.
- Sleeping.
- Mating.
- Defending.

What are the Four Vices of Conditioned Life?

- Illicit sex.
- Gambling.
- Intoxication
- Meat eating.

What is The Sequence of the Production of Matter?

- First is ether.

- From ether comes air.
- From air comes fire.
- From fire comes water.
- From water comes earth.

How Does One Fall Down into Material Entanglement?

- While contemplating sense objects,
- One develops attachment for them,
- From such attachment comes lust,
- Then anger,
- Then illusion,
- Then bewilderment of memory,
- Then comes loss of intelligence,
- Finally one falls down into the eternal cycle of birth and death.

DEVOTIONAL SERVICE AND OTHER RELATED TOPICS

What Makes the Soul Happy?

- Some think it is capitalism.
- Some think it is communism.
- Some think it is socialism.
- Some think it is securalism.
- Some think it is humanitarism.
- Some think it is nationalism.

The real -ism that makes the soul happy is Krishnaism, meaning awaking the dormant love for Krishna.

What Makes Krishna Happy?

Simply chant with sincerity and offenselessly the Hare Krishna Maha-mantra as many times as possible.

**HARE KRISHNA HARE KRISHNA
KRISHNA KRISHNA HARE HARE
HARE RAMA HARE RAMA
RAMA RAMA HARE HARE**

**HARE KRISHNA HARE KRISHNA
KRISHNA KRISHNA HARE HARE
HARE RAMA HARE RAMA
RAMA RAMA HARE HARE**

**HARE KRISHNA HARE KRISHNA
KRISHNA KRISHNA HARE HARE
HARE RAMA HARE RAMA
RAMA RAMA HARE HARE**

**HARE KRISHNA HARE KRISHNA
KRISHNA KRISHNA HARE HARE
HARE RAMA HARE RAMA
RAMA RAMA HARE HARE**

What did Krishna Ask as an Offering from Devotees?

Krishna states "Whoever offers Me with love and devotion a leaf, a flower, fruit or water, I accept them."

- *Patram* - leaf.
- *Puspam* - flower.
- *Phalam* - fruit.
- *Toyam* - water.

What are the Five Non-devotional Philosophies?

- Mayavadi - Sankaracharya - believe in the impersonal Brahman and the world is false.
- Mimamsakas - Jaimini - believe in pious activities.
- Sankhya - Kapila - believe the world is an \ illusion.
- Buddhism - Gautam Buddha - believe the world is void and try to achieve *nirvana*.
- Paramanuvada - Kanada - believe the world is a combination of atoms.

Who were the Two Kapilas?

- One was born at the time of Svayambhuva Manu.
- The other was born at the time of Vaivasvata Manu (present Manu).

What did Krishna Declare?

- Krishna said to Arjuna "May you declare to the world that My devotees are never vanquished" (Bg.9.31)
- Anyone who quits his body, at the end of his life, remembering Me attains immediately to my nature, and there is no doubt of this (Bg.8.5)
- Of all yogis, the one with great faith who always abides in Me, thinks of Me within himself, and renders transcendental loving service to Me is the most intimately united with Me in yoga and is the highest of all. (Bg 6.47)
- Abandon all varieties of religion and just surrender unto Me. I shall deliver you from all sinful reactions. Do not fear. (Bg 18.66)
- If I specially favour a devotee and especially wish to care for him, the first thing I do is to take away his riches.

- When My devotee is bereft of all material riches and is deserted by his relatives, friends, and family members, because he has no one to look after him, he completely takes shelter of My lotus feet.

- I declare that he who studies this sacred conversation of ours, worships Me by his intelligence, and he who listens with faith and without envy becomes free from sinful reactions and attains to the auspicious planets where the pious dwell. (Bg 18.70-71)

- Even if a nondevotee comes from a brahmin family and is expert in studying the Vedas, he is not very dear to Me, whereas even if a sincere devotee comes from a low born family of meat eaters, he is very dear to Me. Such a sincere pure devotee should be given charity, for he is as worshipable as I.

(*Caitanya-caritamrita*)

In what Forms can One Love Krishna?

- Krishna can be loved as the supreme unknown *santa-rasa*.

- Krishna can be loved as the supreme master - *dasya-rasa*.
- Krishna can be loved as the supreme friend - *sakhya-rasa*.
- Krishna can be loved as the supreme child - *vatsalya-rasa*.
- Krishna can be loved as the supreme lover - *madhurya-rasa*.

What are the Varna and Ashrama Systems?

Varna - means the society is naturally divided into four groups which are:
- *Sudra* - working class.
- *Vaisya* - business class.
- *Kshatriya* - ruling class.
- *Brahmin* - intellectual class.

Ashrama - means the growing phases of individuals in society which are four:
- *Brahmachari* - celibate life.
- *Grihastha* - married life.
- *Vanaprastha* - retired life.
- *Sannyasa* - renounced order of life.

What are the Qualities of the Four Varnas?

- Peacefulness, self-control, austerity, purity, tolerance, honesty, knowledge, wisdom and religiousness are the natural qualities by which the *brahmins* work.
- Heroism, power, determination, resourcefulness, courage in battle, generosity and leadership are the natural qualities by which the *kshatriyas* work.
- Farming, cow protection and business are the natural qualities by which the *vaisyas* work.
- Labour and service to others are the natural qualities by which the *sudras* work.

What Types of Yoga are there?

- *Bhakti yoga* - devotional service.
- *Jnana yoga* - acquiring knowledge.
- *Dhyana yoga* - meditation.
- *Karma yoga* - doing one's duty.

What are Accepted as Vedas and Upanishads?

- Sama Veda.
- Rig Veda.
- Yajur Veda.
- Atharva Veda.
- Ramayan.
- Mahabharat.
- Srimad Bhagavatam.
- Svetasvara Upanishad.
- Brahma samhita.
- Vishnu Purana.
- Garuda Purana.
- Katha Upanishad.

Who are the Seven Mothers?

- The real mother.
- The wife of one's guru or teacher.
- The wife of the king or ruler.
- The wife of a *brahmin* or priest.
- The cow because she gives milk.
- The nurse or baby sitter.
- Mother earth because she gives food grains.

What are the Seven Brahminical Qualities?

- Truthfulness.
- Self-control.
- Purity.
- Controlling the senses.
- Simplicity.
- Full knowledge.
- Engagement in devotional service.

What Types of Loving Exchanges are There?

- One who reciprocates as much as he gets from his or her lover.
- One who reciprocates in spite of getting no reciprocation of love from his or her lover.
- One who is neutral to the loving gestures of his or her lover because he has fixed his heart, mind, and body on the Supreme God Krishna. He is called *atmarama*.
- One who is neutral to the loving gestures of his or her lover because he is callous and ungrateful. He is called *gurudruhah*.

What are the Nine Devotional Services?

- *Sravanam* - hearing.
- *Kirtanam* - chanting.
- *Smaranam* - remembering.
- *Pada-sevanam* – serving the lotus feet.
- *Arcanam* - worshiping.
- *Vandanam* - praying.
- *Dasyam* - offering service.
- *Sakhyam* - friendship.
- *Atma-nivedanam* – self surrender.

What are the Thirteen Locations for Vaisnava Tilaka and their Symbolic Representations?

- Forehead - Keshava.
- Belly - Narayana.
- Chest - Madhava.
- Throat - Govinda.
- Right waist - Vishnu.
- Right forearm - Madhusudhana.
- Right shoulder - Trivikrama.

- Left waist - Vamadeva.
- Left forearm - Shridhara.
- Left shoulder - Hrisikesh.
- Upper back - Padmanabha.
- Lower back - Damodara.
- Top of head - Vasudeva.

What are the Qualities of Divine Nature?

- Fearlessness.
- Charity.
- Self-control.
- Austerity.
- Fortitude.
- Cleanliness.
- Gentleness.
- Modesty.
- Simplicity.
- Nonviolence.
- Truthfulness.
- Renunciation.
- Tranquility.
- Vigor.
- Forgiveness.

- Determination.
- Purification of one's existence.
- Cultivation of spiritual knowledge.
- Performance of sacrifice.
- Study of the Vedas.
- Freedom from anger.
- Aversion to fault finding.
- Compassion for all living entities.
- Freedom from covetousness.
- Freedom from envy.
- Freedom from the passion for honor.

What are the Qualities of Demoniac Nature?

- Pride.
- Arrogance.
- Conceit.
- Unclean work.
- Untruthful.
- Insatiable lust.
- Anger.
- Harshness.
- Ignorance.

- False ego.

- False prestige.
- No intelligence.
- Angry.
- Illusioned.
- Self-complacent.
- Impudent.
- Deluded by wealth.
- Does not know the aim of life.
- Improper behavior.
- Say the world is unreal and false.
- Say the world has no control by god.
- Say the world is produced by sex desire.
- Attracted by the impermanent.
- Attracted by sense gratification.
- Secure money by illegal means.
- Perplexed by anxieties.
- Take pleasure in physical and mental strength.
- Engage in unbeneficial, unethical, and horrible works, meant to destroy the world.
- Does not follow rules and regulations of sacrifice.
- Envious of the Supreme Personality of Godhead, Krishna.
- Blaspheme real religion (*sanatana dharma*).

What are Siddhis (Mystic Perfections)?

- *Mahima siddhi* - one can expand.
- *Anima siddhi* - one can contract.
- *Laghima siddhi* - one can become light.
- *Prapti siddhi* - one can get what he wants.
- *Isitva siddhi* - to appear & disappear at will.
- *Vasita siddhi* - can influence anyone.

What are the Four Types of Brahmacaris?

- *Savitra*—upholds celibacy for three days.
- *Prajapatya*—upholds celibacy for one year.
- *Brahma*—upholds celibacy till the end of one's education.
- *Naisthika*—upholds celibacy for one's whole life.

What are the Main Vaisnava Sects?

- Madhva Sampradaya—from Madhvacharya.
- Ramanuja Sampradaya—from Ramanujacharya.

- Visnusvami Sampradaya—from Visnu Swami.
- Nimbarka Sampradaya—from Nimbarka.

What are the Four Tasks of a Devotee Family?

- Chant, alone or in a group, the *Hare Krishna Mahamantra*.
- Eat or distribute the remnants of *prasadam* or food offered to Lord Krishna.
- Discuss or read or preach the teachings of *Bhagavad-gita* and *Srimad Bhagavatam*.
- Do Deity worship and offer prayers to Lord Krishna and His devotees.

What are the Five Topics of Bhagavad-gita?

- *Isvara*, the supreme controller.
- *Jivas*, the controlled living entities.
- *Prakrti*, material nature.
- *Kala*, eternal time.
- *Karma*, activity.

What Is Complete Knowledge?

- Humility.
- Pridelessness.
- Nonviolence.
- Tolerance.
- Simplicity.
- Cleanliness.
- Steadiness.
- Self-control.
- Detachment.
- Approaching a bonafide spiritual master.
- Renouncing the objects of sense gratification.
- Absence of false ego.
- The perception of the evil of birth, death, old age and disease.
- Freedom from the entanglement with children, wife, home and so on.
- Even-mindedness amid pleasant and unpleasant events.
- Constant and unalloyed devotion to Krishna.
- Aspiring to live in a solitary place.
- Detachment from the general mass of people.
- Accepting the importance of self-realization.
- Philosophical search for the Absolute Truth.

Who is a Transcendentalist?

- He who does not hate illumination, attachment and delusion when they are present, or long for them when they disappear.
- He who is unwavering and undisturbed through all the reactions of the material qualities, remaining neutral and transcendental, knowing that the modes alone are active.
- He who is situated in the self and regards happiness and distress alike.
- He who looks upon a lump of earth, a stone and a piece of gold with an equal eye.
- He who is equal towards the desirable and the undesirable.
- He who is steady, situated equally well in praise and blame, honor and dishonor.
- He who treats alike both friends and enemies.
- He who has renounced all material activities.

How many Phases can Krishna be Realized?

Krishna can realized in three phases:
- Brahman - individual soul, like the sunshine.

- Paramatma - super soul, like the surface of the sun.
- Bhagavan - Krishna Himself, like the sun itself.
- It is said that the individual soul, *jivatma,* and the Supersoul, the *Paramatma,* are like two birds sitting on a tree. One is eating the fruit of karma while the other is witnessing the act.

Who were the Great Charitable Persons of the World?

- Bali—gave all his kingdom to a *brahmin.*
- Karna—gave his natural armour to a *brahmin.*
- Hariscandra—gave up his kingdom to keep up a vow to tell truth.
- Rantideva—lived on grains picked from the fields.
- Mudgala—lived on grains picked up in fields.
- Sibi—gave his life in charity to save a pigeon.

TEACHINGS FROM THE BIBLE AND VEDIC SCRIPTURES

Jesus Christ was born some 2000 years ago in Bethlehem, Israel. His advent was also known to the Vedic people as was evidenced by the journey of the three wise men from the east, who followed a celestial star. According to the Judeo-Christian tradition, Jesus was believed to have worked as a shepherd during his age of 12 to 30. However according to Oriental history, Jesus traveled to India during those missing years learning about life and God.

Jesus teachings could be properly understood in the light of Vedic wisdom. According to Judeo-Christian tradition, He was crucified on the cross and rose to heaven on the third day. However according to other oriental believes, Jesus survived the crucifixion and traveled to India, where he lived the rest of his life in spiritual pursuit.

Jesus the Son, Krishna The Father

What did Jesus say about His Supreme Father?

- Father, forgive them. They know not what they are doing.
- Why do you call me good? No one is good but God alone. **(Mark 10.8)** & **(Luke 18.19)**
- I go unto the Father: for my Father is greater than I." **(John 14.28)**
- Thou shall love thy Lord with all thy heart, and with all they soul, and with all thy mind. **(Matthew 22.37)**
- Ask, and it will be given to you; search, and you will find; knock, and the door will be opened for you. For everyone who asks receives, and for everyone who searches finds, and for everyone who knocks, the door will be opened. Is there anyone among you who, if your child asks for bread, will give a stone? Or if the child asks for a fish, will give a snake? If you then, who are evil, know how to give good gifts to your children, how much more will your Father in heaven give good things to those who ask Him. **(Matthew 7.7-11)**
- Do not worry about anything: look at the birds of the air, they neither sow nor reap nor gather

into barns, and yet your heavenly Father feeds them. Are you not of more value than they?

- Father, Your kingdom come, Your will be done, on earth as it is in heaven. (**Matthew 6.10**)
- And lo a voice from heaven, saying, "This is my beloved son, in whom I am well pleased." (**Matthew 3.17**)
- For it is written, thou shalt worship the Lord thy God, and Him only shalt thou serve. (**Matthew 4.10**)
- Blessed are the pure in heart, for they shall see God. (**Matthew.5.8**)
- Let your light so shine before men, that they may see your good works, and glorify your Father which is in heaven. (**Matthew 5.16**)
- That ye may be the children of your Father which is in heaven, for He maketh his sun to rise on the evil and on the good, and sendeth rain on the just and on the unjust. Be ye therefore perfect, even as your Father which is in heaven is perfect. (**Matthew 5.45,48**)
- Take heed that ye do not yours alms before men, to be seen of them: otherwise ye have no reward of your Father which is in heaven, that thine alms may be in secret: and thy Father which seeth in secret Himself shall reward thee openly. (**Matthew 6.1,4**)

- But thou, when thou prayest, enter into thy closet, and when thou hast shut thy door, pray to thy Father which is in secret: and thy Father which seeth in secret shall reward thee openly. For your Father knoweth what things ye have need of, before ye ask Him. **(Matthew 6.6)**
- For if you forgive men their trespasses, your heavenly Father will also forgive you: but if you forgive not men their trespasses, neither will your Father forgive your trespasses. **(Matthew 6.14-15)**
- That thou appear not unto men to fast, but unto thy Father which is the secret: and thy Father, which sees in secret, shall reward thee openly. **(Matthew 6.18)**
- No man can serve two masters: for either he will hate the one, and love the other; or else he will hold to the one, and despise the other. You cannot serve God and man. **(Mat 6.24)**
- If God so clothe the grass of the field, which today is, and tomorrow is cast into the oven, shall He not much more clothe you. O yee of little faith. **(Matthew 6.30)**
- Take no tought, saying, what shall we eat? or, what shall we drink ? Or, wherewith all shall we be clothed ? For your heavenly Father knoweth that you have need of all these things.

seek you first the kingdom of God, and his righteousness; and all these things shall be added unto you. **(Matthew 6.31-33)**

- Not ever one that saith unto me, Lord, shall enter into the kingdom of heaven: but he that doeth the will of my Father which is in heaven. Many will say to me in that day, Lord, have we not prophesied in thy name have cast out devils? And in thy name done many wonderful works? And then will I profess unto them, I never knew you: depart from me, you that work iniquity. **(Matthew 7.21-23)**

- But that you may know that the son of man has power on earth to forgive sins (then saith he to the sick of the palsy). "Arise, take up thy bed, and go unto thine house". And he arose, and departed to his house. **(Matthew 9.6-7)**

- For it is not you that speak, but the spirit of your father which speaketh in you.
(Matthew 10.20)

- The disciple is not above his master, nor the servant above his Lord." **(Matthew 10.24)**

- I thank thee, O Father, Lord of heaven and earth, because Thou hast hid these things from the wise and prudent, and hast revealed them unto babes. **(Matthew 11.25)**

- Whosoever speaketh a word against the son

of man, it shall be forgiven him: but whosoever speaketh against the holy ghost, it shall not be forgiven him, neither in this world, neither in the world to come. (**Matthew 12.32**)

- For whosoever shall do the will of my Father which is in heaven, the same is my brother, and sister, and mother. (**Matthew 12.50**)
- Then shall the righteous shine forth as the sun in the kingdom of their father. (**Matthew 13.43**)
- Every plant, which my heavenly Father hath not planted, shall be rooted up. (**Matthew 15.13**)
- Even so it is not the will of your Father which is in heaven, that one of these little ones should perish. (**Matthew 18.14**)
- You shall drink indeed of my cup, and be baptised with the baptism that I am baptised with: but to sit on my right hand side, and on my left hand side of the throne, is not mine to give, but it shall be given to them for whom if is prepared of my Father. (**Matthew 20.23**)
- And call no man your father upon the earth: for one is your father, which is in heaven. (**Matthew 22.9**)
- But of that day and hour knoweth no man, no, not the angels of heaven, but my Father only (**Matthew. 24.36**)

What does Srimad Bhagavatam say about Krishna?

- In this age of Kali, people who are endowed with sufficient intelligence will worship Lord Krishna, who is accompanied by His associates, by performance of *sankirtana-yajna*. Other *yajnas* prescribed in the Vedic literatures are not easy to perform in this age of Kali, but the *sankirtana yajna* is easy and sublime for all purposes.

- My Lord, those who are favoured by even a slight trace of the mercy of Your lotus feet understand the greatness of Your personality. But those who speculate to understand the Supreme Personality of Godhead are unable to know You, even though they continue to study the Vedas for many years **(SB.10.14.29)**

- Kunti Devi said to Lord Krishna "A person who is proudof his birth, opulence, knowledge and beauty cannot achieve Your lotus feet. You are available only to the humble and meek and not to the proud. **(SB.1.8.25)**.

What did Brahma say about Krishna?

- The Supreme Personality of Godhead is Krishna, who has body of eternity, knowledge, and bliss. He has no beginning, for he is the beginning of everything. He is the cause of all causes. (*Brahma Samhita* **5.1**)
- I worship the Primeval Lord, Govinda, who is always seen by the devotee whose eyes are anointed with the pulp of love. He is seen in His eternal form of Shyamasundara, situated within the heart of the devotee. (*Brahma Samhita* **5.38**)
- Maha-Vishnu, into whom all the innumerable universes enter and from whom they come forth again simply by His breathing process, is a plenary expansion of Krishna. Therefore I worship Govinda, Krishna, the cause of all causes. (*Brahma Samhita* **5.48**)
- Let me worship, the Supreme Personality of Godhead, Govinda (Krishna), who is the original person and under whose order the sun, which is the king of all planets, is assuming immense power and heat. The sun represents the eye of the Lord and traverses its orbit in obedience to His order. (*Brahma Samhita* **5.52**)

What others have to say about Krishna?

- Whoever is protected by Krishna, no one can kill him and whoever is destined to be killed by Krishna, no one can protect him.

- One who has unflinching devotion for the Supreme Lord Krishna and is directed by the spiritual master, in whom he has similar unflinching faith, can see the Supreme Personality of Godhead by revelation. One cannot understand Krishna by mental speculation. For one who does not take personal training under the guidance of a bonafide spiritual master, it is impossible to even begin to understand Krishna.

  (Svetasvatara Upanisad 6.23)

- I offer my respectful obeisances unto Krishna, who has a transcendental form of bliss, eternity and knowledge. I offer my respects to Him, because understanding Him means understanding the Vedas and He is therefore the supreme spiritual master.

  (Gopala-tapani 1.1)

- A *brahmin* qualified to offer sacrifices is better than an ordinary *brahmin*, and better than such a *brahmin* is one who has studied all the Vedic scriptures. Among many such *brahmins*, one who is a devotee of Lord Vishnu is the best, and among many Vaisnavas one who fully engages in the service of Lord Krishna is the very best. (**Garuda Purana**)

• Krishna is the Supreme Personality of Godhead and He is worshipable.

• Krishna is one, but He is manifested in unlimited forms and expanded incarnations.

KRISHNA

SPEAKS THE

BHAGAVAD-GITA

BHAGAVAD-GITA

(The Condensed Version)

Chapter Two

O Arjuna, the nonpermanent appearance of happiness and distress, and their disappearance in due course, are like the appearance and disappearance of winter and summer seasons. They arise from sense perception, and one must learn to tolerate them without being disturbed. The person who is steady in happiness and distress is certainly eligible for liberation. **Text 14-15**

That which pervades the entire body you should know to be indestructible. No one is able to destroy that imperishable soul. However the material body is perishable. **Text 17-18**

Neither he who thinks the living entity the slayer nor he who thinks it slain is in knowledge, for the self slays not nor is slain. **Text 19**

For the soul there is neither birth nor death at any time. He has not come into being, does not come into being, and will not come into being. He is unborn, eternal, ever existing and primeval. He is not slain when the body is slain. **Text 20**

As a person puts on new garments, giving up old ones, the soul similarly accepts new material bodies, giving up the old and useless ones. **Text 22**

The soul can never be cut to pieces by any weapon, nor burned by fire, nor moistened by water, nor withered by the wind. **Text 23**

This individual soul is unbreakable and insoluble, and can be neither burned nor dried. He is everlasting, present everywhere, unchangeable, immovable and eternally the same. **Text 24**

One who has taken his birth is sure to die, and after death one is sure to take birth again. **Text 27**

All created beings are unmanifest in their beginning, manifest in their interim state, and unmanifest again when annihilated. **Text 28**

Do thou fight for the sake of fighting, without considering happiness or distress, loss or gain, victory or defeat—and by so doing you shall never incur sin. **Text 38**

Men of small knowledge are very much attached to the flowery words of the Vedas, which recommend various fruitive activities for elevation to heavenly planets, resultant good birth, power, and so forth. Being desirous of sense gratification and opulent life, they say that there is nothing more than this. **Texts 42-43**

In the minds of those who are too attached to sense enjoyment and material opulence, and who are bewildered by such things, the resolute determination for devotional service to the Supreme Lord does not take place. **Text 44**

You have a right to perform your prescribed duty, but you are not entitled to the fruits of action. Never consider yourself the cause of the results of your activities, and never be attached to not doing your duty. **Text 47**

By thus engaging in devotional service to the Lord, great sages or devotees free themselves from the results of work in the material world. In this way they become free from the cycle of birth and death and attain the state beyond all miseries (by going back to Godhead). **Text 51**

When a man gives up all varieties of desire for sense gratification, which arise from mental concoction, and when his mind, thus purified, finds satisfaction in the self alone, then he is said to be in pure transcendental consciousness. **Text 55**

One who is not disturbed in mind even amidst the threefold miseries or elated when there is happiness, and who is free from attachment, fear and anger, is called a sage of steady mind. **Text 56**

One who is able to withdraw his senses from sense objects, as the tortoise draws its limbs within the shell, is firmly fixed in perfect consciousness. **Text 58**

One who restrains his senses, keeping them under full control, and fixes his consciousness upon Me, is known as a man of steady intelligence. **Text 61**

While contemplating the objects of the senses, a person develops attachment for them, and from such attachment lust develops, and from lust anger arises. From anger, complete delusion arises, and from delusion bewilderment of memory. When memory is bewildered, intelligence is lost, and when intelligence is lost one falls down again into the material pool.
Texts 62-63

One who is not connected with Me can have neither transcendental intelligence nor a steady mind, without which there is no possibility of peace. And how can there be any happiness without peace?
Text 66

As a strong wind sweeps away a boat on the water, even one of the roaming senses on which the mind focuses can carry away a man's intelligence. **Text 67**

A person who has given up all desires for sense gratification, who lives free from desires, who has given up all sense of proprietorship and is devoid of false ego—he alone can attain real peace. **Text 71**

That is the way of the spiritual and godly life, after attaining which a man is not bewildered. If one is thus situated even at the hour of death, one can enter into the kingdom of God. **Text 72**

Chapter Three

Not by merely abstaining from work can one achieve freedom from reaction, nor by renunciation alone can one attain perfection. **Text 4**

One who restrains the senses of action but whose mind dwells on sense objects certainly deludes himself and is called a pretender. **Text 6**

On the other hand, if a sincere person tries to control the active senses by the mind and begins karma-yoga [in Kṛṣṇa consciousness] without attachment, he is by far superior. **Text 7**

Perform your prescribed duty, for doing so is better than not working. One cannot even maintain one's physical body without work. **Text 8**

Work done as a sacrifice for Vishnu has to be performed, otherwise work causes bondage in this material world. Therefore, perform your prescribed duties for His satisfaction, and in that way you will always remain free from bondage. **Text 9**

In the beginning of creation, the Lord of all creatures sent forth generations of men and demigods, along with sacrifices for Vishu, and blessed them by saying, "Be thou happy with this *yajna* [sacrifice] because its performance will bestow upon you everything desirable for living happily and achieving liberation." **Text 10**

The demigods, being pleased by sacrifices, will also please you, and thus, by cooperation between men and demigods, prosperity will reign for all. **Text 11**

In charge of the various necessities of life, the demigods, being satisfied by the performance of *yajña* [sacrifice], will supply all necessities to you. But he who enjoys such gifts without offering them to the demigods in return is certainly a thief. **Text 12**

The devotees of the Lord are released from all kinds of sins because they eat food which is offered first for sacrifice. Others, who prepare food for personal sense enjoyment, verily eat only sin. **Text 13**

A self-realized man has no purpose to fulfill in the discharge of his prescribed duties, nor has he any reason not to perform such work. Nor has he any need to depend on any other living being. **Text 18**

Therefore, without being attached to the fruits of activities, one should act as a matter of duty, for by working without attachment one attains the Supreme. **Text 19**

Kings such as Janaka attained perfection solely by performance of prescribed duties. Therefore, just for the sake of educating the people in general, you should perform your work. **Text 20**

Whatever action a great man performs, common men follow. And whatever standards he sets by exemplary acts, all the world pursues. **Text 21**

O Arjuna, there is no work prescribed for Me within all the three planetary systems. Nor am I in want of anything, nor have I a need to obtain anything—and yet I am engaged in prescribed duties. **Text 22**

For if I ever failed to engage in carefully performing prescribed duties, O Arjuna, certainly all men would follow My path. **Text 23**

As the ignorant perform their duties with attachment to results, the learned may similarly act, but without attachment, for the sake of leading people on the right path. **Text 25**

The spirit soul bewildered by the influence of false ego thinks himself the doer of activities that are in actuality carried out by the three modes of material nature.
Text 27

One who is in knowledge of the Absolute Truth, O mighty-armed, does not engage himself in the senses and sense gratification, knowing well the differences between work in devotion and work for fruitive results. **Text 28**

Bewildered by the modes of material nature, the ignorant fully engage themselves in material activities and become attached. But the wise should not unsettle them, although these duties are inferior due to the performers' lack of knowledge. **Text 29**

Therefore, O Arjuna, surrendering all your works unto Me, with full knowledge of Me, without desires for profit, with no claims to proprietorship, and free from lethargy, fight. **Text 30**

Those persons who execute their duties according to My injunctions and who follow this teaching faithfully, without envy, become free from the bondage of fruitive actions. **Text 31**

But those who, out of envy, do not regularly follow these teachings are to be considered bereft of all knowledge, befooled, and ruined in their endeavours for perfection. **Text 32**

It is far better to discharge one's prescribed duties, even though faultily, than another's duties perfectly. Destruction in the course of performing one's own duty is better than engaging in another's duties, for to follow another's path is dangerous. **Text 35**

It is lust only which is born of contact with the material mode of passion and later transformed into wrath, and which is the all-devouring sinful enemy of this world. **Text 37**

As fire is covered by smoke, as a mirror is covered by dust, or as the embryo is covered by the womb, the living entity is similarly covered by different degrees of this lust. **Text 38**

Thus the wise living entity's pure consciousness becomes covered by his eternal enemy in the form of lust, which is never satisfied and which burns like fire. **Text 39**

The senses, the mind and the intelligence are the sitting places of this lust. Through them lust covers the real knowledge of the living entity and bewilders him. **Text 40**

The working senses are superior to dull matter; mind is higher than the senses; intelligence is still higher than the mind; and he [the soul] is even higher than the intelligence. **Text 42**

Thus knowing oneself to be transcendental to the material senses, mind and intelligence, one should steady the mind by deliberate Kṛṣṇa consciousness and thus by spiritual strength—conquer this insatiable enemy known as lust. **Text 43**

Chapter Four

This supreme science was thus received through the chain of disciplic succession, and the saintly kings understood it in that way. But in course of time the succession was broken, and therefore the science as it is appears to be lost. **Text 2**

That very ancient science of the relationship with the Supreme is today told by Me to you because you are My devotee as well as My friend and can therefore understand the transcendental mystery of this science. **Text 3**

Many, many births both you and I have passed. I can remember all of them, but you cannot. **Text 5**

Although I am unborn and My transcendental body never deteriorates, and although I am the Lord of all living entities, I still appear in every millennium in My original transcendental form. **Text 6**

Whenever and wherever there is a decline in religious practice, and a predominant rise of irreligion—at that time I descend Myself. **Text 7**

To deliver the pious and to annihilate the miscreants, as well as to re-establish the principles of religion, I Myself appear, millennium after millennium. **Text 8**

One who knows the transcendental nature of My appearance and activities does not, upon leaving the body, take his birth again in this material world, but attains My eternal abode. **Text 9**

Being freed from attachment, fear and anger, being fully absorbed in Me and taking refuge in Me, many, many persons in the past became purified by knowledge of Me—and thus they all attained transcendental love for Me. **Text 10**

As all surrender unto Me, I reward them accordingly. Everyone follows My path in all respects. **Text 11**

Men in this world desire success in fruitive activities, and therefore they worship the demigods. Quickly, of course, men get results from fruitive work in this world. **Text 12**

According to the three modes of material nature and the work associated with them, the four divisions of human society are created by Me. And although I am the creator of this system, you should know that I am yet the nondoer, being unchangeable. **Text 13**

There is no work that affects Me; nor do I aspire for the fruits of action. One who understands this truth about Me also does not become entangled in the fruitive reactions of work. **Text 14**

One who sees inaction in action, and action in inaction, is intelligent among men, and he is in the transcendental position, although engaged in all sorts of activities. **Text 18**

One is understood to be in full knowledge whose every endeavor is devoid of desire for sense gratification. Abandoning all attachment to the results of his activities, ever satisfied and independent, he performs no fruitive action. **Text 19-20**

He who is satisfied with gain which comes of its own accord, who is free from duality and does not envy, who is steady in both success and failure, is never entangled, although performing actions. **Text 22**

A person who is fully absorbed in Kṛṣṇa consciousness is sure to attain the spiritual kingdom because of his full contribution to spiritual activities, in which the consummation is absolute and that which is offered is of the same spiritual nature. **Text 24**

Having accepted strict vows, some become enlightened by sacrificing their possessions, and others by performing severe austerities, by practicing the yoga of eightfold mysticism, or by studying the Vedas to advance in transcendental knowledge. **Text 28**

Persons who are inclined to the process of breath restraint to remain in trance, practice by offering the movement of the outgoing breath into the incoming, and the incoming breath into the outgoing, and thus at last remain in trance, stopping all breathing. Others, curtailing the eating process, offer the outgoing breath into itself as a sacrifice. All these performers become cleansed of sinful reactions, and, having tasted the nectar of the results of sacrifices, they advance toward the supreme eternal atmosphere. **Text 29-30**

Without sacrifice one can never live happily on this planet or in this life: what then of the next? All these different types of sacrifice are approved by the Vedas, and all of them are born of different types of

work. Knowing them as such, one will become liberated. The sacrifice performed in knowledge is better than the mere sacrifice of material possessions. All sacrifices of work culminate in transcendental knowledge.
Text 31-33

Just try to learn the truth by approaching a spiritual master. Inquire from him submissively and render service unto him. The self-realized souls can impart knowledge unto you because they have seen the truth.
Text 34

Having obtained real knowledge from a self-realized soul, you will never fall again into such illusion, for by this knowledge you will see that all living beings are but part of the Supreme, or, in other words, that they are Mine. **Text 35**

As a blazing fire turns firewood to ashes, O Arjuna, so does the fire of knowledge burn to ashes all reactions to material activities. **Text 37**

But ignorant and faithless persons who doubt the revealed scriptures do not attain God consciousness; they fall down. For the doubting soul there is happiness neither in this world nor in the next. **Text 40**

One who acts in devotional service, renouncing the fruits of his actions, and whose doubts have been destroyed by transcendental knowledge, is situated factually in the self. Thus he is not bound by the reactions of work. **Text 41**

Chapter Five

The renunciation of work and work in devotion are both good for liberation. But, of the two, work in devotional service is better than renunciation of work. **Text 2**

Only the ignorant speak of devotional service [karma-yoga] as being different from the analytical study of the material world [Sankhya]. Those who are actually learned say that he who applies himself well to one of these paths achieves the results of both. **Text 4**

Merely renouncing all activities yet not engaging in the devotional service of the Lord cannot make one happy. But a thoughtful person engaged in devotional service can achieve the Supreme without delay. **Text 6**

A person in the divine consciousness, although engaged in seeing, hearing, touching, smelling, eating, moving about, sleeping and breathing, always knows within himself that he actually does nothing at all. Because while speaking, evacuating, receiving, or opening or closing his eyes, he always knows that only the material senses are engaged with their objects and that he is aloof from them. **Texts 8-9**

One who performs his duty without attachment, surrendering the results unto the Supreme Lord, is unaffected by sinful action, as the lotus leaf is untouched by water. **Text 10**

When, however, one is enlightened with the knowledge by which nescience is destroyed, then his knowledge reveals everything, as the sun lights up everything in the day time. **Text 16**

When one's intelligence, mind, faith and refuge are all fixed in the Supreme, then one becomes fully cleansed of misgivings through complete knowledge and thus proceeds straight on the path of liberation. **Text 17**

The humble sages, by virtue of true knowledge, see with equal vision a learned and gentle brahmin, a cow, an elephant, a dog and a dog-eater. **Text 18**

A person who neither rejoices upon achieving something pleasant nor laments upon obtaining something unpleasant, who is self-intelligent, who is unbewildered, and who knows the science of God, is already situated in transcendence. He enjoys unlimited happiness, for he concentrates on the Supreme. **Text 20-21**

An intelligent person does not take part in the sources of misery, which are due to contact with the material senses. Such pleasures have a beginning and an end, and so the wise man does not delight in them. **Text 22**

Before giving up this present body, if one is able to tolerate the urges of the material senses and check the force of desire and anger, he is well situated and is happy in this world. **Text 23**

One whose happiness is within, who is active and rejoices within, and whose aim is inward is actually the perfect mystic. He is liberated in the Supreme, and ultimately he attains the Supreme. **Text 24**

Those who are beyond the dualities that arise from doubts, whose minds are engaged within, who are always busy working for the welfare of all living beings, and who are free from all sins achieve liberation in the Supreme. **Text 25**

Those who are free from anger and all material desires, who are self-realized, self-disciplined and constantly endeavouring for perfection, are assured of liberation in the Supreme in the very near future. **Text 26**

Shutting out all external sense objects, keeping the eyes and vision concentrated between the two eyebrows, suspending the inward and the outward breaths within the nostrils, and thus controlling the mind, senses and intelligence, the transcendentalist aiming at liberation becomes free from desire, fear and anger. One who is always in this state is certainly liberated. **Texts 27-28**

A person in full consciousness of Me, knowing Me to be the ultimate beneficiary of all sacrifices and austerities, the Supreme Lord of all planets and demigods, and the benefactor and well-wisher of all living entities, attains peace from the pangs of material miseries. **Text 29**

Chapter Six

One who is unattached to the fruits of his work and who works as he is obligated is in the renounced order of life, and he is the true mystic, not he who lights no fire and performs no duty. **Text 1**

What is called renunciation you should know to be the same as yoga, or linking oneself with the Supreme, for one can never become a *yogi* unless he renounces the desire for sense gratification. **Text 2**

For him who has conquered the mind, the mind is the best of friends; but for one who has failed to do so, his mind will remain the greatest enemy. **Text 6**

For one who has conquered the mind, the Supersoul is already reached, for he has attained tranquility. To such a man happiness and distress, heat and cold, honour and dishonour, pebbles or gold, are all the same.
Text 7-8

A person is considered still further advanced when he regards honest well-wishers, affectionate benefactors, the neutral, mediators, the envious, friends and enemies, the pious and the sinners all with an equal mind. **Text 9**

A transcendentalist should always engage his body, mind and self in relationship with the Supreme; he should live alone in a secluded place and should always carefully control his mind. **Text 10**

He should hold his body, neck and head erect in a straight line and stare steadily at the tip of the nose. Thus, with an unagitated, subdued mind, freedom from desires, feeling of possessiveness, completely free from sex life, he should meditate upon Me within the heart and make Me the ultimate goal of life. **Texts 13-14**

There is no possibility of one's becoming a *yogi*, if one eats too much or eats too little, sleeps too much or does not sleep enough. **Text 16**

As a lamp in a windless place does not waver, so the transcendentalist, whose mind is controlled, remains always steady in his meditation on the transcendent self. **Text 19**

From wherever the mind wanders due to its flickering and unsteady nature, one must certainly withdraw it and bring it back under the control of the self. **Text 26**

For one who sees Me everywhere and sees everything in Me, I am never lost, nor is he ever lost to Me. **Text 30**

He is a perfect *yogi* who, by comparison to his own self, sees the true equality of all beings, in both their happiness and their distress. **Text 32**

A transcendentalist engaged in auspicious activities does not meet with destruction either in this world or in the spiritual world; one who does good, My friend, is never overcome by evil. **Text 40**

The unsuccessful *yogi*, after many, many years of enjoyment on the planets of the pious living entities, is born into a family of righteous people, or into a family of rich aristocracy or into a family of transcendentalists. Such a birth is rare in this world. **Text 41-42**

And when the *yogi* engages himself with sincere endeavour in making further progress, being washed of all contaminations, then ultimately, achieving perfection after many, many births of practice, he attains the supreme goal. **Text 45**

A *yogi* is greater than the ascetic, greater than the empiricist and greater than the fruitive worker. **Text 46**

Of all *yogi*, the one with great faith who always abides in Me, thinks of Me within himself, and renders transcendental loving service to Me—he is the most intimately united with Me in yoga and is the highest of all. That is My opinion. **Text 47**

Chapter Seven

Out of many thousands among men, one may endeavour for perfection, and of those who have achieved perfection, hardly one knows Me in truth. **Text 3**

Earth, water, fire, air, ether, mind, intelligence and false ego—all together these eight constitute My separated material energies. **Text 4**

Besides these, there is another, superior energy of Mine, which comprises the living entities who are exploiting the resources of this material, inferior nature. **Text 5**

All created beings have their source in these two natures. Of all that is material and all that is spiritual in this world, know for certain that I am both the origin and the dissolution. **Text 6**

O Arjuna! There is no truth superior to Me. Everything rests upon Me, as pearls are strung on a thread. **Text 7**

O Arjuna, know that I am the taste of water, the light of the sun and the moon, the syllable *om* in the Vedic mantras; I am the sound in ether and ability in man; I am the original fragrance of the earth, and I am the heat in fire. I am the life of all that lives, and I am the penances of all ascetics; I am the original seed of all existences, the intelligence of the intelligent, and the prowess of all powerful men; I am the strength of the strong, devoid of passion and desire. I am sex life which is not contrary to religious principles.
Text 8-11

Know that all states of being—be they of goodness, passion or ignorance—are manifested by My energy. I am, in one sense, everything, but I am independent. I am not under the modes of material nature, for they, on the contrary, are within Me. **Text 12**

Deluded by the three modes of material nature, the whole world does not know Me, who am above the three modes of material nature and inexhaustible.
Text 13

This divine energy of Mine, consisting of the three modes of material nature, is difficult to overcome. But those who have surrendered unto Me can easily cross beyond it. **Text 14**

Those miscreants who are grossly foolish, who are lowest among mankind, whose knowledge is stolen by illusion, and who partake of the atheistic nature of demons do not surrender unto Me. **Text 15**

Four kinds of pious men begin to render devotional service unto Me—the distressed, the desirer of wealth, the inquisitive, and he who is searching for knowledge of the Absolute. **Text 16**

Of these, the one who is in full knowledge and who is always engaged in pure devotional service is the best. For I am very dear to him, and he is dear to Me. **Text 17**

After many births and deaths, he who is actually in knowledge surrenders unto Me, knowing Me to be the cause of all causes and all that is. Such a great soul is very rare. **Text 19**

Those whose intelligence has been stolen by material desires surrender unto demigods and follow the particular rules and regulations of worship according to their own natures. **Text 20**

I am in everyone's heart as the Supersoul. As soon as one desires to worship some demigod, I make his faith steady so that he can devote himself to that particular deity and obtain his desires. But in actuality these benefits are bestowed by Me alone. **Text 21-22**

Men of small intelligence worship the demigods, and their fruits are limited and temporary. Those who worship the demigods go to the planets of the demigods, but My devotees ultimately reach My supreme planet. **Text 23**

Unintelligent men, who do not know Me perfectly, think that I was impersonal before and have now assumed this personality. Due to their small knowledge, they do not know My higher nature, which is imperishable and supreme. **Text 24**

I am never manifest to the foolish and unintelligent. For them I am covered by My internal potency, and therefore they do not know that I am unborn and infallible. **Text 25**

O Arjuna, as the Supreme Personality of Godhead, I know everything that has happened in the past, all that is happening in the present, and all things that are yet to come. I also know all living entities; but Me no one knows. **Text 26**

All living entities are born into delusion, bewildered by dualities arisen from desire and hate. **Text 27**

Persons who have acted piously in previous lives and in this life and whose sinful actions are completely eradicated are freed from the dualities of delusion, and they engage themselves in My service with determination. **Text 28**

Intelligent persons who are endeavouring for liberation from old age and death take refuge in Me in devotional service. They know Me, the Supreme Lord, to be the governing principle of all material manifestation, of all the demigods, and of all methods of sacrifice. They can understand and know Me, as the Supreme Personality of Godhead, even at the time of death. **Text 29-30**

Chapter Eight

The indestructible, transcendental living entity is called Brahman, and his eternal nature is called *adhyatma*, the self. Action pertaining to the development of the material bodies of the living entities is called *karma*, or fruitive activites. **Text 3**

The physical nature, which is constantly changing, is called *adhibhuta* [the material manifestation]. The universal form of the Lord, which includes all the demigods, like those of the sun and moon, is called *adhidaiva*. And I, the Supreme Lord, represented as the Supersoul in the heart of every embodied being, am called *adhiyajna* [the Lord of sacrifice]. **Text 4**

And whoever, at the end of his life, quits his body remembering Me alone at once attains My nature. Of this there is no doubt. **Text 5**

Whatever state of being one remembers when he quits his body, O Arjuna, that state he will attain without fail. **Text 6**

He who meditates on Me as the Supreme Personality of Godhead, his mind constantly engaged in remembering Me, undeviated from the path, he is sure to reach me. **Text 8**

For one who always remembers Me without deviation, I am very easy to obtain because of his constant engagement in devotional service. **Text 14**

After attaining Me, the great souls, who are *yogis* in devotion, never return to this temporary world, which is full of miseries, because they have attained the highest perfection. **Text 15**

From the highest planet in the material world down to the lowest, all are places of misery wherein repeated birth and death take place. But one who attains to My abode, never takes birth again. **Text 16**

By human calculation, a thousand ages taken together form the duration of Brahma's one day. And such also is the duration of his night. **Text 17**

At the beginning of Brahma's day, all living entities become manifest from the unmanifest state, and thereafter, when the night falls, they are merged into the unmanifest again. **Text 18**

Again and again, when Brahma's day arrives, all living entities come into being. And with the arrival of Brahma's night they are helplessly annihilated. **Text 19**

Yet there is another unmanifest nature, which is eternal and is transcendental to this manifested and unmanifested matter. It is supreme and is never annihilated. When all in this world is annihilated, that part remains as it is. **Text 20**

That which the Vedantists describe as unmanifest and infallible, that which is known as the supreme destination, that place from which, having attained it, one never returns—that is My supreme abode. **Text 21**

The Supreme Personality of Godhead, who is greater than all, is attainable by unalloyed devotion. Although He is present in His abode, He is all-pervading, and everything is situated within Him. **Text 22**

Those who know the Supreme Brahman attain that Supreme by passing away from the world during the influence of the fiery god, in the light, at an auspicious moment of the day, during the fortnight of the waxing moon, or during the six months when the sun travels in the north. **Text 24**

The mystic who passes away from this world during the smoke, the night, the fortnight of the waning moon, or the six months when the sun passes to the south reaches the moon planet but again comes back. **Text 25**

A person who accepts the path of devotional service is not bereft of the results derived from studying the Vedas, performing austere sacrifices, giving charity or pursuing philosophical and fruitive activities. Simply by performing devotional service, he attains all these, and at the end he reaches the supreme eternal abode. **Text 28**

Chapter Nine

My dear Arjuna, because you are never envious of Me, I shall impart to you this most confidential knowledge and realization, knowing which you shall be relieved of the miseries of material existence. **Text 1**

Those who are not faithful in this devotional service cannot attain Me, O conqueror of enemies. Therefore they return to the path of birth and death in this material world. **Text 3**

.

By Me, in My unmanifested form, this entire universe is pervaded. All beings are in Me, but I am not in them. **Text 4**

And yet everything that is created does not rest in Me. Behold My mystic opulence! Although I am the maintainer of all living entities and although I am everywhere, I am not a part of this cosmic manifestation, for My Self is the very source of creation. **Text 5**

At the end of the millennium all material manifestations enter into My nature, and at the beginning of another millennium, by My potency, I create them again. **Text 7**

The whole cosmic order is under Me. Under My will it is automatically manifested again and again, and under My will it is annihilated at the end. **Text 8**

All this work cannot bind Me. I am ever detached from all these material activities, seated as though neutral. **Text 9**

This material nature, which is one of My energies, is working under My direction, producing all moving and non-moving beings. Under its rule this manifestation is created and annihilated again and again. **Text 10**

Fools deride Me when I descend in the human form. They do not know My transcendental nature as the Supreme Lord of all that be. **Text 11**

Those who are thus bewildered are attracted by demonic and atheistic views. In that deluded condition, their hopes for liberation, their fruitive activities, and their culture of knowledge are all defeated. **Text 12**

Those who are not deluded, the great souls, are under the protection of the divine nature. They are fully engaged in devotional service because they know Me as the Supreme Personality of Godhead, original and inexhaustible. **Text 13**

But it is I who am the ritual, I the sacrifice, the offering to the ancestors, the healing herb, the transcendental chant. I am the butter and the fire and the offering. **Text 16**

I am the father of the universe, the mother, the support and the grandsire. I am the object of knowledge, the purifier and the syllable *om*. I am also the Rig, the Sama and the Yajur Vedas. **Text 17**

I am the goal, the sustainer, the master, the witness, the abode, the refuge and the most dear friend. I am the creation and the annihilation, the basis of everything, the resting place and the eternal seed.
Text 18

O Arjuna, I give heat, and I withhold and send forth the rain. I am immortality, and I am also death personified. Both spirit and matter are in Me. **Text 19**

Those who study the Vedas and drink the soma juice, seeking the heavenly planets, worship Me indirectly. Purified of sinful reactions, they take birth on the pious, heavenly planet of Indra, where they enjoy godly delights. **Text 20**

When they have thus enjoyed vast heavenly sense pleasure and the results of their pious activities are exhausted, they return to this mortal planet again. Thus those who seek sense enjoyment by adhering to the principles of the three Vedas achieve only repeated birth and death. **Text 21**

But those who always worship Me with exclusive devotion, meditating on My transcendental form—to them I carry what they lack, and I preserve what they have. **Text 22**

Those who are devotees of other gods and who worship them with faith actually worship only Me, but they do so in a wrong way. **Text 23**

I am the only enjoyer and master of all sacrifices. Therefore, those who do not recognise My true transcendental nature fall down. **Text 24**

Those who worship the demigods will take birth among the demigods; those who worship the ancestors go to the ancestors; those who worship ghosts and spirits will take birth among such beings; and those who worship Me will live with Me. **Text 25**

If one offers Me with love and devotion a leaf, a flower, a fruit or water, I will accept it. **Text 26**

Whatever you do, whatever you eat, whatever you offer or give away, and whatever austerities you perform—do that as an offering to Me. **Text 27**

In this way you will be freed from bondage to work and its auspicious and inauspicious results. With your mind fixed on Me in this principle of renunciation, you will be liberated and come to Me. **Text 28**

I envy no one, nor am I partial to anyone. I am equal to all. But whoever renders service unto Me in devotion is a friend, is in Me, and I am also a friend to him. **Text 29**

Even if one commits the most abominable action, if he is engaged in devotional service he is to be considered saintly because he is properly situated in his determination. **Text 30**

He quickly becomes righteous and attains lasting peace. O Arjuna, declare it boldly that My devotee never perishes. **Text 31**

Engage your mind always in thinking of Me, become My devotee, offer obeisances to Me and worship Me. Being completely absorbed in Me, surely you will come to Me. **Text 34**

Chapter Ten

Neither the hosts of demigods nor the great sages know My origin or opulences, for, in every respect, I am the source of the demigods and sages. **Text 2**

He who knows Me as the unborn, as the beginningless, as the Supreme Lord of all the world—he only, undeluded among men, is freed from all sins. **Text 3**

Intelligence, knowledge, freedom from doubt and delusion, forgiveness, truthfulness, control of the senses, control of the mind, happiness and distress, birth, death, fear, fearlessness, nonviolence, equanimity, satisfaction, austerity, charity, fame and infamy—all these various qualities of living beings are created by Me alone. **Texts 4-5**

The seven great sages and before them the four other great sages and the Manus [progenitors of mankind] come from Me, born from My mind, and all the living beings populating the various planets descend from them. **Text 6**

The thoughts of My pure devotees dwell in Me, their lives are fully devoted to My service, and they derive great satisfaction and bliss from always enlightening one another and conversing about me. **Text 9**

To those who are constantly devoted to serving Me with love, I give the understanding by which they can come to Me. **Text 10**

To show them special mercy, I, dwelling in their hearts, destroy with the shining lamp of knowledge the darkness born of ignorance. **Text 11**

I am the Supersoul, O Arjuna, seated in the hearts of all living entities. I am the beginning, the middle and the end of all beings. **Text 20**

Of the Adityas I am Vishnu (The Lord of Universal Maintainance).
Of lights I am Surya (the radiant sun).
Of the Maruts I am Marici (the Superintendent of the Subtle Wind and Space).
Among the stars I am the moon.

Of the Vedas I am the Sama Veda.

Of the Demigods I am Indra (the king of heaven).

Of the senses I am the mind.

In living beings I am the living force (consciousness).

Of all the Rudras I am Lord Siva
(The Lord of Universal Destruction).

Of the Yaksas and Raksasas I am Kuvera
(the Superintendent of wealth).

Of the Vasus I am Agni (the fire God).

Of mountains I am Meru.

Of priests I am Brihaspati
(The Chief Priest of Heaven).

Of generals I am Kārtikeya (The Commander-in-chief
of the Heaven's Military Force).

Of bodies of water I am the ocean.

Of the great sages I am Bhrigu.

Of vibrations I am the transcendental *om*..

Of sacrifices I am the chanting of the holy names
(*japa*).

Of immovable things I am the Himalayas.

Of trees I am the banyan tree.

Of the sages among the demigods I am Narada.

Of the Gandharvas I am Citra-ratha (Celestial Singer).

Among perfected beings I am the sage Kapila
(Sankhya Philosopher).

Of horses I am Uccaihsrava (produced during the
churning of the celestial ocean for nectar).

Of lordly elephants I am Airavata
(The carrier of Indra).
Among men I am the monarch.
Of weapons I am the thunderbolt.
Among cows I am the surabhi (Celestial Cow).
Of causes for procreation I am Kandarpa
(the god of love).
Of serpents I am Vasuki (a celestial serpent).
Of the many-hooded Nagas I am Ananta
(the serpent bed of Visnu).
Among the aquatics I am the demigod Varuna
(the Water God).
Of departed ancestors I am Aryama
(the Lord of Ancestor World).
Among the dispensers of law I am Yama
(the lord of death).
Among the Daitya demons I am the devoted Prahlada.
Among subduers I am Kalacakra (eternal time).
Among beasts I am the lion (the King of the Jungle).
Among birds I am Garuda (the celestial bird carrier
of Lord Vishnu).
Of purifiers I am the wind.
Of the wielders of weapons I am Rama.
Of fishes I am the shark.
Of the flowing rivers I am the Ganges.
Of all sciences I am the spiritual science of the self.
Among logicians I am the conclusive truth.

Of letters I am the letter A.
Among compound words I am the dual compound.
I am also the inexhaustible time
Of creators I am Brahma (the Lord of universal creation).
I am all-devouring death.
I am the generating principle of all that is yet to be.
Among women I am fame, fortune, fine speech, memory, intelligence, steadfastness and patience.
Of the hymns in the Sama Veda I am the Brihat-sama.
Of poetry I am the Gayatri mantra.
Of months I am Margasirsa ([November-December).
Of seasons I am flower-bearing spring.
I am also the gambling of cheats.
Of the splendid I am the splendor.
I am victory.
I am adventure.
I am the strength of the strong.
Of the descendants of Vrishni I am Vasudeva.
Of the Pandavas I am Arjuna.
Of the sages I am Vyasa.
Among great thinkers I am Usana.
Among all means of suppressing lawlessness I am punishment.
Of those who seek victory I am morality.
Of secret things I am silence.
Of the wise I am the wisdom.

I am the generating seed of all existences.
Text 21-39

Know that all opulent, beautiful and glorious creations spring from but a spark of My splendour. But what need is there, Arjuna, for all this detailed knowledge? With a single fragment of Myself I pervade and support this entire universe. **Text 41-42**

O Arjuna, see here the different manifestations of Adityas, Vasus, Rudras, Asvini-kumaras and all the other demigods. Behold the many wonderful things which no one has ever seen or heard of before. **Text 6**

Chapter Eleven

O Arjuna, whatever you wish to see, behold at once in this body of Mine! This universal form can show you whatever you now desire to see and whatever you may want to see in the future. Everything—moving and non-moving—is here completely, in one place. **Text 7**

But you cannot see Me with your present eyes. Therefore I give you divine eyes. Behold My mystic opulence! **Text 8**

Arjuna Saw the Universal Form of Krishna

Arjuna saw in that universal form unlimited mouths, unlimited eyes, unlimited wonderful visions. The form was decorated with many celestial ornaments and bore many divine upraised weapons. He wore celestial garlands and garments, and many divine scents were smeared over His body. All was wondrous, brilliant, unlimited, all-expanding. **Texts 10-11**

If hundreds of thousands of suns were to rise at once into the sky, their radiance might resemble the effulgence of the Supreme Person in that universal form. **Text 12**

Then, bewildered and astonished, his hair standing on end, Arjuna bowed his head to offer obeisances and with folded hands began to pray to the Supreme Lord. **Text 14**

Arjuna Said:

My dear Lord Krishna, I see assembled in Your body all the demigods and various other living entities. I see Brahmā sitting on the lotus flower, as well as Lord Śiva and all the sages and divine serpents. **Text 15**

O Lord of the universe, O universal form, I see in Your body many, many arms, bellies, mouths and eyes, expanded everywhere, without limit. I see in You no end, no middle, and no beginning. **Text 16**

Your form is difficult to see because of its glaring effulgence, spreading on all sides, like blazing fire or the immeasurable radiance of the sun. Yet I see this glowing form everywhere, adorned with various crowns, clubs and discs. **Text 17**

You are the supreme primal objective. You are the ultimate resting place of all this universe. You are inexhaustible, and You are the oldest. You are the maintainer of the eternal religion, the Personality of Godhead. This is my opinion. **Text 18**

You are without origin, middle or end. Your glory is unlimited. You have numberless arms, and the sun and the moon are Your eyes. I see You with blazing fire coming forth from Your mouth, burning this entire universe by Your own radiance. **Text 19**

Although You are one, You spread throughout the sky and the planets and all space between. O great one, seeing this wondrous and terrible form, all the planetary systems are perturbed. **Text 20**

All the hosts of demigods are surrendering before You and entering into You. Some of them, very much afraid, are offering prayers with folded hands. Hosts of great sages and perfected beings, crying "All peace!" are praying to You by singing the Vedic hymns. **Text 21**

All the planets with their demigods are disturbed at seeing Your great form, with its many faces, eyes, arms, thighs, legs and bellies and Your many terrible teeth; and as they are disturbed, so am I. **Text 23**

O all-pervading Vishnu, seeing You with Your many radiant colours touching the sky, Your gaping mouths, and Your great glowing eyes, my mind is perturbed by fear. I can no longer maintain my steadiness or equilibrium of mind. **Text 24**

O Lord of lords, O refuge of the worlds, please be gracious to me. I cannot keep my balance seeing thus Your blazing deathlike faces and awful teeth. In all directions I am bewildered. **Text 25**

O Lord of lords, so fierce of form, please tell me who You are. I offer my obeisances unto You; please be gracious to me. You are the primal Lord. I want to know about You, for I do not know what Your mission is. **Text 31**

Krishna said:

Time I am, the great destroyer of the worlds, and I have come here to destroy all people. With the exception of you [the Pandavas], all the soldiers here on both sides will be slain. **Text 32**

Therefore get up. Prepare to fight and win glory. Conquer your enemies and enjoy a flourishing kingdom. They are already put to death by My arrangement, and you can be but an instrument in the fight. **Text 33**

Arjuna Said:

Thinking of You as my friend, I have rashly addressed You "O Krishna," "O Yadava," "O my friend," not knowing Your glories. Please forgive whatever I may have done in madness or in love. I have dishonoured You many times, jesting as we relaxed, lay on the same bed, or sat or ate together, sometimes alone and sometimes in front of many friends. O infallible one, please excuse me for all those offences. **Texts 41-42**

Thus I fall down to offer You my respectful obeisances and ask Your mercy. As a father tolerates the impudence of his son, a friend the impertinence of a friend, or a wife the familiarity of her partner, please tolerate the wrongs I may have done You. **Text 44**

Krishna Said:

No one before you has ever seen this universal form of Mine, for neither by studying the Vedas, nor by performing sacrifices, nor by charity, nor by pious activities, nor by severe penances can I be seen in this form in the material world. **Text 48**

You have been perturbed and bewildered by seeing this horrible feature of Mine. Now let it be finished. My devotee, be free again from all disturbances. With a peaceful mind you can now see the form you desire. **Text 49**

Arjuna Saw the Original Form of Krishna

When Arjuna thus saw Krishna in His original form, he said: O Janārdana, seeing this humanlike form, so very beautiful, I am now composed in mind, and I am restored to my original nature. **Text 51**

Krishna Continues to Speak the Bhagavad-gita:

My dear Arjuna, this form of Mine you are now seeing is very difficult to behold. Even the demigods are ever seeking the opportunity to see this form, which is so dear. **Text 52**

The form you are seeing with your transcendental eyes cannot be understood simply by studying the Vedas, nor by undergoing serious penances, nor by charity, nor by worship. It is not by these means that one can see Me as I am. **Text 53**

Only by undivided devotional service can I be understood as I am, standing before you, and can thus be seen directly. Only in this way can you enter into the mysteries of My understanding. **Text 54**

Chapter Twelve

Those who fix their minds on My personal form and are always engaged in worshiping Me with great and transcendental faith are considered by Me to be most perfect. **Text 2**

For those whose minds are attached to the unmanifested, impersonal feature of the Supreme, advancement is very troublesome. By controlling the various senses and being equally disposed to everyone, such persons, engaged in the welfare of all, at last achieve Me. **Texts 3-5**

Just fix your mind upon Me, and engage all your intelligence in Me. Thus you will live in Me always, without a doubt. **Text 8**

If you cannot fix your mind upon Me without deviation, then follow the regulative principles of bhakti-yoga. In this way develop a desire to attain Me. **Text 9**

If you cannot practice the regulations of bhakti-yoga, then just try to work for Me, because by working for Me you will come to the perfect stage. **Text 10**

If, however, you are unable to work in this consciousness of Me, then try to act giving up all results of your work and try to be self-situated. **Text 11**

If you cannot take to this practice, then engage yourself in the cultivation of knowledge. Better than knowledge, however, is meditation, and better than meditation is renunciation of the fruits of action, for by such renunciation one can attain peace of mind. **Text 12**

Chapter Thirteen

The Supersoul is the original source of all senses, yet He is without senses. He is unattached, although He is the maintainer of all living beings. He transcends the modes of nature, and at the same time He is the master of all the modes of material nature. **Text 15**

The Supreme Truth exists outside and inside of all living beings, the moving and the non-moving. Because He is subtle, He is beyond the power of the material senses to see or to know. Although far, far away, He is also near to all. **Text 16**

Although the Supersoul appears to be divided among all beings, He is never divided. He is situated as one. Although He is the maintainer of every living entity, it is to be understood that He devours and develops all. **Text 17**

He is the source of light in all luminous objects. He is beyond the darkness of matter and is unmanifested. He is knowledge, He is the object of knowledge, and He is the goal of knowledge. He is situated in everybody's heart. Only My devotees can understand this thoroughly and thus attain to My nature. **Text 18-19**

Material nature and the living entities should be understood to be beginningless. Nature is said to be the cause of all material causes and effects, whereas the living entity is the cause of the various sufferings and enjoyments in this world. **Text 20-21**

Yet in this body there is another, a transcendental enjoyer, who is the Lord, the supreme proprietor, who exists as the overseer and permitter, and who is known as the Supersoul. **Text 23**

Some perceive the Supersoul within themselves through meditation, others through the cultivation of knowledge, and still others through working without fruitive desires. **Text 25**

One who sees the Supersoul accompanying the individual soul in all bodies, and who understands that neither the soul nor the Supersoul within the destructible body is ever destroyed, actually sees. **Text 28**

One who sees the Supersoul equally present everywhere, in every living being, does not degrade himself by his mind. And one who can see that all activities are performed by the body, which is created of material nature, and sees that the self does nothing, actually sees. **Text 29-30**

When a sensible man ceases to see different identities due to different material bodies and he sees how beings are expanded everywhere, he attains to the Brahman conception. Those with the vision of eternity can see that the imperishable soul is transcendental, eternal and beyond the modes of nature. **Text 31-32**

The sky, due to its subtle nature, does not mix with anything, although it is all-pervading. Similarly, the soul situated in Brahman vision does not mix with the body, though situated in that body. **Text 33**

O Arjuna, as the sun alone illuminates all this universe, so does the living entity, one within the body, illuminate the entire body by consciousness. **Text 34**

Chapter Fourteen

The total material substance, called Brahman, is the source of birth, and it is that Brahman that I impregnate, making possible the births of all living beings. I am the seed-giving father. **Text 3-4**

Material nature consists of three modes—goodness, passion and ignorance. When the eternal living entity comes in contact with nature, he becomes conditioned by these modes. **Text 5**

The mode of goodness, conditions one to happiness and knowledge. Passion conditions one to fruitive actions. Ignorance binds one to madness, indolence and sleep.
Text 6-9

Sometimes the mode of goodness becomes prominent, defeating the modes of passion and ignorance. Sometimes the mode of passion defeats goodness and ignorance, at other times ignorance defeats goodness and passion. In this way there is always competition for supremacy. **Text 10**

When one dies in the mode of goodness, he takes his birth in the higher planets of the great sages.
When one dies in the mode of passion, he takes birth among those engaged in fruitive activities.
When one dies in the mode of ignorance, he takes birth in the animal kingdom. **Text 14-15**

Action done in the mode of goodness results in purity.
Action done in the mode of passion results in misery.
Action performed in the mode of ignorance results in foolishness. **Text 16**

When the embodied being is able to transcend these three modes associated with the material body, he can become free from birth, death, old age and their distresses and can enjoy nectar even in this life. **Text 20**

One who engages in full devotional service, unfailing in all circumstances, at once transcends the modes of material nature and thus comes to the level of Brahman. **Text 26**

And I am the basis of the impersonal Brahman, which is immortal, imperishable and eternal and is the constitutional position of ultimate happiness. **Text 27**

Chapter Fifteen

That supreme abode of Mine is not illumined by the sun or moon, nor by fire or electricity. Those who reach it never return to this material world. **Text 6**

The living entities in this conditioned world are My eternal fragmental parts. Due to conditioned life, they are struggling very hard with the six senses, which include the mind. **Text 7**

The living entity in the material world carries his different conceptions of life from one body to another, as the air carries aromas. Thus he takes one kind of body and again quits it to take another. **Text 8**

The living entity, thus taking another gross body, obtains a certain type of ear, eye, tongue, nose and sense of touch, which are grouped about the mind. He thus enjoys a particular set of sense objects. **Text 9**

The foolish cannot understand how a living entity can quit his body, nor can they understand what sort of body he enjoys under the spell of the modes of nature. But one whose eyes are trained in knowledge can see all this. **Text 10**

The splendor of the sun, which dissipates the darkness of this whole world, comes from Me. And the splendor of the moon and the splendor of fire are also from Me. I enter into each planet, and by My energy they stay in orbit. I become the moon and thereby supply the juice of life to all vegetables. I am the fire of digestion in the bodies of all living entities, and I join with the air of life, outgoing and incoming, to digest the four kinds of foodstuff. **Text 12-14**

I am seated in everyone's heart, and from Me come remembrance, knowledge and forgetfulness. By all the Vedas, I am to be known. Indeed, I am the compiler of Vedanta, and I am the knower of the Vedas. **Text 15**

There are two classes of beings, the fallible and the infallible. In the material world every living entity is fallible, and in the spiritual world every living entity is called infallible. Besides these two, there is the greatest living personality, the Supreme Soul, the imperishable Lord Himself, who has entered the three worlds and is maintaining them. **Text 16-17**

Because I am transcendental, beyond both the fallible and the infallible, and because I am the greatest, I am celebrated both in the world and in the Vedas as that Supreme Person. **Text 18**

O Arjuna, whoever knows Me as the Supreme Personality of Godhead, without doubting, is the knower of everything. He therefore engages himself in full devotional service to Me. **Text 19**

O Arjuna, this is the most confidential part of the Vedic scriptures, O sinless one, and it is disclosed now by Me. Whoever understands this will become wise, and his endeavours will know perfection. **Text 20**

Chapter Sixteen

O Arjuna, in this world there are two kinds of created beings. One is called the divine and the other demoniac. Divine qualities are conducive to liberation, whereas the demoniac qualities make for bondage. **Text 5-6**

The demoniac say that this world is unreal, with no foundation, no God in control. They say it is produced of sex desire and has no cause other than lust. Following such conclusions, the demoniac, who are lost to themselves and who have no intelligence, engage in unbeneficial, horrible works meant to destroy the world. **Text 8-9**

The demoniac person thinks: "So much wealth do I have today, and I will gain more according to my schemes. So much is mine now, and it will increase in the future, more and more. He is my enemy, and I have killed him, and my other enemies will also be killed. I am the lord of everything. I am the enjoyer. I am perfect, powerful and happy. I am the richest man, surrounded by aristocratic relatives. There is none so powerful and happy as I am. I shall perform sacrifices, I shall give some charity, and thus I shall rejoice." In this way, such persons are deluded by ignorance. Thus perplexed by various anxieties and bound by a network of illusions, they become too strongly attached to sense enjoyment and fall down into hell. **Texts 13-16**

Bewildered by false ego, strength, pride, lust and anger, the demons become envious of the Supreme Personality of Godhead, who is situated in their own bodies and in the bodies of others, and blaspheme against the real religion. **Text 18**

Those who are envious and mischievous, who are the lowest among men, I perpetually cast into the ocean of material existence, into various demoniac species of life. Attaining repeated birth amongst the species of demoniac life, such persons can never approach Me. Gradually they sink down to the most abominable type of existence. **Text 19-20**

There are three gates leading to this hell—lust, anger and greed. Every sane man should give these up, for they lead to the degradation of the soul. **Text 21**

The man who has escaped these three gates of hell performs acts conducive to self-realization and thus gradually attains the supreme destination. **Text 22**

He who discards scriptural injunctions and acts according to his own whims attains neither perfection, nor happiness, nor the supreme destination. **Text 23**

Chapter Seventeen

According to one's existence under the various modes of nature, one evolves a particular kind of faith. The living being is said to be of a particular faith according to the modes he has acquired. **Text 3**

Those who undergo severe austerities and penances not recommended in the scriptures, performing them out of pride and egoism, who are impelled by lust and attachment, who are foolish and who torture the material elements of the body as well as the Supersoul dwelling within, are to be known as demons. **Texts 5-6**

Even the food each person prefers is of three kinds, according to the three modes of material nature. The same is true of sacrifices, austerities and charity. Now hear of the distinctions between them. **Text 7**

From the beginning of creation, the three words *om tat sat* were used by transcendentalists at the start of activities. They perform their activities without desire for fruitive results, and with the ultimate aim of pleasing the Supreme Lord. **Text 23-27**

Anything done as sacrifice, charity or penance without faith in the Supreme, is impermanent. It is called '*asat*' and is useless both in this life and the next. **Text 28**

Chapter Eighteen

The giving up of activities that are based on material desire is what great learned men call the renounced order of life [*sannyasa*]. And giving up the results of all activities is what the wise call renunciation [*tyaga*]. **Text 2**

Acts of sacrifice, charity and penance are not to be given up; they must be performed. They purify even the great souls. All these activities should be performed without attachment or any expectation of result. They should be performed as a matter of duty. That is My final opinion. **Text 5-6**

If one gives up his prescribed duties because of illusion, such renunciation is said to be in the mode of ignorance. **Text 7**

Anyone who gives up prescribed duties as troublesome or out of fear of bodily discomfort is said to have renounced in the mode of passion. **Text 8**

When one performs his prescribed duty only because it ought to be done, and renounces all material association and all attachment to the fruit, his renunciation is said to be in the mode of goodness. **Text 9**

It is indeed impossible for an embodied being to give up all activities. But he who renounces the fruits of action is called one who has truly renounced. **Text 11**

For one who is not renounced, the threefold fruits of action—desirable, undesirable and mixed—accrue after death. But those who are in the renounced order of life have no such result to suffer or enjoy. **Text 12**

The place of action [the body], the performer, the various senses, the many different kinds of endeavor, and ultimately the Supersoul—these are the five factors of action. **Text 14**

Whatever right or wrong action a man performs by body, mind or speech is caused by these five factors. Therefore one who thinks himself the only doer, not considering the five factors, is certainly not very intelligent and cannot see things as they are. **Text 15-16**

One who is not motivated by false ego, whose intelligence is not entangled, though he kills men in this world, does not kill. Nor is he bound by his actions. **Text 17**

Knowledge, the object of knowledge, and the knower are the three factors that motivate action; the senses, the work and the doer are the three constituents of action. They are all influenced by the three different modes of material nature. **Text 18-19**

There is no being existing, either here or among the demigods in the higher planetary systems, which is freed from these three modes born of material nature.
Text 40

Brahmins, kshatriyas, vaisyas and *sudras* are distinguished by the qualities born of their own natures in accordance with the material modes. Every man can become perfect by following his own qualities of work. **Text 41, 45**

By worship of the Lord, who is the source of all beings and who is all-pervading, a man can attain perfection through performing his own work. **Text 46**

It is better to engage in one's own occupation, even though one may perform it imperfectly, than to accept another's occupation and perform it perfectly. Duties prescribed according to one's nature are never affected by sinful reactions. **Text 47**

Every endeavor is covered by some fault, just as fire is covered by smoke. Therefore one should not give up the work born of his nature, O son of Kunti, even if such work is full of fault. **Text 48**

Though engaged in all kinds of activities, My pure devotee, under My protection, reaches the eternal and imperishable abode by My grace. **Text 56**

In all activities just depend upon Me and work always under My protection. In such devotional service, be fully conscious of Me. If you become conscious of Me, you will pass over all the obstacles of conditioned life by My grace. If, however, you do not work in such consciousness but act through false ego, not hearing Me, you will be lost. **Text 57-58**

The Supreme Lord is situated in everyone's heart, and is directing the wanderings of all living entities, who are seated as on a machine, made of the material energy. **Text 61**

O Arjuna, surrender unto Him utterly. By His grace you will attain transcendental peace and the supreme and eternal abode. Thus I have explained to you knowledge still more confidential. Deliberate on this fully, and then do what you wish to do. **Text 62-63**

Always think of Me, become My devotee, worship Me and offer your homage unto Me. Thus you will come to Me without fail. I promise you this because you are My very dear friend. **Text 65**

Abandon all varieties of religion and just surrender unto Me. I shall deliver you from all sinful reactions. Do not fear. **Text 66**

For one who explains this supreme secret to the devotees, pure devotional service is guaranteed, and at the end he will come back to Me. There is no servant in this world more dear to Me than he, nor will there ever be one more dear. **Text 68-69**

The Final Conclusion

Sanjaya said:

Wherever there is Kṛṣṇa, the master of all mystics, and wherever there is Arjuna, the supreme archer, there will also certainly be opulence, victory, extraordinary power, and morality. That is my opinion. **Text 78**

About the Author

The author, Bhakta Vijai, was born in India in 1969 in a Hindu and Christian family. Going to churches and temples has been a natural activity from his early childhood. He learned the Vedic values of life from his maternal grandmother and grandfather through stories and the Christian values of life from his paternal grandmother.

He extensively studied both the Hindu and Biblical religious books but he was dissatisfied. He eventually got peace and bliss while studying His Divine Grace A. C. Bhaktivedanta Swami Prabhupada's *Bhagavadgita As It Is*. It was a turning point in his life and ever since then, he has been steadily progressing on the spiritual path of life.

This will be the author's first spiritual book to be published and distributed internationally. He was inspired to produce it while preaching in Muslim countries. The aim of the book is to introduce Krishna to those who are not familiar with Vedic traditions and to encourage further research into the eternal science of Vedic knowledge.

The author plans to extensively distribute this book in many languages of the world. He also intends to periodically review it and add more and more information to make it richer in content.

For correspondence with the author please write to: bhaktavijai@yahoo.com

References

Bhagavad-gita As It Is: His Divine Grace A.C. Bhaktivedanta Swami Prabhupada.
Free online book at:
http://www.webcom.com/ara/col/books/bg/gita/contents.html

Srimad Bhagavatam: His Divine Grace A.C. Bhaktivedanta Swami Prabhupada.
Free online book at:
http://www.webcom.com/ara/col/books/clas/bhag

Krishna the Supreme Personality of Godhead:
by His Divine Grace A.C. Bhaktivedanta Swami Prabhupada.
Free online book at:
http://www.krsnabook.com

Krishna and Jesus: His Divine Grace A.C. Bhaktivedanta Swami Prabhupada.
Free online book at:
http://www.geocities.com/athens/ithaca/1388/christ.html

Feedback

We'd like to hear from you.

1. From where did you get this book?
   (a) Bookstore (b) Library c) Friend
   (d)Internet (e) Others

2. How would you rate this book?
   (a) Extremely interesting
   (b) Moderately interesting
   (c) Seldom interesting

3. What else do you think should be added?

4. What needs to be altered or be removed?

Please send your feedback to:
bhaktavijai@yahoo.com

Richard Harland  land, in
1947 a   After a
period   t-time
poet, he   NSW.
In 1987,   ty of
Wollongo   ses on popular fanta   of the imagination.

His theoretical books, *Superstructuralism* and
Beyond Structuralism, have been published internationally, but fiction writing has always been his
greatest love. He is the author of a comic horror
novel called *The Vicar of Morbing Vyle*, published in
1993 to cult success.

The Dark Edge is the first of a series featuring
Central Inspector Eddon Brac and Parapsych Vail ev
Vessintor. In 1996, he resigned his lectureship in
order to devote his time to the writing of further
Eddon and Vail adventures.

THE DARK EDGE

RICHARD HARLAND

Pan
Australia

First published 1997 in Pan by Pan Macmillan Australia Pty Limited
St Martins Tower, 31 Market Street, Sydney

National Library of Australia
cataloguing-in-publication data:

Harland, Richard. 1947– .
The dark edge.

ISBN 0 330 36007 8.

I. Title.

A823.3

Typeset in 11/13.5pt Rotis Semi Sans by Post Pre-press Group
Printed in Australia by McPherson's Printing Group

For Van:
one of the true believers

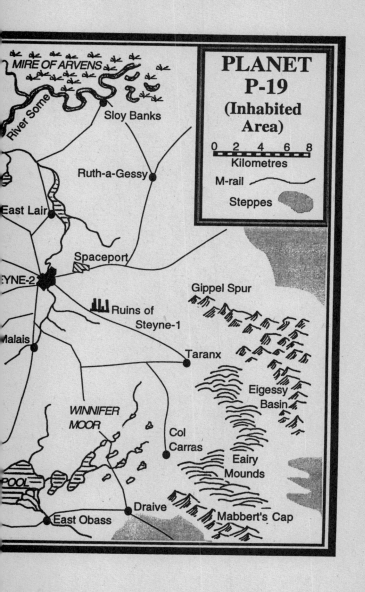

PLANET P-19
(Inhabited Area)

0 2 4 6 8
Kilometres

M-rail

Steppes

MIRE OF ARVENS

River Some

Sloy Banks

Ruth-a-Gessy

East Lair

Spaceport

EYNE-2

Malais

Ruins of Steyne-1

Taranx

Gippel Spur

Eigessy Basin

WINNIFER MOOR

Col Carras

Eairy Mounds

POOL

East Obass

Draive

Mabbert's Cap

PART ONE
Planet P-19

1

Coming out of cryonic freeze, there was always a tingling on the skin and a taste like almonds in the mouth. When you opened your eyes, a million tiny pinpricks of colour danced across your retina like interference on a holo-screen.

Eddon Brac lay motionless for the regulation two minutes. Then he shook his head and blinked. The pinpricks of colour vanished. He flexed his muscles, feeling the circulation return. It felt good to be alive.

He was lying in a shallow cryo-bath – 'coffin' in the Spacers' jargon. The defrost had long since finished, the gas had been drawn off, and the hood was open. Over his head the sonic alarm continued its *ping-ping-ping*.

Across in the next bath, the young woman stirred and made a noise in her throat like the purr of a cat. Her eyelids fluttered faintly, but she didn't open her eyes.

He reached up and turned his alarm off. He wanted to leap out onto the floor and swing his arms. But not yet — give the body time to recover, he told himself. One by one he detached the monitoring electrodes.

There was a floss-towel laid out ready. He sat up in his bath and wiped off the gel from under the electrodes. The young woman's sonic was still ping-pinging relentlessly. Two months in deep sleep, but she seemed in no hurry to come back to consciousness.

My assistant, he thought with a grimace. Long greeny-black hair, pale face, a gash of purple lipstick. Her eyelashes were spangled with fluctuating chrysolite, and double rings of kohl circled her eyes like bulls-eye targets.

At once he remembered everything he already hated about this assignment. It was the worst sort of crazy sicko murderer case — the sort of case every detective at Central tried to avoid. Totally random killings that you either solved by chance or you didn't solve at all. And right out on the edge of the galaxy, on some insignificant frontier planet a million miles from anywhere. The only thing that could make it worse was being lumbered with a parapsych assistant who dressed like a ghoul and acted like a sorceress. And here she was.

Again she made the noise in her throat. Her bare arms unfolded and slipped to her sides, hands stroking over her hips. Her legs moved slowly in an undulating, caressing motion. Under the gash of lipstick she seemed to be smiling.

4

Like a goddamned snake in the sun, he thought. How long is she going to stay comatose? It's almost as if she enjoys it.

He stood up and walked over to the stool and washstand. He gargled a glass of tangozine from the drinks server, swilling away the taste of almonds. He felt nearly back to normal now.

There was a privacy screen for dividing the cabin into two halves. He pulled it across and started to dress. Official Central Inspector uniform: black wing-jacket, hoofers and webbing. On the other side of the screen there was a sudden silence as the alarm was turned off.

'Welcome to the world,' he said breezily, sarcastically.

'Hiya, Eddon — I mean, Inspector Brac. What a drift!'

'A what?'

'You know, a drift. Mmm. I could do that any time.' She had a drawling, dreamy voice. 'Are we nearly there?'

'Near enough.'

There was a pause. Then:

'We hardly met before, did we? Parapsych Vail ev Vessintor reporting for duty.' She gave a sort of giggle.

Straight out of seminary, he thought despairingly. One of those posh psychoseminaries where they pranced around like little witches. All sophisticated style and no bloody experience.

'I know your name, PP. And you're not on duty till you're dressed.'

'Oh-aah, yeah. Now where's my wardrobe?'

Eddon finished dressing. He snapped shut his last pop-stud and spoke in the direction of the screen.

'So. You've read the report, PP?'

'Have I read the report? No, I don't think I have. What report?'

'The four murders. You must've been given the report when they put you on this assignment.'

'I suppose. I'm not very good at reading reports. I mean, I don't always get much out of them.'

'You *can* read?'

'Oh-aaah. Yeah.'

'I only ask. I thought maybe you just sniffed the paper and absorbed the psychic aura.'

'I didn't think there was any hurry. This *is* my very first case, you know.'

'Not *your* case, PP. *My* case. You're only an assistant on it. And as an assistant I expect you to do some hard work. Real hard work.'

'Sorry, CI.'

'CI? What's that?'

'I'm PP for Parapsych, so you must be CI for Central Inspector.'

Eddon gritted his teeth. 'Have you finished dressing?'

'Are you joking? I've hardly started.'

Eddon took his portacase from the stow-all on the wall and drew out the report file. On the other side of the screen he could hear clothes rustling and the sound of a zipper being zipped.

'Listen up. I'll give you the main details. You need to know this before we land. Perhaps you can direct a portion of your attention this way.'

'As long as I can keep seventy-five percent for getting dressed. Eighty-five percent when I come to make-up.'

Eddon made a face to himself. She wouldn't be so chirpy after hearing what was in the report, he suspected. It had even given him a queasy feeling the first time he'd read it through.

2

'OK, so the first killing reported took place on the night of 17–4–660 — that would be about six standard months ago. Victim was, quote, *Janna II MetHannig, female, 61 years old.* Hmmm. They all seem to have names like that on P-19. All with that numeral in the middle. *The body was found in open moorland, in the south of the Brennag.* Must be a deserted area — *no habitation within one kilometre of the scene of the crime.* Yet three families reported hearing distant sounds of screaming in the night. *Sounds continued for approximately twenty minutes.* Nobody went to investigate though.'

'Why not?'

'Doesn't say. But plenty of people went to investigate the next morning — there's a whole list of names given. They found the old woman by a path *trampled into the ground.* That's what it says, *trampled into the ground.* And blood smeared everywhere — *within a ten-metre radius around the body. Death may be attributed to kicking and stamping and repeated violent blows continuing over a long period of time.* The killer must've had a thing against the human skeleton: every single bone in the old woman's body was broken.'

He skimmed through to the end of the page.

'No suspects, no motive established. *The victim's clothing did not appear to have been disturbed. However, around the body they found samples of,* quote, *a white sticky liquid like spittle.*'

'Ugh! Gross!'

'Euphemism for something else? The report just says *like spittle.* There's no record of any chemical analysis performed.'

Eddon flipped over to the next page.

'Second murder reported — though it might have been the first committed. The body was discovered in the storage room of a metalwork shop in Steyne–2. Steyne–2 is the largest settlement on P-19.

'So. *Shop foreman Wex III Wellamaker said that workers had noticed an unpleasant smell for several weeks, but blamed it on sewerage problems. Storage room was rarely used. When source of smell became obvious, 29–5–660, the room was opened up, and a body was discovered in state of partial decomposition. Identified as sixteen-year-old male, Arram V* — I can't pronounce the surname.

8

'The report says the victim had been dragged to the storage room from two streets away. Must've been some kind of evidence, doesn't say what. Killer dragged him there and then set to work on him with, quote, *a five-pound hammer and cold chisel . . . found beside the body.* The boy's skull was completely pulverised, broken up into a thousand fragments. Just the skull. Strange obsessive sort of frenzy, huh? It'd take a long time to reduce a human skull to that condition, don't you think?'

There was no reply from the other side of the screen.

'What do you think, PP?'

Still silence.

'Are you all right there? Hey?'

'I'm okay.' Her voice sounded subdued. 'Just finished dressing.'

She pulled back the screen, opening up the cabin to its full area again. Eddon had forgotten how tall she was. He was 180 centimetres himself, but she was half a head above him. Tall and thin, with a strange drooping posture.

She was wearing the black PP uniform, with its cloak, high collar and soft-hose. Her face was dramatically pale against the black. A sash of scarlet royalette was slung around her waist — not an official part of her uniform, Eddon suspected.

'Make-up,' she said. 'I'll need to use that mirror behind you. Can I take over your stool?'

They traded places across the cabin. Eddon took up a position leaning against the wall. Vail lifted a drum-shaped bag out of the stow-all, then sat down facing the mirror.

'Ready for killing number three?'

She nodded. She reached into her bag and drew out a selection of phials, brushes, wands and squirters.

'This is a multiple slaying, this one. Happened in an isolated house at a place called Malais — wherever that is. I couldn't find the name on the old maps. A family of three was butchered in the night. Mother, father and son, the Magham family. The killer used, quote, *table knives taken from the cutlery drawer in the kitchen.*

'There were signs that he'd got in through the roof — doesn't say how. A neighbour discovered the shambles on the following morning, 2–8–660. They'd been taken apart organ by organ. Kidneys, lungs, stomachs, bowels, liver, the lot. *Chest cavities and abdomens cut open and the internal organs removed.* And not only removed but thrown around in a kind of frenzy — suggested by marks and bloodstains on the walls of the main living room.'

Vail had stopped repainting the circles around her eyes. The paintwand was suspended in midmovement, inches away from her face. With a visible effort, she controlled her shaking hand and started work again.

Eddon continued relentlessly. 'It gets worse. The butchery was so insane that even the organs ripped out and scattered around the room *appeared to have been individually subjected to attack.* Livers hacked apart, hearts cut and stabbed, eyeballs

10

sliced open. The whole thing must've gone on for hours. Unbelievable. And here's that stuff again — sticky white liquid found around the room. Only now it's described as *like mucus*.'

Vail gave up the struggle with her make-up. She put the paintwand down, took out a comb, and started combing her greeny-black hair. She kept her face deliberately turned away from Eddon.

He ran his eyes down over the fourth and final page of the report. 'The last one took place on 5-9-660 — about ten standard weeks ago. Another night-time killing. The victim was *Perla III Erridge*.'

'I suppose I have to listen to all this?' Vail broke in suddenly. Her voice was no longer drawling, but tight and constricted.

Eddon stuck out his jaw aggressively.

'What did you expect? This is policework. That means ugly, nasty, not nice. You'll get used to it in time.'

'You're *used* to this?'

'I've been around a long while. Serving at Central, you get to see just about every kind of crime sooner or later.'

'Even this?'

'No, not usually as sick as this.'

'How old are you anyway? You look kind of young for an Inspector. Twenty-five, thirty?'

'Twenty-eight. Seven years older than you.' He turned back to the report. '*Perla III Erridge*. Obviously a very important person, *twenty-year-old great-niece of Headman ev Ghair*. Sounds almost

11

tribal. Perhaps he's the top boss on P-19. High up enough to make them call for outside help anyway. It was after this murder they finally contacted us.'

Vail continued combing her hair.

'*Attack occurred at 2.15 and continued until 2.30.* They can be precise about this one because she was attacked in her own bedroom, dozens of people heard the screaming. Continuous loud screaming. I guess this was in some sort of palace or large house with many rooms. The witnesses heard screaming and violent movements through the door, but the killer had bolted it from inside. Must've been a very solid door if it took that long to break down. Incredibly, the sicko was still there when they burst in. *Male, aged about thirty, seen crouching on floor over the body of the victim. Immediately leaped out through an open window...*'

Eddon frowned as he read. 'Doesn't even say he was pursued. Maybe he was wearing a mask. Else they'd've surely picked him up, with so much to go on.

'Anyway, here's how she was killed: *a writing pen had been driven through the left eye socket and into the brain.* That must've taken some force. Also her clothing had been completely stripped off and she had been *pierced and slashed on all parts of the body with the pin of a brooch.* Her own brooch, presumably. Helluva way to commit a murder — how could you kill anyone like that? *Over two hundred incisions, leading to profuse bleeding.* Here's the real lulu, though. Guess what he was doing when they burst in? *Shoe was found forced down into the victim's gullet, and another shoe had been inserted into the mouth.* Can you believe it? He was stuffing her own shoes down her throat. What do you think of that for crazy?'

'I think —' She hesitated, then swung around suddenly on the stool to face him. The corners of her mouth were pulled down in a look of distaste. 'I think you're enjoying telling me all this.'

Eddon bristled. 'This is the report you should've already read yourself.'

'But you have to pick out all the most sickening bits.'

'I'm giving you what's in the report. Here.' He held the report out for her to take. She shook her head violently. Her long greeny-black hair swung from side to side.

'Where's the details? Where's the evidence? It doesn't even sound like a proper police report!'

'Because it isn't. This is what they recorded at Central Police when P-19 contacted us for assistance. A brief microdot transmission.'

'A microdot transmission? Not fast-text?'

'Seems they don't have fast-text facilities on P-19. Probably no police force either. That would explain why the report is so amateurish.'

'Probably? Probably no police force? How come you don't know?'

'What do you mean? I don't know because nobody knows. P-19 has been cut off from the rest of the galaxy for over seventy years. We're their first visitors for seventy years.'

'Why cut off?'

'They cut themselves off. Hey, didn't you check up on the political history of P-19.'

'No, how could I?'

'When you were told you were being sent on this assignment? Didn't you have a look at a visi-text or something?'

'They don't have visi-texts on political history in our library. I mean, at the psychoseminary.'

Eddon snorted in disgust. 'No books on political history? Too practical and worldly perhaps?'

'It's not their job to teach us history. Their job is to train our psychic talents.'

'Oh, right. So they have books on magic spells, huh? *1001 Curses For Beginners*? *Advanced Potions and Brews*?'

Vail compressed her lips and said nothing.

'Let's get one thing straight, PP Vail ev Vessin-tor. As you may or may not have guessed, I don't have much time for parapsych assistants. I'm not against them, I know cases where they've paid their way — though none of the cases I've been on. But I don't think they're the most wonderful thing that ever happened to police investigation. And I don't think a few smart-ass talents and flairs does away with the need for a whole lot of bloody hard work. Just because you don't belong in the regular force doesn't mean you're on holiday. I expect —'

'To give me orders like some sort of junior policeman?'

'You know what we call you at Central? All you

14

parapsych assistants? We call you witches. God-damned witches.'

'Ha!' She gave an imitation witchy cackle. 'Sounds to me like you're afraid. Typical. Afraid of what you don't understand.'

'What's to be afraid of?'

'Oh, plenty. I've got powers that'd make your hair curl. You want witches, you got the best right here, CI Brac. Some of the highest results ever recorded at St Alda's Psychoseminary. You'd better watch out for yourself.'

Eddon was about to reply. But suddenly she turned her eyes on him, very wide and staring.

'I feel a terrible man-devouring spell coming on,' she murmured.

She pointed the comb at his forehead and began drawing circles in the air with her other hand. Her eyes seemed to be growing larger and larger . . .

Eddon blinked and shook his head. Instinctively he raised his hand to cover his eyes.

'Stop that stuff!' he burst out. 'Don't try your witchy tricks on me!'

Vail gave another imitation cackle. Then she laughed.

'Only pretending! You don't think I can cast spells as easy as that?'

Eddon lowered his hand. She had started combing her hair again.

'Psychic science isn't supernatural, you know,' she said. 'You just have to be aware of the energies

15

and how to use them. What you call spells or curses work by intelligible laws like anything else.'

'I know that.'

'But you're still superstitious.'

Suddenly the interspeak crackled and came to life.

'Hi, everyone. Flightman Zeno Berrit here. Hope you're up and about. We're well inside the Walder-J solar system, and planet P-19 is now visible ahead. We'll be decelerating in about ten minutes.'

Vail gave one last sweep to her hair and tossed the comb into her bag.

'I'm going forward to take a look. You?'

Eddon shook his head. She rose to her feet. Her half-finished make-up was more garishly bizarre than ever.

'I know. You've got more serious things to do. Excuse my frivolity!'

The drawl was back in her voice. Slinky as a cat, she stooped through the doorway and headed forward towards the Flight Cabin.

3

Flightman Berrit was in his chair with his audiphones on. He jumped when Vail glided suddenly into the seat beside him. He removed the audiphones and turned to take a look at her. He jumped again.

'Whooo-hupp!' he exclaimed. 'You startled me.'

'Yeah, I have that effect on people.'

He was clean-cut and fresh-faced, with a square jaw and sandy-coloured eyebrows. His hair was quiffed up neatly in the style of a 'Spacers' peak'.

'Take a seat,' he said. 'Enjoy the view.'

'I did. I am. So you've been piloting us for the last two months?'

'Sure have. Flightman Zeno Berrit. My friends call me "Beano".'

'Beano?'

'It's made up from the "eno" of "Zeno" and the "B" of "Berrit".'

'I like your sleeves,' she said, stroking the two-tone red-grey material of his Spacers' flight jacket. 'What do you do in your time off, Beano?'

'Whooo-hupp!' Beano exclaimed again. He leant forward to twiddle a knob. 'Hey! Let me show you the Walder-J solar system!'

Vail curled and curved herself more comfortably into her chair. Looking forward through the Flight Cabin view-screen, she could see a thousand points of light shimmering in the blackness of space. Some brighter, some fainter. The far right-hand side of the view-screen was lit up by a single huge fiery mass.

'That,' said Beano, pointing to the fiery mass, 'is the Walder-J star itself, the sun of this solar system. A blue-white giant — we call them "Blueys" in Spacers' jargon. We've been passing close and using its gravitational pull to slow our speed.'

17

He pointed to a glowing spot of light in the centre of the view-screen. 'And that's planet P-19, where we're heading.'

Vail frowned. 'What's those dark lines I can see? Behind P-19 and across in front of the stars over there?'

'Can you see that?' Beano was surprised. 'Most people wouldn't be able to pick it out. That's the Anti-Human.'

'I've heard of it. What is it?'

'It's like a dark web between the stars, cutting off the light. Much larger than you can see from here. We'd get a clear view if we were closer.'

Vail shivered. 'Close enough for me.'

'Yep, we're right on the edge of the galaxy here. P-19's the furthest out inhabited planet in the P Sector. This is the end of the road.'

'What'd happen if we went on into it?'

'Into the Anti-Human? Maximum zero! Mash-out!'

'But what exactly?'

'Not known. No ship has ever gone into the Anti-Human and returned. It's an area where human beings can't survive. There's thirty-two similar areas recorded on the charts now. Like a ring around the inhabited universe. This one beyond Walder-J was one of the first discovered.'

'Is it a force field or what?'

'Not known. It doesn't exist in any form that we can understand. Some scientists believe it's a malign intelligence.'

'Brrrr! Horrible. Talk about something else.'

'Sure. Accepted.' Beano fiddled with the knobs on the control panel, lighting up some dials and darkening others. 'Down to 200,000 k.d.s. now. Slowing at 1,000 per second. Time to broadside. That's Spacers' jargon for an interspeak message.'

He swung a bob-mike across in front of his mouth.

'Flightman Zeno Berrit here. We shall commence deceleration in five minutes approx. Please take your seats in the Flight Cabin.'

Vail smiled to herself.

'Is it very difficult?' she asked. 'Bringing a ship in?'

Beano whacked his knee with the flat of his hand. 'Nothing to it!' Then his face fell. 'Nothing at all when it's fully automated. The ship's computer looks after everything nowadays. See that screen.'

She nodded.

'Those intersecting circles on the screen represent the navigation beams from P-19. They came through five, six minutes ago, when I did the first broadside on the interspeak. The ship's computer guides us in along those beams, works out where and when to decelerate, everything. No bandwork, no handwork.'

He sat silent for a moment. Then he whacked his knee with the flat of his hand again.

'What about you? You're a parapsych, right? On the police force?'

'*Attached* to the police force.'

'And we're going in to P-19 because of some crime? You two are going to solve it?'

'Me and Inspector Brac? Oh, I think he's going to solve it. He's going to work at it so hard, the murderer will surrender just to save him from a heart attack. I'm only along for the ride. Take in a few auras, enjoy the psychoscenery, you know?'

Beano looked puzzled. Vail lowered her eyelashes.

'So I guess I'll have plenty of spare time. How about you, Beano?'

Beano jumped as if he'd been stung.

'Yip! Yep! Sure! My orders are to wait around until you two are ready to return. Whooo-hupp!'

He twiddled knobs all over the control panel, muttering 'Zag-a-doo!' and 'Owzie-wowzie!' under his breath.

Then he decided it was time for another broadside.

Three minutes before deceleration. Could you please come forward and take your seat in the Flight Cabin, Inspector.

'We have to strap in?' asked Vail.

'Totally required. Where's your Inspector?'

'Oh, he's tough, he'll bounce around. Don't worry. Tell me something about this planet we're landing on.'

'You want the physical data?'

'And the ecology. And profile of the inhabitants.'

'Can't tell you about ecology and inhabitants.

That sort of stuff isn't important to Spacers. All we worry about is the condition of the spaceport. A De Luxe or a Hopstop or a Crumbly. This one's a Crumbly for sure — been out of use so long. Hey, we're the first ship to land here in seventy years.'

'I know. So tell me the physical data about the planet.'

'Heavy metal. 3,300 k diameter. 1.22 SEG. Daily rotation takes 22 hours 9 minutes.'

'Heavy metal? Is that more Spacers' jargon?'

'Nope. That means its mineral composition is over 90% metallic, so it has a heavy gravitational pull. 1.22 SEG means 1.22 times greater than Standard Earth Gravity.'

'Terrific. So every time I move it's like lifting a quarter as much extra weight again?'

'Nearly a quarter.'

'I'm exhausted already. Maybe I'll just stay lying down the whole time.'

Beano looked at her, then looked away again.

'The mineral composition is mainly ferrous, iron and cupro-nickel. Plus a high proportion of lead and zinc on the surface.'

'Oh-aaah. So there'd be a strong electro-magnetic field?'

'A real juicer. Very strong.'

There was a bump and a thump from behind. Inspector Eddon Brac grunted to announce that he had arrived. He settled himself into a seat behind the two front seats.

'One minute twenty seconds to deceleration,'

21

said Beano. 'Here we go, folks. You'll feel a jerking sensation when I switch on the inertial exchange system. Also breathlessness and a sort of floating in the chest. Don't worry about it. It'll happen seven or eight times. Like suddenly having a rug pulled from under your feet.'

He pressed a switch on the control panel. A shield rose up over the Flight Cabin view-screen, blocking the view.

'Nipper shipper, down the dipper! Spacers' jargon! Let's put this baby in the cot!'

4

Everything had changed angle by ninety degrees. The ship had decelerated, retro-reversed and docked. Now it sat on its tail in the spaceport. Their seats were facing skywards.

'I'll go get the portables,' said Eddon. 'I'll wait on Entry Deck.'

He reached for the nearest ladder and swung himself out of his seat. Hand over hand he clambered down the wall of the Flight Cabin, disappearing through the doorway which had now become a trapdoor.

Beano turned and spoke into a second bob-mike.

'HP4107 to Ground. Commencing internal check and shutdown.'

A speaker overhead responded.

'*Ground here. All okay. Exit steps are on their way.*'

Vail still hadn't moved. She was slumped out in her seat like a dying fish. Her eyes were closed and her nostrils dilated.

'Hey!' Beano looked across and realised. 'You okay? Have you fainted?'

One eyelid lifted lazily.

'Hmm. How could I tell you I'd fainted if I'd fainted?'

'I thought the deceleration might have —'

'Loved it. I always close my eyes when I'm enjoying something. Don't you?'

She unclipped the straps on her seat and stretched luxuriously. A voice came suddenly from the speaker overhead.

'*Ground here. Ready for you to disembark.*'
Beano frowned.

'*HP4107 here. Will be disembarking when check and shutdown completed. Five minutes approx.*'

He began switching switches and pressing buttons.

'You're welcome to go down to Entry Deck if you want,' he suggested. 'Inspector Brac said he'd be there with the baggage.'

'Yeah, I heard him.'

There was a ladder, now vertical, on the wall beside her. With a sinuous twist, she swung herself out of her seat and onto the ladder. She clung there for a moment, surveying the Flight Cabin.

'Everything looks different, don't you think? More solid and massive?'

'Because of the gravity? They say it's because you feel heavier in yourself. A subjective illusion.'

'My illusions are always completely objective,' said Vail, with a swirl of her cloak.

She started to descend, down through the Flight Cabin and out through the doorway. What had been the corridor was now a vertical shaft like a well. Rung by rung she lowered herself past bulwarks, past air-vents, past the entrance to the Passenger Cabin.

She went slowly, turning her head in every direction, trying to take an impression of the change. It was as though the materials of the ship had become more densely present, more heavily *there*. The very walls seemed to be pressing in and somehow closer together than they were before.

She climbed down through another doorway. Entry Deck was now directly below her, dimly lit in an orangey light. She could see the top of Eddon Brac's head.

'Where've you been?' he said, without looking up.

'Practising dark magic. Secrets of the coven.'

She descended to the floor of Entry Deck. She jumped the last two rungs, dropping to the ground with her arms flung wide and her cloak spreading out like the wings of a bat.

Entry Deck served mainly as a cargo hold. It was bare and unfurnished, with stores and equipment boxed and clipped along the walls. There was a stack of baggage in the centre of the floor: three foldaways, three bags and a portacase. Two of the bags and all of the foldaways bore the initials *V ev V*. Eddon was standing beside the exit door.

'Be ready when the door opens,' he said. 'There could be a whole crowd out there to meet us. Remember, we're the first outsiders to visit this planet in seventy years.'

'Wow, big occasion!' She draped herself, half sitting, half leaning, on the baggage. 'How many people live on this planet anyway?'

'Not many. About two thousand at the time of the Breakaway. Wouldn't have increased much since then.'

He was eyeing her make-up disapprovingly: the wavering slash of lipstick, the incomplete rings of kohl. Vail showed her teeth in a grotesquely brilliant smile, like a parody of a holo-film star.

'This is my new look,' she announced. 'The half-finished look. I've decided to make it fashionable.'

Eddon snorted. 'Guess it doesn't matter. After seventy years they'll hardly know what's normal in the rest of the galaxy.'

'No, maybe they'll think it's you that's the weirdo.'

Eddon rolled his eyes heavenward, and murmured something under his breath. They stood in silence for a while.

Vail studied him discreetly. Good-looking enough, she thought. A wry mobile face, full of expression, with jutting eyebrows and a strong jaw.

25

His blue eyes roamed ceaselessly this way and that. Everything about him was forceful, restless, pugnacious. Yes, good-looking enough – but seriously lacking in style. His dark brush-like hair shot out at all angles and he seemed in need of a shave. Even in Police uniform he looked somehow unkempt.

'So here we are waiting then,' she said at last. 'Let's pass the time pleasantly. Would you like to tell me the history of P-19?'

'"Like" in the sense of: enjoy, take pleasure in?'

'"Like" in the sense of: proceed to second-best option. Since I didn't learn it all up beforehand.'

Eddon looked at her thoughtfully for a moment, then nodded. He began rattling out facts in a rapid-fire voice.

'Planet P-19 was first colonised 170 years ago. Human expansion across the galaxy was still in full swing then. P-19 had suitable oxygen atmosphere, suitable sunlight, suitable H_2O conditions. Not exactly the same as Standard Earth Environment, but not too different. Main disadvantage was the metallic composition of the terrain.'

'Mainly iron and cupro-nickel,' Vail added helpfully. 'With a high proportion of lead and zinc on the surface.'

She smiled back at Eddon's quirked eyebrows.

'No, I didn't read it up. Let's just call it witches' intuition.'

'Okay. So with a metallic composition like that, the planet needed tending. A nursling planet. You know about nursling planets?'

'Oh-aaah. The plant life has to be built up very gradually. Beginning at the bottom of the chain, first lichens, then mosses. You try and get the lower forms started, drawing on available minerals. When the lichens and mosses can sustain their own life-cycle, they become eco-factories producing more and more organic material. Eventually there should be enough organic material to start growing edible plants. Over a thousand years you can make a whole planet fertile.'

'Right. After about 80 years, nearly one twen-tieth of the surface of P-19 was covered with lichen. The colonists had enough land under culti-vation to look after their own food supply. "Colonists" meaning, in this case, administrators, scientists and agricultural workers. The administra-tors and scientists were sent out by the Hegemony on term contracts, to provide control and exper-tise. The agricultural workers were permanent — political drop-outs, anti-urbanites, ex-crims, the usual volunteers. Anyone mad enough to prefer a bare survival existence at the edge of the galaxy to the civilised pleasures of a well-settled planet. No brain-power required, just manual labour. Hence the nickname "peasants".'

'Sort of similar to the nickname "witches"? I like them already.'

'Yeah? You'll find plenty to like on P-19 then, because it's only the agricultural workers that are left now. They took over in the Breakaway — their revolution against the Hegemony. At first it was peasants and scientists versus administrators. Then the scientists changed sides after the original Governor was stripped of power. The Hegemony brought in troops and the rebels were driven out into the uninhabitable zones. They were starving to death, almost finished, when suddenly this one scientist turned up on the rebel side — Argid ev Ghair. Ring a bell?'

'In the report. The Headman whose great-niece was murdered — his name was ev Ghair.'

'Got it. Presumably this Headman now would be a son or grandson of Argid ev Ghair — unless they have a Headman almost a hundred years old. Anyway, the rebels under Argid ev Ghair developed new tactics. The rebellion went on for two years, and in the end the Hegemony called it quits. They shipped out the troops and administrators and the rest, and left the planet to go its own way.'

'So what started the revolution in the first place?'

'The original Governor. He had this thing about the Anti-Human. You know about that? There's a huge patch of it just beyond the frontier here, beyond the Walder-J system. When they discovered it, this fool of a Governor wanted to become a conqueror. Thought he could overcome the Anti-Human by sending out ships to wipe out the webs. I suppose nobody knew the size of it then. Still, this Governor must've been a raving megalomaniac. It was when he tried to conscript the agricultural workers into forming a military force that the

Breakaway began. All totally unnecessary. Should never have happened.'

'Hmmm.'

'Hmmm indeed. So now you realise why we're being sent to P-19.'

'I thought it was to catch a serial killer?'

'It's political. The Hegemony wants to draw P-19 back into the fold. These drop-out planets usually come around to seeing the benefits of membership in the Hegemony after a while. We're being sent here in order to create links. The people on P-19 need help over these killings, so we have to show them how useful the Hegemony's help can be.'

'You don't like this assignment, do you?'

'Of course I don't. I didn't join the force to become a goddamned diplomat. I'm not into polite speeches and formalities.'

'Yeah, I noticed.'

'And you see what it means?'

'Do I?'

'Don't be so naive. It means we *have* to make an arrest. We're expected to come up with a result one way or another. This whole assignment is a pain in the ass.'

Vail flicked her long greeny-black hair to the side.

'Ah well, that's something anyway.'

'What is?'

'That it isn't just me you don't like.'

'Oh you. You're only a small twinge in the buttock.'

Vail was about to reply when a green light began flashing above the exit door. There was a whirr of hidden machinery and a sudden suck of air from around the doorseal.

'Door's been released,' said Eddon. 'Get yourself upright, PP. We're on.'

He unclipped the safety-fast, opened up the masterlock, and rotated the handle of the exit door.

There was no crowd and no welcoming reception. The mobile steps had been wheeled up and adjusted to the level of the exit door. Eddon and Vail came out onto the top of the steps. A single figure stood waiting at the bottom.

'Hello, peasants,' said Vail to the non-existent crowd. 'Not one of my greatest star appearances.'

'What a dump,' said Eddon.

It was a dreary desolate world, weighed down under heavy skies. Everything was in shades of grey. A cold rain was drizzling all around and the ground was covered in mist. Far off in the distance the tops of several tall buildings loomed out above the mist; closer in, the rounded hump of the spaceport control tower was vaguely visible. It was the sort of scene that seemed to have been standing there since the beginning of time.

There was a clatter on the ladder behind them,

and a cheery 'Whooo-hupp!' Beano had come down to the Entry Deck.

'We need to shift this baggage,' he called out. 'Any auto-porters?'

'Not as such,' said Vail.

'No? We'll have to carry it ourselves then,' said Beano. 'The ship has to be closed up before we leave. Can't have curious sightseers wandering around inside.'

'Sightseers?' Eddon snorted. 'Curious?'

Beano had brought down his own portacase. They went back inside and picked up two items of baggage each. One large bag and one foldaway remained.

'I'll come back for those,' said Beano.

They started down the steps in the rain. Below them, the landing pad on which the ship stood was a crisscross grid of rusty metal. In some parts the rust had eaten away the surface completely.

'Whango-prango,' muttered Beano. 'This is prehistoric. It's a miracle we didn't crash on landing.'

The man on the ground watched impassively as they descended. He wore high-boots and a kind of semi-transparent coat with a hood. His clothing was dark, but shot through with strange glints of silver and pewter and bronze. Metal bangles hung from his arms and wrists, and a small triangle of mirror-glass was pinned to his chest like a badge.

Only when they came to the bottom of the steps did he make a move. He held out a hand.

'Welcome to Independent P-19.'

His voice was slow and deliberate, with an

oddly deep resonance. He did not smile. There were heavy lines etched into his face, though he did not appear old. Thick black eyebrows matched thick black moustache. His skin had a ghastly leaden hue, with deep hollows of darkness around the eyes.

Eddon remembered the old-fashioned ceremony of shaking hands as a sign of greeting. He stepped forward and shook hands.

'Inspector Eddon Brac, Central Police,' he said. 'And this is my assistant, Vail ev Vessintor. And Flightman Berrit.'

The hand-shaking ceremony was repeated with Vail and Beano. The man seemed less surprised at Vail's bizarre neo-gothic appearance than at her height. He himself was solid and stocky, half a head shorter than Beano and a whole head shorter than Eddon.

'My name is Masilin III Crouth,' he said. He pointed to the mirror-badge on his chest. 'I am a Senior Leader here. You would say perhaps: guardian, or supervisor. We have no officialdom or bureaucracy on planet P-19.'

Beano set down the baggage he was carrying, turned and headed back up the steps for the remaining bag and foldaway.

There was a moment of silence. Masilin was staring up at the ship. Vail shook herself like a cat.

'Brrr,' she said. 'I hate rain.'

Masilin brushed a hand across his forehead. The metal bangles jangled on his arm.

'Ah, I have brought vannamaks for you. You are not used to our weather on P-19?'

He reached into a pocket, drew out two tightly rolled bundles of material and passed them across to Vail and Eddon. Opened up, they turned out to be lightweight coats with hoods, exactly like the one he was wearing himself.

'Your weather is *always* like this?' asked Vail. She draped the coat over her cloak. It came down only as far as her waist.

'Sometimes rain, sometimes shower, sometimes mist.'

'No sun?'

'There is our sun.' Masilin gestured to one side of the sky. A wan white orb glimmered through the cloud. 'Late afternoon. Soon it will be sunset.'

Again he stared up at the ship. The exit door was now closed and locked. Beano came back down the steps to rejoin the group.

'Whooo-hupp! These bags weigh a megaton!'

'The gravity of our planet is new to you,' said Masilin. 'Avoid over-exertion until your body has adjusted. Otherwise you may cause damage to your heart and muscles.'

He spoke flatly, distantly, as though his mind was on something else. He handed Beano a third vannamak, then picked up the two leftover items of baggage.

'Let us not delay,' he said.

He turned and set off into the mist. Eddon caught him up and walked alongside, with Vail and Beano following behind.

Beyond the landing pad, the ground was flat

and smooth as if wave-worn. Grey mineral ground, striated with fine veins of coppery blue-green. It clanged under their feet like beaten metal. Here and there were sad pools of standing water and patches of velvety moss. Masilin led them around the pools of water on a twisting turning route.

'Where are we heading?' Eddon asked.

'To the M-rail. Junior Leader Wyvis and Junior Leader Oaves will meet us there. They have been in the control tower, sending out the navigation beams which guided your ship down.'

'And this M-rail — we ride on it?'

'Yes. To Steyne-2. The main settlement and capital of P-19.'

'Right. I think I saw it already.'

At ground level, the mist completely obscured the distant buildings whose tops they had seen before. But Eddon nodded in the approximate direction.

'Over there, isn't it?'

Masilin frowned. 'No. What you saw was the Old Settlement. Steyne-1. Nothing but shells and ruins. Nobody lives or works there now.'

'How's that?'

'The Old Settlement was the centre for administration in the time before the Breakaway. Administration and research and manufacturing. Those buildings were built with materials shipped in from other planets. Hegemony buildings. They don't belong on P-19.'

'You abandoned them for political reasons?'

'For reasons of pride and self-respect. And

because everything in the Old Settlement ran on fuels we don't have here. There's no fissionable nuclear material and no organic fossil fuels on P-19.'

'What do you use then?'

'We have developed our own technologies. We live with our planet, we use what it gives. You will see when we come to the M-rail.'

They walked on in silence. The pools of water, the mist, the patches of moss — everything seemed endlessly the same. The only sound was the eerie clanging of their footsteps.

'Masilin,' said Eddon suddenly, 'are you in charge of this business?'

'Business?'

'These four killings.'

Masilin seemed momentarily taken aback.

'Four killings. Of course. You received our message. In what way do you mean, in charge?'

'In charge of the investigation. In charge of the people working on the case.'

'We have no police force on P-19.'

'Right, I guessed that. But still, you must have people working on the case?'

'No, that is your role. My role is to look after you and render assistance.'

Eddon grimaced to himself. 'So you're the one I have to ask for information?'

'You can ask me. Or Junior Leader Wyvis. Or Junior Leader Oaves.'

'First question then. Have there been more killings?'

'More killings?' Masilin appeared to be digesting the question.

'Yes. Since we received your message over two months ago. You looked surprised when I said four.'

Masilin's brain seemed to have come to a standstill. It was a long while before he finally spoke.

'No, there is nothing new.'

'He's lying low then, this psychopath. Perhaps after his close escape that last time . . . ?'

'So it would appear.'

'And have you uncovered any new facts? In the last two months?'

Masilin turned his leaden-hued face to look directly at Eddon. 'You are in a hurry, Inspector Brac? You want to solve this case and return to your Central Police?'

'Sure. Solving cases quickly is my speciality.'

'Things do not happen quickly on P-19.' Masilin's tone was final. 'The information on the case we can discuss tomorrow.'

He raised his voice and spoke to include Vail and Beano. 'We are nearly at the M-rail. Now you can see it ahead.'

Something like a low wall loomed through the mist in front of them. It was a girder of continuous metal, rising up about half a metre from the ground.

'Let me guess,' Vail called out from behind. 'M-rail stands for Magnetic railway.'

'Your guess is correct,' said Masilin. 'We use the planet's own magnetic field as a power source to propel the railcar.'

As they came closer they could distinguish a smaller strip of metal running all the way parallel to the larger girder. Whereas the girder was a dull black colour, the smaller strip glittered like polished steel. Both girder and strip were fastened to the ground with clamps and bolts.

'The railcar has not yet arrived,' said Masilin. 'We will wait for them here.'

Beano put down his bags and went forward to inspect the rails. He was fascinated by this new technology.

'So how does it work?' he asked.

'The small rail is a ferrous alloy which polarises under the planet's influence. The large rail is non-ferrous and magnetically uncharged. The railcar's propulsion unit works by using the difference between them.'

'What sort of power do you get?'

'Low power. But constant and inexhaustible.' Masilin put down his bags and moved forward beside Beano.

'The unit's rotor touches the steel rail,' he explained. 'The rotor oscillates to make and break contact.'

Beano had a hundred questions to ask. They started discussing field-sequences and transductors and electro-magnetic gradients.

Eddon was fuming. He turned to Vail.

'Look at him now,' he growled. 'Willing enough to talk about propulsion units.'

'Yeah, but not serial killings. I heard.'

'"Things do not happen quickly on P-19" — what's that supposed to mean?'

'Mmm. They send an urgent request for help, get us to come half way across the galaxy. And when we arrive this guy doesn't even care.'

'Oh, he cares.' Eddon was very definite.

'He does?'

'He cares about *something*. Very strongly. Only he's holding it in.'

'I didn't know you had psychic talents.'

'Hnh, nothing psychic about it. Observation of ordinary voice-cues. There's some sort of feeling churning him up inside. Maybe hope, maybe fear, I'm not sure.'

'Is it a feeling about us?'

Eddon was about to reply when suddenly a dark shape appeared out of the mist. The railcar had arrived. It glided along the two rails in absolute silence. Then it slowed smoothly to a halt.

The railcar was little more than a trolley: six wheels, a chassis and a fabric roof mounted upon poles. In front was a seat where the driver sat, behind were two rows of seats facing in towards a central aisle. To Beano's disappointment, the propulsion unit was hidden away under the chassis.

Junior Leader Oaves and Junior Leader Wyvis

were short and muscular like Masilin. They too wore vannamaks and metal bangles on their arms. Only the badge of mirror glass on their chests was different: circular instead of triangular.

Masilin performed the introductions. Oaves and Wyvis shook hands and smiled, but somehow the smile stopped short of their eyes. Wyvis helped load the baggage into the back of the railcar, while Oaves remained sitting in the driver's seat.

Then the group climbed in and took their places. Eddon, Vail and Beano sat on one side of the aisle, Masilin and Wyvis on the other. Oaves shifted a lever, and the railcar moved off.

For a time they talked about the journey out to P-19. Wyvis seemed very interested in space travel. Although he had worked the equipment to transmit the navigation beams, he still didn't understand how the guidance system operated. Beano was happy to explain.

Eddon studied Wyvis's face. He seemed younger than Masilin and wore no moustache, but his face had the same leaden hue and dark shadows around the eyes, almost like bruising. His manner, though slow, was taut and tense. He had a habit of blinking and wincing his eyes as he spoke.

The railcar reached its top speed and glided along steadily at about twenty kilometres an hour. The rain was falling more heavily now, thrumming on the roof, but the mist had started to clear.

After a while they left the area of the spaceport and came to a new kind of scenery. The bare metallic ground and pools of water were replaced by fields of crops, mainly tubers and green vegetables. The fields were very small and divided by intersecting drainage channels. Some were enclosed within high walls of solid metal.

A little further on, the first buildings came into view. They were long and low like humped-up ridges of the ground itself. They glistened a bluey-grey gun-metal colour in the rain. They had odd little spires at the corners and deep-set windows edged with mouldings of silver and bronze. Their walls blended in with their roofs and their roofs were softly rounded at the top. Nowhere were there any sharp angles or geometrical straight lines. They looked as though they had been made out of soft wax.

'Now you see how we build on P-19,' said Masilin. 'Our planet gives us metal ores which are naturally malleable, naturally easy to hammer and shape. Everywhere there is building material at hand. Why should we need to manufacture microplastic or fibre steel?'

'What are the spires for?' asked Eddon.

'What for? For decoration, ornamentation. What else should they be for?'

'Of course.' Eddon made an effort to be diplomatic. 'My Hegemony way of thinking. I'm used to a purely functional architecture.'

'Ah yes. Functional glass towers and mega-domes and skybridges. Doubtless our buildings do not seem very impressive when that is what you are used to.'

Masilin's voice was sarcastic. Wyvis came in quickly to smooth over the harshness.

'Hegemony architecture has its own way of being impressive,' he said. 'On P-19 we have gone in a different direction. You will see more clearly as we approach the centre of Steyne-2.'

'You will see an art that exists nowhere else in the galaxy,' said Masilin.

They travelled on in silence. Gradually the M-rail rose up above the ground, running along an embankment. The buildings became more and more frequent. Now they were arranged in clusters and rows, linked together by huge pipes. Sometimes the walls were dull or covered in lichen, sometimes they were polished and bright. There seemed to be very few people around — only an occasional figure glimpsed in the distance, hurrying along under the rain. Eddon, Vail and Beano twisted around on their seats, trying to look out on all sides.

'The building coming up on the left,' said Masilin, 'is the house of the Peresall family.'

It was a building with taller spires and a crest of metalwork along the roof. The spires were grooved around and around like barley sugar, and the metalwork crest was fretted into intricate shapes of lace. The mouldings around the windows spread out across the walls in bands of metallic silver and coppery green. The whole building looked like a fantastically patterned jewellery box.

'The patterns remind me of vegetation,' said Vail. 'Vines or roses or something.'

41

'That is our Classical style of decoration,' explained Wyvis. 'It developed after the Breakaway and reached a peak about thirty years ago.'

'Expressing your dreams perhaps,' mused Vail. 'You wanted to make plants grow here on this planet, so your craftsmen created a style of rich tangled vegetation. In metal.'

'Must take a helluva long time,' said Eddon. 'If it's all done by hand.'

'Yes, it is all done by hand,' said Masilin. 'We have plenty of time on P-19. Patience is something one must learn on a nursling planet. We do not have the entertainments and amusements which keep you so busy at the Centre of the Hegemony.'

'Anyway, I think it's a drift,' said Vail. 'Really beautiful.'

The railcar carried them on into the heart of Steyne-2. The white orb of the sun was now almost totally clouded over, and the light had started to fade. Looking down from the height of the embankment, they could see streets and alleys and quiet deserted squares carpeted in green moss. Water-filled channels ran down the sides of the streets and dark iron pipes crossed over from building to building. Many of the buildings were decorated with bronze wrought tracery on the walls, or gold fillets inlaid on the roofs, or lavishly embellished porches. There seemed no end to the variety of ornamentation.

Masilin called out some of the names as they passed by.

'The Saith family house.'

'Over there with the silver beading — the Curtelhouse.'

'The house of the Clavendars and Bredes.'

Vail pointed to a building that hadn't been named. 'And what's that one?'

It was Wyvis who answered. 'The Golgass Market.'

'Is that a different style?'

'Yes, that's what we call the Extravagant style.'

The Golgass Market bristled with dozens of spires, each one ending in a pointed barb. Taut wires were strung out in a web-like pattern from spire to spire. Around the windows and doors was a profusion of metalwork wrought into strange skeletal shapes. Strangest of all was the bright rusty red colour of the walls themselves. The over-all effect was savage and discordant.

'Is it an older style?' asked Vail. 'Before the Classical?'

'No, it is more recent,' said Wyvis.

'I thought because of the rust —'

'The rust is part of the style.'

'Oh-aaah. Are there many buildings in the Extravagant style?'

'Not many. There hasn't been much building work done recently on P-19.'

Masilin broke in abruptly. 'Our finest buildings are in the Classical style,' he said. 'Soon we will come to the Big House, which is the finest of all.'

The line of the M-rail on which they were

43

travelling came to an intersection with another line. Junior Leader Oaves threw a lever to the side. With a loud click the railcar came to a halt on the point of the intersection, then swung around through 45 degrees. Another loud click, and it accelerated off along the new line.

The new line took them in a direction where the ground rose steadily uphill. The embankment shrank away beneath them. Soon they were travelling along on a level with the streets. They passed by more decorated buildings, including another in the Extravagant style.

In one street, they saw a woman walking fast, head down, keeping close to the walls of the houses. She wore the usual semi-transparent vannamak and had the usual solid build. She did not look up as the railcar went by.

'Not many people around,' Eddon commented.

'It is getting late,' said Masilin. 'Almost everyone is indoors by now.'

'They must go to bed very early,' said Vail. 'This is my usual waking up time.'

Masilin looked at her out of the dark pits around his eyes. 'Ah, you are being humorous.'

'How many people in Steyne-2?' asked Eddon.

'About four thousand.'

'As many as that? What about P-19 as a whole?'

'About six and a half thousand. You seem surprised?'

'I thought there were only two thousand left here at the time of the Breakaway.'

'Of course. We have grown. Did the Hegemony imagine we would dwindle away without their help?'

'No, but —'

'In the first thirty years of independence our population doubled. Ten years ago we could support a population of seven thousand.'

Wyvis coughed. 'We have had a few bad harvest years since then.'

While they were talking, the M-rail had dipped down below the level of the ground. Now only the bottom parts of the houses were visible, cut off between the rising banks and the roof of the railcar. Everyone fell silent as the gloom deepened. Wyvis seemed rigid and tense, Masilin brushed his hand across his forehead. A few seconds more, and the banks blocked out the view completely. Their faces were dim ovals in the semi-darkness.

But already the railcar was slowing down. Up ahead, the cutting terminated in a blank wall. This was the end of the line. A queue of three railcars stood parked one behind the other. Oaves worked his levers and brought their own railcar to a halt, bumping gently up against the tail of the queue.

'Now we shall take you to the Big House,' said Masilin.

There was a path running along at the side of the cutting, leading to a flight of iron steps. The three P-19ers clambered out and gathered up most of the baggage. Eddon, Vail and Beano followed with the rest. They walked to the end of the path and climbed the steps.

It was still raining. One by one they emerged from the gloom, out into the fading light of the late afternoon. Wide open space was all around. They had come out into the centre of an immense square, a square of black metal inlaid with rays of gold. Three sides of the square were surrounded by grandly decorated houses. On the fourth stood the Big House itself.

The Big House was a glittering miracle. It was only a single storey high, like all the buildings on P-19, but its facade was almost a hundred metres wide. It had no overall symmetry, with rooms and wings tacked on at random, and a chaotic superstructure of spires and domes and pinnacles. Every part of the facade was covered with shining mirror glass: a hundred thousand mirrors cut into irregularly shaped panels. The whole facade seemed to shift and change as one moved, like the scales of some great creature coiling and uncoiling in the light.

Eddon, Vail and Beano stood gazing and recovering their breath. Unaccustomed to the heavy gravity, they were exhausted by the climb up the steps.

Masilin put down the two bags he was carrying and pointed proudly.

'See the large arch and doorway on the left? That's the Major Portal. And over there, the roof with the star design? That's the roof of the Old Hall.'

'Whose house is it?' asked Vail.

'Headman ev Ghair lives there all the time, and his family. Along with whoever is doing their turn as Leader or Reeve. There are one hundred and forty-nine rooms altogether. Including the guest rooms, where you'll be staying.'

'Let us go on!' Junior Leader Oaves broke in. He gestured towards the darkening sky. 'It is growing dark.'

He set off across the square. Masilin picked up his two bags again, and the whole party followed.

'Can we just have a walk along in front of the facade?' suggested Vail. 'So beautiful!'

'Tomorrow,' said Wyvis over his shoulder. 'You'll appreciate it more in the light.'

Eddon lengthened his stride and moved up to walk alongside Masilin.

'I'll be wanting to report back to Central, of course.'

'Why?'

'Why not?'

'To tell them that you've arrived?'

Eddon clenched his fists. 'Because I feel like it.'

'You would have to have approval from our Headman to use the Messages Centre. You would need to see him.'

'So I'll see him. I expect to see him. Why shouldn't I see him?'

Masilin looked uncomfortable. 'He may not want to see you.'

'What do you mean? He sent a request asking for urgent assistance. His own great-niece was one of the victims. Of course he'll want to see me.'

'We sent the request.'

'We? Who's we?'

'Junior Leader Oaves, Junior Leader Wyvis, and myself.'

'Goddamnit, what sort of a system do you run here? Was it an official request or not?'

Masilin shrugged. 'Ev Ghair knew about it. He didn't stop us from sending it. But he didn't encourage it either.'

Eddon glared at him, eyeball to eyeball. 'Okay, Masilin III Crouth. I can't do my job if I don't have everyone's full cooperation. Either I get to see your Headman, or I turn right round and tell my Flight-man to take us back.'

'No!' There was a sudden intensity in Masilin's voice. 'No. You mustn't do that. I'll try to arrange a meeting.'

'Try immediately. Today.'

'Very well.'

They came to the doorway that Masilin had called the Major Portal. Up close, one could see that the walls behind the mirror glass were moulded out of some dark blue metal. The door itself was a massive iron construction, studded and barred.

As they approached, a slot slid back in the door

and a pair of eyes stared out. Then came the sound of locks being turned and chains being unhooked. Finally the door swung smoothly open. Oaves led the way in.

Inside it was dry and warm. There were small yellowy lights like fairy lights dotted everywhere overhead. Even added all together, their tiny glows still left the hallway full of shadows. The ceiling was decorated with silver pendants, reminiscent of stalactites in a cave. Nowhere were there any soft-enings of cloth or carpet. The vibration of their footsteps set the metal walls ringing.

Oaves exchanged a few words in a low voice with the man behind the door. Then he led the party down the hallway and along a corridor. Beano swerved to the side of the corridor and touched a hand against the walls.

'Hey, I thought so!' he exclaimed. 'These walls are warm.'

'Heated by an electric current,' said Wyvis. 'All the walls in our houses are the same.'

'Must use a lot of electricity.'

'We tap the planet's own electro-magnetism. The charge builds up through long coils of ferrous alloy, running across from building to building.'

'Inside those pipes we saw?' Vail hazarded.

'Yes,' said Wyvis. He pointed to the tiny lights overhead. 'And the same charge powers our lighting.'

They came to a large hexagonal room with sev-eral exits. In each corner of the room was a huge brass sphere mounted like a globe. Complicated lines and shapes were incised on the surfaces of the spheres.

'The guest rooms are this way,' said Oaves, heading left.

'First we have to meet your Headman,' said Eddon.

Oaves looked at Masilin, who nodded unhappily.

'Yes, go to the Old Hall,' he confirmed.

They took an exit to the right and proceeded along another larger corridor. This corridor curved in a semicircle, and there were small niches let into the walls at regular intervals. Each niche contained a holo-image of some helmeted man or woman, carrying a gun.

Down at the far end of the corridor was a doorway surrounded by a whole arc of clustered lights. Masilin, Wyvis and Oaves seemed to tread more carefully and quietly as they approached. The door was slightly ajar.

There were voices within, raised in animated discussion. One deep voice boomed out above the rest.

'That is Headman ev Ghair,' whispered Wyvis.

'So what are we waiting for?' Eddon demanded.

The P-19ers exchanged dubious glances.

'The three of us will go in first and tell him you're here. Then if he's willing to see you . . .'

Masilin, Wyvis and Oaves put down the bags they were carrying and entered the Old Hall. They entered around the side of the door, allowing the visitors no view of the interior. Once in, they swung the door smartly shut behind them.

Eddon and Vail took a pace forward and bent their ears to the door. But the thickness of the metal muffled all sounds. Eddon swore and turned away. He began walking impatiently up and down.

Vail looked at him with raised eyebrows. 'Did you mean what you said before?' she asked. 'About turning round and going back?'

'You overhear a lot, don't you? No, I wouldn't be too popular with Police Commissioner Magendor if I did that.'

'Only bluffing. I thought so.'

'Politics, politics, politics.' Eddon scowled. 'We've landed right in the middle of some petty little intrigue, some stupid faction fight or something.'

'You think so?'

'Don't you? Don't you have any of your famous parapsychic intuitions about it?'

'Mmmm, I have lots of intuitions.'

'Like what?'

'Oh, nothing that'll be much help to you.'

'Try me.'

'There's something wrong about this place.'

'In what sense wrong?'

'Just wrong. Not right. Discrepancies.'

'Masilin and his merry band?'

'More than them.'

'Headman ev Ghair?'

'More. More than political intrigue. It's a feeling I keep getting about this whole place.'

'Nothing definite, huh?'

'I told you it wouldn't be any help.'

51

'Phhuh.' Eddon expelled a contemptuous snort. 'Know what I don't like about you parapsychs? You suggest so much and then deliver so little. You create mysteries and then —'

He stopped in mid-sentence. There was another voice, a voice of thunder and passion. Muffled but booming, it was audible even through the thickness of the metal door. It was the deep voice of Headman ev Ghair, launching into a tirade.

'Do you think I don't know why you brought them? I'm not too old to see through you! What's in your hearts? Nothing! You have no hearts! I wash my hands of you! You and your Hegemony fools! Do what you want! Only get out of my sight!'

There was a tremendous banging, as of metal striking metal. The door opened and Masilin, Wyvis and Oaves shuffled backwards out of the Old Hall. A final furious shout of 'OUT OF MY SIGHT!' accompanied their exit.

Oaves closed the door. They were white-faced, all three of them. Masilin forced a smile.

'Not a good time to ask. I think you heard the answer.'

Eddon gave him a cold hard look. 'Okay. I'll see him tomorrow then.'

'Perhaps.'

'Perhaps?'

'Yes, later tomorrow. Let us show you to your rooms.'

As they picked up the baggage again, Vail bent over towards Wyvis and remarked, 'That was an old man's voice, wasn't it? Your Headman is an old man?'

'Yes.'

'Nearly a hundred years old?'

'Ninety-five.'

'So your Headman is still the same ev Ghair. The original leader of the revolution against the Hegemony.'

'Argid,' said Eddon, snapping his fingers. 'Argid ev Ghair.'

'Yes. He is still our leader.'

'Not bad for ninety-five,' said Vail. 'Powerful voice.'

They went on down the corridor towards the guest rooms.

Vail drew another looping line of kohl from the corner of her eye around and down to her left cheekbone. She had two half moons of glittering chrysolite above her eyebrows and her lips were submerged in an alternating pattern of red and purple lipstick. The dim lighting of the bedroom gave a dim reflection in the mirror, but that only made her all the more inventive. She was feeling pleased with herself.

They had eaten a meal in their rooms two hours ago, a simple meal of chicken and vegetables. Vail had arranged an exchange of rooms with Beano, so that his bedroom was now in the middle, between hers and Inspector Brac's. Privacy was important. She didn't want Brac listening on the other side of the wall when Beano came visiting her tonight.

She just hoped Beano would be able to rise to the romantic spirit of the evening. He didn't even know he was going to come visiting yet. But he'd get the idea when she was ready. She carried the kohl from her cheekbone to her ear, then finished off with a final twirl.

It was true, Beano wasn't as good-looking as Eddon Brac. But Brac wasn't her type — too speedy and aggressive. And too domineering. It was bad enough having to be ordered around as his assistant. No way was she going to get emotionally involved with *him*.

She remembered all the corny jokes about Police Inspectors and their PP assistants. It was almost a regular expectation. But she didn't intend to be that kind of PP assistant.

She tossed the wands, brushes and squirters into her make-up bag and tossed the make-up bag onto the floor. All her other baggage lay already scattered around on the floor — the foldaways containing her clothes, the bags containing her parapsych equipment. She didn't believe in cupboards and nor, it seemed, did the inhabitants of P-19.

Everything about the room pleased her. The heavy coppery-coloured curtains and drapes, the massive bed and bedside table, the dresser and mirror and stool. Everything was moulded in flowing lines, in sinuous shapes suggestive of growing plants. All so different from the abstract Hegemony style, with its flat bright surfaces and geometrical angles. This style had mystery and atmosphere. Above all, she liked the tiny dim lights and soft shadows and dark corners of the room. It was perfectly, excitingly neo-gothic.

She stood in front of the mirror and looked at herself with approval. She was wearing her sexiest slinkiest clothing: a tightfitting sheathsuit. *Very* tightfitting. It clung to her body like a second skin.

She swayed languidly from side to side. Her long greeny-black hair curled around one hip, then around the other.

'Purrrrrr!' she said to herself, feeling feline.

She took up a yellowy-gold flask of perfume. It was her own concoction — 'Uncanny Number 3' she called it. Hot like chilli and cool like mint. She dabbed it generously over her neck and wrists.

Then she lay down full-length on the bed. It was important to be fully relaxed for psychosummoning. She stretched and arched luxuriously.

She felt the heavy gravity pulling her down into the quilt, the weave of the quilt pressing up against her skin. Her feet extended beyond the end of the bed, but she was used to that. She settled and waited until she felt fully relaxed. Then she put her hands to the sides of her face and prepared to call Beano.

She thought of everything she'd seen him do

during the day. She ran through her memories from the time she'd sat beside him in the Flight Cabin to the time she'd said goodnight after the evening meal. The way he walked, spoke, gestured, even the way he breathed — slowly she sank herself into the essential impression of him.

Then she projected the impression forward into the way he was now. She imagined how he was lying in bed in his room. He would be asleep, of course, fast asleep like a baby . . .

With her mind focussed so intently upon Beano, she was not aware of the male presence advancing along the corridor. She did not hear when the footsteps halted outside her own bedroom.

Instead she began to murmur Beano's name in her mind: *Flightman Berrit.* Then: *Come and knock on Vail's door.* She smiled. It would take time to complete the connection, but she was in no hurry. *Flightman Berrit. Come and knock on Vail's door. Flightman Berrit —*

Suddenly she realised that someone was already at her door. Someone was taking a grip on the door handle. Not Beano. Who — what — why?

It was like a bucket of cold water thrown over her. She struggled to re-focus her perceptions, flooding back into herself.

There was a faint creaking sound as the door handle began to turn, very slowly.

Vail reached out to the bedside table, found the light-switch stand, and turned off the lights. At the same time, she slid snake-like across the quilt. As the door swung open, she dropped off the side of the bed.

The bed was built into the floor with solid metal side-panels. She lay stretched out against the side-panels, hoping she hadn't been heard.

A figure entered the room. For a moment he was visible against the light in the corridor: stocky and muscular, a typical P-19er. He held something like a cloth in one hand. With the other hand he closed the door carefully behind him.

She held her breath. She remembered Perla III Erridge, hideously murdered in one of the rooms in the Big House.

Who to call for help? She was desperate. She'd lost all connection with Beano. Eddon Brac would be a better bet. If only he wasn't asleep . . .

Frantically she ran through her memories of Eddon, trying to capture an exact impression. She remembered his way of moving and talking, his mobile face, his brusque manner, his scowl. Then she projected her impression forward into the present, imagining him in his bedroom at this very moment. She felt sure he wasn't asleep.

The intruder came forward on the other side of the bed. He stood by the top of the bed and reached out towards the bolster. There was a faint sound of indrawn breath. He had touched the bolster and found no-one there. Now he patted the bolster from end to end and felt with his hands all over the quilt.

Vail put her hands to the sides of her face. She

began to call Eddon Brac in her mind: *Eddon Brac. Vail needs help. Eddon Brac. Vail needs help...*

But she couldn't stop thinking about the intruder. It was impossible to get into the appropriate state of relaxation. She could hear the man's breathing and the rustle of his clothes. What was he doing now?

She sensed him stretching out across the bed. He was reaching for the bedside table. He must be intending to turn on the lights. Vail raised an arm, hooked her fingers around the light-switch stand and lifted it out of his way. She lifted it down from the table and onto the floor beside her.

'Zah!' He gave a sudden sharp hiss. Perhaps he had heard her movement. There was a moment's silence.

Vail willed herself to relax. She called up more memories of Eddon Brac. Again she projected her impression forward into the present. She had an idea that he was sitting on the side on his bed, leafing through a sheaf of papers.

Eddon Brac. Vail needs help. She murmured it over and over in her mind, forcing herself to remain calm. *Eddon Brac. Vail needs help. Eddon Brac. Vail needs help.*

And there it was! She felt the tiny tug of the connection being made. Her imagined impression of Eddon shifted and became a real apprehension. She slipped into the real position of his body sitting, the angle of his head, his hands holding the sheaf of papers. The message was getting through at last.

Suddenly the intruder made a lunge all the way across to Vail's side of the bed. He swept his hand through the air, missing her by inches. She felt the wind of his fingers passing just in front of her face.

Eddon Brac. Vail needs help. Vail needs help. Vail needs help.

The intruder withdrew. But only momentarily. Then she heard his footsteps moving around the bed. He was coming around from his side to her side.

She refused to panic. She would have to try and kick at him with her feet. Still flat on her back, she drew back her legs. There was a sharp ripping sound as her tightfitting sheathsuit split along the seams.

Now he knew exactly where she was. He began to bend down towards her. She steeled herself. Suddenly the door burst open.

Eddon stood in the doorway, silhouetted against the light of the corridor. He held some sort of gun in his hand.

'Ev Vessintor? What's going on?'

Looking into the darkened room, naturally he couldn't see a thing. The intruder whirled and rushed straight at him. There was a crunch and a thump. Eddon staggered sideways.

The intruder kept on going, out of the room and away down the corridor. Limping heavily, Eddon rushed out after him.

'To the left!' Vail called. She heard the sound of Eddon's footsteps going off to the left.

She gathered herself together and stood up.

Too quickly. There were more ripping sounds from her sheathsuit.

She stooped and felt around for the light-switch stand on the floor. She put it back on the table and turned on the lights. Looking down at her sheathsuit, she saw that the material had opened up all along the thighs and down the front.

Damn! And already she could hear Eddon's footsteps returning. He must have lost track of the intruder almost immediately.

She didn't want to get into complicated explanations. There was only one thing to do. She climbed into bed and slipped in under the quilt.

'Couldn't see which way he went,' said Eddon. 'Kicked me in the shin, the sonovabitch.'

He hobbled across to the stool and sat down. He was still wearing his daytime clothes. Vail kept herself well hidden with the quilt pulled right up to her chin.

'Did you get a look at him?' she asked.

'No. Did you?'

'Only that he was solid and muscular, like all these P-19ers.'

'Could he have been —?'

'The serial killer? I don't think so. More like a burglar.'

'A burglar? What's to burgle?' Eddon surveyed the room. 'Your parapsych equipment, I suppose.'

'But did he even know it was me in this room? I swapped with Beano, remember.'

'Oh, yeah. Hmm.'

Eddon was sniffing curiously. The strange fragrance of Uncanny Number 3 lingered in the air. He quirked an eyebrow but made no comment.

'Thanks for saving me anyway,' said Vail.

'Lucky I came round, huh? I must've heard a noise, gave me the idea you were in danger.'

He frowned for a moment, as if trying to remember something. Then he shook his head.

'What makes you think this wasn't the serial killer?'

Vail shrugged. 'I dunno. Too deliberate, too cautious.'

'That doesn't rule anything out. Just because psychopaths can be incredibly violent doesn't mean they can't be very cautious too.'

'I'll take your word for it. But this didn't *feel* like a serial killer.'

'Feel? What does a serial killer feel like?'

'I didn't get a sense of evil.'

'Evil?'

'You don't believe in evil, do you?'

'No. Not the way you parapsychs mean it. In my experience, there's always a psychological motive for any criminal act. Someone wants something. It might be a form of satisfaction that seems totally insane and bizarre to a normal person, but it's real for them. If you can work it out, their behaviour becomes explicable.'

'So, what've you worked out for this serial killer?'

'Nothing much yet. I've been studying the report for the last half hour. Do you know what's so unusual about this killer?'

'Slaughtering whole families and throwing their intestines around? Slashing people to ribbons with their own brooch-pins?'

A flicker of a grin passed over Eddon's face.

'Compared to other serial killers, I mean. What's so unusual is there's no pattern to his killings.'

'Explain.'

'Serial killers almost always have a definite modus operandi. Certain actions turn them on, excite them, a particular routine becomes an inflexible ritual. They're like addicts. Even the clever ones who vary their routine still select a very specific type of victim. But each of these four killings has been completely different. Old women, young women, males as well as females.'

'And completely different methods of attack.'

'Yeah. And notice how the murder weapon has always been something at hand, never deliberately taken along to the scene of the crime. As though the impulse to murder takes over on the spur of the moment.'

'Still, there's one similarity between all the killings.'

'Which is?'

'An absolute hatred of the human body.'

'Right. You picked up on that. The one similarity is this urge to utterly destroy the bodies of the victims. Every bone broken ... the boy's skull pulverised to a paste ... internal organs individually mutilated ... the slashing with the brooch pin. Extraordinary savagery. It's as though — why are you wearing a sheathsuit in bed?'

Too late Vail realised that she had let the quilt slip down, exposing her shoulders.

'Oh-aaah!' She gave a sort of giggle and pulled the quilt back up.

'Do you always go to bed in evening wear?'

'That's my business. Not relevant to our professional relationship.'

Eddon was still staring. '*Ripped* evening wear.'

'It was too tight.' Vail tried not to look him in the eyes. 'The seams split.'

Eddon rose from the stool and came across towards the bed. For a moment Vail wondered what he was going to do. Then he drew something out of his pocket.

It was a small black gun, the same gun he'd been brandishing earlier. He placed it with a clink on the bedside table.

'I'll leave this with you. In case of more burglars.'

Vail looked at it.

'This is a punchgun, isn't it? I've heard about them.'

'Yeah. I've got another back in my room.'

'Are they legal on this planet? Does anyone know you brought in punchguns?'

63

'Nobody asked. Do you know how to use it?'

Vail sat up higher in the bed. With one hand she clutched on to the quilt, keeping her shoulders well covered. With the other hand she reached out and picked up the gun. She held it close in front of her face and half shut her eyes. She didn't seem to be observing it so much as thinking about it. For a few moments she rotated it this way and that.

'It fires two sorts of projectiles,' she said slowly. 'Lethal and stun. There's a safety on the top, trigger in the usual place, and the shunt for lethal or stun is on the underside of the barrel. I think it works by pressure-coil, therefore almost silent. Right?'

She opened her eyes wide again. Eddon had a puzzled look on his face.

'I'm not right?'

'Yeah, totally right. I was just wondering how you did that.'

'Absorption interfacing. Witchcraft to you.'

'Hmm, well. So you can use a punchgun now?'

Vail nodded.

Eddon turned away and headed towards the door. Then he paused. He wheeled around to look at Vail again, pensively scratching his chin.

'Something the matter, Cl?'

'The noise I heard, that made me think you were in danger. Did I really hear a noise?'

'No. I called you.'

'I don't remember a call.'

'Not a call out loud. I planted a suggestion in your mind.'

'You mean, telepathy?'

'We call it psychosummoning. It's like a hypnotic suggestion. The receiver can't exactly remember it afterwards.'

'So you summoned me to come to your room?'

'It's only possible with someone known and familiar. Someone you can have an empathetic connection with.'

'Empathetic connection? Between you and me?'

'Hard to believe, isn't it?'

Eddon shook his head wonderingly. 'And all of you can do this? You parapsychs?'

'Some more, some less. I'm about as good as there is. I'm the witchiest.'

Momentarily forgetting about her sheathsuit, she waved her arms in a dramatic witchy gesture. The quilt slipped off her shoulders, accompanied by a loud sound of ripping.

Eddon breathed in sharply. The sheathsuit had split open all the way to her navel.

Quick as a flash she dived back down under the quilt. She dived down so far that her feet stuck out at the bottom of the bed.

'Professional relationship, Inspector,' she cried. 'Don't forget it!'

Eddon was staring at her hotly, almost angrily. He seemed to be contemplating the outline of her body under the quilt. Then he narrowed his eyes and looked away.

When he spoke, it was in his usual brusque, cynical voice.

'Don't let your feet get cold,' he said. 'I'll see you in the morning.'

He went out quickly, closing the door behind him.

PART TWO
Draive

1

Breakfast consisted of boiled egg, a kind of rye bread and marmalade, and a hot brew made from roasted barley seeds. Everything, especially the egg, had a faintly metallic taste.

'Same as the vegetables last night,' said Beano.

The food was served by Masilin's wife, Vanna, and Oaves' wife, Hillvey. It seemed as though the families of Masilin, Wyvis and Oaves were exclusively responsible for looking after the interplanetary visitors.

Eddon was planning ahead.

'Forget the intruder in Vail's bedroom,' he said. 'Almost certainly irrelevant. The serial killings are what we're here for. Number one priority is to get the full files on all four murders. And any additional information from Masilin and co. Then we'll start the investigation with the murder that happened right here in the Big House.'

'Blam! Zap! Powee!' said Vail unenthusiastically.

She looked still half asleep. 'I was hoping you'd stay in bed and nurse your bruised shin.'

'Recovered,' said Eddon. 'First, we'll need to interview all the witnesses. Everyone who broke into the bedroom and saw the killer escape.'

'Does this 'we' include me?' asked Vail. 'Doesn't sound like there's much work for a parapsych.'

'Maybe not, but there's plenty of work for a parapsych who's also an assistant. Lining up the witnesses for one thing. Recording interviews for another.'

Vail pulled a face. 'Pressing buttons on a voice-recorder. Sheez, what fun!'

'Next we'll focus on that other murder in Steyne-2. See if there are any leads there.'

'And what are your plans for today, Beano?' Vail asked, turning towards Flightman Berrit.

'Ah! Whooo! Guess I'll just go for a walk and take a look around town.'

'Sounds like heaven,' said Vail dreamily.

She sipped at her drink and picked half-heartedly at her bread and marmalade. Beano ate his last slice of bread and pushed his plate away. Eddon had finished his breakfast five minutes before.

They were sitting in a small room adjoining a large kitchen. The early morning light came in through two deep-set windows. It seemed a brighter day than yesterday.

Vail was still sipping her drink when Masilin, Wyvis and Oaves came in. The hollows around their eyes looked darker than ever.

'Good morning,' said Masilin. 'I hope you had a peaceful night's sleep.'

'As a matter of fact,' Vail began, 'my night was dramatically interrupted.'

But Masilin wasn't listening. 'There's been another killing,' he announced.

'The message came in this morning,' added Wyvis. 'A young man found murdered in Draive. A violent, senseless attack.'

'Hmm.' Eddon snapped his fingers. 'This changes our priorities.'

'You should follow it up straight away,' said Masilin. 'Get out to Draive immediately. It's about fifteen kilometres away.'

Eddon turned to Vail. 'Looks like your parapsychic powers will be needed after all.'

Vail groaned.

Masilin pulled out a map and unfolded it on the breakfast table. It was a map of the inhabited area of P-19. He pointed with his forefinger.

'We're here, at the centre of P-19. And Draive is over here. It's one of our outer settlements. There's an M-rail all the way out.'

He refolded the map and handed it to Eddon.

'This is for you. These too.'

He nodded to Oaves, who stepped forward and held out two circular pieces of mirror glass.

'These are Junior Leaders' badges. You are entitled to wear them while officially working on this case. People will understand that you have authority.'

Eddon and Vail each took a badge. Vail started

to pin hers onto the high collar of her cloak, but Oaves shook his head.

'No, it must be worn in the middle of the chest.'

'Not even on the lapel?'

'In the middle of the chest.'

'Draggy,' murmured Vail. 'Loses all effect.' But she re-positioned the badge.

Meanwhile Hillvey Oaves had brought in two bottles and two packages wrapped in metal foil.

'These are your provisions for the day,' said Masilin. 'Junior Leader Oaves will show you how to operate the M-rail.'

'Hold it!' Eddon raised a hand. 'There's a mis-understanding here. You don't expect us to head off to this Draive place on our own, do you?'

The three P-19ers looked uncomfortable.

'We cannot come with you today.'

'Why not?'

'Other urgent tasks.'

'More urgent than this? Okay, then find some-one to come with us who doesn't have urgent tasks.'

Masilin, Wyvis and Oaves exchanged glances.

'You are experts in criminal investigation,' said Oaves, spreading his hands. 'You have solved crimes all across the Hegemony. How could our limited abilities help you?'

'I don't need help solving the crime,' said Eddon. 'I need help talking to people. Practical help. I need to be told how things work on this planet.'

'Our ways are not very different.'

'Yes they are.'

'If you show your badges...'

'No.'

Masilin signalled to Wyvis and Oaves, and all three moved across to the side of the room. For a minute they conferred in low whispers. Then Masilin turned back to Eddon and Vail.

'Junior Leader Oaves will accompany you to Draive and give what assistance you require. Is that satisfactory?'

'Fine.' Eddon rose from the table. 'Let's get moving then.'

Vail sighed. 'I'll go collect my parapsychic equipment.'

Oaves sat in the driver's seat at the front of the railcar, Eddon and Vail sat behind. He didn't try to talk to them and they didn't try to talk to him.

Eddon studied the map he'd been given. It was all very different compared to the old maps from pre-Breakaway times. The inhabited area extended at least thirty-five kilometres east-west and twenty-five kilometres north-south. There were more settlements everywhere, and many new names.

He looked for the locations named in the original murder report. The Brennag was about thirty kilometres south-west of Steyne-2. Malais was about five kilometres due south of Steyne-2. Neither was anywhere near Draive.

Vail was content to watch the scenery glide by. There was only a light cover of cloud over the sun, and the air seemed full of brightness. Everything swam in an early morning haze. She gazed at the buildings shining with gleams of blue and bronze, and the people out working in the tiny fields. It was strange that so many of the fields were enclosed within high walls.

After about twenty minutes the scenery changed. The cultivated fields came to an end and were replaced by an endless spread of dark green moss. It was as though a velvet cloth had been spread out over the ground, shaped to every underlying rise or swelling. No trees or bushes or plants interrupted the smooth surface.

Eddon was following their route on the map. 'We're crossing the Winnifer Moss-moor,' he announced. 'The cultivated land only extends for ten kilometres around Steyne-2.'

Now the settlements were few and far between. For many kilometres there were only isolated houses. Paths ran across the moors like thin silvery snails' trails, worn down into the metallic ground beneath the moss.

It was beautiful country. Lakes were scattered everywhere, interconnected by countless small streams and channels. They seemed to swallow up the light, they were so utterly black and still. Even when the M-rail skirted beside them it was impossible to see down into their depths. Vail, half-closing her eyes, imagined them as bottomless holes.

It was beautiful country, but it had an odd smell. A dark smell, fetid and sour. Perhaps it came from the moss, perhaps from the stagnant lakes. It hung in the air like a vapour, like the sweat of the earth itself.

'Draive is right out on the edge of the moor,' said Eddon, consulting his map. 'Then the lichen-steppe begins.'

It was another twenty minutes before they saw the first patch of lichen. Vail pointed it out: an area of variegated colour, light green and chalky grey.

'Right,' said Eddon. 'Must be getting close now.'

Soon the moss thinned out, like velvet wearing away to baldness. More areas of lichen appeared, in varied colours: browny-red, lilac, maroon and a sort of tawny yellow. Away in the distance, bluffs and ridges rose up a hundred metres above the moor, also covered in blotchy lichen. They had a raw craggy look.

Then Oaves turned and called out over his shoulder.

'This is Draive up ahead on the left.'

Up ahead was a cluster of about forty buildings, huddled together on a small rise at the side of the M-rail. Silvery paths converged towards it from every direction.

Vail leaned forward to speak to Oaves. 'What do people do in Draive?' he asked. 'There's no farming here?'

'There is farming of a different kind,' said Oaves.

75

'The people in Draive are responsible for fifty square kilometres of the lichen-steppe. They spread the lichen spores and get the moss started, making the land fertile for future cultivation.'

The railcar crossed over a channel of dark water and glided in to the foot of the rise. The buildings had their backs turned towards the M-rail and seemed somehow blank and unfriendly. They were moulded out of soft grey metal, with the usual spires at the corners.

Oaves switched the railcar onto a sideline. There were two other railcars already standing parked there. Oaves brought their own railcar to a halt, parking in close behind. Eddon jumped out, followed more slowly by Vail. She carried her bag of parapsychic equipment.

The buildings were arranged on either side of a single street which went up and over the rise. Oaves led them along a path to the bottom of the street. As they started up the hill, the loose gravel crunched loudly under their feet.

'Seems strangely quiet and peaceful,' commented Eddon. 'Where's everyone?'

'They know we're here,' said Oaves. 'They're staying inside because of the murder.'

Eddon raised his eyebrows, but said nothing.

There were no pipes running between the buildings in Draive. Nor was there much decoration around the windows or doors. In spite of the mild weather, the windows were shuttered and the doors were closed. Some of the doors had been completely covered with sheet metal, others had been padlocked on the outside. Every window was barred.

'Where are we going?' asked Eddon. 'Where's the body?'

'You'll see,' said Oaves flatly.

At the top of the rise the street widened out into a plaza. Here some of the buildings were grander, with decorated porches and ornamental roof-crests. But the shutters and bars were as heavy as ever. In the centre of the plaza was a monument, a seven-foot pyramid of black metal capped by a golden globe.

'That's the Independence Monument,' said Oaves.

There was a sickly taint of blood in the air, and a sound like the buzzing of innumerable flies. Both smell and sound came from somewhere behind the Independence Monument.

They continued forward. There were dark red stains on the metal of the Monument, and spots of blood spattered widely around on the ground. And something else also spattered on the ground: small blobs of creamy whitish liquid.

Eddon bent down to take a closer look.

'So this is the white stuff?' he asked Oaves. 'The same that was found at the scene of the other killings?'

'Yes.'

'It's definitely not semen,' Eddon announced.

'No,' said Oaves. 'Of course not.'

Beyond the Monument the street started to

slope downhill again. There in the middle of the street lay what looked like a dark floppy bundle of clothes.

A great mass of flies rose up as they approached. Small black grass-flies and large blue mud-flies. They swarmed around and around in frenzied circles.

The clothes were male clothes. They were ripped and torn with wide gaping holes. Shredded human flesh showed through the holes. The body of the victim was mutilated beyond recognition.

Vail stared at the victim's head. 'Where's his face?' she asked.

Eddon pointed.

'That's where it *was*.'

There were no eyes or cheeks or nose, only a raw oval of bleeding red. Where the mouth had been was now an open lipless cavity. Minute fragments of metallic material were embedded in the red.

Eddon turned to Vail. She was very pale. So inexperienced, he thought. He had almost forgotten that this was her first ever case. 'Do you think you can do a memoscopy on that?' he asked.

'I can try.' She was clearly making an effort to control her voice. 'The skull has been broken, but not badly. The brain should be intact.' She put down her bag. 'I'll do the photography first.'

'Okay. And we'll collect a sample of this white stuff too.'

Without a word, Vail fished in her bag and drew out a small glass sample tube. She passed it across to Eddon. Then she drew out a special scan-camera and various attachments. She snapped on one attachment and started taking pictures, moving around the body for different angles.

Eddon scooped up a quantity of the glutinous cream-like stuff. He capped the tube and replaced it in Vail's bag. Then he began searching the ground, working away from the body in wider and wider circles.

Vail snapped another attachment onto her camera and took a second set of pictures.

'The different attachments are for different types of picture,' she explained to Oaves, who was looking on curiously. He had his hand clasped over his nose against the smell. 'Pictures by ordinary light, by thermal radiation, by sonic wave, by electrostatic imaging, and so on. We record the condition of the interior as well as the exterior of the body. The pictures will tell us the exact nature of the injuries, the time of death, everything.'

She snapped on a further attachment. Eddon was prowling around the Independence Monument. Vail continued clicking until she had several dozen pictures.

Then she put the camera back in her bag. She took out a spraycan and held it out to Oaves.

'Insect spray,' she said. 'I need silence for the memoscopy. See if you can get rid of these flies.'

Oaves was still spraying when Eddon came back from his inspection.

'Okay, I've got it,' he said. 'The killer picked the

victim up by the feet and dashed him against the Monument. Flogged the body against the metal edges.'

Vail was still very pale. 'That would explain the blood being scattered so far around,' she said.

'Right. Also the broken legs and arms and the holes ripped in his clothing. There are fibres from his clothing still sticking in the dried blood on the Monument.'

'Insane hatred against the human body?'

'Yeah, same again. Only one thing I can't understand. There ought to be more blood.'

'*More* blood?'

'This isn't much. Considering the body's almost bloodless.'

Oaves handed back the spraycan, having driven off the flies. Vail delved into her bag and came up with two pairs of ultra-thin plastic gloves.

'I'll need you to adjust the head,' she said to Eddon. 'For the memoscopy.'

Eddon pulled on the gloves and crouched down beside the body.

'Face up?'

'In a minute.'

Reaching once more into her bag, she produced a strange contraption of polished brass. Strut by strut she unfolded and opened it out. It was about the size of a hand, with four spindly extensions like four long fingers.

'Now. Very carefully.'

Very carefully Eddon rotated the head until the

back of the skull rested on the gravel and what had been the face pointed up towards the sky. Then Vail lowered her brass apparatus over the victim's temples. The spindly extensions fitted on either side of the forehead and just above the ears. She tightened various screws and fixed it in place.

'Try to hold the head absolutely still,' she told Eddon, diving into her bag again.

This time she brought out a black ergalite box and a tangle of wires. Some of the wires terminated in tiny plugs, others in silvery discs; at the other end they all fed into the box. It took Vail a while to disentangle them.

'It's a brain-reading device,' Eddon explained to Oaves. 'When someone dies, the last activities of the brain remain as traces in the synapses. Minute differences in electro-chemical voltage. The ETP machine scans and measures those differences.'

'And what does that do?'

'A trained parapsych can interpret the traces empathetically. She'll get her brain into exactly the same state as the victim's brain was in. I don't know how. They say it's like receiving the same experiences. Living through the same last impressions that were recorded in the memory before death.'

Vail lifted a hand for silence. Now she had four wires terminating in plugs and four wires terminating in discs. She connected the plugs to four tiny sockets in the apparatus over the victim's head, and attached the discs to her own head: two on either side of the forehead and two just above the ears.

The discs seemed to have their own power of adherence.

Next she adjusted herself into a crosslegged sitting position. She began breathing in and out, very slowly, very steadily. Her face was completely expressionless. After a while her breathing became so quiet that she hardly appeared to be breathing at all.

Then she touched a switch on the box and closed her eyes.

3

The impressions started on the very edges of her mind. Like miniature floating worlds they were, separate and impersonal, as if belonging to no-one at all.

She reached towards them, emptying her consciousness at the centre, expanding outwards. Now she began to feel and know them: flashes of colour, rudimentary sounds, bodily sensations.

And pain. Hints of some terrible pain, hidden and glinting like the fires in an opal. But she mustn't try to avoid or steer round it. The pain had to be brought out too.

The difficult thing was to make the impressions fall into an order. It was easy to get a total simultaneous rush, an explosion of colours and sounds and sensations all together. Any parapsych could do that. But it took patience to find one's way into the proper sequence of remembering.

She waited until she came to the furthest, faintest, outermost impression. An impression of climbing. She felt her legs moving in the action of someone going up a hill. And going with careful steps, as if trying not to make a noise.

What was the scene? She could find only fragments. Passing by a wall. The darkness of the night. And something like the backs of houses, glimpsed up ahead.

More decipherable was the inward emotion. A feeling of excitement like a glow in the pit of the stomach. It was associated with some particular destination, some room with a low ceiling and —

The blow came out of nowhere at all. She reeled. For a moment she was paralysed with stun and shock. She couldn't even tell where the blow had fallen. There was only a sense of amazed incredulity.

Hands held her. One gripped her by the collar, one clamped over the back of her skull. She could feel the fingers clenching her hair. Enormously powerful hands and fingers.

She was aware of being carried forward, half-lifted off the ground. Then a clang. She had fetched up against an iron door. An iron door studded with iron studs.

The impressions were coming clearer and stronger all the time. She cast about for a glimpse of the attacker. Nothing. Her head was held in an inexorable vice. And the vice was pressing her face against the door.

Screaming, screaming, screaming! The studs tore through the skin of her cheeks. He was rubbing her face up and down against the studs of the door. Shredding and grating it off!

The agony was beyond belief. There was a taste of blood in her mouth, the bones cracked in her nose. A film of red spread in front of her eyes. Then her sight went blank. There was a horrible pulpy wetness, something rounded and rolling.

She couldn't think, she couldn't register. All she knew were pure vivid streaks of pain etched in a black void. Going up and down, up and down. And endless high-pitched screaming!

Up and down, back and forth, up and down...

Until suddenly all sensation ceased, and consciousness went out like a light.

Eddon and Oaves, watching anxiously, saw her slump forward where she sat. At a gesture from Eddon, Oaves came forward to support her shoulders from behind.

It was a while before she opened her eyes. She shuddered, reached out a hand and turned off the switch on the box.

'You okay?' asked Eddon.

'Do I look it?'

'I wouldn't go through that for anything,' said Oaves.

She took a number of slow deep breaths. Spasms of shaking still ran through her body.

'I didn't get much,' she said. 'The victim never saw his killer's face. There were no words spoken either.'

Gradually the shaking subsided. Vail removed the silvery discs that had been fixed over her head. Then she bent forward and removed the brass apparatus from the victim's head. She laid everything out in front of her on the ground.

Eddon stood up and pulled off his plastic gloves.

'We could see you making movements,' he said. 'Like someone dreaming, half-acting out the dream.'

'The victim wasn't killed in the plaza here,' said Vail. 'He was coming up the hill, but not up the main street. I think it must've been some narrow lane between the houses. The first he knew of the killer was a blow struck from behind.'

'Right. We saw you give a sudden jerk.'

'The killer grabbed him and pushed him forward. There was this door, a side door of one of the houses. An iron door with iron studs. He rubbed my face — his face —'

She broke off as another spasm of shaking ran through her.

'Sorry. The killer rubbed the victim's face up and down against the studs of the door.'

'We saw the up–down movements of your head. Seemed to go on a long time. And your mouth kept opening.'

'I suppose the victim was screaming, I kept hearing screams. I don't think the killer was in any hurry to finish him off. Just to destroy his face.'

'Any indication of the killer's feelings? Anger, hatred, sexual thrill?'

'Nothing. No feelings that I could read. I've

heard that insane people are impenetrable — I guess someone totally mad is just totally impenetrable.'

'And no other clues?'

'No.'

Eddon turned to Oaves. 'Okay. First objective is to find the place where the victim was attacked. I'm looking for a narrow lane coming up a hill.'

'Very steep,' added Vail.

Oaves pointed. 'That's the steepest side. The lanes go down in the gaps between the houses. See? There and there and there.'

'Right. That's where we'll start.'

Vail uncrossed her legs and tried to stand. But her legs trembled and she started shaking all over. She collapsed back into a sitting position.

'It was a bad one,' she said faintly.

'Take it easy.' Eddon's voice was less abrasive than usual. 'You stay here and recover. I expect I can recognise the place by myself.'

He turned again to Oaves. 'While I do that, you fetch the people out of their houses. Bring them out and line them up in the plaza.'

'Everyone?'

'Everyone. I want to see the whole settlement.'

Oaves shrugged and headed towards the nearest house. Eddon headed towards the nearest gap and laneway.

The gap was about a metre and a half wide. The lane dropped sharply between the side walls of the houses. It was very steep, and there were two doorways visible further below.

He started down. The surface of the lane was covered with a powdery metallic dust. His feet sank softly into it at every step. Behind in the plaza, he could hear Oaves knocking on the houses and calling people out.

The first door was made of iron, but without studs. The second door was completely covered over with wire mesh and bars. No signs of blood, no signs of a struggle. Wrong lane.

He kept on going down to the bottom of the lane. At the bottom was a path turning off to the left and right. He followed it to the left, circling around the foot of the rise. After about thirty metres he came to another lane leading back up to the plaza. Another very steep lane between houses, with doorways at the sides of the houses. It looked like the second lane that Oaves had pointed out.

Almost immediately he had the feeling that this was the one. He climbed quickly uphill, past metal walls and windowless buildings like outhouses. The first thing he saw were the marks on the ground. Deep depressions in the dust, followed by a kind of trough. 'Someone dragging their feet,' he muttered. 'Someone being carried dragging their feet.'

The trough led uphill to a particular doorway. As he approached he could see the studs on the door. The whole door was covered in the dark red of dried blood. The blood had trickled down to the bottom of the door and formed a pool behind the sill. Now coagulated, the pool was almost black.

'*Knew* there had to be more blood,' said Eddon to himself.

He pulled a pad and scriber out of his pocket and began jotting down the details. He made a diagram of the door and studs. There were shredded morsels of human flesh still caught in the crevices around the studs. He didn't see any of the cream-like liquid.

Next he took out a measuring tape and recorded the exact distances. The trough was five hundred and fifty-nine centimetres long. There were deep depressions in the dust around the doorway as well as the depressions he had first seen. Evidently the footsteps of the killer, when he was supporting the extra weight of the victim. But the dust was too soft to give clear prints.

Eddon bent down and measured the dimensions of the depressions. So far as he could tell, the dimensions suggested feet about two sizes smaller than his own. Probably about average for a P-19er, he supposed.

It took him about five minutes to draw and record everything he wanted. He made one last inspection all around. Then he pocketed his pad and scriber, and started walking uphill again.

It was interesting that although the deep footprint depressions continued uphill, there were no signs of dragging feet, no trough. The killer must've either slung the victim over his shoulder or carried him under his arm, Eddon decided. All the way to the Monument. Whatever the size of his feet, he clearly possessed exceptional strength. But then madmen often did . . .

Studying the marks on the ground, Eddon came up towards the top of the rise. He'd almost forgotten that he had asked Oaves to fetch everyone out of their houses. But they were all there waiting for him when he emerged onto the plaza.

4

They stood in a semicircle on the far side of the body. There were about seventy of them — men, women and children. They looked as if they had just woken up from a heavy sleep. They stood there rubbing their eyes and blinking in the bright, hazy light.

Both males and females wore leggings and boots. Today at least they had not put on their vannamaks, but were dressed in loose grey blouses, reinforced with straps at shoulders and waist. To Eddon, the P-19ers they'd met so far all looked very similar; but these seemed darker around the brows and even more leaden under the eyes.

Oaves and Vail stepped forward. Vail was back on her feet, but still swaying and unsteady.

'Everyone's here,' said Oaves. 'Except for three families who are out on the steppe, and the Shadd family staying in Steyne-2 this week.'

'Still doesn't seem many for a settlement this size.'

'Not all the houses in Draive are occupied,' explained Oaves.

Eddon took up a position to address the crowd, facing them across the mutilated body. There were flies around the body once again, buzzing and settling on the raw red flesh.

The crowd stared at him, eyes swivelling to follow his every movement. They muttered and passed comments behind their hands. Eddon had the impression that the comments weren't friendly.

'They've never seen anyone from off-planet before,' said Oaves. 'If you want to speak you'd better start now.'

Eddon coughed for silence and began in a firm voice. 'Okay, listen up. I'm Inspector Brac from Central Police. I'll be asking you some questions about this murder.'

He gestured towards the body, but the eyes of the crowd never left his face. The muttering grew louder and clearer.

'Who does he think he is?'

'He's from the Hegemony.'

'So's she.'

'Why are they wearing Junior Leaders' badges?'

'We don't want policing.'

Vail leaned across to Eddon. 'Be diplomatic,' she murmured.

Eddon gritted his teeth. 'We're here at the request of your government —'

'We don't have a government!' somebody called out.

'This is Independent P-19!' cried someone else.

'We're here to help find and arrest this serial killer. We have considerable experience with serial killers at Central Police, and we've developed some very sophisticated techniques for investigating cases of this kind.'

The muttering turned into jeering and outright catcalling.

'Thinks he knows all about it!'

'"Considerable experience with serial killers"!'

'Bloody outsiders!'

'We take care of our own problems.'

'Doesn't understand a thing!'

'Go back to your own planet!'

Oaves stepped hastily forward to intervene.

'These two people are not enemies,' he said. 'Our Headman himself called them in and personally appointed them as Junior Leaders. He expects you to cooperate and answer their questions as fully as possible.'

The jeering ceased and the hubbub quietened down to a low muttering again. Oaves turned to Eddon and Vail.

'I could've told you this wasn't the way. You'll have to interview them separately. One family at a time, in their own homes.'

Eddon was bristling with anger. But he could see the truth of Oaves' words. He nodded agreement.

'Who do you need to interview?' asked Oaves.

'First, the victim's family. Second, anyone who might've been the last to see him alive.'

91

Oaves shook his head. 'The dead man doesn't come from a Draive family. Must be from another settlement. Nobody saw him until this morning.'

'They told you that?'

'Yes. They don't know who he is, not with his face gone. They've already looked in his pockets.'

'Hmm. Have they now.'

'They said there was nothing there.'

Eddon raised his eyes despairingly heavenwards. 'What a nightmare,' he said to no-one in particular. 'We don't even get to examine the evidence untampered.' He spoke again to Oaves. 'Okay. We'll start with the people in those two houses over there.'

'Why them?'

'They're beside the lane where the killer first attacked.'

'Very well. Only the left-hand house is occupied though.'

Oaves directed his voice towards a particular cluster of people at one end of the semicircle. 'The MetGivon family! Yes, all of you. You'll be the first to be interviewed this morning.'

Five faces scowled resentfully.

'Then all the families living around the plaza here,' added Eddon, again addressing the crowd himself. 'We'll be calling to interview you during the day. Please be in your homes when we call.'

'Where else would we be?' sniffed one old man.

There were more resentful looks, but nobody voiced any objection.

'That's all for now,' said Oaves. 'Meeting's over.'

As the semicircle broke up, he turned to Eddon and Vail. 'Give them a while before you start the interviews. Let them get settled in their homes again. You can't hurry things here.'

'I could do with something to eat,' said Vail. 'I'm still sort of shaky.'

Eddon nodded. 'We'll go get the food from the railcar.' Then, to Oaves: 'Can you arrange for the body to be moved? It's just gathering flies in the open. Somewhere cool.'

Oaves pointed to one of the buildings on the plaza. 'That's the community hall. There should be a storage cellar underneath.'

'Fine. If you can arrange some people to carry it there. On a tarpaulin or blanket, as carefully as possible. We'll need to keep it for eventual identification.'

Oaves went off and began rounding up helpers. Half the crowd had left the plaza already. Eddon and Vail walked past the Independence Monument and down the street.

'Do you need a shoulder to lean on?' asked Eddon.

'What's this? Gallantry?'

'You can hardly walk straight.'

'I'm enjoying the role of being heroic,' said Vail.

But she leaned on his shoulder nonetheless. They descended towards the bottom of the hill. Eddon forced himself to walk slowly.

'Makes Masilin and Wyvis and Oaves look good, doesn't it?' said Vail. 'We thought they weren't very welcoming, but they're the height of hospitality compared to this lot.'

'Peasants,' said Eddon harshly. 'The name fits.' He spread his hands. 'What happens if they won't answer questions? What authority do I have?'

'I don't think anyone has much authority on P-19. Except this Headman.'

'Yeah, that was the magic word, wasn't it? Oaves must be taking a chance, lying his head off like that.'

They came to the encircling path at the bottom of the hill and walked around to the M-rail.

'We'll sit in the railcar to eat,' said Eddon.

They climbed into the back of the railcar. Eddon reached in under the seat and pulled out the packages of food and bottles of drink.

'What do you want?'

'What've we got?'

Eddon opened up one of the packages. It contained six slices of rye bread, two pickled onions, two cucumbers and a small jar of chutney.

'Plain and simple,' said Eddon.

'Just like me,' said Vail. She picked out a slice of bread and a cucumber. Eddon took a drink from one of the bottles: water flavoured with berry juice. The flavour of the juice barely masked the metal taste of the water.

They ate in silence for a while. Vail's long legs stuck out more than halfway across the aisle. She folded them one over the other to allow Eddon more room. Eddon couldn't help staring. She was wearing tight black soft-hose, and the perfect shape of her legs was visible from calf to thigh. Slender and shapely and spectacularly long.

Vail finished her cucumber. She picked up the jar of chutney.

'So this is our food for the whole day,' she commented.

'Yeah. I suppose we have to share it with Oaves too.'

'Here he comes now,' said Vail, pointing.

Oaves had just appeared in view, walking down the street between the houses. He descended to the bottom of the hill and turned along the path towards them.

'Huh,' snorted Eddon. 'I meant him to supervise the moving of the body. He's just given orders and left them to it.'

Oaves came rapidly along the path. He seemed displeased by the sight of all the food spread out on the seat.

'You shouldn't make a display of your food like that,' he said. 'Unless you're going to eat it all immediately.'

'Why not?'

'People will see.'

'So?'

'So —' He shrugged. 'Very well. It's your choice. I'll show you how to drive the railcar now.'

'Drive the railcar? Why?'

'For when you want to come back to Steyne-2.'

'You'll be taking us back.'

'Sorry. I have to leave now.'

'For what?'

'Something that has to be done with Masilin and Wyvis at Steyne-2. I've set up things for you here as much as I can. You're the ones who conduct the interviews. You're the experts from Central Police, with all the sophisticated techniques of investigation.'

It was hard to tell if he was being sarcastic.

'I'm not happy about this,' said Eddon.

'I have to go. Take your time. You don't need to do all the interviews in one day.' He pulled out some sort of timepiece that hung like a pendant around his neck. 'You've got four and a half hours of daylight left.'

'Only four and a half hours? What is this? I thought you had a daily rotation of twenty-two hours here?'

'Yes, but only seven hours of daylight. Our nights are very long at present.'

'You mean this is the middle of your winter?'

'That's right. The middle of our winter. Now if you'll watch I'll show you the driving controls. You can watch while you continue eating.'

5

Beano was not impressed. He'd been tramping around Steyne-2 for two hours. He had gone down countless narrow alleys, crossed dozens of M-rail lines, stooped under a hundred metal pipes. But nowhere had he found the kind of thronging thoroughfares you'd expect in a spaceport metropolis. No holo-dromes, no food-bars, no buzz-parlours. If there were any shops at all, they didn't reveal themselves by signs or display windows.

Instead of entertainments and excitements, Steyne-2 had memorials. Metal sculptures rose on pedestals in the centre of every square, polished plaques were set into the paving of every second street.

'In Honour of the Judder Family, Who Gave Up Their Lives for the Cause of Independence'

'In Memory of Alloquin Spey and Shannoth Wryell, Who Died in the Bombing of Gormoy Bend'

'Muir and Aurie Sheaves: Battle of Silloth Pond, 3–6–588'

Beano soon lost interest in reading the inscriptions. It seemed strange that such tiny local conflicts could produce so many memorials.

He was more curious about the examples of P-19 technology. As well as the M-rail and the heating pipes, he came across certain mysterious black tanks and rows of pylons. All connected with the use of electro-magnetic power, he was sure. He would have liked to ask, but he couldn't find anyone willing to stop and talk.

Not that the people in the streets were busy or hurrying. They seemed more like sleepwalkers. They moved along slowly with lowered heads, lost in their own private dreams. At first Beano tried calling out a cheery good morning, but they only scowled and passed by with averted eyes. It was almost as if they'd been found out doing something illegal.

After two hours he'd had enough. He made his way back to the Big House. He had some visi-texts he could watch in his room. Lucky he'd brought his own, because they probably didn't have visi-texts on this out-cold planet. Probably didn't even link in to a Galactic news service!

Beano re-entered the Big House not by the Major Portal but by a small side-door. Masilin had shown him how to use it when he'd gone out earlier. 'This entrance is closer to your rooms. But remember it gets locked an hour before nightfall.'

He walked along the corridor. It was much darker inside the Big House, but also much warmer. He turned the corner and gave a whistle of surprise. The doors of their rooms were all open.

At first he thought it might be someone doing the cleaning. But when he looked in through the doorway of Eddon's room, there were papers and clothes scattered all over the floor.

'Holy hooley-boopers!' he exclaimed.

He hurried on down the corridor. He remembered what Vail and Eddon had said over breakfast, about the attempted break-in last night. Vail's room was similarly disordered, with personal belongings strewn everywhere.

'The place has been ransacked!' he muttered aloud.

He came to his own room. Even as he strode in through the door, he could see his clothes tossed around and his bags opened up and emptied.

And then he stopped short. There on his bed sat Masilin and Wyvis.

'Ah,' said Masilin. 'Back from your walk at last.'

'What's been going on?' Beano came further into the room and stared at the chaos all around. 'Do you know who did this?'

'This?' Masilin pursed his lips. Wyvis got up and went across to close the door.

'What were they looking for?'

Masilin took out a large square of white cloth and folded it into a pad. 'They didn't find it,' he said.

'Didn't find what?'

'I'll show you.' Masilin reached across towards a yellow plastic ampoule on the bedside table.

'That? That's not mine.'

Masilin placed the ampoule on the pad. 'No, but it's *for* you.'

Wyvis gave him a sudden push and hooked his feet away from behind. He fell forward onto his knees. As he fell he could see Masilin's hand closing the pad over the ampoule, bursting the plastic.

'Hey! Whaddayya —!'

Masilin pulled his face down into the pad. A biting chemical vapour entered his nose and mouth. Wyvis grabbed both his arms and twisted them up behind his back.

Beano tried to break free, tried not to inhale. But already his head was floating and his body seemed to belong to someone else. There was a hot, burning sensation in his throat. His struggles grew increasingly remote and faraway. He gasped, and the vapour rushed down into his lungs. For a moment the room went spinning around and around. Then nothing. Unconsciousness.

6

The door was opened by an old woman.

'Interview,' said Eddon. 'You're first.'

'We're all in the parlour. You'd better come in. I don't know why you bother.'

She led them down a dimly lit hallway.

'Shall I start the talking?' Vail whispered to Eddon.

'Why?'

'I'll try and soften them up, get them on side.'

'You don't think I can do that?'

Vail made no reply.

'Okay, Okay. You start.'

They entered the parlour. Four other members of the MetGivon family were seated around a massive silver table. There were ornamental chains of silver hanging from the walls and looped across the ceiling. The walls themselves were padded with some kind of thick quilting material.

The old woman neither sat down herself nor offered them a chair. Vail looked around the room with interest. She went across and touched the quilting on the walls.

'This is different,' she said. 'Why the quilting?'

'Insulation,' the old woman answered grudgingly.

'Where we stayed last night the walls were heated by electrical elements. Not here?'

This time it was one of the men at the table who replied. 'We're beyond the electricity grid here.'

'Mmm. So that's why there's no pipes running between the houses in Draive?'

'That's right.'

'What do you do for power?'

'Batteries. Lead-nickel batteries for lighting and cooking.'

'Ah, there's so much to learn about P-19.' Vail pulled a spare chair up to the table. 'Why don't we all sit down,' she said. 'I'm Inspector Brac's PP assistant, Vail ev Vessintor. And you are . . . ?'

She went round them one by one. The old man who had been answering the questions was Gerraid III MetGivon. The woman who had opened the door was his wife, Fladda III MetGivon. Their son and daughter-in-law were Dennott IV MetGivon and Magda IV MetGivon. There was also a teenage granddaughter, Sperry V MetGivon.

'I'm beginning to understand those numbers in your names,' said Vail. 'They go by descending generations, right?'

'Counting from the time of Independence,' said the old man. 'The first generation is the generation of the Breakaway.'

'Only six of them still alive,' added the old woman.

'But your Headman is first generation, of course?'

'Of course. You met him?'

'We were very impressed. He seemed so — so wise and sensible. He gave us our Junior Leaders' badges last night. Then this morning he told us about this latest killing and sent us here to investigate.'

She leaned back and waved a languid hand towards Eddon.

'That's why we have to do this interview. Inspector Brac will be asking the questions.'

'Right.' Eddon leaned forward. 'Now, the victim died from injuries received —'

Magda, the younger woman, suddenly covered her face with her hands. Her husband Dennott spoke up for her.

'She looked out of our side door this morning and saw the mess across the lane. She's still upset.' He didn't seem so much upset himself as hostile and angry. 'You don't have to spare our feelings. We know why there was no face on the body.'

'Okay. You know. Tell me, why *is* the house across the lane unoccupied?'

'It belongs to the Lauders family. They moved to Steyne-2 a month ago.'

Vail quietly reached into her bag and turned on a voice recorder. Eddon surveyed the five heavy faces around the table.

'Next question then. Did anyone hear or see anything last night?'

The old man and woman shook their heads. The young wife still had her face in her hands, the young husband still looked angry. The granddaughter brushed her fingers across her forehead.

'We have reason to believe there was screaming. For several minutes at least.'

'We were all asleep,' said old Gerraid firmly.

'From what time? When did you go to bed?'

'Nightfall.'

'You slept the whole night through? But your nights are, what, fifteen hours long?'

'Yes.'

Eddon shrugged. 'Let's talk about the victim then. Does anyone have any information about him? Any ideas about who he is or where he came from?'

Magda lowered her hands, stared, then broke into a kind of choking fit. Her breast heaved and she rocked back and forth in distress. She seemed to be trying to say something.

'Are you all right?' asked Eddon. 'Is there something —'

'She knows who he is and so do I.' Dennott, the young husband, spoke up suddenly. 'Eriph IV Sivanne. From the settlement of Col Carras, about three kilometres away.'

'How do you know it's him?'

'He used to work with me. I recognised his boots. And that braided belt he always wore.'

'Can you be sure?'

'Sure enough. What do you want?'

His voice was raised aggressively. Eddon frowned.

'You didn't say this earlier. Why not?'

'What difference does it make?'

'Why would Eriph have been coming to Draive?'

'How should I know? He always was a fool. Walking all that way in the dark.'

'He'd've known other people in Draive?'

'Yes.'

'But they didn't recognise the body this morning.'

'Like I said, you had to remember his boots and belt.'

'Which way is Col Carras from here?'

Dennott thought about it, but his wife was quicker.

'North-east,' she said, pointing a direction. 'That way.'

She had recovered from her choking fit, but her voice was very quavery.

'Hmm. So why would he have been coming up this lane? If Col Carras is in that direction, surely you'd expect him to come into Draive walking up the main street?'

Eddon had turned to address Magda, but it was Dennott who broke in again.

'What's this got to do with the murder?'

'Maybe nothing,' said Eddon. 'But it's possible the killer knew the victim beforehand. I assume there aren't many people out walking around at night.'

Dennott gave a short harsh laugh. 'You could say that.'

'So how did the killer know when and where to attack?'

'Saw him coming across the moor and hid in wait for him?'

'But why would the killer be in Draive in the first place? Are you suggesting he *lives* in Draive?'

'You're the clever one, you tell us.'

'But then he'd have to do a lot of travelling, given the other murders in other places.'

'The great detectives,' said Dennott sarcastically. 'Got it almost solved, have you?'

'Nope. But we'll keep on working at it till we have.'

'Why don't you just go on back to your own world? Your nice, bright, smart Hegemony!' Dennott seemed to be working himself up into a rage. 'We're just peasants, hey? Isn't that how you think of us?'

He banged the table with his fist. His wife had her face in her hands again.

Old Gerraid stood up. 'We've answered your questions as well as we can. You've had some help from us now.'

'Have we?'

'You've learned the name of the victim and where he lived. I reckon we've done our bit.'

Vail reached into her bag and switched off the voice recorder. 'Perhaps for the time being. What do you think, Inspector Brac?'

Eddon stood up. 'Yeah. But we may be getting back to you later.'

'Go and stick your noses into someone else's lives,' growled Dennott sullenly.

The old man escorted them out of the parlour and back down the hallway to the street door.

Someone was shaking him. Then a hand slapped across his face. Beano opened his eyes. A bleary sea of swimming colours. The hand slapped him again. Slowly the colours came into focus.

It was the face of a young woman bending over him. Heavy brows, strong jaw, dark under the eyes — the typical face of a P-19er. Beano remembered where he was, remembered Masilin and Wyvis.

'That's better,' she said. 'Keep your eyes open, stay conscious. I'll go and get someone to help.'

Her face withdrew out of focus. He listened and heard her footsteps going away. How long had he been unconscious?

He tried to move but his movements were restrained in some way. His throat felt raw and burning. He swallowed and it was like knife-blades going down his gullet.

Time passed. His eyes closed, but he forced them open again. He was lying on the bedroom floor. His hands seemed to be tied behind his back and his ankles fastened together.

Then two sets of footsteps entered the bedroom.

He swivelled his eyes in their direction. The same woman had come back with another, older woman. The older woman was carrying a satchel. She had steely-grey hair and wore many strands of silver jewellery around her neck.

She knelt down beside him and opened the satchel.

'Don't move yet.' Her voice was calm and unhurried.

Inside the satchel were bottles and tubes and bandages, a complete medical kit. She took out a pair of scissors, leaned across and snipped at the ties around his wrists and ankles. As the ties fell away, he felt the circulation coming back into his arms and legs.

'That's right. Now you can flex and stretch a bit.'

Her eyes were as calm as her voice — clear and serene and grey. She had an ageless kind of face, smooth-skinned everywhere except around the eyes.

'How's your throat?' she asked. 'Can you speak?'

It's fine, Beano started to say. But the only sound that came out was a croak. The knife-blades twisted in his gullet and tears ran out at the corners of his eyes.

The older woman nodded. 'I thought so. You've been made to inhale SJP solution. I thought I could smell it when we came into the room.'

She selected a bottle of dark brown liquid. She set the bottle on the floor, along with a medicine glass and a kidney bowl.

'Give him 20 ml to gargle now, and another 20 ml in three minutes time,' she instructed the younger woman. 'I'll go and tell Argid what's happened.'

She rose to her feet.

'This treatment will ease your throat,' she told Beano. She had a slow thoughtful smile that irradiated her whole face. 'I'll be back soon.'

The younger woman crouched down on her haunches. She measured a quantity of brown liquid into the glass.

'That's Mairie ev Ghair,' she whispered to Beano as the older woman left the room. 'She's the wife of our Headman here.'

She propped up Beano's head and held the glass to his mouth. Her arms were brawny and muscular. Beano took the glass from her and tilted it back himself. He gargled the liquid in his throat for half a minute.

'Now spit here,' she said, holding out the kidney bowl.

Beano spat.

'I'm Hannema, by the way. I was cleaning the rooms along this corridor and I knocked on your door but no-one answered. So then I took a peek inside. That's how I found you.'

She pointed to something around his neck. 'Here's the gag that was over your mouth. I worked it loose and pulled it down.'

She picked up the scissors and cut through the gag. She held it up in front of his face: a white

108

cloth wound into a long roll. It looked like the same cloth that Masilin had previously folded to use as a pad.

Suddenly Beano realised that he was no longer wearing his flight jacket. Masilin and Wyvis must have stolen it. So *that* was what they'd been after all along! He tried to speak.

'Mas-lin,' he croaked. 'Wyv —'

Hannema tut-tutted. 'Don't try to talk yet. There's nothing to be done till Mairie gets back. Your voice will be better after your second dose.'

Beano gave up and waited. In three minutes time, Hannema measured out his second dose. He had just finished gargling when Mairie ev Ghair returned. Hannema held out the bowl for him to spit into, then rose to her feet.

'Argid says he knows who did it,' said Mairie. 'Masilin, Wyvis and Oaves.'

'I think that's what he was trying to tell me just now,' said Hannema.

They looked to Beano for confirmation. Beano swallowed and discovered that the knife-blades had gone from his throat.

'Masilin and Wyvis,' he husked.

'He says he knows why they did it too. They were after the control keys for your spacecraft.'

Beano nodded. 'In my jacket,' he husked, gesturing to show that his flight jacket had been stolen.

'So they've got the control keys and now they'll

109

be trying to fly out.' Mairie seemed as calm and unruffled as ever. 'In that case, Argid said to find Junior Leader Jaralax and ask him to head out to the spaceport with half a dozen men. See if they can be stopped.'

'I saw Jaralax in the Octagon a little while ago,' said Hannema.

'Perhaps you could find him and tell him then.' Mairie smiled her slow smile. 'You move faster than me.'

'I want to go there too.' Beano's voice cracked as he tried to speak louder. 'Spaceport.'

'I doubt you're recovered enough,' said Mairie.

For answer, Beano struggled up off the floor and stood upright. He swayed a little, but kept his balance.

'All right.' Mairie turned to Hannema. 'Ask Jaralax to call back here before he starts off.'

Hannema nodded and went out.

'Sit down while you wait,' said Mairie, pointing to the bed. Beano sat.

'Why — they want to steal a spaceship?' he husked.

'They want to leave P-19. There are no regular spaceflights here, remember. And we have no spacecraft of our own. My husband says that's why they called you here in the first place. Their message to Central Police was a way to get a Hegemony spaceship to land on P-19.'

'Not murders?'

'Oh, the murders are real enough. But that's not

the reason they contacted Central Police. They didn't care who came out on the ship. All that mattered was the ship itself.'

Beano blinked. His head was spinning with this new view of things.

'What about us?' he asked finally.

'If they fly out in your ship? You'll be stranded here, won't you?'

'Until?'

Mairie shrugged. 'Until whenever.'

Beano's heart sank. Stranded on P-19! He could understand why Masilin, Wyvis and Oaves would want to leave. They'd be heading for the Galactic Centre, heading for the excitement of the great metropoli on Rion or Salph or even Terra itself. While he'd be stuck here on this boring planet for eons and eons. What a total zunk-out!

He was still thinking about it when he heard the sudden sound of boots approaching along the corridor. A man strode into the room, young and stocky, with a black rope-like moustache. Rings hung from his ears and bangles jangled on his arms. He carried a lightweight T-gun over one shoulder.

'Where's this Hegemony flightman? You? I'm Jaralax IV Fallender.'

Beano stood up from the bed. Jaralax swung around to address Mairie.

'It's Masilin, Wyvis and Oaves all right. They've taken their families with them. Their rooms are empty.'

He swung back towards Beano.

'Okay, flightman. Let's go.'

8

The journey to the spaceport was maddeningly slow. The two railcars moved along steadily at their maximum speed of twenty kilometres per hour. Beano felt he could jump out and run faster.

He sat in the front car with Junior Leader Jaralax and three of his men. They seemed utterly stolid and impassive. Everyone except Beano carried a T-gun.

'We're never going to get there in time,' he exclaimed in frustration. His voice was now fully recovered.

'They haven't taken off yet,' said Jaralax.

'Blang-a-dang!' Beano whacked his hand on his thigh. 'At least it'll take them a while to set the navigation beams.'

The railcars passed through the outskirts of Steyne-2, past the cropfields and the last of the houses. Not much further to the spaceport. Beano gazed eagerly ahead, but everything was veiled in the bright hazy air.

He turned to Jaralax. 'There's something I don't understand. If your Headman knew what these characters were planning to do, why didn't he stop them?'

'There's no law against leaving P-19. It might be disloyal but it's not illegal.'

'But stealing a spaceship to do it!'

'You can't jail people for what you think they're planning to do. That would be tyranny. Anyway, it's not a very serious crime.'

'Not serious? Stealing a Hegemony spaceship?'

'No, not serious. In case you haven't noticed, we don't much care for the Hegemony around here. What happens to Hegemony property is no concern of ours.'

'But I'll be left stranded on —'

'On Independent P-19,' said Jaralax fiercely. Beano was glad he hadn't completed the sentence himself. He'd been about to say 'this boring planet'.

The cropfields came to an end and the M-rail began to cross the wide flat expanse of the space-port. Now the control tower was visible through the haze, straight ahead. And over to the side —

'Whooo-hup! There she is!' cried Beano, pointing.

The spaceship still stood on its tail on the land-ing pad. Sleek and silvery, with its cutaway fins and tube-like hull. Beano felt a surge of possessive pride.

Slowly the railcars glided on. They passed over the bare metal ground, over patches of moss, over pools of water. As they came closer, Beano could see the mobile steps wheeled into position, leading up to the spaceship's exit door. The door itself seemed to be closed. There was no sign of Masilin, Wyvis, Oaves or their families.

'Either not arrived or already inside,' Beano muttered to himself.

Jaralax gave a signal and the two railcars slowed to a halt.

'Okay. This is where we get off.'

The men dismounted: seven of them altogether. They unslung their T-guns and moved forward in the direction of the spaceship.

Beano followed behind Jaralax. They moved at a fast trot, swerving around the pools of water. Beano was soon puffing and panting. Although he'd adjusted to the gravity, he still wasn't naturally adapted to it like the shorter and more muscular P-19ers.

Suddenly a great roar shook the air. A vivid violet light burst from the tail of the spaceship. It beat against the grid of the landing pad and radiated out in throbbing brilliant waves. Clouds of white steam arose as the water in the nearby pools was vaporised.

Louder and louder, higher and higher in pitch, the roar intensified. It mounted to a whining crescendo. But still the spaceship stayed where it was. Beano gaped.

'They haven't reversed the IE system!' he cried.

The light cut out and the noise stopped as suddenly as it had started. Billowing clouds of white steam drifted across the spaceport.

'What did you say?' asked Jaralax.

'The inertial exchange system. They forgot to reverse it. This way the ship is cancelling out its own thrust. Like trying to go backwards and forwards at the same time.'

'Maybe they don't know that it has to be reversed.'

'Hey, yeah! Or they don't know the right controls! Zag-a-doo!'

Jaralax showed his teeth in a sudden wild grin.

'Everybody spread out,' he shouted. 'Encircle the ship.'

They resumed the advance. Jaralax veered to the left of the spaceship and Beano kept close behind him. They passed through a cloud of warm steam. They were about fifteen metres away when another roar broke forth.

Again the violet light sluiced down onto the landing pad.

'Down!' yelled Beano.

Jaralax didn't need to be told. They hit the ground together as the radiating light fanned out over their heads. At this distance, the waves of light were like prismatic bands, like folds rippling through a curtain.

Once more the roar built up into a whine. They clamped their hands over their ears. Deep quaking vibrations passed through the ground beneath them. The whine doubled and trebled in volume. Flying pads of moss whizzed past in the air, dislodged by the blast. The air itself seemed glowing with heat.

On and on it continued, twice as long as the first time. But eventually the light was quenched and the noise and vibrations died away.

'Hah!' said Jaralax triumphantly, rising to his feet.

Beano rose too. The spaceship was still standing on its tail on the landing pad. The landing pad was half blown away, the mobile steps were twisted and buckled. But the spaceship itself had never moved.

The other men also rose to their feet. They had their T-guns raised and pointing. They kept on circling around until the spaceship was surrounded on all sides. But they didn't approach any closer.

For several minutes, nothing happened at all. Then the exit door opened. Very cautiously, two faces looked out.

'Vanna Crouth and young Elphie Wyvis,' commented Jaralax. He signalled to his men to close in.

More faces appeared in the door. Beano recognised Masilin, Wyvis and Oaves.

'Okay, the great escape is over,' shouted Jaralax. 'Bring the control keys with you.'

The faces turned to one another and there was animated discussion and gesturing. Masilin seemed to be giving orders. Jaralax and his men formed a ring around the bottom of the mobile steps.

Then, one by one, the families came out onto the steps and began to descend. First the children, then the old people, then the wives. They struggled to clamber over the places where the steps were buckled and missing. When they reached the bottom, they stood huddled together with downcast eyes.

Jaralax and his men waited patiently. Masilin, Wyvis and Oaves were the last to descend. Masilin carried Beano's flight jacket in one hand. In the other he held a bundle of black mica rods.

'Are those the control keys?' asked Jaralax.

'That's them,' said Beano.

Masilin, Wyvis and Oaves arrived at the foot of the steps. Jaralax gestured towards Beano.

'Give him his jacket and the keys.'

Masilin walked up to Beano, holding out the flight jacket and the bundle of rods. But instead of handing them over, he flung them suddenly in Beano's face.

'Run!' he yelled, and dodged past Beano and out of the ring.

It was the signal for all of them. The huddled group exploded outwards in every direction. Men, women and children rushed past the armed men and fled across the spaceport.

The men swivelled and aimed, but didn't shoot.

'No!' shouted Jaralax, lowering his own gun. 'Don't shoot!'

'You're going to let them get away?' cried Beano in amazement.

'Yes. They know they haven't done anything we'd be prepared to shoot them for.'

'But resisting arrest?'

'This isn't the Hegemony, flightman. You've got your keys back, haven't you?'

The fleeing figures dwindled in the distance. Jaralax's men shouldered their guns and relaxed.

'There's nowhere to run very far on P-19, you know,' said Jaralax. 'They might try to survive out on the steppes for a week or so. But sooner or later they'll have to come back.'

He pointed to the control keys. 'Why don't you check your spaceship? Lock up anything left unlocked. We'll wait for you here.'

Beano nodded, and started off up the twisted steps. Jaralax's men chatted together as they watched him go.

'If I was him, I'd fly out right now,' said one.

'Half his luck,' said another.

'If I had the chance —'

'That sounds like disloyalty,' said Jaralax, glancing across with a frown.

'Aw, come on Jaralax, wouldn't you if you could? Get out before it gets any worse?'

Eddon and Vail were disheartened and frustrated. They had spent the whole day interviewing people in the houses around the plaza, and everywhere they'd met with sullenness and hostility. None of the families had refused to answer questions, but they had answered unwillingly, grudgingly, giving as little information as possible. Eddon and Vail flaunted their Junior Leaders' badges and invoked the name of the Headman, but it was like beating their heads against a brick wall. The inhabitants of Draive just didn't seem to care about catching the killer.

There was only one significant breakthrough. The first four families interviewed had all denied hearing any sounds in the night. But in the fifth interview, Eddon began posing his question in a different way, asking 'Did you hear the screaming from this house *too*?' The Gildert family fell into the trap and agreed that, yes, they'd heard sounds of screaming round about three o'clock.

'So you looked out of the window?'

'No. It would've been too dark to see anyway. There's no streetlights in Draive and no-one keeps house-lights on through the night.'

'You didn't go outside to see if someone needed help?'

That question brought shakes of the head and a sort of derisive silence. They seemed surprised that Eddon would even suggest such a thing.

The response in subsequent interviews was similar. The screaming had been heard around three o'clock, and had gone on for at least five minutes. But no, they hadn't seen anything, and no, they hadn't done anything about it. One young man in one family said, 'I thought perhaps it was a dream.'

That was as much information as Eddon and Vail had been able to extract. And, to complete their frustration, when they returned to the railcar ready for a late afternoon snack, they discovered that their remaining food package and bottle of drink had been stolen.

'I knew criminal investigation wasn't all fun and games,' said Vail, 'but I never thought it'd be as draggy as this.'

They rode the M-rail back to Steyne-2. Vail

wanted to drive, so Eddon sat behind. The bright haze had long since gone, and the light was fading.

'Do you get the feeling that we're out of our depth on this planet?' said Vail.

Eddon leaned forward to speak over her shoulder. 'I get the feeling they're withholding something all the time. Something so basic and obvious that they despise us for not knowing it.'

'Mmm-yeah. Remember that last house, that tiny woman with the apron. She was almost sneering at us.'

'And the Scallow family, with the twins. They treated us like we'd just hatched out of the shell.'

'Yet they're all so desperate and defensive too, don't you think? Tragic even. As if they're under some terrible burden but too proud to admit it.'

'Are you thinking of that Vace family?'

'Yeah, them especially. Did you ever see such grim, despairing faces? And the old one, the man with no teeth . . .'

'Looked as though he had the ultimate hangover.'

'You know what it reminds me of? Like they're the natives and we're the tourists. They see us as outsiders come to gawp at their horrors, and they hate being gawped at.'

'Yeah. As if we're intruding on their privacy. I guess they'd rather go to hell in their own way than be helped in ours.' Eddon snorted. 'If I was going by the way they act, I'd arrest the whole lot of them as guilty.'

The railcar was approaching the cropfields, leaving the moss-moors behind. There were no figures out working in the fields now. Vail altered speed from time to time, just for the pleasure of fiddling with the controls.

'More interviews tomorrow,' said Eddon. 'We'll have to check out that other settlement, where the victim came from.'

'What're we trying to find out?'

'Why Eriph whatsisname came visiting Draive in the middle of the night.'

'You think it's relevant?'

Eddon grunted. 'Who knows what's relevant in a serial killer case? You can go around uncovering all sorts of connections and causes, and in the end maybe none of them mean a thing. If this killer is killing completely at random ... But we have to follow up the leads we've got.'

'Hmm. Do you think the people in this other settlement will be more willing to talk?'

'Nope.'

'It'd be easier if I put them under hypnosis.'

'Against their will?'

'Why not? Get them on their own and —'

'It's contrary to police procedure.'

'Oh, who cares about police procedure?'

'I do.'

'It can be great fun.'

'*Fun?*'

'Yeah. Think of all the little secrets we could uncover under hypnosis! I bet these settlements are real sexual hotbeds under the surface. More exciting than a visi-series!'

'Don't you parapsychs have any sense of responsibility?'

'Nope. Hey, I bet they're all secretly screwing each other! I bet —'

'Whoa!' Eddon nearly leapt out of his seat.

'What?'

'What you just said!'

'What did I say?'

'Where's your voice recorder? Still in your bag?'

'Yeah. Be careful! Please don't mess up my equipment!'

But Eddon was already digging around in the bag. He pulled out the recorder and pressed the rewind.

'That first interview with the MetGivon family. Is that where the recording starts?'

'Yeah.'

'Okay. Stop the railcar. I want you to listen.'

Vail brought the railcar to a halt. They were not far from the outskirts of Steyne-2. She turned around in the driver's seat to listen.

It took several minutes to play the whole interview through. Eddon paid special attention to the parts involving the young husband and wife, Dennott and Magda. Dennott explaining angrily why his wife was upset... Magda's distressful choking fit... Dennott breaking in to admit that they both knew the murder victim...

'You hear?' demanded Eddon. 'Listen to the voices!'

'You think —?'

'That's the sound of a jealous husband.'

Vail nodded slowly.

'And a young woman who's found her lover brutally murdered. Magda had been having an affair with Eriph. Which is why he was visiting in the middle of the night. And why he came up the back lane.'

'Mmm-yeah. Clever.'

'It all fits together.'

'And the memoscopy too. I didn't tell you. Eriph was in a state of excited anticipation when he came up the lane. I couldn't pick what it was. But, yeah, like someone going to a rendezvous with a lover. He was thinking of a particular room with a low ceiling — that would have been their secret meeting-place. Maybe a store or cellar at the bottom of the house.'

Eddon snapped his fingers. 'We'll have to follow this up immediately. Let's move! Back to Draive!'

'But it's getting dark.'

'Half an hour to nightfall. We can be back in Draive in just over twenty minutes. I want to put these MetGivons on the spot.'

'All right. You're the boss, boss.'

'Can you put this thing in reverse?'

Vail engaged reverse, and the railcar glided backwards along the line in the direction of Draive.

'Is this the fastest you can do?' asked Eddon, after a few minutes.

'It doesn't seem to have the same speed in reverse as forwards.'

'Okay, Okay.' Eddon was fuming with impatience.

'We'll have to go forwards then. Head towards Steyne-2, until we find an intersection where we can turn right around.'

By the time they found an intersection, they had wasted nearly ten minutes. It took another three minutes to get back to the place where Eddon had had his moment of revelation.

Slowly, inexorably, the day was failing. As they sped across the cropfields, the watery disc of the sun dimmed and disappeared. As they passed across the moss-moors, the light ebbed out of the sky and the shadows settled deeper over the ground.

'It's going to be one dark night if this planet doesn't have a moon,' remarked Vail.

There was no moon. By the time they came towards Draive, the last glimmer of twilight was gone. Vail had to slow down to see where the side-line turned off. By the time they finally dismounted from the railcar, an absolute blackness had swallowed the world.

The night air was growing cool. They put on their vannamaks and Vail carried her bag. They made their way along the path around the base of the settlement, unable to see even the ground beneath their feet. There seemed to be no lights on anywhere. They came to the main street and started up the hill.

'It's incredible,' said Vail.

'What?'

'Do they all go to bed the moment it gets dark?'

'Maybe it's because they only have batteries to power their lights.'

'I don't like it.'

They sensed rather than saw the houses on either side of the street. Their own hands were mere blurs of paleness, scarcely visible. They kept close together, almost tripping over each other.

They came to the plaza at the top of the hill. Here were a few houses with lights on in the windows. But the windows were shuttered and the lights appeared only in thin yellowy slits. Away from the windows, the plaza was as dark as ever.

'Doesn't it seem to you like there's something *wrong* here?' asked Vail.

'Don't spook me. What's the problem? You've got your punchgun.'

'No, I haven't. I left it back at the Big House.'

'You're joking?'

'You never told me we were going to come creeping around in the dark.'

'Creeping? Who's creeping?'

'We are.'

It was true. They were both stepping softly and carefully, instinctively trying to minimise the noise of their feet on the gravel.

'The MetGivon house is somewhere over there,' said Eddon.

'Betcha they won't come to the door.'

'Maybe, maybe not.'

They crossed the plaza to the house by the lane. Vail shivered as she looked down the lane. She felt an empty space of blackness breathing up at her.

Eddon stood in front of the door. The windows of the MetGivons' house were dark and lightless. He pressed on the doorbell button.

There was a loud ringing deep inside the house. Then silence. Eddon bent down and put his ear to the door. There was no sound of anyone stirring within.

'I'll give it another go. Check and see if anyone looks out the windows.'

Vail backed away a few paces until she could observe the entire house. Eddon took out his punchgun and reversed it in his hand. Using the butt as a hammer, he struck half a dozen times on the door. Metal on metal, the reverberation echoed thunderously across the plaza.

Still no-one came to the door. Eddon put his punchgun back in his pocket.

'Anything?' he called out.

'Not that I could see.'

'Damn stupid peasants.'

'They're all fast asleep and dreaming.'

'Hey!'

'What?'

'Who's that?'

'Where?'

'There!'

Eddon stared into the darkness. 'Where?'

Then he saw. Someone was standing in the shadow of the walls, two houses away. Whoever it was seemed to be turned in the other direction, not facing them.

'Hey you! Who're you?'

The figure turned its face towards him. It started screaming.

Eddon advanced. The figure raised its arms and hands defensively, covering its face. It screamed as if in extreme agony.

'Calm down,' shouted Eddon. 'I'm not going to do anything to you!'

He took another step forward.

Then the hands dropped away, revealing the face. It was a man — but not a man. His mouth was wider than any human mouth was ever meant to open. Screaming in utter insanity. Between his teeth hung strings of something white, like a mucus.

Eddon drew his punchgun out of his pocket. Simultaneously the killer sprang.

There was no warning, no transition. Only Eddon's instant reactions saved him. As he jumped aside, the killer caught him a raking blow with one extended arm.

Eddon went sprawling. The punchgun flew from his hand, fell to the ground with a clatter.

The killer didn't stop. Now he was heading towards Vail. She dropped her bag and backed away. The killer reached out, grasping for her neck.

Eddon scrambled to his feet and threw himself forward. He slammed into the killer from behind.

But the killer stayed upright, scarcely even staggering. Eddon got an arm around his throat.

The killer took hold of Eddon's arm with one hand. The strength in that hand was incredible. Slowly Eddon's arm was levered away. The killer reached back over his other shoulder and grabbed a fistful of Eddon's vannamak.

Vail wasn't watching. She had heard where Eddon's punchgun had hit the ground. She darted after it, detouring around the two combatants.

The killer bent forward, hoisting Eddon like a sack of coals over his back. Eddon felt his feet leave the ground. He gouged at the killer's eyes with the fingers of his free hand. But it made no difference. The killer threw him bodily across the plaza. For a moment he was sailing, weightless, revolving in the air. Then he smashed head-first into the Independence Monument.

There was a tremendous clang of bone striking metal. As if in slow motion, Eddon slid down the side of the Monument and slumped to the ground. The killer strode towards him.

But now Vail had located the punchgun. She snatched it up with a wordless prayer. As the killer stooped over Eddon's motionless body, she pulled the trigger and fired.

The killer gave a slight shudder. Nothing more. Vail knelt down on one knee and took aim very carefully. Again she fired, straight for the heart. It was as if she hadn't fired at all. The killer twitched and turned to face her.

Again he screamed his unbelievable ear-splitting scream. The slavering white stuff in his mouth was like thick cream. He left Eddon and advanced upon Vail.

She felt for the shunt on the gun. It was set to stun. She switched it across to lethal. Once more she fired. The shot took him in the chest.

This time he stumbled and twisted. The scream changed to a voiceless shriek, a kind of grating rasping sound. He backed away and turned as if to run.

She fired another three shots. Every shot hit home. The killer took a dozen wavering steps across the plaza. Then his legs seemed to give out. He collapsed and lay still.

Vail jumped up and ran across to Eddon. He was lying in a heap at the base of the Monument. No movement, no sign of life.

She took his wrist and felt for a pulse. Yes, there it was! She breathed a sigh of relief.

She loosened his collar.

'Uh-uhhh,' he moaned.

'You okay?'

He blinked and opened his eyes. His eyes had a dazed, glassy look, wandering erratically from side to side.

'You've been concussed,' she told him. 'Lie still. Relax.'

'What happened?' he asked in a wavering voice.

'You saved my life. The serial killer. He threw you against the Monument.'

'Oh yeah. I remember.'

'I saved your life too. I shot him with your punchgun. I had to use the lethal setting.'

'You killed him?'

'Had to.'

'Where is he?'

'Over there.' She gestured vaguely.

Eddon blinked several times. He seemed to be trying to focus.

'No.'

'What?'

'Nothing there.'

Vail spun around. Behind her, the plaza was empty. The killer had gone. She jumped to her feet and stared in every direction.

'Impossible,' she breathed. 'He couldn't have! I shot him four times.'

The darkness was impenetrable. The killer might be still in the plaza, lurking in the shadows. He could return and attack at any moment. They had to find shelter.

She struggled to stay calm. She considered the houses around the plaza. What about the windows where the lights were on? Surely there was someone still awake?

'We'll knock on the windows,' she said. 'Someone will have to let us in.'

But Eddon didn't reply. She looked down and saw that his eyes were once again closed. He seemed to have sunk back into his state of concussion.

'Maybe for the best,' she muttered.

She crouched down beside him and cupped his head in her hands. She ran her thumbs over his skull, slowly down and around on either side. She was marking out an arc from ear to ear.

Eddon's eyelids flickered open. 'What're you —?'

'Temporary semiothesia,' said Vail. 'An elementary parapsychic technique. This was one of the first lessons we learnt at the psychoseminary.'

She spoke in a quiet soothing tone, repeating the motion with her thumbs and applying a steady gentle pressure.

'I'm creating a kind of bulwark across the middle of your cortex. You'll be able to use your basic motor functions. But the frontal lobes of your brain will be damped down.'

'Brain?' Eddon mumbled. He tried to roll his head to the side. 'I don't want your spells in my —'

He stopped speaking in mid-sentence. His eyelids stayed open but his eyeballs were as if locked in position.

Vail moved her thumbs across his skull a few more times.

'Now,' she said. 'You'll be able to move your body without conscious thought. Let's stand up.'

Eddon propped himself up on his elbows. Then slowly but steadily he rose to his feet. Vail gripped him under the elbow and guided him upright. He stood firmly planted with legs apart.

'Hey, this is great,' she said. 'Pity you can't be like this all the time.'

She turned him to face the nearest lighted window.

'Okay, let's go.'

They walked slowly across the plaza. Vail still gripped him under the elbow. His feet shuffled and crunched in the gravel. Vail wasn't sure if she could hear other footsteps as well, or only an echo of the noise Eddon was making. She kept the punchgun ready in her free hand, constantly swinging it around in every direction.

The window was protected by shutters, and a cage of metal bars in front of the shutters. Vail reached in between the bars and hammered on the shutters with the butt of the punchgun.

If the killer attacked now, she'd be helpless, unable to shoot. But there was no attack.

There was no movement inside the room either. Vail brought her face up against the bars and peered through the slits in the shutters. Through one slit, she could see the side of a bed; through another, the top of a cupboard; through another, a pair of boots on the floor. She had the strong impression that there was someone lying on the bed, although she couldn't get a view of the room in that direction.

Again she reached in and hammered with the butt of the gun.

'We're in danger out here,' she called, directing

her voice through the shutters. 'Please let us in. I know you're there.'

But again there was no response. The room was almost unnaturally still. If anyone was lying on the bed, they were holding themselves motionless.

She turned away, fighting down her fear and anger.

'What's wrong with these people?' she muttered. 'Okay, we'll try that window over there.'

She directed Eddon towards another lighted window, two houses further on. Eddon walked beside her, eyes staring rigidly ahead.

There were no metal bars over the next window, but the shutters were fastened with a heavy brass padlock. Vail brought Eddon to a halt and peered through the slits.

Inside, the room looked like a washroom. She could see a basin, a mirror and two towels on a rack. The walls were panelled with stainless steel. The light was not in the room itself, but shone through the open door from a corridor beyond.

Vail hammered violently on the shutters with the butt of the gun. The shutters shook and rattled under her blows. Then suddenly the light went off.

Vail stopped her hammering and waited. But in vain. Nothing further happened. Whoever had turned off the light didn't intend to open the door.

'Scumbags!!' Vail was ready to scream. 'Brown-ass mothersucking scumbags!!'

At that moment, from the other side of the plaza, came the sound of a door opening.

Her first assumption was that someone was looking to help them. She felt overwhelming relief.

'We're over here!' she shouted at the top of her voice. 'We'll walk across to you!'

But even as she shouted, some other instinct, some other part of her mind, gave a warning. The feeling of relief turned into a kind of creeping chill.

From across the plaza came the sound of the same door closing. Vail froze. She stood staring into the darkness. But there was nothing further.

Instead Eddon started mumbling quietly to himself.

'Mmmuh . . . Mmmmah . . . Mmm.'

The semiothesia was wearing off. For a moment she considered bringing him out of it. She wanted help, she needed support. But no, that would be unfair. And cowardly.

She pushed Eddon forward again. The next house on this side of the plaza had no lighted window — but it did have a porch. A porch would offer some protection.

'Come *on*,' she muttered, trying to hurry him along. But Eddon couldn't be hurried.

The house was one of the more ornate buildings on the plaza. The porch was decorated with wrought iron tracery, a grand entranceway for a front door. It had solid walls at the sides and a step at the front.

Vail guided Eddon in up the step. He moved forward as far as the door, then halted.

Vail stood in the entrance of the porch, gazing

out across the plaza. The darkness seemed very wide and open. But nothing stirred. Her beating heart began to slow down. She turned back to the interior of the porch. She didn't even bother trying to knock on the door.

'Lie down now,' she said to Eddon in a low voice. She pressed lightly on his shoulders. 'Here in front of the door.'

Eddon was still mumbling quietly to himself. He lay down crosswise at the back of the porch, curling his legs to fit in.

'Now close your eyes and sleep.'

Eddon settled more comfortably and the mumbling died away. Within a minute, his breathing had taken on the slow, heavy rhythm of sleep.

Vail sat down in front of him, facing out from the porch. She crossed her legs and cradled the punchgun in both hands. If the killer attacked, he would have to attack from straight ahead — she was protected on the other three sides. She willed herself to relax, to remain alert without over-focussing. She would have to keep guard all through the night. It was going to be a long and weary vigil.

It rained three times during the night. Short sharp showers, sweeping across the settlement, then passing rapidly away. The rain angled into the porch, forcing Vail to sit further back, pressed up against Eddon's legs.

It was during the first shower that Vail thought she heard once more the sound of a door opening on the other side of the plaza. But this time there was no sound of the door closing afterwards. She strained to hear above the noise of the rain as it beat down on metal roofs and gravel. She gripped the punchgun tighter, silent as a statue, hardly breathing. Moment by moment she waited for that terrible mad face to materialise out of the darkness. But nothing happened.

Later on, after the shower had passed, she remembered her bag. She had dropped it out in the plaza when the killer attacked. Thinking of her bag, she also remembered the coil of whipperwire that was packed inside it. A plan began to form in her mind.

Eddon was sleeping soundly. She rose and tiptoed out into the plaza, punchgun at the ready. She found the bag lying just where she'd expected. She snatched it up and returned to the porch.

Her plan relied upon the wrought iron ornamentation around the porch's outer entrance. The intricacies of the metal offered numerous notches and openings through which to thread the wire. She anchored one end with a triple stay-knot, then started to weave a web from side to side across the entrance. By the time she had used up all the wire, there was a taut network of thirty or forty strands crisscrossing the front of the porch. It might not

136

stop the killer for long, but it would certainly hold off any sudden attack.

She sat down crosslegged again, feeling a little more secure. Eddon slept on peacefully. A tempting drowsiness crept up over her too. She had to shake herself to keep awake.

The second shower came and went, and the third.

She started to think about St Alda's Psycho-seminary, back on Terra in the Centre of the Hegemony. And her old teachers — so wise and learned, yet so remote from the real world. They'd always wanted her to stay and develop her talents in research, couldn't understand why she'd turned down the excellent post they offered. 'Not exciting? That's a rather immature attitude, ev Vessintor!' She wondered what they'd say about her present situation, hiding in a porch while some crazed serial killer roamed the night...

A sudden scream jerked her out of her thoughts. The same terrible, mad scream, the killer's scream — but far away in the distance now. It sounded like the drawn-out howl of an animal.

Over and again it rose and fell. Vail listened in a kind of awe.

'It's out on the moors,' said a voice behind her.

Eddon was awake. The scream had penetrated even his deep slumber. He hadn't moved, but his eyes were wide and staring.

'Must be at least half a kilometre away,' he added. 'Can you tell what direction it's from?'

Vail gestured with the hand that held the punchgun. 'Somewhere over thataway, I think.'

Still the blood-chilling sound continued. But the screams grew gradually weaker, separated by longer and longer intervals. Finally they stopped altogether. The night seemed suddenly, overpoweringly silent. Eddon rubbed his eyes and sat up.

'So we know one thing now,' he said. 'We know it wasn't the murder victims screaming. Those screams described in the report.'

'No. It was the killer himself. Even the screaming I heard when I did the memoscopy.'

'And we know something else too. We know where the white liquid stuff comes from.'

'Yeah. Foaming at the mouth. Isn't that what madmen are supposed to do?'

'Except foaming at the mouth is just spittle. This stuff is something different.'

He stretched and shook himself. He massaged the circulation back into his legs.

'How long until dawn?' he asked

'About two hours. How do you feel?'

'Me? Fine.'

'No headache?'

'No. Just a bit stiff in the legs. And you? Have you been keeping watch all night?'

'Yeah.'

'Okay. Then it's your turn to get some sleep.'

'While you keep watch?'

'Yeah. I couldn't go back to sleep now anyway.'

'Fine by me.'

Vail passed the punchgun across and they traded places. Eddon moved to the front of the porch and sat propped up against one side of the entrance. Vail moved to the back and lay down with her spine against the door. Because of her long legs she had to double up into an almost foetal position.

'Don't go walking off anywhere,' she said.

'Relax. I'll be right here.'

'Or you'll walk into my wire across the front of the porch.'

She took three deep breaths and immediately fell asleep.

Eddon reached out and touched the strands of wire. Ingenious, he thought to himself, a sort of invisible barrier. She must've rigged it up after bringing him to the shelter of this porch. Though he couldn't exactly remember being brought...

It was strange, the way she'd taken charge of things. In some ways she seemed so young and irresponsible, in other ways so old. He couldn't decide about her at all.

Slowly, slowly the hours went by. Once, twice, Vail shifted in her sleep, pressing her legs against the small of his back. He tried not to move. Her legs were warm and stirred slightly as she breathed. There was a tiny whiffle of a snore every time she exhaled.

He remembered the usual sayings about PP assistants. Amoral as cats, sexed-up and ready to go. The inspectors back at Central had many other

names for them as well as 'witches'. But this one ...
this one was a mystery.

There were no further screams or noises
through the night. Eddon rested his head against
the side of the porch, using his hand as a pillow.
The bruise on the back of his skull was sore and
aching.

But at last the dawn arrived. He watched and
waited as the light grew stronger. Now he could see
the silvery web of whipperwire in front of him. But
he couldn't see out across the plaza. The air was
thick and damp with fog. It was like staring into a
sea of dim grey nothingness.

He gazed round at Vail, folded up at the back of
the porch. No slinky sophistication about her now.
She had her head buried in the crook of her arm
and her greeny-black hair flopped forward over her
face. He wondered what she looked like beneath
her make-up. She might be really attractive or
really ugly. But the more he gazed, the more he
imagined her as attractive ...

He thought of waking her up. He was impatient
to find out what had happened to the killer. But
what could they do in this fog? He decided to let
her sleep on.

Another half hour passed. Now Eddon could
just glimpse the looming shapes of houses on the
other side of the plaza. But still the fog rolled and
stirred in slow dense swirls. It was like being inside
a cloud.

There were no signs of activity from the people

of Draive. If they were up from their beds, they still weren't coming out of their houses. The whole place was as silent as a ghost town.

Suddenly the silence was broken. From the other side of the plaza came a violent rattle and clatter: the rattle of bolts being drawn, the clatter of shutters flung open. Through the fog, Eddon caught a glimpse of a woman's head and shoulders thrust forward out of a window.

'It's Jaith, it's Jaith!' she cried. Her voice was on the very edge of hysteria. 'Jaith is the killer!'

Eddon had to shake Vail by the shoulder to wake her up. By the time she opened her eyes the woman had vanished. But she nodded when Eddon pointed the direction across the plaza.

'Looks like the same house where I heard the door open and close,' she said.

Eddon slid out from the porch flat on his back, squeezing under the bottom strand of the wire. Vail wriggled out on her belly. They jumped to their feet and hurried across through the fog. There were sounds of front doors opening tentatively all around the plaza.

'Did we interview the family in this house?' asked Vail.

'Yeah, the Scallow family.'

'With the twins?'

'Right. Husband's name was Jaith.'

'I remember. And the wife was Roah.'

They came to the window from which Roah had called out. The shutters were still wide open. The window was set high above the ground, higher than the level of Eddon's head. But Vail standing on tiptoe was just tall enough to see in.

A strange scene met her eyes. The room was a bedroom, but it looked almost bare. Most of the furniture had been shifted across and piled up in a great barricade against the door. Bedstead, chest, table, chairs — the barricade reached right up to the ceiling.

Roah herself sat crouched in a far corner of the room. She had her face in her hands and she appeared to be shivering. She was wearing a loose nightgown that was ripped and grimed in many places.

The only piece of furniture not piled against the door was a massive clothes cupboard. With a start of surprise, Vail realised that two pairs of eyes were peering down at her from the top of the cupboard. There in the darkness were two small pale faces, two bobs of dark hair. It was the twins. They had made a hiding place for themselves on top of the cupboard.

She called out softly to the woman. 'Roah. Roah.'

Roah lowered her hands and looked up. Her eyes were wide like staring lamps.

'It's all right, Roah. You're safe now. Take down your barricade and let us in.'

Roah seemed to be in a state of shock. 'He tried to kill me in the night,' she said dully.

Eddon meanwhile was watching the activity in the plaza. The people of Draive were coming out of their houses, converging through the fog. They gathered in a crowd before the Scallows' front door. The door was already ajar.

Vail tried again.

'Jaith has gone, Roah. Take down your barricade.'

Roah stood up, then hesitated. 'Where is he then?'

'Out on the moors. A long way away.'

Roah seemed to make up her mind. She went over to the barricade and began pulling at the furniture. She worked slowly at first, but gradually her movements became more purposeful.

'Damnation,' Eddon exclaimed suddenly. 'They're starting to go in. Let's move.'

He caught Vail by the arm and drew her away from the window. They hurried across to where the crowd was starting to push forward through the front door into the Scallows' house. Eddon and Vail joined in at the rear.

'Damn, damn, damn,' said Eddon. 'They're sure to touch everything.'

A woman in front looked round at him. It was Fladda, the old woman from the MetGivon family.

'So what?' she demanded truculently. 'What difference does it make?'

'We can't work from evidence that's been tampered with.'

'Who needs evidence? We know Jaith is the killer, what else do we need to know?'

The crowd pressed forward along a hall and into a kind of parlour. There were several armchairs with high backs, and a huge quilted sofa. People stood around muttering and pointing. They seemed to be pointing especially at an area in the middle of the parlour.

Eddon elbowed his way forward and Vail followed in his wake. In the middle of the parlour was a low glasstop table and a rug. The rug was thick with blood and there were blobs and trails of sticky white stuff all around. Beside the table lay a box with a red cross insignia — a medicine chest. Its contents had been spilled out over the floor.

Eddon knelt down and inspected the contents of the medicine chest.

'The bandages have been taken,' he announced. 'He must've been bandaging his wounds.'

Several faces turned towards him.

'Wounds?'

'What wounds?'

'Who wounded him?'

Eddon rose to his feet. 'The killer attacked us last night,' he said. 'We shot him — my assistant shot him.' He drew out the punchgun and held it up. 'With this. He should've been killed outright, but he was only wounded. Now he's out on the moors.'

'How do you know?'

144

'We heard him there afterwards, screaming. He must've come here for bandages first. He's probably —'

Eddon was about to say that Jaith was probably hiding somewhere on the moors, unable to go further with the wounds he'd sustained. But at that very moment the bedroom door swung open. Roah had finally finished dismantling her barricade.

She stood for a moment framed in the doorway. She saw the crowd and gave a sort of sob. She looked half ready to laugh and half ready to cry. She advanced unsteadily into the room, arms raised and hands clasped in a gesture of thankfulness.

'Oh, it's true ... he's gone ... you're here ... I thought I'd never be safe again ...'

She hardly seemed to know what she was saying. A dozen paces into the room, her eyes rolled up and her body went limp. Gentle hands caught her before she could fall to the ground.

'Get her to the sofa!'

'She's completely out!'

'Somebody bring water and a towel!'

'Her pulse is very slow!'

'Open a window! Let some air in!'

'Where's that medicine chest?'

They carried Roah across to the sofa. Everyone seemed suddenly very busy, milling around the unconscious woman. Vail turned to Eddon.

'They'll take care of her. Why don't we go and check up on the children?'

Eddon grunted agreement. They slipped away from the crowd and went through the door into the bedroom. The furniture from the dismantled barricade lay in a jumble on one side of the room. The twins were still looking down from their hiding place on top of the cupboard.

Vail approached and nodded up at them.

'Hey, you two! Are you okay?'

'Where's Papa? Can we come down now?'

'Yeah, come down. We'll help you.'

The eyes vanished. Two pairs of feet appeared over the edge of the cupboard, then two pairs of legs, dangling in mid air. Vail reached up and grabbed the first pair of legs, Eddon reached up and grabbed the second.

'Okay, we've got you.'

The children slid down further and let go. Vail and Eddon caught hold of them by the waist, lowered them to the ground.

'Phew, you sure weigh a ton!' said Eddon.

They were identical twins, a girl and a boy. They had bare feet and were dressed for bed in grey night-tunics. They seemed grave and solemn and oddly unchildlike.

'How old are you?'

'Eight,' said the girl. 'I'm Dairsie.'

'I'm Keal,' said the boy. 'Where's Papa?'

Eddon and Vail exchanged troubled glances. How much had they seen, how much should they be told?

'He wanted to kill us,' said Dairsie. 'Did you know?'

'Let's all sit down and talk,' said Eddon.

He went over to the jumble of furniture and

146

pulled the mattress from the top of the bed. He dragged it out into the centre of the room and sat down on it. Vail sat down too, and the twins sat between them.

'You say your Papa wanted to kill you?' asked Eddon.

'He turned.'

'Do you want to tell us about it?'

They nodded.

'He came back in the middle of the night,' said Keal.

'We didn't know he'd been going out,' said Dairsie.

'I dreamed he was in the parlour,' said Keal. 'I dreamed there were sounds in the parlour. Then I woke up and heard them.'

'I was asleep all the time,' said Dairsie. 'I didn't hear Keal getting up.'

'I got up very quiet. I went to the parlour and turned on the light. I saw Papa on the floor. His legs were all wrong. He was on the floor and blood all over him.'

'Go on,' said the girl.

'I said "What's wrong Papa?" I wanted to cry. His face was different and he was changed. He looked like he didn't remember me, but then he did. He said he was hurt and I had to bring him the medicine chest.'

'I wouldn't've brought it,' said Dairsie.

'Yes, you would've,' said Keal. 'You don't know what it was like. It wasn't like anything normal. It was like in a dream.'

'So you brought the medicine chest?' prompted Vail.

'Yes. I got muddled. I kept going to the bathroom and coming back, and he kept telling me where it was and I kept forgetting. His voice was all thick and wet and horrible. Then I brought it and Papa —'

The boy's eyes filled suddenly with tears. But he blinked them away and went on.

'Papa knocked it over and got the bandages out. He was tying them round himself. I asked to help but he didn't notice. There was this bandage to go round his back and he couldn't make it go right. I went to help because I thought I ought. I nearly touched him. Then he opened his mouth at me. He was — he —'

Eddon and Vail waited as the boy struggled to find the words.

'Like it made him sick to look at me. I wanted to go away, but I couldn't move. He finished doing the bandages. Then he said to come and put my head on the table.'

'Put your head on the table?'

'Yes. I had to put my head on the table.'

Eddon looked across at Vail. 'Must've been the glasstop table by the rug,' he murmured.

'I was scared. He had these scissors out of the medicine cabinet. He was holding them funny. He was sitting on the floor waiting for me to put my head on the table. I started shouting.'

'He shouted "Mum! Mum! Mum!"' said Dairsie. 'Real loud. It woke me up.'

'Papa was looking at me with his eyes. I was so scared. But I wouldn't put my head on the table! I wouldn't! I wouldn't!'

The boy shook and shuddered and pushed out with his fists, as if to drive something away. He was completely submerged in the memory. Eddon, sitting next to him, put an arm over his shoulder.

'It's okay, Keal,' he said gently. 'Take it easy.'

The boy quietened down and went on.

'Then Mum came rushing in and picked me up. Papa didn't have time to move. She was so quick. She picked me up and ran into the front bedroom. She slammed the door. She started putting things against the door so he couldn't open it. But he didn't come after us anyway.'

'He came after me instead,' said Dairsie. 'I was lying in bed. I heard the shouting and Mum running out in the parlour, but I didn't understand what it was. I looked at Keal's bed but he wasn't there. Then I heard this slow dragging sound, closer and closer.'

The girl shook her head as if she still couldn't believe it.

'Then there was this face coming in at the door. He was crawling. I didn't even know it was Papa at first. There was stuff in his mouth like something horrid.'

'I saw it too,' said Keal, breaking in. 'Ugh!'

'I jumped out of bed and he started following me. He was all blood and bandages. I jumped back on the bed so he couldn't reach me. But he sort of lifted himself up over the edge.'

'He couldn't stand upright?' asked Eddon.

'No. He had one leg dragging behind all the time. I jumped from the bed up onto the dresser. He came round after me on the floor. I thought I was safe because I was so high. But he got up with the handles. He pulled himself up until he could grab at my ankles.'

She lifted her night-tunic up to her knees.

'See what he did?'

Her legs and feet were red with dried blood. There were a dozen deep cuts on her calves and ankles.

'But those are cuts,' said Eddon. 'He didn't do that just by grabbing at you.'

'No. He was grabbing at me at first. I was kicking at his hands and moving around on top of the dresser. I was so fast he couldn't catch hold of me. So then he started stabbing at my legs with something in his hand.'

'The scissors!' Keal interrupted. 'It was the scissors.'

'Yes, okay, the scissors. He cut me and cut me and I was bleeding all over the dresser. But I wouldn't stop moving around. I picked up my mirror on the dresser and smashed him over the head. But it didn't make any difference. I couldn't hurt him. And he kept making this sound with his mouth like — like he was — like I was —'

'Like you made him feel sick,' said Keal

Dairsie nodded. 'It went on and on. I was getting tired and starting to slip on the blood. I was thinking to jump off the dresser and run somewhere else. But he'd only keep coming after me. I didn't know what to do. I thought Mum had forgotten about me.'

'We were busy piling the stuff against the door,' said Keal. 'Mum was doing it and I was helping her. We thought he was going to be coming after us. We were making so much noise we didn't hear anything else. Then we stopped when it was all piled up. Then we heard him in the other bedroom.'

Dairsie sniffed. 'About time.'

'Mum went frantic. She was crying and going "Dairsie! Dairsie! Dairsie!" We had to pull all the stuff away from the door again. We did it so fast. Mum was like crazy. She ran out to save you.'

Eddon turned from Keal to Dairsie. 'So then what, Dairsie?'

'I saw Mum at the bedroom door. She was holding out her arms. Papa heard her and turned round, sort of snarling. Then I did this huge leap from the dresser, right over the top of his head. I nearly knocked Mum over. He started coming to get us, but we ran out through the door first.'

'They came back into the front bedroom with me,' said Keal. 'I put a chair against the door as soon as they came in.'

He pointed to the jumble of furniture. 'That one there. Then we all started piling stuff up again. We pushed the big bed across and the other stuff against it.'

'He couldn't get in,' said Dairsie. 'He came up to the door and he was turning the handle. We heard it.'

'Mum made us get on top of the cupboard. She said to shush and hide.'

'But he couldn't get in.'

'We stayed up there all night.'

'I think you're both very brave,' said Eddon. 'And your Mum too.'

'What'll happen now?' asked Dairsie.

'We don't have a Papa any more,' said Keal.

'Will he have to be caught and killed?'

'Well, he'll have to be caught, yes.'

'And killed?'

Eddon shrugged and looked at Vail. Vail shrugged and looked back at Eddon. They weren't sure what to say. They were saved from answering when a voice spoke up suddenly from the doorway.

'Ah! The children are here!'

It was a young woman looking in from the other room.

'Yes, they're fine,' said Vail.

'Roah was asking for them,' said the woman. 'She's just recovered.'

'Mum!' the two children exclaimed simultaneously. They jumped up from the mattress and ran out to the parlour.

The young woman nodded and smiled and disappeared from the doorway again.

Eddon rubbed his chin and looked thoughtful.

'Know what I'm thinking?' he said.

'What?'

'I'm thinking we might be able to get these people to help.'

'Help?'

'Help search the moors. Find the killer.'

'Yeah. They don't seem so hostile today. Maybe because we shot the killer for them.'

'Maybe. Or because we've become involved in everything now. I think they might help.'

'Worth a try.'

'I'll ask.'

15

The people of Draive were not difficult to persuade. They were willing to search for the killer on the moors if Eddon could narrow down the area to be searched. When they assembled half an hour later in the plaza, virtually the whole population of the settlement was there.

They came armed with a variety of makeshift weapons. Some brought hammers, some brought metal bars, some brought strange agricultural implements. There were tooth-edged zaroths and auto-rakes and battery-powered strippers. Most common of all were the seed-drills: sharply pointed metal tubes up to three metres long, carried by means of grips and a harness.

The fog was as dense as ever in the plaza, and even more dense when they descended to the level of the surrounding moss-moor. Everyone formed up in a long line, facing in the direction from which the last screams had come. Once Eddon had pointed out the direction, no further organisation was needed. The people of Draive took up position as if they knew exactly what to do, spacing themselves out at four metre intervals. Four metres was about the limit of effective vision in the fog.

Then the line moved off. They walked at a measured pace over the velvety green moss, everyone adjusting their stride to keep up with their neighbours. It was a weird and eerie procession. When anyone spoke, the fog distorted the sound, making voices either muffled and remote or oddly loud and booming. But there wasn't much speaking. Most of the time, the only sound was the soft swish of boots over the moss, the dull thud of boots on the ground.

The ground was mainly moss-covered in the direction they were heading. Sometimes they came upon stretches of greeny-grey or yellowy-grey lichen, sometimes they passed by humps of rock where neither moss nor lichen had been able to take hold. There were countless tiny pools of water and a few larger ponds. They had to swerve around the larger ponds, temporarily separating and re-forming the line on the other side.

They walked on steadily for ten minutes. Eddon didn't expect any sign of the killer close to the settlement. But after ten minutes he called out:

'Watch out now! He could be hidden some-where in a hollow! Watch out he doesn't spring at you suddenly!'

The message was passed on down the line by successive voices. The people of Draive held their weapons pointing forward, at the ready. Eddon drew his punchgun from his pocket. Only Vail was weaponless.

The fog seemed to be settling down thicker than ever. Vail could see the figures closest to her in the line: Eddon on her left and a muscular young adolescent on her right. Further away, the next figures on either side were grey and indistinct; further away again, the next figures were mere ghostly shadows. And beyond them, nothing.

Still there was no sign of the killer. Vail swore as her foot sank into a half-hidden pool of water.

'Oh slag it! That's the third time!'

'Keep watching,' said Eddon, non-committally.

'I'm not equipped for this,' snapped Vail. 'I'm a parapsych. I haven't got proper boots or anything.'

Eddon grinned to himself. 'This wasn't in your psychoseminary training, hey?'

'Hah! I'm supposed to use intuition and insight. Not plodding around the goddamn countryside.'

'So use it. Apply your intuition and tell us where this sicko killer has hidden himself.'

'Oh yeah. You know I've got nothing to work from.'

'How should I know how you work? Do

something supernatural. Tune in to vibrations in the air or something.'

'Okay.' Vail pointed dramatically. 'He's over there on the right.'

'Why there?'

'Just the first direction that came into my mind.'

'Very helpful, I'm sure.'

'You want intuition, that's my intuition.'

Eddon was about to reply when a shout came suddenly from over on the right.

'Here! Here! I've found his trail!'

It was the very direction where Vail had been pointing. She gave Eddon one of her brilliant starry smiles.

'Hnh!' Eddon snorted disbelievingly. 'A fluke!'

'But of course. I cultivate flukes.'

Everyone was running in the direction of the shout. Eddon and Vail turned and ran too. Now there were many voices shouting.

'This trail is fresh!'

'He can't be far!'

'We've got him now!'

'Let's go!'

The trail was a line of bloodspots. Bright red blood on the deep rich green of the moss. Eddon and Vail were among the last to arrive.

Eddon bent down to inspect.

'He was crawling,' he announced after careful examination. 'No proper footprints. And this mark dug into the moss — like he was still dragging one leg behind.'

He turned back to the beginning of the trail, in a small hollow in the ground half encircled by a low outcrop of bare rock. The moss in the hollow was not spotted but smeared with blood.

'Here's where he spent the night,' he said. 'Curled up here. See the imprint of his body on the moss?'

'It's like a kind of nest,' said Vail.

'Yeah. I guess the bandages staunched the bleeding for a while. But eventually the blood must've soaked through. He probably got up and headed off again after dawn. Or maybe when he heard us starting to hunt for him.'

'Er, I think we're getting left behind,' said Vail.

She was looking in the other direction. The people of Draive had already vanished into the fog, continuing the hunt, following along the trail.

'Right,' said Eddon. 'What are we waiting for?'

They set off running. They didn't need to track the bloodspots on the ground. It was easier to follow the clamour of the people up ahead. They were all shouting and yelling and cheering each other on.

'Slag it! Slag it!' exclaimed Vail as she sploshed through two more pools of water.

Up ahead, the shouting and yelling and cheering died suddenly away. There was a sort of gasp, followed by an intent silence.

'They've found him,' muttered Eddon between puffs. 'They'd better not do anything to him.'

For the last twenty metres the blood on the moss was not merely in spots but ran in a continuous wavering line, like a stripe of red paint across the green. Eddon and Vail skidded to a halt as grey human shapes loomed out of the fog in front of them. The people of Draive were formed up into a ring. They stood as if listening to something. Their weapons were all directed in towards the centre of the ring.

Eddon and Vail came forward. Now they could hear it too: the faint failing sound of a voiceless scream, cold and harsh and rasping.

Vail was tall enough to get a glimpse over the heads of the people. In the centre of the ring was a reddish-coloured figure, stretched out, head down. He lay half on the moss and half in a pool of water. On all sides he was surrounded by the menacing points of seed-drills, the cutting edges of auto-rakes, zaroths and strippers.

Eddon couldn't see over the people's heads. He pushed his way forward into the ring.

'Let me through!' he cried.

On the ground, the killer raised his head and snarled.

The killer's body looked oddly distorted, limbs twisted and askew. He was bandaged around the torso and legs, but so clotted with blood and mud that it was difficult to tell where bandages ended and clothing began. Some of the bandages had come undone, and trailed loose ends over the ground or in the pool. The water in the pool was a dark and murky red.

Again and again he snarled. He reached out and made tearing clawing movements with his hands. His mouth opened and closed, champing savagely on empty air. But when he tried to crawl forward, the points of the weapons forced him back.

Voices called out from around the ring, voices filled with repulsion and disgust.

'Look at his eyes!'

'He's turned completely!'

'Destroy him!'

'Into the water with him!'

'No!' shouted Eddon at the top of his voice. 'Wait!'

But the people of Draive paid no attention. With the points of their weapons they pushed and prodded at the figure on the ground. The sharp ends of the seed-drills pierced deeply into his flesh. But it was the sheer weight of the weapons that made him move. Gradually he was turned around and forced to face the pool. Then they drove him headfirst towards the water.

'Stop this!' yelled Eddon. 'We have to interrogate him!'

But still they drove him forward, deeper into the water. They shifted the points of their weapons and pressed down on the back of his head and neck. His head went down under the surface, and stayed down. He was starting to drown.

Eddon pulled out his punchgun and waved it in the air.

'Stop or I shoot!'

The people paused. For a moment they stopped. But they didn't draw their weapons away.

Eddon selected someone at random. He flicked the punchgun onto the setting for stun, and took deliberate aim.

'Back off now!'

The man stepped back. Eddon swivelled and pointed his gun at one person after another.

'And you! You too! Back off! And you!'

Gradually the ring fell back.

'What's the use of interrogating him?' someone cried angrily. 'It's a waste of time!'

'I don't think so,' said Eddon, 'and I'm responsible here.' He indicated the circular piece of mirror glass, the Junior Leader's badge on his chest. 'Your Headman appointed me responsible.'

Vail came forward and stood beside Eddon.

'He told us to bring the killer back alive,' she declared. 'Those are our specific orders from Argid ev Ghair.'

There was much scowling and grumbling and muttering.

'Don't believe you.'

'Why would he order that?'

'Doesn't make sense.'

But the confrontation was over. People were shrugging their shoulders, lowering their weapons.

'You'll take him right away from here?'

'Of course,' said Eddon. 'We'll be taking him back to Steyne-2. For trial and sentencing.'

There was mocking laughter from around the ring.

'Trial and sentencing? That's a Hegemony notion!'

'We don't do that on P-19.'

They seemed perfectly serious. Eddon and Vail glanced at each other in surprise.

'But what's your system of justice?'

'We don't need one.'

'Our Headman takes care of judging and punishing.'

'*Behind you*!' said someone suddenly, in a different tone of voice.

Eddon and Vail spun around. Jaith had dragged himself out of the pool. No longer controlled by the people's weapons, he was crawling towards them inch by inch. There was an inhuman, murderous look in his eyes.

'Doesn't he ever stop?' cried Vail. 'Doesn't he know he's just about dead? What *is* this thing?'

'Hold him down!' yelled Eddon. 'Keep him pinned face down!'

The people lifted the points of their weapons and forced the killer to a halt. He lay flat on the ground, silent and immobilised. Eddon put his punchgun back in his pocket. From another pocket he drew forth a pair of lightweight carbonite handcuffs.

'Try and get his arms out at the sides!'

More jabbing and prodding. The auto-rakes and strippers came into play, hooking around Jaith's arms and pulling them out from under his body. Now he lay completely spreadeagled.

Eddon launched into action. He took three steps forward, placed a knee across the killer's legs, caught hold of his wrists and swung his arms up behind his back. It was the smooth practised movement of a professional police officer. But nothing in Eddon's experience could have prepared him for the sound that followed. The moment Eddon touched his wrists, the killer screamed as if red-hot needles were running through his flesh. A scream so loud and high and pure, it was almost beyond the range of human hearing. It was like the screech of metal on glass, a million times magnified.

Eddon would have given anything to clamp his hands over his ears. But he didn't flinch or falter. He brought the wrists together, snapped on the cuffs, then stepped back again.

The moment he stepped back, the screaming ceased. The killer writhed on the ground like a cut worm, convulsively, without coordination.

'Those handcuffs'll never hold him,' someone said scornfully.

'They're tested to a force of over two hundred kilos,' said Eddon.

'He'll tear himself free even if he breaks every bone in his hand.'

Vail was curious. 'How do you know so much about him?'

'He's mad. Don't you understand? Incredible strength. Just because he's half dead doesn't mean he's lost his strength.'

Vail turned to Eddon. 'Perhaps they're right, CI. We're not dealing with a normal case here. I shot him four times and he survived.'

'Hmm. I suppose we can tie him down. We'll make a stretcher. Tie him down on a stretcher and carry him back to Steyne-2.'

'Yeah, and I can drug him too. I've got some ethobirynol in my bag. An injection of that'll knock anything out.'

'Good.' Eddon thought for a moment. 'Best if I stay here and you go back for your bag. Take half a dozen helpers and get some materials for making a stretcher. You know the kind of thing?'

'You want the de luxe or executive model stretcher?'

'I think the serial killer special, with safety features.'

Vail selected half a dozen helpers from around the ring. The people of Draive had no objections to the plan.

'As long as we don't have to touch him.'

'Just get him away from here.'

'He's all yours, and welcome.'

Vail drove the railcar and Eddon watched over the killer in the back. The stretcher was laid out along the left-hand row of seats while Eddon sat facing across on the right. He kept the punchgun balanced on his knee, with the setting on lethal.

The stretcher had been constructed from an old cupboard door bolted onto metal poles. The killer was held down by three buckled belt-straps, and by Vail's whipperwire wound around every part of his body. He lay comatose all the way back to Steyne-2.

They came to a halt at the M-rail terminus in front of the Big House. Eddon stayed in the car while Vail went on ahead to get help with carrying the stretcher.

'We've got him!' she exclaimed triumphantly to the guard at the Major Portal. 'The serial killer!'

'Where from?'

'Draive.'

'Ah, Draive. My family comes from East Obass, just west of Draive.'

He seemed totally unimpressed by the fact that they had captured the killer — and in a mere three days. Vail pulled a face, her triumph flattened.

The guard went and called another man over, and together they followed her back to the M-rail. They introduced themselves: Clon IV Quidder and Ewart IV Paig. They were both Reeves, both wearing the Reeve's badge of diamond-shaped mirror-glass. Stolid, phlegmatic characters they seemed; but they eyed the killer nervously as they descended the steps to the railcar.

'So he's drugged, is he?' asked Ewart.

'Won't wake up for another hour, hour and a half.'

'You're sure?'

'Sure I'm sure. You're not scared are you?'

'I don't like the look of him. I'm not scared of anything normal. This is different.'

They picked up the stretcher, holding the metal poles by the very tips, as far away as possible. They carried it up the steps and across the square. Eddon and Vail walked alongside, Vail with her bag and Eddon with his punchgun.

Half way across the square, the killer's head rolled suddenly to the side. Clon panicked and almost dropped his end of the stretcher.

'You jogged him, he didn't move by himself,' said Vail. 'Keep going.'

They entered the Big House through the Major Portal. Another two Reeves and a Junior Leader had gathered in the corridor behind the door. They were obviously curious, though they didn't approach the stretcher too closely.

Eddon spoke to the Junior Leader. 'We need Masilin to come and look at this. Can you call him?'

'Masilin's not around.'

'Well, Wyvis or Oaves then.'

'They've gone too.'

'So who do we report to? Go and tell your Headman. Tell him we've captured the killer.'

'I can tell him. But you don't expect him to come here to you, do you?'

Eddon snorted. 'No? Then we shall have to go to him, won't we? I suppose he's in the Old Hall?'

Vail coughed.

'I think perhaps we should do the interrogation first,' she said.

'What? But we can't do that until the drug wears off.'

'Even so . . .'

She gave Eddon a meaningful look. Eddon raised an eyebrow. Vail responded with an almost imperceptible nod of the head. Eddon turned to the Junior Leader.

'Okay, we'll go to the Old Hall later. Right now we need a room for the interrogation. Preferably small, table and chairs, lockable door.'

The Junior Leader thought for a moment. 'The Filing and Records Room,' he said.

He went across and took down a key from a board on the wall. He passed it across to Eddon.

'Forward to the Filing and Records Room,' cried Vail.

Clon and Ewart moved off with the stretcher. Eddon and Vail followed, dropping a little way behind. Vail leaned towards Eddon and spoke in a low murmur.

'When I said they jogged him. They didn't. He moved his head.'

'The drug's worn off already?'

'He's coming out of it. I don't understand how. I just hope nothing more happens before we get to this room.'

They turned off from the main corridor and the Filing and Records Room was immediately before them. It was windowless and dark until Eddon turned on the lights. Clon and Ewart lowered the stretcher onto the table where Eddon directed.

From the killer's throat came a faint sound, harsh and rasping. Clon and Ewart jumped back.

'What's that?'

'Just a reaction of the autonomic nervous system,' said Vail.

The two Reeves weren't convinced. They made for the door and left in a hurry.

Eddon was surveying the room with approval. Small lights glowed in strips along the ceiling. The walls were completely bare. There were two upright chairs near the door, and two filing cabinets standing in opposite corners.

'Two filing cabinets for six and a half thousand people.' Eddon shook his head wonderingly. 'This must be the ultimate non-bureaucracy!'

Vail put down her bag and studied the killer's face.

'How do we get him to talk?' she mused. 'He'll probably just scream or make noises.'

'He can talk if he wants to,' said Eddon. 'Remember, he spoke to the boy when he told him to fetch the medicine chest.'

'But if he doesn't want to?'

Suddenly the killer opened his eyes. Eddon turned and locked the door, putting the key in his pocket. Vail sat down on one of the chairs.

The killer's hands were still handcuffed behind his back. He was tied down in a position half on his back and half on his side. As he became aware of his bonds he began to struggle. Eddon and Vail watched in silence.

There was little visible movement, the wire and the belts were fastened so tightly. His arms and torso strained and quivered, his head rocked from side to side. Patches of bright new red appeared on the bandages, spreading across the old dark red, seeping out over mud and clothes. He was bleeding from all of his wounds again. The stretcher shook and rattled on the table.

But the wire and belts defeated him. After a few minutes he gave up and lay still. Small trickles of blood ran out over the stretcher and gathered in pools on the table.

'I reckon he's fully conscious now,' said Eddon. 'Hand me the voice recorder.'

Vail reached into her bag, took out the voice recorder and passed it across. Eddon switched it on and spoke in a clear formal voice:

'Interview with Jaith, er, Scallow. Inhabitant of Draive.' He glanced at his timeband. 'Date 20–11–660. Starting at 2.24 p.m.'

He approached the bloody figure on the stretcher.

'Right. Let's hear it.' He thrust the recorder towards the killer's face. 'You know we can pin the murder of Eriph IV Sivanne on you. Now we want to hear about the rest.'

The killer stared back at Eddon with eyes as impenetrable and cold as a lizard's. If he was listening, he made no response.

'You want me to list them? Okay.'

Eddon began pacing up and down the room.

'One. Janna II MetHannig, who was trampled to death on the Brennag moors six months ago. Two. The sixteen-year-old boy, Arram, the one with the pulverised skull. Body found in the storage room of a metalwork shop in Steyne-2. Three. The Magham family in Malais. Father, mother and son all slaughtered. Four. The murder of Perla III Erridge in her own bedroom right here in the Big House.'

Eddon stopped pacing. He came up by the side of the stretcher and directed the voice recorder once more towards the killer.

'Four murders, and they all look like your work, Jaith. Tell us about them.'

Still the killer made no response. Eddon's voice took on a harsher tone.

'You're wasting my time. You were seen in Perla's bedroom, so there's witnesses to identify you. Start talking.'

The killer's mouth opened slowly, very slowly. For a moment it seemed that he was about to speak. Eddon bent forward more closely.

Then the jaws snapped suddenly, savagely shut. Eddon jerked back, an instinctive reaction. The eyes stared at him with a look that might have been triumph.

'Very smart!' Eddon spoke through clenched teeth. He kicked at the leg of the table. 'Now talk, goddam you! Talk!'

Again and again he kicked. The table shook and

juddered. The puddled blood ran off the edge and dripped down onto the floor. But the killer's mouth stayed shut.

Eddon cursed. He walked away to the far side of the room.

'Sheez, I'd like to —' He slammed his fist into the palm of his hand.

'He's beyond being hurt,' said Vail. 'Physical violence isn't a threat to him.'

'I know that. Why do you think I'm not using it?'

'Let me have a try.'

'What can you do?'

'I could put him under.'

'Under?'

'Under hypnosis.'

'Hmm. Anything said under hypnosis is worthless as evidence.'

'So? There's no justice system on P-19. No courts, no trials. We don't need that sort of evidence.'

'True.' Eddon nodded. 'Okay, if you think you can do it. Be my guest.'

18

Vail herself wasn't sure if she could do it. She knew she had the talent to hypnotise any ordinary subject, no matter how unwilling, but she didn't know if her talent would work on so strange a mind as this. She would have to apply full technique, that was obvious.

From her bag she drew out a luminator, a miniature control-box, and an extension lead. She used the lead to connect the luminator and control-box. Eddon watched with interest. The luminator looked like a glass globe mounted on a black plinth.

'That must be your crystal ball,' he said.

'Hang around and you'll get to see real magic spells being chanted,' said Vail.

She placed the luminator on the floor in the middle of the room. Then she moved her chair up close beside the stretcher, level with the killer's head. She sat just out of his line of sight with the control-box on her lap.

'If you can turn the lights off,' she said to Eddon. 'Don't come up close till I give the signal. Like this.' She made a beckoning hand-gesture. 'Then start recording.'

'Right.' Eddon went across to the light-switch by the door. 'See if you can get him to admit specific details.'

'Details?'

'Things that no-one but the actual murderer could know.'

'Got it. Okay, lights off.'

Eddon flipped the switch. For a moment the room was in darkness. Then the globe of the luminator began to glow: on-off, on-off, on-off. Ripples of light moved over the walls and ceiling, successive ripples spreading and fading to a steady pulse.

Vail watched the killer intently. She adjusted a knob on the control-box and the ripples of light changed rhythm slightly. Eddon realised that she was timing the pulse to the rhythm of the killer's own breathing.

Then she began to chant.

> '*Munnnn. Daaaaa.*
> *Immm. Vaaaaa.*
> *Munnnn. Daaaa.*
> *Immm. Vaaaaa.*'

It was an eerie incantation, timed to the rhythm of the luminator and pitched very low. It made the hairs stand up on the back of Eddon's neck. He had the impression of attending some cultish religious ceremony, with Vail in the role of high priestess.

But he saw what she was doing. Little by little the incantation slowed down, little by little the frequency of the ripples decreased. She wasn't just following the rhythm of the killer's breathing, she was also influencing it. Insistently, imperceptibly, she dragged it back.

Finally she lifted her hand from the control-box. The rhythm continued at a constant rate, quietening, calming, numbing. Eddon even found that he was breathing to the same rhythm himself. For five minutes it continued. Then Vail spoke.

'Jaith, Jaith, can you hear me? My words are entering your mind, Jaith. My words are entering your ear-drums, my words are passing along the nerves to your brain. Can you hear them inside your head, Jaith?'

The killer lay still, very still. Vail's voice was drawling, languorous, unhurried.

'Your mind feels huge, Jaith, huge and hollow. My words are very tiny in your mind. Like a thin silver line, my words, threading their way amongst your thoughts. They're heading towards your speech centre, Jaith. Broca's area, where your brain processes speech and language.'

She paused, watching intently.

'But you don't want them in your mind, do you Jaith? You don't want them to unlock your speech centre. You try to resist. You don't want to speak. You clench your muscles, yes, very tight. But my words are so thin, so tiny. They're moving towards the left, veering towards the left-hand side of your head. That's where your speech centre is, Jaith. You can't help thinking about them moving towards the left. You can't stop them veering towards your speech centre. Can you feel them coming, Jaith? And now they've reached it. Answer me! Can you feel them there?'

'Yes.' The answer came in a slurred and distorted voice, almost foreign-sounding.

Vail made the hand signal to Eddon. He switched on the voice recorder and came up to stand just behind her shoulder.

'Think about my words, Jaith. Concentrate on them. Now they're heading towards another area of your mind. They're going back into your memories. They're leaving the present behind. Leaving your body behind, your arms and legs, leaving this room behind. Sights and sounds in this room don't matter, Jaith. All those perceptions are falling away. Only my words matter. And now they're moving forwards. Upwards. To the right. Sifting through your memories. So many memories stored inside your head. But they're seeking out a particular memory. A particular night six months ago. A night when you were on the Brennag, Jaith. Do you know that memory?'

'No!' Jaith licked his lips. 'Not there.'

He began to writhe and twist under his bonds.

'No, of course. You have to resist going there, don't you? Now you're willing my words to retreat. Back, back. And they do retreat, Jaith. They're very small and remote now. But they're still there. You have to fight very hard against them. Fight them off! Don't let them through! But they're so very tiny, so very silvery. They keep slipping through, they keep returning. Seeking and seeking. Looking for the memory of that night on the Brennag. Six months ago, Jaith. A dark night. An old woman.'

'Coming along the path.'

'Who was it, Jaith?'

'Old Janna. She always came that way. I was there. I sprang out and knocked her down.'

He spoke in a monotone, still slurred and foreign-sounding. Eddon held the recorder forward to capture the confession.

'Her body was on the ground. Old woman's body. I stamped on it ... break the bones.'

Eddon whispered in Vail's ear. 'Ask him how long.'

'And you had to keep stamping, didn't you?' said Vail. 'How long did you keep doing it?'

'Twenty minutes. Old, wrinkled body ... hideous ...'

His voice fell away into a mumble. His mouth continued to move, but he was no longer audible.

'Relax, Jaith. Relax and be quiet. My words are moving away again. Away from that memory. They make a thin silvery line through your mind. Now they're seeking another memory. Something that happened in Steyne-2. In a metalwork shop, in the storage room of a metalwork shop. Someone you dragged there, Jaith, a young boy ...'

'Sixteen years old,' whispered Eddon behind his hand.

'A sixteen-year-old boy. Do you remember, Jaith? Do you remember smashing his skull to powder?'

The killer made no reply. Vail intensified the note of authority in her voice.

'Where is that memory, Jaith? My words are circling around it. Around and around. Coming towards it, closer and closer. They're almost there. The metalwork shop. The boy's skull. Tell me — now.'

'Pounding the skull,' came the slurred monotone again. 'I held his head in one hand. I hit at it with a hammer. The brains came out ... wet and slithering around. I smashed them and squashed them. Little bits. The skull had to be destroyed. I used a chisel as well as the hammer.'

Vail glanced round at Eddon, who nodded. Their faces appeared in the light of each spreading ripple from the luminator, then vanished again in the next moment's darkness. On-off, on-off, on-off.

'Keep focussing on my words, Jaith. They're starting to move forward now, forward through time. There are memories on every side, rows and banks of memories. But we have to find the right one, Jaith. It's a memory of Malais and the Magham family. You know the settlement called Malais. You remember the Magham family.'

'Malais. Magham.'

'The memory is starting to unfold, Jaith. My words are unfolding it. There's a father, Jaith, and a mother and son. Can you see them?'

'They're running away from me. I drop down from the skylight in the roof. The boy screams but I scream louder. Into the kitchen. I take a knife to cut them with.'

'What sort of knife, Jaith?'

'A carving knife. The cutlery drawer. I slice him and her. And the other one. Their insides all opened up. I throw their insides against the walls. I keep slicing more and more ... slicing ... slicing ...'

'Relax, Jaith. Now my words are moving on —'

'Slicing ... slicing ... slicing ...'

'That memory is finished, Jaith. My words penetrate through it, like a silvery thread. Drawing you, leading you out. Out and on. You don't want to move on, but the memory is fading, growing dim. Only my words are bright. Every syllable sharp and clear as silver. Yes, Jaith. Taking you forward to another memory. Here it is, Jaith, this other memory. A memory of a bedroom in the Big House. Look into the bedroom, Jaith. Climb in through the window. There's a young woman there.'

'I know. She's sitting in front of her mirror.'

'Perla III Erridge in front of her mirror. What happens next, Jaith?'

'She sees me reflected in the mirror. I want to rip her into nothingness. I stab something through her eye.'

'What sort of something, Jaith?'

'Don't know. Don't notice. I take her brooch that she's wearing and rip her skin. I rip her all over.'

He opened his mouth and snapped his teeth. Opened and snapped, opened and snapped. His arm jerked in tiny restricted movements, back and forth under the belts and whipperwire. He seemed to be reliving the experience, trying to repeat the ripping action.

'And what happens then?'

'People shouting and yelling outside. Knocking on the door. I have to do something to her. I see her shoes. Make her swallow her shoes. I want to —'

There was a sudden sharp knock on the door of the Filing and Records Room.

The killer's voice came to a halt. Eddon turned

round and stared angrily at the door. Vail frowned. She took a deep breath and began speaking again in her quietly intense tone.

'Jaith. Jaith. Jaith. Keep concentrating on my words. We're going to move on to another memory now. A very recent memory, two nights ago in Draive. Jaith? Can you still hear me? Keep —'

The knock came again, louder than before.

Vail threw up her hands in frustration. Eddon put the voice recorder down on the floor, and went across to open the door.

It was Beano. He stood there in his flight jacket, with a cheery grin on his face.

'Hey-upp! There you are! They told me you were in the Filing and Records Room.'

Eddon glowered and Vail groaned. But Beano was impervious to anything being wrong.

'I wondered where you'd got to last night. Is that a suspect? Zag-a-doo! Hey, why don't you turn on the proper lights?'

'Hushhhh!' hissed Eddon. 'Interrogation under hypnosis.'

'Oh, sorry!' said Beano. Then, lowering his voice to a whisper, 'Whoops!'

Vail started chanting again:

'*Munnnn. Daaaaa.*

Immm. Vaaaaa.
Munnnn. Daaaa.
Immm. Vaaaaa.'

For two minutes she tried. Then she gave a shake of the head. Her long greeny-black hair switched like a horse's tail.

'Too late,' she said. 'I've lost him. Total blank. He's closed himself off.' She turned around with a downcast expression on her mouth. 'There's nothing more I can do.'

'Hey, doesn't matter!' cried Eddon. He strode across, picked up the voice recorder and clicked it off. 'It's all in here. You've done great. Case closed!'

'But what drove him to do it? How did he choose his victims?'

'Who knows? You can't make sense of a sicko.' He patted the voice recorder. 'Main thing is, we've got what we need to nail him for those four other murders.'

He swung around to Beano. 'Turn on the lights, Flightman!'

'Sorry,' said Beano, still in apologetic mood. He turned on the lights.

Eddon took another look at the figure on the stretcher. Now the lizard-like eyes were closed, and there was a tiny trickle of white liquid at the corner of the mouth. Beano came forward and took a look too.

'Yurrrk!' he murmured. 'He's all busted open.'

'Yeah, he had a bad night,' said Eddon. He put the voice recorder in his pocket. 'And now it's time

179

to take him to see Headman ev Ghair. Do you know how to get to the Old Hall from here?'

'Yes, but . . .' Beano seemed doubtful.

'Good. We hand this sicko over to him. Then we clear off out of here.'

Vail raised an eyebrow. 'No more diplomacy and building bridges? Encouraging P-19 to rejoin the Hegemony?'

'Forget it. I've had enough of P-19. We're going to get back to the real live world.'

'Where murders are murders and crims are crims?'

'Yeah. Good wholesome murders and proper decent law-breaking criminals. We'll get a message sent through to Central saying we're ready to come home.'

Eddon swivelled the stretcher crosswise on the table, so that the metal poles stuck out over the sides. There was no sound or movement from the killer.

'Okay, Flightman. Let's you and me carry this stretcher. You take the front end and lead the way.'

Beano was still hesitant. 'Do you think Headman ev Ghair will want to see us?'

'He'll be seeing us whether he wants to or not. Sheez, I may be only a cop but I'm not a servant. I still expect thanks for a job well done. He's not too high and mighty for that.'

Beano shrugged and moved to stand between the front end poles.

'I know why he didn't want to see us before,' he

said. 'There's been a lot going on while you've been away.'

'Like what?'

'Like Masilin and Wyvis and Oaves. You wouldn't believe what they were planning to do.'

'Okay, tell us about it as we go,' said Eddon. 'Hup!'

He lifted the poles at the back and Beano lifted the poles at the front. They manoeuvred the stretcher clear of the table and headed towards the door. Vail followed behind.

'It's a long story,' said Beano. 'Yesterday morning I came back to my bedroom...'

The Old Hall was a round theatre, about twenty metres across and lit by skylight windows from above. The floor fell away in concentric circles of steps, seemingly cut into the very ground on which the Big House stood. Polished like marble, the steps gleamed with metallic veins of greeny-blue and silver, the pattern of the rock's own ores.

At the bottom of the steps in the centre of the room was a short thick pillar. It too was made of polished rock, but a different type of rock striated with horizontal bands of brilliant red and gold. A spiral staircase of wrought iron wound around the pillar, leading up to a balustraded pulpit at the top.

Vail, Eddon and Beano entered through the same door that they had waited outside three days ago. It was just one of the four doors symmetrically arranged around the circumference of the hall. They stood for a moment surveying the scene.

About twenty people were gathered in the centre of the hall. There was no doubt which one was the Headman. He was sitting on the steps of the spiral staircase. Seen from behind, the only obviously striking thing about him was his shock of pure white hair. He wore no special regalia, no cap or chain or circlet. His tunic was plain grey, the bangles on his arms were simple iron and brass. The black staff in his hand seemed nothing more than a walking-stick. Even the way he sat on the steps was informal and casual. Yet there was something about him which immediately drew the attention and made him the focal hub of the whole room.

'Argid ev Ghair,' breathed Vail. 'Ninety-five years old.'

'Let's go,' said Eddon

They descended towards the centre of the room, coming around in an arc. It was impossible to avoid tilting and jolting the stretcher as they went. But the blood-soaked body remained inert, the killer's eyes stayed closed.

Coming around in an arc, they were soon able to see the Headman's face. He had the typical leaden hue of all P-19ers, but his complexion seemed even more startling in contrast with his sheer white hair. His face was relatively unlined except on the far left side. There, in a patch running between ear and cheek and jawbone, the skin was as gnarled and dry as the bark of an old tree. It was as though all the furrows from the rest of his face had moved across and collected in that one blasted patch.

The people around the pulpit stood murmuring amongst themselves and glancing towards ev Ghair. Many of them wore gilded star-shaped badges. Their voices were low and dull and dismal-sounding. One at a time they came forward to address the Headman. Ev Ghair replied in a loud growl: an old man's voice, but deep and powerful.

'You must wipe out and quarantine,' he was saying to the particular young man before him. 'I know, I know, five squares wasted. But it has to be done. We'll get you some help from the next settlement. They're not so badly off in Spallam, they can help out!'

The young man nodded gravely and extended his hand, palm up. Ev Ghair put his own right hand underneath and pressed his left hand down on top. For a long moment he held the young man's hand between his own two hands, almost as if imprinting some sort of stamp. Then he released it without another word. The young man drew back and someone else prepared to step forward.

But Eddon broke in first.

'Headman ev Ghair!' he called out. 'Something to show you here!'

Pushing from behind, Eddon drove Beano forward through the crowd until they stood with the stretcher right at the foot of the staircase.

'Here's your killer,' said Eddon. 'Name's Jaith. From the settlement of Draive.'

Argid ev Ghair rested his hands on the pommel of his staff.

'And what's *your* name?' he asked calmly. 'I don't remember meeting you before. Who are your family?'

'I'm Central Inspector Eddon Brac. This is Flight-man Zeno Berrit. And my parapsych assistant, Vail ev Vessintor.'

'Ah yes. You're Hegemony, aren't you? You're the ones who were summoned by Masilin, Wyvis and Oaves. They're still hiding out on the steppes, did you know?'

'I only heard the story a minute ago.'

'And now you've come to show me this murderer.' Ev Ghair turned his eyes to look at the bloody figure on the stretcher. 'I see you've got him tightly bound.'

'Down,' said Eddon to Beano. They lowered the stretcher and set it carefully on the floor. Then Eddon took the voice recorder out of his pocket. He set the recording to play from the start of Vail's questioning.

'My assistant interrogated him under hypnosis. We recorded him admitting to all the murders.'

'He admitted to all the murders?' Ev Ghair raised an eyebrow. His eyebrows were as white as his hair.

'More than admitted. He gives details that only the murderer could know. Your serial killer problems are over.'

'All the murders?'

184

'Yeah. Listen.'

Eddon clicked the recorder on, and Vail's slow hypnotic voice filled the room.

'*Think about my words, Jaith. Concentrate on them...*'

Eddon lowered the volume temporarily.

'You'll hear him in a minute. When she starts asking about the murder of Janna II MetHannig.'

Ev Ghair made a soft growling sound and stood up. He was tall, taller than Eddon and almost as tall as Vail. He came down the staircase, supporting himself on his staff. One side of his body seemed to have been affected by a partial paralysis: his left leg moved stiffly and his left shoulder was askew, several inches lower than the right. The skin on his left hand was withered and furrowed like the patch on his face.

He bent over the killer on the ground.

'So. Jaith IV Scallow. Who'd have thought of you as a murderer?'

The killer's mouth moved slightly and released a small flow of thick creamy liquid.

'That white stuff —' Eddon began.

'I know about the white stuff,' said ev Ghair. He turned and glared suddenly at the voice recorder. 'Turn that ridiculous thing off!'

'Wait,' said Eddon, raising the volume again. 'Here's where he talks and confesses.'

'*Old Janna. She always came that way. I was there...*'

Ev Ghair transferred the staff from his left hand to his right, and swung it whirling through the air. The

185

end of the staff struck the recorder a smashing blow and sent it spinning from Eddon's grasp. It hit one of the P-19ers on the chest and fell broken to the floor.

Eddon was taken completely by surprise. The P-19ers retreated a step backwards.

Ev Ghair changed his grip on the staff again, clasping both hands over the pommel. He held it up vertically over the figure on the stretcher. Jaith opened his eyes and mouth. Perhaps he was going to scream. But the scream never came.

With tremendous force, ev Ghair drove the staff downwards, point first, straight through the killer's face. The staff went in all the way through to the back of the head. There was a sound of shattering bone.

No-one spoke or moved. Ev Ghair put his boot against the head and yanked his staff free. A large round hole had appeared in the place where the killer's nose had been.

Ev Ghair raised the staff again, again drove it down through the shattered face. Again and again he struck, ten times. The strength and violence of the act were extraordinary.

Then it was over. All that remained of the killer's head was the hemisphere of his skull and a slushy mess of red and grey. Ev Ghair's boots were spattered with morsels of flesh, brain and bone.

Beano was the first to recover.

'Phew!' he said disbelievingly, shaking his head.

Eddon had been as if stunned with shock. Now he was white with anger.

'What was that? Is that your system of justice? Is that what you call it?'

The Headman paid no attention. He was breathing heavily. He wiped the point of his staff against the killer's leggings.

'Tevyn. Eilsa.' He singled out two of the P-19ers from the crowd. 'Get this mess cleared up, can you?'

Then he slowly reascended the spiral staircase and sat down on the same step as before. He seemed to have become suddenly very old and very tired. Once more he rested his hands on the pommel of his staff, and his chin on his hands.

'Halber.' He singled out another P-19er from the crowd. 'Go with these Hegemony people. Repeat your report to them. Tell them what you were telling me earlier. Take them outside into the corridor.'

The man addressed wore a star-shaped badge and a netcord jerkin over his vannamak. He had a long chin and lugubrious drooping moustaches. He nodded to Eddon, Vail and Beano, indicating that they should follow.

But Eddon hadn't finished saying his say. He was still smouldering. He faced ev Ghair and started to speak. But the Headman's voice overrode him.

'Go now, Eddon Brac. I have other more important problems to deal with. Come back if you have something further to show me.'

They were dismissed. The two P-19ers assigned to clean up the mess pulled the stretcher out of the way. Another P-19er stepped forward and began to talk to ev Ghair — something about some kind of food reserve running out, and various fields that had had to be abandoned.

Vail put a hand on Eddon's shoulder and guided him away.

'No use now,' she said. 'Let's go hear this report.'

They moved out of the crowd, with Beano following. Halber was already half way up the steps. He had halted and was waiting for them. When he saw them approach, he turned and continued on up towards one of the doors. He held it open for them to pass through.

It was not the same door as the one where they'd entered. But the corridor behind was much the same, with decorative stalactites of metal hanging from the ceiling and small dotted lights glowing all around. It seemed very dark after the light from the skylight windows in the Old Hall.

Halber came through behind them and closed the door.

'Well?' Eddon asked brusquely.

'I'm a Warden in East Lair,' said Halber, pointing to his badge. 'I came in to report the murder of Tharmony III Leggen. She was murdered last night in her own home.'

Five minutes later, Eddon, Vail and Beano were heading back towards the guest rooms. Beano led the way, with Eddon and Vail trailing along behind. Their heads were still spinning over Halber's report.

'He said the woman was cut up into tiny pieces,' said Vail.

'And discovered this morning.'

'It doesn't make sense. Jaith was in Draive last night. We know he was.'

'Unless the remains had been lying around for much longer.'

'But he was in Draive the previous night too. Killing Eriph whatsisname.'

Eddon snapped his fingers. 'Maybe it was a copycat killing.'

'Copycat serial killing?'

'It's not uncommon. Some crazy watches a murder on the news and goes straight out to do exactly the same thing. There was a case on Terra just before we left.'

'On Terra, I believe it. But on P-19? Do they even have broadcast news on this planet?'

'No news, no entertainment, no nothing!' Beano called back over his shoulder. 'Primeval!'

'Okay,' said Eddon. 'So maybe it wasn't a crazy. Maybe someone carried out a planned murder and tried to make it look like the serial killer. Not know-ing that the serial killer had just been put out of action.'

'Hmm. Do you believe that?'

'I don't know what I believe. I wish to hell we could interrogate Jaith again under hypnosis. But thanks to ev Ghair —'

'Whango!' cried Beano triumphantly, rounding a corner. 'Here's our corridor.'

'Great landing, Beano,' said Vail. 'Hey, where can we get something to eat? I'm famished.'

'The guest kitchen,' said Beano. 'Next to the room where we had breakfast yesterday. We can help ourselves.'

He led them into the small room with the breakfast table, then on through a swing door into the adjoining kitchen. The kitchen contained three large stoves, three cold-bins and numerous lead-lined storage cupboards.

Beano went around opening cupboard doors and lifting the lids off bins.

'Dark bread here. Waferbread here. Beanspread. Margarine. Pickled eggs. Fishcakes. Some sort of vegetables like potatoes. Flatcakes in syrup. Soup-stock. Preserved wineberries. Oatmeal.'

'Let me at it,' said Vail. 'Nothing that needs cooking.'

She found a tray and began loading it up. Eddon and Beano followed suit.

'I blame myself,' said Eddon, pursuing his own thoughts. 'I should've stopped ev Ghair at the time.'

'Whooo! Not easy!' said Beano.

'I should've tried.'

'None of the locals did.'

'Maybe they're used to his mad behaviour. I still ought to have done something. I don't know why I didn't.'

'I do,' said Vail.

'Hey?'

'You came up against an overpowering force of personality.'

'Force of personality? What's this, some sort of aura stuff?'

'If you like. There's an extraordinary strength of will in that old man. Normally old people become less focussed, more diffuse. But not ev Ghair. When he destroyed our murderer, it was as though every nerve in his body and every thought in his mind was directed into the act. The total mental weight of a ninety-five-year-old life. I've never known anything like it. It was like being hit on the head and stunned.'

'Yeah. I was sort of stunned.'

'And you felt as though you couldn't make up your mind what to do?' Vail went on. 'Couldn't think clearly, couldn't decide? That's how it seemed to me.'

Eddon reflected. 'Yeah, that was it.'

'Me too,' said Beano. 'Does he have some sort of psychic power then?'

'No. Not in the sense that a parapsych has psychic power. Ev Ghair has no talents, no sensitivity, he's not deliberately projecting. It's just sheer raw force of will. He's an amazingly *simple* person.'

'I feel like a psychological weakling,' said Eddon.

'Compared to that man, we're all psychological weaklings.'

They took their trays out to the other room. Already the light through the two windows was growing dim. Beano went across and turned on the ceiling lights. They sat down at the table and began to eat.

'I can't work it out,' said Eddon, between mouthfuls. 'Ev Ghair behaves like a mad tyrant, and still these people are always talking about how P-19 is democratic and anti-authoritarian and better than the Hegemony. Are they stupid or what?'

Vail paused half way through a slice of bread and beanspread. 'I don't think we understand the half of what's happening here.'

'And never will if we go on like this. Why won't anyone explain anything to us? They're all as tight as clams.'

'Maybe Jaralax,' mumbled Beano, chewing.

'What?'

'Maybe I could ask Junior Leader Jaralax. I got to talk to him when we went out to the spaceport chasing Masilin. He seemed sort of more outgoing than the rest. Do you want me to try?'

'Why not?'

'I'll look around for him tomorrow then. What are your plans for tomorrow?'

'Our plans?' Eddon pursed his lips. 'We're heading out to East Lair, of course.'

'Of course,' said Vail. 'Are we?'

'I want this last murder cleared up quick. We'll head out first thing in the morning.'

'Just us? Without a guide?'

'We can drive the M-rail okay. We'll have to ask around when we get there. Wasn't that Warden going back this afternoon?'

'Halber? Mmmm-yeah.'

'We can ask where he lives. Get him to help.'

Eddon pushed his tray to one side. He fished out the map that Masilin had given him and spread it out flat on the table.

'Here it is. East Lair.' He picked up a syrupy flat-cake and continued eating as he traced out the route. 'North of Steyne-2, beside a sort of lake. It's in the cropfields area, not very far at all. Only about four kilometres. Hmm.'

He took a look at his timeband.

'Whoa!' cried Vail. 'Don't even think about it! It's already starting to get dark. All the doors would be shut by the time we arrived. Anyway, I need my beauty sleep. I only slept a couple of hours last night.'

Eddon shrugged. 'Okay. But first thing tomorrow morning. We get up at dawn. Beautiful or not beautiful.'

'Brrrrr.' Vail gave an expressive shudder.

PART THREE
East
Lair

1

Finding the way out to East Lair was more difficult than anticipated. There were no signs to tell which line was which at the M-rail intersections, and nothing to indicate the names of the settlements. They followed one line in a false direction and wasted nearly an hour. It was 10.30 a.m. by the time they finally came towards East Lair.

The settlement was larger than Draive, spreading along the foreshore of a long brown lake. The roofs of the houses were bright with green and gold, and numerous coppery-coloured spires rose up into the air. Some of the spires were sharply barbed and interlaced with crisscross wires in the style that Wyvis had called 'the Extravagant Style'.

The M-rail curved in along the edge of the lake. As they approached, Eddon and Vail could see dozens of boats tied up at piers or beached on the foreshore. Groups of people in sleek dark coats were moving around with nets, ropes and oars. Vail stopped the railcar at the first group they came up to.

'We're looking for Halber!' Eddon called out.

Three men turned around. Their boat was flat like a punt, made of thin sheet metal.

'Halber III Domevair or Halber IV Wranx?'

'Don't know. He's a Warden here.'

'That's Halber IV Wranx. He'll be in his bottom field.'

The speaker fell silent, as though there was nothing more needing to be said. Then after a long pause he added:

'Take the next line branching right. To the end of the line. Then follow the path. You'll see him soon enough.'

The three men stood watching as Eddon and Vail moved off. They were still watching when Vail swung the railcar to the right, and still watching when she brought it to a halt at the end of the line, just fifty metres later.

'Here's the path,' said Eddon. 'I guess this is where we get out and walk.'

The path led away from the settlement, winding around small cropfields and vegetable patches. There were several squat buildings with humpbacked metal roofs, but they seemed more like sheds than houses. Eddon and Vail kept to the main path, ignoring the many lesser paths which cut across their route.

They passed fields of mustard cress and wet-oats, flowering yellowroot and parsley. Several of the fields lay fallow, exposing furrows of thin grey-black soil like iron filings. There were patches of fruit bush and strange vines on poles and trellises. But the most intriguing fields were the ones enclosed behind walls, such as they had seen elsewhere.

'I wonder what they grow there?' Vail pondered. 'Must be some very valuable crop to need protecting like that.'

The walls were about two and a half metres high, too high for even Vail to see over. Nor were there any crannies through which to peer. The metal of the walls was solid moulded lead. Sometimes there were doors into the enclosures, but they were locked. Even the cracks around the doors were tightly sealed.

But then the path ran past one particular enclosure where the walls were a little lower.

'Wait a minute,' said Vail. 'I should be able to see over here.'

She dropped her bag, reached up and got a grip on the top of the wall. Then she jumped upwards, pulling with her arms. Almost immediately she fell back down again — but not before catching a momentary glimpse over the top.

'That's odd,' she said, in a puzzled voice.

But Eddon wasn't listening.

'Let's go,' he said. 'I think that's Halber up ahead.'

She attempted another jump. This time she managed to stay up for several seconds before falling back down.

'It's totally overgrown,' she said. 'The plants are just running wild. Not a cultivated crop at all.'

But Eddon was no longer there. He had walked on without her. Vail shrugged and followed behind.

The figure that Eddon had seen was indeed Halber IV Wranx. He was working in a patch of wineberry bushes. His moustaches were as drooping and lugubrious as ever. When Eddon called out, he came across to the path.

'We need your help with the murder investigation,' said Eddon. 'Tharmony III Leggen.'

'Ah. Tharmony.'

'The same. First thing is to inspect the body.'

'It's not exactly a body.'

'Can you take us there? Now?'

Halber nodded slowly. He was carrying a pair of pruning shears which he wiped and clipped onto his belt. Without another word, he set off along the path, back towards East Lair. Eddon and Vail walked beside him.

'What other facts can you give us?' asked Eddon. 'Tell us some more about Tharmony.'

'I told you. She was a widow, fifty years old. Her husband died two years ago. Yuel III Leggen. He was famous as a metal-caster and pattern-maker. Most of the best work in East Lair is the work of Yuel or his father or grandfather.'

'Did she have family living with her?'

'No. She was alone in the Leggen house. Far too big for her. Her sons wanted her to move out and live with them, but she refused. She wouldn't even close up the parts of the house she didn't use. Impossible to defend, windows all over the place.'

'So the killer came in through a window?'

'No. He didn't need to. She had a spare key for the front door that she kept outside in a special niche. When we found her yesterday morning, the front door was open and the spare key was in the lock.'

Eddon nodded. 'Obviously suggests someone with local knowledge. This key was well hidden?'

'Only if you didn't know,' said Halber. 'But she was always using it, always forgetting her other keys. Half of East Lair would've known where it was.'

He veered suddenly off the main path onto a side path. Eddon and Vail followed. The side path was so narrow that they had to walk in single file. Eddon postponed further questioning for a while.

Halber was leading them around the back of East Lair. They passed more small cropfields of yellowroot and parsley. Dark black clouds had moved up over the sky, threatening rain. The air was heavy with an ominous quality of silence and oppression.

They walked on until they came to a small river. It was penned between artificially raised straight banks, flowing towards the centre of the settlement. The side path led up the nearside bank and joined onto a larger path running along the top. Halber turned and followed the larger path towards East Lair.

Approached from the back, East Lair seemed a much less attractive place. The houses were built very close together and had a gloomy brooding appearance. The rusted walls in the Extravagant Style were particularly depressing. Everywhere were massive metal pipes crossing over from building to building.

Soon they passed in amongst the outlying houses. The path changed to an alley running along by the edge of the river. Then the river itself changed. The water flowed over a weir and into a large square slope-sided basin. Here the water was still and stagnant, and partly covered over with khaki-green algae. Half a dozen channels issued out on the other side, threading between the houses like small canals.

They skirted the basin and crossed over an iron footbridge. Their footsteps clanged and echoed in the silence. Perhaps it was the closeness of the buildings, but the day seemed to be growing darker and darker.

Halber led the way along beside one of the channels. He was short enough to pass upright under the overhead pipes, but Eddon and Vail had to keep ducking. Water lapped and sucked at the walls of the houses.

They crossed another bridge and turned further corners. Left, right, right, left. It was like walking through a maze. They saw other bridges that were blockaded with metal barriers, they passed by alleys that were closed off behind wire fences with bolted gates.

'Why the blockades?' asked Eddon. He had moved up to walk alongside Halber again.

'Safety at night,' said Halber. 'People feel more secure.'

He led them along by another channel, where a greeny-grey scum mantled the surface of the water.

'You can't be sure of anyone these days,' he

added bitterly. 'You can't trust anyone outside your own family. If Tharmony hadn't been so trusting, if she'd been more careful about security . . .'

He turned another corner and pointed.

'There. That's the Leggen house ahead.'

It was a large building in the Extravagant Style, with angled wings and irregular extensions. Its walls were rusted to a bright orangey-red, its porch and windows were decorated with strangely wrought, strangely barbaric tracery. At the front it faced onto a small quay; elsewhere the walls plunged straight down into the water.

They crossed another bridge onto the quay and walked up to the porch. A sign saying DO NOT ENTER had been chalked on the door. Halber indicated a particular hollow in amongst the fantastic intricacies of metal carving around the porch.

'Here's where she used to hide the spare key,' he said. 'I've taken charge of it since.'

He pulled out a keyring with at least two dozen keys on it. He unlocked the door and went in.

Eddon and Vail followed behind. For a moment the place was in darkness, then Halber turned on the lights. Eddon and Vail found themselves surrounded by twisting tortured shapes of metal, rising up like a forest. Shapes of bronze, shapes of steel, shapes of brass and silver. The lights were set low on the walls and created an eerie network of shadows across the ceiling.

'This is Yuel's old display room,' said Halber. 'Exhibiting some of his designs.'

'Creepy!' said Vail with approval.

'Works of art,' said Halber sternly. 'Yuel was one of the earliest leading craftsmen in the Extravagant Style.'

He pointed to an open arched doorway on one side of the room.

'That's the way to his workshop. That's where the killer must've gone. For the tools.'

'The tools?'

'Used in the murder. Tharmony was slaughtered with her husband's own metal-carving tools. You'll see them still there in the bathroom.'

'Is that where the body is?'

'Yes. Not exactly a body. Do you want to examine the workshop first, or the bathroom?'

'Bathroom.'

Halber led them across the room to a different doorway, curtained with strands of beaded metal. The strands jingle-jangled as he passed through. He turned on the lights to illuminate the next room.

This was another spacious room, but mostly empty. The furniture had been pushed back against the walls and covered with dust sheets. The floor was magnificent, a glittering mosaic of metal, coloured stones and glass. Huge gilded arms projected from the walls, unfolding into sprays of tiny glowing lights. The arms were vaguely reminiscent of organic vegetable forms, but somehow distorted and sinister.

'The entertaining room,' Halber announced. 'The Leggens used to hold grand dinners here, and music and dancing. Of course, that was many years ago.'

He crossed the mosaic floor to another doorway on the far side of the room. A similar doorway, curtained with hanging metal beads. Halber reached in through the beads and turned on a further set of lights. Through the beads Eddon and Vail could see two steps descending to a long curving corridor.

'The bathroom is the second door on the left.'

'Fine,' said Eddon. 'Lead the way.'

Halber pulled at his moustaches, making his face look more lugubrious than ever.

'I've been inside once,' he said. 'I'm not going inside again.'

'Hnnh.' Eddon scowled. 'You'll wait out here then?'

'No. Why?'

'There'll be further questions to ask.'

'Ask the people in the houses around. They know as much about it as I do.'

Before Eddon could insist more firmly, Halber turned on his heel and walked off. Eddon stared at his retreating back. Then he looked across at Vail and shrugged. Vail returned the shrug.

They passed through the bead curtain and down the steps. The sickly sweet smell of blood came drifting faintly along the corridor.

'Where's the lights?'

'I'm looking,' said Eddon. 'Don't touch anything.'

'I'm not.'

They spoke with their hands clamped over their mouths and noses. Inside the bathroom the smell was overpowering. It was not a smell of fresh blood, but tainted and slightly putrescent.

'Ow!' cried Vail suddenly.

'What?'

'I think I just stepped on one of those metal-carving tools.'

The lights in the corridor cast scarcely any illumination into the bathroom. Eddon ran his hands over the walls by the door, searching for the light-switch. At last he found it.

The tiny glowing lights seemed to spring out from all sides, reflected and multiplied in sheets of mirror glass. There were mirrors set into the walls, and mirrors set into the panelling around the bath. The bath itself was made of stainless steel, with brass taps sculptured into fantastically contorted shapes.

Eddon looked around for the body. There were smears of blood everywhere. The tools used by the killer lay scattered on the floor, along with various articles of clothing. But no body.

Vail dropped her bag with a bang. She let out a gulping choking sound.

'In the bath,' she said.

The bath was half-filled with a murky slop, dark red with bits of pink and browny-purple. The pink bits were segments of human flesh, the browny-purple were human organs. They protruded above the surface of the slop like meat in a casserole.

Eddon stepped up beside her.

'Ugh!' he said. 'Dismembered. He must've chopped her up right here in the bath. I wonder how they could be sure it was Tharmony?'

'Maybe the clothes?' Vail suggested.

She went around the room inspecting the scattered articles of clothing. She was glad to turn away from the bath.

'Strange,' she said. 'Seems like there's two sets of clothing. You don't think —?'

'Don't touch anything!' snapped Eddon.

'But why would he take his clothes off? And go away naked afterwards?'

Then she noticed a large bathtowel hanging on the back of the bathroom door. A once-white bathtowel, now soiled and red.

'Look! Must be where he dried his hands!'

Eddon swung around to look. He shook his head. He went across for a closer inspection.

'No,' he said slowly. 'This isn't from drying his hands. Too much blood and other stuff. This is from wiping himself dry all over.'

'You mean —?'

'He got into the bath with the dismembered body. He wallowed around in the blood and slop. And then he —'

Vail gagged. She ran for the door, her stomach heaving. Out in the corridor, four paces to the right, she could hold on no longer. She leaned against the wall and vomited. Again and again, until there was nothing left to bring up. She stood doubled over with tears in her eyes, trying to recover her breath.

Eddon put his head out of the bathroom door. He looked pale in the face himself, but he spoke steadily enough.

'You all right?'

Vail nodded mutely.

'Take your time. I'm going to get some gloves out of your bag, okay?'

Another mute nod. Eddon's head disappeared.

Vail walked up and down the corridor to calm herself. Then she sat down on the steps leading up to the entertaining room. She practised some of the meditation techniques that she'd learned at the psychoseminary: the slowing of bodily rhythms, the successive narrowing and expanding of consciousness. After about five minutes she felt sufficiently recovered to return to the bathroom.

Inside the bathroom, Eddon was bending over something on the floor. He had a long-handled bath loofah in one hand and a gouging iron in the other — evidently one of the tools that the killer had left behind. He was wearing plastic gloves and a triangle of white cloth over his mouth and nose.

'What're you doing?'

Eddon looked up. 'Make yourself a mask,' he said in a muffled voice. 'Tear off a strip from the towel in the handbasin. Wet it and pour on some eau-de-cologne. Helps to keep out the smell.'

He went back to what he was doing: arranging body-parts on the floor. He had been fishing them out of the bath and reassembling them. There were bits of rib and pelvis and thigh-bone, sections of torso and shoulder and arm. Vail could see the outline form of a human being beginning to take shape on the floor.

She crossed to the handbasin and picked up the towel. It was a clean white handtowel, with one large strip already torn off. The bottle of eau-de-cologne stood on a shelf above the basin. She turned on the tap and washed her face.

'One thing's for sure,' said Eddon, speaking over his shoulder. 'This wasn't a planned murder that someone just tried to make look like a serial killing. Only a complete sicko could've done this.'

Vail made herself a mask as Eddon had described. When she fastened the ends around the back of her neck, the pungency of the eau-de-cologne made her cough. But it was better than the sickening stench of blood.

'Another thing.' Eddon fished something bluey-purple out of the bath. He had released the plug and let the blood drain out, exposing the body-parts more clearly. 'This murder was committed when Halber said. Otherwise the corpus would be in a more advanced state of putrescence. I don't see how Jaith could've done it.'

Vail went to her bag. She took out a pair of plastic gloves and snapped them on.

'I'm ready to help,' she said.

'Yeah?'

'Yeah.'

'If you say so.' Eddon finished arranging the bluey-purple thing. 'I'll lift the bits out and you can arrange them on the floor. I'll tell you where.'

Using the loofah and gouging iron like a pair of chopsticks, he began fishing out pieces of flesh and bone and passing them across to Vail. Vail knelt on the floor and pushed the pieces into position with her gloved hands.

'Lower part of right foot. Over there.'

'Right forearm.'

'Section of colon. Goes below the intestine.'

'I know where the colon goes,' said Vail, grimly.

'Right ear.'

'Portion of lungs.'

'Little finger of left hand.'

'Part of —'

'Wait a minute!' Vail exclaimed suddenly. 'We've already got a complete left hand. Are you sure it's not a right-hand little finger?'

Eddon reached down and gathered the blood-soaked object in his gloved palm. He carried it across to the basin and washed it off under the tap. Then he scrutinised it again, more carefully.

'It's the way the tendons go,' he pronounced at last. 'Has to be a left-hand little finger.'

'And here's another little finger already on the left hand,' cried Vail, pointing. 'Look!'

Eddon whistled. 'Are you thinking what I'm thinking?'

'What?'

'His insane urge to destroy human flesh. He was

in a frenzy. Hacking and slicing at the body in the bath. He accidentally sliced off his own little finger.'

'Without even noticing?'

'Or perhaps he only noticed afterwards. When it was too late, and the missing finger was lost in amongst all the other chopped up bits and pieces.'

'It didn't stop him from taking a bath.'

'No.'

Vail shook her head incredulously. She stared again at the object in Eddon's hand.

'And that's an actual piece of the man we're after?'

'Yeah. If it is a man.'

Eddon compared the sliced-off finger to his own little finger. The sliced-off finger was noticeably thinner and smaller. He clicked his tongue.

'Hard to tell.' He pointed at Vail's bag. 'You got any preserving jars in there?'

'Better. I've got some sealpacks.'

She drew out a transparent plastic envelope with a miniature Holweg valve. She held it open and Eddon dropped the severed finger in. Then she closed the seal and worked the valve, shrinking the plastic tight around the finger.

'There. Total vacuum. You want it?'

'Keep it in your bag.'

Eddon pulled off his gloves and began pacing around the room.

'This is the most amazing stroke of luck,' he said. 'You realise what this means?'

'We're looking for a nine-fingered killer?'

'That's right, PP. A nine-fingered killer. So easy! No need to bother with any more of this.' His gesture took in the bath, the partly assembled body, the clothes and tools on the floor. 'All we have to do is check out who's missing a little finger on their left hand.'

'In East Lair?'

'Of course. Local knowledge, remember? He knew where to find the key. Probably someone living close by.'

'Halber said half of East Lair knew. There must be a hundred houses in East Lair.'

'So we check out a hundred houses. Family by family. We'll ask some questions like an ordinary interview. But all we need is to get a look at their hands. Like I said — easy!'

'Anything's better than this shambles.' Vail pulled off her gloves. 'Just let me out of here.'

Beano found Junior Leader Jaralax in the armoury. He was sitting on a bench, polishing the barrel of a pommelgun. On another bench sat a second man, also cleaning guns. The second man had the same black eyebrows as Jaralax, and a similar bristling black moustache.

Jaralax looked up.

'Ah! Flightman Berrit! Good morning to you!'

'Morning! Hey, call me Beano, everyone does.'

'Beano? Okay. Beano, this is my younger brother, Tulaic IV Fallender.' He gestured towards the second man, then patted the bench on which he was sitting. 'Take a seat.'

Beano sat and looked around. The armoury was long and low, with white walls and a rounded ceiling like a tunnel. The walls were stacked with metal shelves and racks holding military equipment of every variety. Beano recognised T-guns and kit-bombs, wastemakers and sub-calivers, slow-shells and shock-throwers.

'All a bit old-fashioned?' suggested Jaralax, following the line of his gaze. 'Is that what you're thinking?'

Beano nodded. 'There's no wide-targetters on the guns. And the shells are pre-carbon technology.'

'Not up to the latest Hegemony standards. Hah!' With a sudden swift movement, Jaralax swung the gun he'd been cleaning up against his shoulder and took aim at nothing in particular. 'These are the weapons that defeated the Hegemony. Everything in this armoury comes from the time of the Breakaway.'

'Are those the T-guns you took when we went after Masilin and the rest?'

'Yes.' Jaralax lowered his gun. 'We were authorised to carry guns then. Doesn't happen very often.'

'You have to be authorised?'

'Yes. By our Headman.'

'In the Hegemony, everyone has the right to carry a gun if they take out a licence. It's a guaranteed freedom.'

'Not on P-19.'

'Who makes the rules?'

'Rules? It's a community prohibition. In everyone's interest.'

'But ev Ghair decides when the prohibition can be waived?'

'Yes.'

'And he'd judge and punish anyone who carried a gun otherwise?'

'Of course.'

'He must have a lot of power then. Almost like an old-time autocrat. And living in this palace too.'

'Palace? You mean the Big House?'

'It's a palace compared to everyone else's house.'

'But it doesn't belong to him, it belongs to the people.'

'Maybe, but he still seems to do very well out of it.'

'Ah, you think he's living in luxury, is that it? You should see his bedroom. It's smaller than the guests' bedrooms, where you sleep.'

'But he must have special privileges.'

'Special privileges? Like what?'

'I dunno. Special food. Servants.'

'There are no servants on P-19.' Jaralax twirled his moustache fiercely. 'Listen. The only thing he has different from anyone else is responsibility. He's

214

worn himself out looking after P-19. He's been taking care of every kind of problem for seventy years. Being Headman is a burden not a privilege. I wouldn't be him at any price.'

'He's the father of P-19,' said Tulaic IV Fallender, from the other side of the room.

'That's right,' Jaralax confirmed. 'He led us to independence. The Hegemony would've defeated us except for him.'

He stood up suddenly.

'Here. I want to show you something.'

Beano followed him across to a rack of T-guns on the wall. With a sort of reverence Jaralax placed his hand over the collar of one particular gun.

'This was my great-grandfather's gun,' he said. 'This was what he used when he fought alongside Argid ev Ghair in the battles of the Breakaway.'

'Er — wow,' said Beano politely. 'You must be very proud of your family past.'

'I am,' said Jaralax simply. 'The Fallenders of Strone.'

'Our great-grandfather still lives in Strone,' put in Tulaic. 'It's a part of Steyne-2 now, west of the river.'

'Yes,' added Jaralax. 'One of only six people still alive who actually fought in the Breakaway. The only man still alive, along with ev Ghair — the other four are women. The women fought side by side with the men.'

'He was there in the Battle of Drume. And the Battles of Crawm Lakes.' Tulaic began reciting names like a roll-call. 'The Raid on Dergevar. The

Battle of the Slains. The Ambush on Loin Moor. The Quirion Expedition. The Bombing of Gormoy Bend.'

'I think I heard of that one somewhere,' said Beano, interrupting the recitation.

'Our great-grandfather told us about all those battles,' said Jaralax. 'We used to listen to him for hours when we were kids. The bravery of those times! They were heroes. And ev Ghair — he was almost superhuman. There was nothing he wouldn't dare. Always at the front of the fighting — you wouldn't believe the incredible things he did.'

'I can imagine he must've been a powerfully strong fighter,' said Beano, remembering how ev Ghair had smashed his staff through Jaith's skull.

'Yes. But his determination — that was what made him leader. He never doubted we'd win, not for a moment. He gave everyone new hope. That's what my great-grandfather said. Our people were almost ready to give in. We'd been driven out to the edge of the moss-moors. Due east of —' Jaralax broke off. 'Don't you know about any of this?' he demanded. 'Don't they teach you about the Break-away in your Hegemony schools?'

Beano shook his head. He held back from saying that most people in the Hegemony wouldn't even know of the existence of planet P-19.

'Hah! I'll explain it to you then. A history lesson!' Jaralax knitted his brows. 'I'll need a map to explain it properly.'

He turned to Tulaic. 'We'll just go along to the Map-room. Back in a few minutes.'

Tulaic nodded. Jaralax led Beano out into the corridor, explaining as they went.

'You see, when the Hegemony brought in reinforcements, they also brought in a Proctor-General, over the head of the old Governor. He made overtures to the scientists and researchers. They'd been on our side in the uprising, but now they went over to the Hegemony. We had to continue the struggle with no technology, no computers, no training in warfare — hardly even any weapons. The only thing we knew about was farming and crop-management. While they had the very latest in DCT.'

'Distance Control Telearchics,' murmured Beano. 'Yes, that's still state-of-the-art in military strategy.'

'Every soldier was wired with data reporting devices. Streams of information were transmitted to a central computer, the computer developed a total coordinated strategy, then streams of instructions were transmitted back to the individual troops. My great-grandfather said it was like trying to fight one creature with a thousand tentacles.'

They passed through a vestibule, along another corridor, and came into the Map-room. It was the same hexagonal room that Beano, Eddon and Vail had seen on their first arrival at the Big House, the room with the six brass globes. There were also six large wall-maps, engraved in brass in panels on the walls. It was towards one of these that Jaralax turned.

'This is a map of the inhabited area of P-19 as it was in the time of the Breakaway. Much smaller than it is today. Our forces were driven out to the

217

east here, see, the Eigessy Basin.' He tapped on the spot with his finger. 'Nothing but rock and water and moss. People were so hungry they were chewing the moss for something to eat. And then Argid ev Ghair appeared.'

'Where from?'

'He was one of the scientists in Steyne-1. But he didn't switch over to the Hegemony when the other scientists deserted us. He stayed true to our cause. And he came to join us.'

Jaralax moved his finger towards the extreme edge of the map.

'He came walking in out of the steppes, from even further east. In the early light of dawn. Everyone just stood and stared. He was a huge man, tall and upright. He was only twenty-three years old then, not stooped or shrunken like you see him now. Striding towards our camp with the sun's rays shining behind him.'

'Whoo-eee! Sounds like a scene from a holo-film,' said Beano. 'But real, of course,' he amended, seeing the scowl on Jaralax's face.

'Yes, real. Things are real on P-19. We don't spend our lives watching holo-films like you Hegemony people. What I'm telling you is what my great-grandfather told me. Ev Ghair stood there and said: "The Hegemony doesn't stand a chance. I can show you how to win." And everyone knew it was true. Everyone was ready to follow him there and then, my great-grandfather said. Even when he ordered a fifty mile march.'

Jaralax traced a looping line around the edge of the map.

'They had to circle around outside the inhabited lands. The suffering was terrible — they didn't even have moss to eat on the steppes. But still they were fortunate — a heavy fog came down and hid their route from the enemy's tracking machines. They came around to the River Sorne, just there. Due north.'

'I don't understand. What was the use of that?'

'Because there was a major ore-body of high-grade magnetic zirconium there. You see, ev Ghair had been researching electro-magnetic fields before the uprising. That's why he'd originally come to P-19. And he knew how to make use of the planet's own forces. "The planet will help us against them!" was one of his phrases. He set our people to work mining and casting and shaping the zirconium. It was made into a huge shield, eighty square metres, but in separate segments, so that everyone could carry a piece separately. When it was assembled and wired up and charged by portable batteries, it drew power from the planet's own magnetic field to produce a kind of electro-magnetic storm.'

'Wiping out their DCT transmissions! Whop-a-doo!'

Jaralax grinned. 'For up to a thousand metres in every direction. All communication between their troops and their central computers obliterated. Their strategy was useless. Worse than useless! Because their troops had never been trained to think cooperatively. They had no idea of working by themselves in small teams. Without their DCT, they were just a disorganised mass of individuals. Hopeless!'

He began tracing routes across the map.

'We raided down past the Crawm Lakes here. Then towards the Slains, across here. Later we cut a great swathe to the north of Steyne-1 here. The basic tactic was to move through the countryside in secret, everyone carrying their own piece of shield. Then assemble the shield, attack the troops stationed in the area, destroy the installations. By the time they could gather a major force against us, we'd disappeared and moved on elsewhere.'

'You make it sound like you were there yourself.'

'No, but the Fallender family was! It was like we couldn't lose, my great-grandfather said. We captured weapons from their troops until we were almost equally well armed. In the end they abandoned all the territory they'd conquered except for a small enclave around Steyne-1 and the spaceport. We couldn't attack them there, with all their forces concentrated together. But every time they ventured out, we chopped them to pieces.'

'They could've used atomics on you.'

'They could've. But only at the price of making the planet uninhabitable. They weren't as stupid as that. So the stalemate lasted for eighteen months. Then finally they negotiated a retreat and withdrew. And we became Independent P-19! The fortunate planet!'

'Why fortunate?'

'Because everything went right for us. The planet was on our side. We didn't move into Steyne-1, we built a whole new settlement using the planet's own resources. Steyne-2. Ev Ghair planned it. He worked out how to set up the coils to generate heat electro-magnetically. And how to build the M-rail. He was our inspiration. Everything he said came true. We were the luckiest people in the entire galaxy.'

'Were?'

Jaralax's face fell. 'Until the last ten years, of course.'

'What's happened in the last ten years?'

Jaralax looked at him in surprise. 'You don't know about the last ten years?'

'No.'

'Didn't Masilin tell you?'

'No.'

'I thought that was their excuse for getting you out here.'

'No.'

Jaralax shrugged and turned away. 'Let's head back to the armoury. I'll tell you as we go.'

The dark clouds that had been looming all morning finally opened, disgorging large heavy drops of rain. Vail pulled up the hood of her vannamak.

'I *hate* rain,' she said.

'We don't stop because of a little bit of rain,' said Eddon grimly. 'Have you got that last family down?'

Vail pulled out a sheet of paper, half covered with a scrawl of lines and labelled boxes. The lines represented alleys, bridges and water channels, the labelled boxes represented the houses of families already visited. She sketched another box and wrote in *Saggert family.*

'That's over forty families interviewed so far,' she said. 'We're getting further and further away from where the murder was committed.'

'So? Just make sure we don't miss anyone.'

They were standing by the side of a murky water channel. Raindrops plopped loudly into the water, rippling the scummy surface. There were two boats floating in the channel, moored to bollards on the quay. A rank yellowy smell filled the air.

'Let's go,' said Eddon.

They walked on to the next house along the quay. It was an undistinguished-looking building, with green patches of mildew growing on the walls. Around the windows, the ornamental edgings were speckled and streaked with rust — not the deliberate rust of the Extravagant Style, but the unplanned rust of neglect and decay. The door was a roll-down door of metal shutters, like a warehouse door.

There was no bell-button to ring. Eddon knocked on the shutters, until the whole door shook and rattled. A minute later the door was raised, making even more of a clatter.

A young man stood in the doorway. His wild black hair stood out in every direction. Eddon and Vail noted that he had all of the fingers on his left hand.

'We're from your Headman,' said Eddon, pointing to his badge. 'We have some questions to ask.'

The young man nodded, but made no move to invite them in.

'Questions for the whole family,' said Eddon firmly.

'We're about to eat lunch,' said the young man sullenly. But he moved aside and gestured for them to enter.

'Go on down the hall,' he said, pulling the shutter-door closed again.

The hall was filled with a chaotic jumble of boxes and cases and rolled-up fishing nets. Eddon and Vail had to weave their way through. The young man followed slowly behind.

'Two Junior Leaders here!' he shouted ahead to the rest of the family. Eddon and Vail emerged from the hall and into the living-room.

The living-room was almost as cluttered as the hall, with too many pieces of furniture crammed into too small a space. There were chairs and arm-chairs, a cabinet, a sideboard, a cold-bin, and a table set with plates and cutlery. Everything looked slightly greasy and grubby.

Eddon and Vail surveyed the family, looking for the tell-tale missing finger. There was an older man, a woman in her twenties, a girl of about seventeen, another pair of younger girls, and a very young boy of about four. After a moment, an older woman entered through a further door, carrying a large casserole dish. When she saw Eddon and Vail she carried it out again. A delicious aroma of spicy fish and vegetables lingered in the air.

'What's this about?' demanded the older man. He had prominent yellowing teeth and stubble on his chin. He lounged in one of the armchairs with his hands in his pockets.

'We're investigating the murder of Tharmony III Leggen,' Eddon announced. 'You've all heard about that?'

There was a general nodding of heads. The young man who had answered the door propped himself against the sideboard. The older woman came back in without the casserole dish. She was strong and burly-looking, with a screwed-up mouth and a sour expression. She was still wearing the oven-mitts on her hands.

'Is the whole household here now?' asked Eddon.

'Yes. We're the Craill family.' It was the sour-faced woman who spoke. She was evidently the mother. 'Who are you?'

Eddon and Vail introduced themselves. Then the members of the Craill family gave their own names. The mother was called Drisseg and the father was Settal. Leore was the name of the woman in her twenties, the wild-haired young man was Lexter, and the teenage girl was Phekna. Drisseg herself introduced the three younger children: the girls Triss and Ethnie, and four-year old Dannavie.

Outside the rain was starting to fall heavily. It drummed on the metal roof, echoing through the house with a continuous gong-like reverberation. Water streamed down the panes of the two small living-room windows.

Drisseg sat down at the table. She picked up a knife and began tapping impatiently on the table.

'We can't offer you lunch, I'm sorry,' she said.

'Not expected,' said Eddon.

'We would, but I didn't make enough for guests.'

'Not expected,' said Eddon again.

Already he and Vail had managed to observe the left hands of most of the Craill family. There were no missing little fingers as yet. But Drisseg had her hands in the oven-mitts, while Settal's hands were deep in his pockets.

'We have reason to believe that the killer knew how to get into the Leggen house,' said Eddon.

'Yes, with the spare key,' said Leore. 'We heard about that.'

'And did you know where the key was kept?'

'Yes.'

'Plenty of people did,' added Lexter.

Eddon asked the usual interview questions: where had everyone been the night before last? had they heard any significant sounds during that night? He had to speak loudly to make himself heard above the rain. The answers were predictable.

They were getting nowhere. Settal's hands stayed in his pockets, Drisseg showed no inclination to remove her oven-mitts. Eddon's questioning began to go around in circles.

'We've already answered that,' said Leore sharply.

'Okay. Now there's something I want you to look at.' Eddon threw Vail a meaningful glance. 'Pass me your bag, PP.'

Vail was puzzled, but responded to the glance. She handed her bag across. Eddon set it on the floor and opened it up. He took out the first item of equipment that came to hand: a piece of Y-shaped tubing with attached input valves.

He held it up in the air for everyone to see.

'Any of you ever seen anything like this before?'

'No, what is it?'

'Is it a piece of evidence?'

'Does it have something to do with the murder?'

Eddon swung around and held it out to Settal.

'Can you please take a closer look?'

The trick worked. Settal removed his hands from his pockets in order to receive the piece of tubing. He turned it this way and that, frowning deeply. There was no missing finger on his left hand.

'No, never seen one of these before,' he said at last.

'What about your wife? Drisseg?'

Settal passed the tubing across to Drisseg. She

226

accepted it — but without taking off her oven-mitts. After a moment's inspection she handed it back to Vail.

'Means nothing to me. Why? What does it have to do with the murder?'

'I can't tell you that,' said Eddon. 'Hey! Get out of there!'

It was one of the two little girls. She had crawled up to the bag and was nosing around inside.

'Ethnie!' roared Settal in a savage voice. 'Stop it!'

'Always so inquisitive,' said Drisseg, placatingly.

Ethnie lifted her face out of the bag. She held something clutched in her hand. She opened her hand for her mother to see.

'Mam. They got a finger in the bag. Look! Why they got a finger in the bag, Mam?'

The Craill family gaped at the plastic-wrapped finger. There was a horrified look on every face. Ethnie began to cry.

Eddon reached down and took the finger away from the little girl. He put it back in the bag. Across the room, the other little girl began to cry in sympathy. Then the four-year-old joined in too.

'Okay, okay, I'll explain,' said Eddon, raising his voice. 'That finger was found along with the dismembered remains of Tharmony III Leggen. Since it doesn't belong to her, it must belong to the killer. The person we're looking for has the little finger on their left hand missing.'

He turned to Drisseg.

'You're the only person here who hasn't been checked out. So if you'll take off that mitt, please, and show us your left hand.'

Drisseg sat as if frozen. Her mouth was twisted more sourly than ever.

'Your left hand, *please*.'

Slowly Drisseg brought her right hand round and took hold of the tip of the left-hand oven-mitt. Slowly she pulled it off. She didn't look at what she was doing: her eyes were fixed on Eddon's face. Eddon and Vail stared as the mitt came off. Her hand was perfectly normal, with the little finger perfectly intact.

'Right,' said Eddon, trying to hide his disappointment. 'That's good. This family is in the clear then. Thank you for your cooperation. One last thing. It'll make our investigation simpler if other people know nothing about the missing finger. Please keep that information to yourselves. Okay?'

There was no response from the Craill family. The three children were still wailing and snuffling.

Eddon took silence for consent. 'We'll leave you to your lunch then.'

He turned towards the door. Vail collected her bag and followed behind. He took five steps across the room. Then he stopped. He stopped so abruptly that Vail almost banged into his back. For a moment he stood immobile.

Then he swung around and came back to the middle of the room. He looked thoughtfully at the table. He stared at the members of the Craill family, one by one.

'There are nine plates set out on the table here,' he said in a cold, quiet voice. 'But only eight people in the room. So who's the missing member of the family?'

5

With one accord the family looked towards Drisseg. She lowered her eyes, angry and flustered.

'He's not well,' she said. 'I didn't think he counted.'

'Who is he?'

'My second son.'

'Where is he?'

'In his bedroom. He only comes out for meals. What could he tell you?'

'That's what we're going to find out,' said Eddon.

'He's not well —' Drisseg began.

'LET THEM SEE HIM!' Settal bellowed suddenly.

Drisseg flashed her husband a look of hate. But to Eddon she said, 'I'll go and get him. Wait here.'

She rose and hurried from the room. Eddon and Vail waited. The rest of the family sat on in silence, their faces dark and closed. It was impossible to guess what they were thinking. They didn't look willing to answer questions, and Eddon didn't ask any.

The minutes went by. Eddon and Vail exchanged glances.

'What if she runs off with him?' said Vail in a low voice.

'She'll bring him,' said Settal, overhearing. 'DRISSEG! BRING HIM NOW!'

A voice replied faintly, unintelligibly, from several rooms away.

Still the minutes passed.

'Enough,' said Eddon. 'I'm going to find them.'

But even as he spoke there was a noise in the adjoining room. A moment later, Drisseg showed her head around the corner of the door.

'He's here in the kitchen,' she said. 'He doesn't want to come in the living-room, with everyone around. He says he'd rather talk to you alone in the kitchen.'

'Suits me,' said Eddon. He strode through into the kitchen. Vail followed, still carrying her bag.

The kitchen was filled with steam. Several saucepans were bubbling away on a long stove. The casserole dish sat on a side table, still giving off its smell of fish and vegetables.

At the other end of the room, through the steam, Eddon and Vail could see the figure of a young boy leaning against the kitchen wall. He was slight in build, about fourteen years old. Eddon and Vail gasped in surprise. His left arm was completely missing.

'This is Graem,' Drisseg was saying. 'You can see the finger is nothing to do with him. He doesn't even have a left arm.'

'Let them see for themselves, mother.'

The boy looked up as Eddon and Vail approached. His face was white and as waxy as cheese. Even propped against the wall, he was scarcely able to stand. He seemed very sick indeed.

'You want to ask me questions about the murder of Tharmony III Leggen?'

His manner was calm and oddly adult for his age, but his voice was very low, very weak. He wore loose grey pyjamas, with the left sleeve rolled up and pinned below the shoulder. For a brief moment, Eddon wondered if he could be hiding his arm round behind his back. But only for a moment: there was no mistaking the shape of the stump, visible through the soft material of the pyjamas.

'When did you lose your arm?'

'About two years ago. A fishing accident. I've been like this since I was twelve.'

'What happened?'

'We were trying to moor the boat in a storm. My arm got caught between the boat and the side of the pier. The bone was completely smashed, then an infection started to set in. The whole arm had to be amputated.'

Eddon wiped his brow. He was sweating from the heat and humidity in the kitchen. Suddenly there was a clattering sound from the direction of the hall. Vail raised an eyebrow.

'That sounds like the shutter-door going up,' she said.

She crossed back across the kitchen and peered into the living-room.

'They've gone,' she announced. 'No-one there. They've taken off.'

Eddon swore quietly.

'No point trying to chase after them,' said Vail.

'No.' Eddon shook his head. He turned to Drisseg. 'Now why do you think they'd take off?'

Drisseg curled her lip and shrugged.

'They don't care about me,' said the boy. 'I don't think my father even likes me.'

'Why not?'

'I don't know. Because of being sick.'

'He's been sick for almost three weeks now,' said Drisseg. 'I'm the only one who looks after him.'

'But why did they take off? What are they afraid of?'

'They're fools,' said the boy. 'They make me stay in my own room, away from the rest of the house.'

'I see. And were you in your own room the night before last?'

'Yes, of course.'

'You didn't go out of the house?'

'I never go out of the house. Not since I've been sick.'

He swayed and sagged slightly as he spoke. He was obviously making an effort to remain composed.

'He ought to be back in bed,' said Drisseg sharply. 'Have you finished questioning?'

'No,' said Eddon. Then, to the boy: 'Did you know where Tharmony kept her spare key.'

'Yes. Everyone did. So it's true — the murderer entered straight through the front door?'

'Yes. Then went to the workshop to collect some tools.'

'I heard that too. The tools were found in the bathroom, weren't they? Where the murderer chopped Tharmony up in the bath.'

'Yes.'

'Poor Tharmony. Of all people.'

'Why do you say that?'

'She was a good person. Very kind, very gentle. Did the murderer actually kill her in the bath?'

'Maybe. Or dragged her into the bath after killing her.'

'You don't know which?'

'No, but we know something else.'

'What?'

'We have reason to believe that the murderer climbed into the bath and wallowed around in the victim's blood and remains.'

'Ugh! That's disgusting!' The boy uttered a choking sound and half-turned his face away. 'Why? What for?'

'It's impossible to understand the motives of psychopathic killers,' said Eddon. 'They think in a totally different way to ordinary people.'

'But to —' The boy seemed to be having difficulty speaking. He lifted his sound right arm and dabbed at his mouth with the sleeve of his pyjamas.

'Psychopaths are like another species,' Eddon went on. 'They're not mentally lacking, they're often very intelligent. But there are connections in their minds we can't even begin to understand.'

'I can't understand how anyone could be so abnormal.' The boy had his face almost turned to the wall now. 'How could any human being think of doing that?'

'It's a horrific case,' Eddon conceded.

'Don't tell me any more. I don't want to hear —'

'Why are you telling him such things!' Drisseg cut in shrilly. 'It's morbid! He's not well!'

'I — gggh.'

The boy's voice clogged up completely. Eddon moved around to look at his face. But the boy only twisted further away.

'What did you say?'

'No!!!' shrieked Drisseg.

'Don't turn away! Look at us!'

The boy turned to face them. He was holding something in his mouth, something that filled his cheeks to bursting. Slowly, irresistibly, it began to trickle out between his lips. There was a strange glittering expression in his eyes.

He opened his mouth and a great flow of white liquid spilled out. A thick white creamy mucus pouring over his chin, cascading onto his chest, dripping onto the floor.

Eddon reached into the pocket of his vannamak and drew out his punchgun. The setting was on lethal.

'One move and I shoot,' he said.

The boy gave an explosive spitting laugh that scattered gobbets of mucus in every direction.

'You're finished,' he hissed. 'You're dead!'

The muscles in his face were working as if in some kind of fit. He glared at the punchgun. He was taut and trembling like an overstretched string.

Then Drisseg moved. She flew across the room to stand in front of her son. Arms outspread, she defended him.

'It was my fault!' she cried. 'I didn't do the locks properly! You mustn't hurt him!'

Eddon stepped around to the side, trying to get a clear line on the boy with his gun. But Drisseg moved too, blocking off the angle.

Eddon looked across to Vail. 'Did you bring your punchgun?'

'Right here!'

Vail reached inside her bag and drew out the second punchgun. Training it on the boy and his mother, she began to circle around in the opposite direction to Eddon.

Drisseg could no longer block off both angles. Arms desperately extended, eyes swivelling from side to side, she retreated, pressing backwards into the boy behind her.

The boy started to scream. A thin, high scream of exquisite pain. With his one arm he reached forward, encircling his mother's neck. His fingers sank into her throat.

Drisseg struggled and gasped for air. Her strangled cries mingled with the boy's screams. The fingers continued to tighten their grip.

Eddon stepped up swiftly, around to the side of

Drisseg. He lifted his punchgun close up against the boy's one arm, and fired.

His first shot tore away a mass of flesh. But the arm stayed raised, the fingers still kept their grip on Drisseg's throat. His second shot smashed through solid bone. Blood and splinters flew in every direction.

One more shot and the fingers released their grip. Like a dead weight, the arm dropped down and hung dangling, attached by the merest threads of cartilage. Drisseg staggered away, wheezing and whooping and gulping in great draughts of air.

The boy stopped screaming. He turned back and forth between Eddon and Vail, snapping his teeth. There was a look of unspeakable hatred in his eyes.

But Eddon hooked a foot around his ankle and tripped him up. With one arm missing and one arm dangling, the boy couldn't keep his balance. Like a slowly toppling pillar, he crashed face first down onto the floor.

Then he began to wriggle and squirm. Eddon dived forward and made a grab at him. But the boy's body was like a snake. This way and that he coiled and lashed, banging into the wall, hitting against a table leg. Eddon could only get a hold on the material of his pyjamas. As the boy continued to wriggle and squirm, the pyjama top ripped and split, then pulled away completely.

Eddon whistled. Now the stump of the missing arm was visible. It was enclosed in a plastic bag and bound with string. The boy's torso was visible too. The skin was coloured all over with a dark red stain.

'That's where he wallowed around in the bath,' breathed Vail in horror. 'He didn't even wash it off afterwards.'

'The sicko,' Eddon muttered. 'The filthy sicko.' He aimed his gun directly at the boy's head.

'No! Stop!' cried Vail.

'I'm not going to kill him,' said Eddon, changing the setting on the gun from lethal to stun. 'Get that whipperwire out of your bag, will you?'

With a rapid movement, he pressed the muzzle of the gun into the back of the boy's neck and fired repeatedly. After a dozen shots, the boy went limp.

'Now, quick. Help me tie him up. The stun'll probably wear off in a minute or two. I want him hobbled around the ankles, so he can walk in small steps only. As for *you* —'

He turned and pointed the punchgun at Drisseg. She had recovered her breath and was starting to edge away in the direction of the living-room door.

'As for *you*, you just hang around a while. I've got some business with you in a minute.'

6

By the time Eddon and Vail had finished, the boy was trussed up like a turkey. Only his legs were free to move, and they were hobbled by a short length of wire tied from ankle to ankle. He would be able to walk, but only in very small steps.

'Keep a close watch on him when he starts to recover,' said Eddon.

'Okay. Where are you going then?'

'I want to check out his bedroom.'

He stood up and went across to Drisseg. She was sitting slumped in a corner of the kitchen. She had been massaging the bruised areas of her neck.

'On your feet,' Eddon ordered. 'Show me the way to your son's bedroom.'

Drisseg looked up at him. She shook her head.

'Don't think I won't use this,' said Eddon, waving the punchgun. 'Aiding and abetting. You're virtually the same as a murderer yourself.'

Slowly, unwillingly, Drisseg rose to her feet. Her face was twisted into a mask of bitterness.

'I thought he was too young to be dangerous,' she whined. 'I thought it was just the stuff in his mouth. He'd've been all right if he'd stayed in his bedroom.'

'You can tell me the story as we go,' said Eddon. 'Now, lead the way.'

Drisseg led the way, but she said nothing further. She led Eddon out through a door at the back of the kitchen, into a small room full of brass tanks and copper cylinders. Drying clothes were strung on lines across under the ceiling. The place looked and smelt like a laundry. Eddon had to duck his head low to pass underneath the clothing.

On the far side of the room was a short ladder of half a dozen steps. It led up to a tunnel-like corridor, raised about a metre above ground level. Eddon followed Drisseg up the ladder and into the corridor.

The floor of the corridor clanged with a hollow sound under their feet. The walls were made of thin sheets of tin-metal, and there were clear gaps of daylight between the sheets. Eddon put his eye to one particular gap and saw green water below. The corridor was evidently a kind of covered bridge, built over a channel.

He stood for a few moments watching the rain-drops rippling the surface of the water. It seemed that the worst of the storm had passed. Then he turned and continued on to the end of the corridor. Drisseg had already descended by another ladder into another room.

It was a room without a proper floor, just muddy earth and duckboards. It contained a large number of metal drums, stacked up in rows, and two boats, seemingly under repair. A strong fishy smell hung in the air.

Drisseg followed a circuitous route over the duckboards towards a further door. Eddon's eyes opened wide when he saw it. It was reinforced with bars of solid iron, and there were three great bolts to slot home, top, middle and bottom. At present it stood slightly ajar.

'So you kept him a prisoner,' said Eddon. 'Since when?'

'Three weeks,' muttered Drisseg.

She swung open the door and entered. It was

pitch black inside until she turned on the lights. Eddon followed behind.

The interior of the room was like a cage. Walls, roof and floor were covered with thick steel wire, like some kind of fencing wire. A window at one end had been blocked off with a huge metal slab, riveted into place. There was almost no furniture except for the bed which occupied the centre of the room.

The metal slab was scratched with words and pictures. Eddon went up close for a better look. But the pictures were strange and confusing, and the words incomprehensible.

He took a walk around the bed, peering this way and that. On one side of the bed was a large enamel pot, empty but smelling of urine. On the other side of the bed was a mug and a bottle of drink. And at the foot of the bed, hanging down, was a loop of chain.

'Hah!' exclaimed Eddon. He felt under the bed and ran his hands along the chain. It passed through the bedframe, with a manacle at either end.

'So! You locked his feet while he lay on the bed?'

'At night,' said Drisseg sullenly.

Eddon lifted up one of the manacles and turned it over thoughtfully in his hands.

'I can't understand. How could you keep on hiding him when you knew what he'd done? You knew he was Tharmony's killer, didn't you? Since he managed to escape on the very night of the murder. I suppose you never let on to the rest of the family?'

There was no reply.

Suddenly Eddon noticed something gleaming on the floor underneath the bed. He got down on his knees, reached in with one hand, and pulled out a long-handled kitchen cleaver, with a wide shiny blade. Fresh red blood dripped from the blade.

He set the cleaver to one side and lowered his head to the floor. Now he could see all the way in under the bed. And there it was... just as he'd expected. He gritted his teeth. He reached in again and caught hold of the thing. He dragged it carefully across the floor and out into the light.

It was the boy's arm. The bone and tendon had been severed at a point just below the shoulder. It was a left arm, and the little finger was missing from the hand.

Eddon felt sick to the pit of his stomach.

'So this is why you took so long to fetch him?' he said grimly.

There was no reply. Eddon turned and looked round. Drisseg was nowhere to be seen.

He cursed. She must have taken the chance to slip off while his back was turned. He rose to his feet and sat down heavily on the bed.

He couldn't take his eyes off the severed arm on the floor. He thought he'd seen just about everything, but this took his breath away. A picture of the scene floated into his mind: the mother tying off the arm with string, then picking up her cleaver and . . .

He shook his head. Better not to think about it. But what to do with the arm? He felt reluctant to carry it back to Steyne-2. What about getting Vail to take a picture with her scan-camera? That would be all the evidence needed.

Then he remembered ev Ghair in the Old Hall, smashing his staff down through the first killer's face. There were no court trials on planet P-19. Who cared about evidence anyway?

He stood up. The arm wasn't important to the investigation. Let the Craill family do what they wanted with it. They could have it.

'To hell with the arm,' he said out aloud. The urgent thing was to transport the boy back to the interrogation room in the Big House. Get Vail to question him under hypnosis the same way she'd questioned Jaith. Then maybe they could start making some sense of this case . . .

'My words are inside your head, Graem. Listen to the syllables, clear, silvery syllables. Concentrate on them, forget everything else. They are moving around in your mind, Graem, slipping through all your resistances. You can't keep them out, you can't stop thinking about them.'

Vail's voice was calm and slow and drawling. The globe of luminator glowed on and off, sending rhythmical ripples of light across the walls and ceiling of the Filing and Records Room. Vail sat on a chair beside the table, with Eddon standing just behind her. Everything was exactly the same as before, except now it was Graem and not Jaith who lay on the table.

His eyes were open but vacant, gazing upwards. He was still bound around with whipperwire. The loose ends of the wire, which had served as reins during the journey, were fastened to the tops of the table legs. Eddon and Vail had thrown a vannamak over the upper half of his body, covering the bloodstained torso.

'You can feel my words as they move through your mind,' said Vail. 'They are probing amongst your thoughts, searching and questioning. They're coming to a question about Tharmony III Leggen. Now they form a thin silvery chain around her image in your mind. Coming closer and closer and closer. Do you remember what happened to Tharmony III Leggen?'

'I cut her up.'

The boy spoke flatly, slowly. He seemed to be having difficulty with pronunciation.

'Why did you cut her up?'

'I hated her.'

'You felt a sudden violent rage?'

'I felt clarity.'

'Clarity? What do you mean, clarity?'

'I saw how things ought to be, and I saw how she was. I knew she was wrong.'

'Mmmm.' Vail shook her head, puzzled. Eddon bent forward to whisper in her ear.

'Ask him if it was a copycat murder.'

'Graem. What gave you the idea of killing someone in that way? Were you imitating another murder?'

'No.'

'Did you hear about the murders committed by Jaith IV Scallow?'

'No.'

'And yet they were very similar. He killed an old woman called Janna II MetHannig. And a sixteen-year-old boy in Steyne-2, found dead in the storage room of a metalwork shop. And —'

'I remember.'

'Ah. You remember hearing about those murders?'

'I remember doing them.'

'Doing them?'

'Those people were my victims.'

Eddon and Vail looked at each other.

'*You* were the killer?'

'I was there. Grinding them. Slicing them. Stamping them flat.'

Eddon shook his head.

'The confession syndrome,' he whispered. 'The desire to take credit for murders one didn't commit. It's not uncommon in these cases.'

'You're making it up, Graem,' said Vail. 'Why should I believe you?'

The boy made no response.

'Tell me about these murders then. Give me all the details if you want me to believe you.'

Still silence.

Vail reached for the control-box which regulated the pulsing light from the luminator. Speaking in her quiet soothing voice, she gradually slowed down the rhythm of the pulsations. Her voice dragged slower and slower too.

'Follow my words, Graem. My silvery words, passing down into the memories in your mind. Only your real memories, Graem, only your true experiences. Forget about wishes and imaginings. Leave them behind. My words are going deeper and further back. Back, back, to the very back of your brain. Delving for a memory, Graem, looking for a particular memory of . . . of a boy murdered in the storage room of a metalwork shop. A boy with his skull pulverised. Can you remember that, Graem? Does that memory exist?'

'I was there.'

'Tell me about it. From the beginning.'

'I was walking along Fladdabast Street. It was dark and drizzly. I turned left into Pouley Street.'

'In Steyne-2?'

'Yes. There were five young men walking towards me. They were laughing and shouting. They had been drinking. One was straggling behind, after the rest. I knew he was the one. I hated them all but he was the one I wanted for my victim.'

'Why?'

'To destroy. I kept my face down when the first four went past. I didn't want them to see the look in my eyes. Then the last one came. He was staggering. Distorted, hideous. I raised my face and let *him* see the look in my eyes. He tried to cry out but I closed off his mouth with my hand. I lifted him right off the ground and carried him to the side of the street. I was perfect and strong. I laid him down where it was dark, beside the wall.'

'Describe him.'

'He was very thin. He had close-cropped hair and long eyelashes. His breath smelt of barley-wine. He made me feel sick. I wanted to begin work straight away. I bent over him and stuff from my mouth dropped onto his face and chest. His eyes opened very wide, then his eyeballs rolled up and he went limp and unconscious. Then I started knocking out his teeth.'

'Knocking out his teeth?'

'Hideous small white teeth. I hated them. I hit them with my fist and pulled them out. But then I screamed. I couldn't help it. Those other four heard me and stopped. I was aware of them, further on down the street. They realised their friend was missing. They shouted and came running back.'

The boy moved and strained on the table, but the whipperwire held him tight. The muscles stood out on his neck.

'I picked up my victim and ran. I carried him easily in my arms. I turned one corner, then another, then another. I knew they couldn't catch me. I stood in an alley and blocked off the scream with my coatsleeve in my mouth. I listened to them rushing past in the wrong direction.'

'Go on.'

'Then I had to find somewhere closed and private. Somewhere to work undisturbed. I saw a window not properly locked in a building close by. I dropped my victim in through the window. Then I climbed in after.'

'Where was this?'

'A storage-room. Herroc's metalwork shop.'

'Describe the room.'

'There were slabs of raw iron leaning against the walls. Rolls of copper wire and ingots of solid lead. Bins of bright metal shavings. And shelves stacked high with boxes, tins, tools, pieces of machinery. I looked through the shelves and found a cold chisel and a hammer.'

Eddon and Vail exchanged significant glances.

'What were the chisel and hammer for?' asked Vail.

'For my victim. He was on the floor, starting to come awake. I knelt beside him and he opened his eyes. I could see the horrible fears and feelings squirming around like maggots in his brain. I could see what was going on inside his skull. Filthy, soft, wet brain, all coiled and folded. Gggh!'

The boy's face contorted as he spat.

'He looked and saw how I was aware of his foulness. He knew he was wrong and going to be destroyed. I held his head in one hand and hit it with the hammer.'

'That's exactly what Jaith said,' Eddon whispered to Vail.

'I smashed and squashed the brains all over the floor. The skull had to be destroyed too. I used the chisel as well as the hammer.'

'Almost the same words even,' Vail whispered to Eddon.

'Incredible,' murmured Eddon. 'This case makes less and less sense all the time.'

'How could they both know the same details?'

Eddon beckoned Vail away from the table. He went and stood over by the door. Vail rose from her chair and joined him.

'I'm going to bring ev Ghair here,' he said. 'He has to listen to this.'

'You reckon he'll come?'

'I'll make him come if I have to drag him.'

'Perhaps he can explain it, do you think?'

'I don't know. Can you keep the boy under hypnosis while I'm gone?'

'No problem. Just take care there's no sudden loud noises.'

Eddon nodded and slipped quietly out through the door.

When Eddon returned, he came with a whole group of people. Vail heard the sound of Eddon shushing them outside the door. The boy was still gazing blankly up at the ceiling.

Then the door opened. Eddon entered, followed by ev Ghair, followed by a dozen Reeves and Wardens. Mairie ev Ghair was there too, and so was Beano. Beano gave Vail a silent wave.

Eddon brought ev Ghair up towards the table. The others stood back against the walls. The Headman leaned on his staff as he walked, bearing down heavily on his paralysed side. There was a deep frown on his face, and he looked preoccupied. At first he seemed hardly even to notice the boy on the table.

Eddon pointed. 'There,' he said in a low voice. 'The killer of Tharmony III Leggen.'

Ev Ghair surveyed the boy without interest.

'So? You don't need me to dispose of him, surely? You said there was something extraordinary I had to see.'

'Right.' If Eddon was disappointed, he didn't show it. 'I'll explain. This boy has been put into a hypnotic trance by my assistant. PP Vail ev Vessintor. That light machine over there is an aid to inducing the trance.'

Ev Ghair tapped with his staff impatiently.

'We've been interrogating him under hypnosis. And we've turned up something totally inexplicable.'

Ev Ghair curled his lip. 'A mystery? We've got enough mysteries already. I was hoping you might have some solutions.'

'Wait. This is important.'

'I doubt it. I doubt that it's anywhere near as important as the news I was hearing when you interrupted me.'

'Listen to what he says.'

Eddon signalled to Vail to begin. Vail took a deep breath and bent forward.

'Graem,' she said, in her slow, insistent voice. 'Concentrate on my words, Graem. My —'

'I don't have time for this,' said ev Ghair. 'You said you'd interrogated him already. Just tell me what he answered.'

'You need to hear for yourself. You won't believe it otherwise.'

'There's very little I won't believe,' said ev Ghair grimly. 'Tell me.'

Vail flicked her long greeny-black hair and sat back in her chair.

'Okay.' Eddon shrugged. 'So we had him under hypnosis. First he admitted to the murder of Tharmony. Then he started talking about the murder of that sixteen-year-old who was found with the pulverised skull about five months ago. The one in the storage-room of the metalwork shop. Herroc's metalwork shop, according to the boy.'

'Arram V Eigh,' said ev Ghair. 'I remember.'

'He described how he'd done it in great detail. He knew about the hammer and chisel used on the skull.'

'He was in a state of deep hypnosis,' put in Vail. 'It's not possible for a subject to lie or invent stories in that state.'

'But here's the mystery,' said Eddon. 'When we interrogated Jaith IV Scallow the other day, he said that *he'd* done the killing in the metalwork shop.'

'That was under deep hypnosis too,' said Vail. '*And* he knew about the hammer and chisel.'

'He said almost exactly the same things,' added Eddon.

'So how could they both know?' demanded Vail. 'They couldn't have done it together. Which one was the real killer?'

Ev Ghair sighed wearily.

'Neither of them,' he said. 'We caught the killer soon after the murder.'

Eddon and Vail gaped.

'Arrasay IV Quainne,' ev Ghair explained. 'She'd been hiding for several days in a disused chicken-coop.'

Eddon was the first to recover his voice. 'A woman?'

'Yes.'

'Can we question her?'

'No. She was executed.'

Eddon snapped his fingers.

'Masilin must've known,' he said angrily. 'They must've known that the killer had already been caught when they transmitted their message for help. We were deliberately misinformed.'

'Probably,' said ev Ghair. 'I've no idea what they put in their message.'

'Why? Did they want to make the situation

sound more desperate? Did they think the Hegemony would be more likely to send a ship if they presented as many unsolved murders as possible?'

Beano gave a cough from the other side of the room. 'It's not like you think, Inspector,' he called out in a loud whisper. 'There's something you don't know. I can explain . . .'

But no-one was paying attention. Eddon began pacing up and down.

'How can you be sure this Arrasay was the murderer?' he asked. 'The boy gave us so many details. Pouley Street, Herroc's metalwork shop . . . he said he attacked after the victim's four friends had gone past. Is none of that true?'

'*She* attacked. Everything else is true. Arram's four friends saw enough of the killer to describe her afterwards. That's how we knew it was Arrasay.'

Eddon shook his head. 'I don't understand . . .'

Ev Ghair made a growling sound deep in his throat. '*Nobody* understands.'

Vail turned in her chair to address ev Ghair.

'So how many killers are there? Do we assume as many separate murderers as there are murders?'

Ev Ghair frowned. 'Of course not. Some killers have managed to commit up to a dozen murders before getting caught.'

There was a moment's silence. Eddon stopped pacing.

'What are you saying?' he demanded. 'How many of these murders have there been?'

'Including the very latest ones?'

'Yes.'

Ev Ghair calculated. 'Two hundred and twenty-three.'

There was an even longer silence.

'That's what I was trying to tell you,' said Beano from across the room.

Eddon nodded slowly to himself, thinking it through.

'We were told there had been just four murders,' he said dully. 'Four murders up to the time we arrived.'

Ev Ghair banged on the floor with the end of his staff.

'You fools!' He laughed a strange, violent laugh. 'We're in a much worse state than that! Much much worse than that! And you thought there were only four! What a mockery!'

Again and again he banged on the floor with his staff. His laugh became a kind of raging jeer. There were echoes of laughter from all around the room, harsh, jangling laughter.

'So you thought you'd come out here and solve our little problems! The great detectives! The Hegemony experts! You must've thought it was hardly worthy of your talents! A few miserable murders! Came out here to save us, did you?'

The boy on the table twitched and stirred. The noise of the jeering and laughter had broken through his hypnotic trance. He licked his lips and moved his eyes this way and that. Vail noticed but said nothing.

Ev Ghair lifted his staff high in the air and brought it down on the floor with a tremendous final crash. His laughter stopped as suddenly as it had started. Then he swung on his heel and turned towards the door.

But Eddon stepped across to stand in his way.

'Wait,' he said. 'You haven't explained everything yet. Are these all the same kind of murders?'

Ev Ghair's face darkened. He was trembling with barely suppressed emotion. But when he answered, his voice was quiet and controlled.

'Different methods of killing. But always at night or in the dark. And always insanely brutal. Trying to destroy the victim completely.'

'And the white stuff?'

'Yes, that's present in most cases. All the killers seem to produce it.'

'And the screaming?'

'As far as we can tell, yes.'

'And do they all know about each other's doings? I mean, the way this boy and Jaith seemed to know about the murder of Arram.'

Ev Ghair shrugged. 'The killers we've caught have never admitted anything. We've never been able to get them to talk.'

'Ah. That's something for further investigation then.' Eddon was beginning to regain his equilibrium. 'And how long since these murders started?'

'Ten years.'

'Ten years? Hhhn. No wonder we couldn't work out what was going on.'

'The first murder was ten years ago. One in the first year, a couple in the second. But gradually it built up. A year ago, there was an average of a murder every month. Then it became more like one or two a week. Until now...'

'Now what?'

'Until now they seem to be happening almost every hour. Four new murders reported yesterday. And today I've had reports of six murders already. What do you think I was doing when you came and interrupted me?'

'There's another murder to report too,' said one of the Reeves, stepping forward from the wall. 'From Sloy Banks. I was waiting to tell you.'

'And another from Cark-a-Truel,' said a grim-faced Warden, also stepping forward. 'Discovered an hour ago.'

Ev Ghair cried out and put his hands to his head as if in pain. His staff fell with a clatter to the floor.

'Eight! Eight! It's moved onto a new level again! I —'

He was interrupted by a sudden sound of violent spitting. It was the boy on the table. He spat and sputtered and shrieked:

'We're taking over! You're all dead! It's our time now!'

The vannamak slid off and exposed the red-stained skin of his torso. His mouth worked furiously, gathering more liquid to spit. Vail jumped up from her chair and retreated.

'You're finished! We're the ones! It's our time now!'

Ev Ghair growled an animalistic growl. He approached the table and stretched out with his hands to encircle the boy's throat. He was quivering with rage.

But Eddon sprang forward. He put out his own hands protectively in front of the boy's throat.

'No!' he cried.

Ev Ghair halted in mid-action. His hands were still arched, still ready to grip and strangle.

'Why not?'

'We haven't finished with him,' said Eddon. 'He's our evidence. We need to do further tests and examinations.'

Ev Ghair broke into violent laughter, harsh and jeering as before. He drew back away from the table.

'So you think you can solve this case, do you?' he mocked. 'You didn't even understand what needed solving until two minutes ago! Do you even understand it now?'

Eddon's mouth was a thin hard line. He didn't answer. His hands were covered with slimy wetness from the boy's spitting. He picked up the vannamak that had fallen to the floor and wiped his hands on it.

'Catching individual killers doesn't solve anything!' cried ev Ghair. 'However many you catch, there'll always be more! The only thing that matters is to discover the source. What makes people turn insane and become killers? You don't have to find a murderer — you have to find the cause of the murderousness!'

He was working up into a blazing passion. On the paralysed side of his face, the furrowed patch of skin was livid and almost black. He whirled and pointed to the P-19ers standing by the wall.

'See these people!' he shouted. 'Good people! Honest people! Decent people! Once happy and contented people! Here, Ervin IV Wray. Stuis III Spiddal. My own wife, Mairie II ev Ghair. But they can turn. We all can, any one of us. We all know we might be the next murderer. Suddenly, out of nowhere — madness and the rage to kill! Why?'

He whirled again and glared at Eddon. His voice rose to a thunderous volume.

'Ah, I know what you Hegemony people think! That P-19ers are a low breed. Descended from drop-outs, ex-criminals, anti-social eccentrics. Just the sort of people to develop some odd genetic warp. Bad blood! Is that what you think? Wrong! We had a wonderful society here on P-19! We're not the cause of this curse! Don't ever suggest it! Don't ever believe it!'

Again and again he whirled, swinging to face in every direction. It was almost as if he were being attacked, as though the madness he described were rushing towards him from all sides of the room. He seemed scarcely able to focus his eyes. His white hair stood out wildly all around his head.

There was a sudden smash as he bumped into

the table. He gripped the edge of the table with savage hands and stared in the direction of the young murderer.

'Take him then! Take him and carry out your tests. Much good it'll do you! Do you think I haven't already explored every possible explanation? Do you think I'm not scientifically trained myself? Ten years I've been working on this thing, ten years carrying out tests and experiments. Night after night and day after day! And do you know what I've discovered? Do you? Do you?'

He seemed to be shouting at no-one in particular. His partially paralysed leg and arm were in spasm, jerking uncontrollably as he staggered around. Vail darted across the room and snatched up her luminator before he could walk into it.

'There is no explanation!' he roared. 'That's what I've discovered! No cause! No source! No answer! There's no sense or meaning to it! You want to look for explanations? THERE IS NO EXPLANATION!'

He knocked into the chair on which Vail had previously been sitting. There was a crash as the chair fell over, and another crash as he kicked it away. Then he stopped. The spasms departed from his limbs, and the rage and the fury drained out of him. He stood there, suddenly still, an old man in the middle of the room. Tears were streaming down his face.

'Lead me out of here,' he muttered. 'I can't see very well. Why is it so dark?'

Mairie came up and took him by the arm. One

of the Reeves picked up his staff from the floor. Someone turned on the main ceiling lights, someone else held open the door.

Guided by his wife, ev Ghair walked slowly out of the room. One by one the P-19ers followed, looking troubled, shaking their heads gloomily.

9

'I was trying to tell you,' said Beano. 'Jaralax explained the whole story to me this morning.'

Beano, Eddon and Vail were the only ones left in the Filing and Records Room, along with the boy on the table. They were still shaken and white-faced. The boy was making quiet spitting noises to himself.

'I can't believe what fools we've been,' groaned Vail. 'It was all so obvious and we never even guessed. We never even doubted what Masilin told us.'

Eddon snapped his fingers.

'So we've been fools. So forget it. Let's re-think. New start, new problem.'

Vail heaved an exaggerated sigh and gazed away at the wall.

'New problem,' Eddon repeated. 'It's like ev Ghair said. We're no longer searching for a murderer. We're searching for the cause of the murderousness.'

Vail turned back to look at him. She shook her head slowly, wonderingly.

'You're incredible,' she said.

'Huh?'

'Don't you feel even a little bit dispirited? Flattened, brought down, made to feel ridiculous?'

'Sure.'

'But it doesn't bother you?'

'Happens all the time in criminal investigations. Someone misleads you, you find out your guesses were all mistaken. False trail. You just get on with the job.'

'Zap! Blam! Powee!' said Vail with heavy irony.

She was leaning against one of the room's two filing cabinets. Her pose conveyed the very image of exhausted languor.

'I thought criminal investigations involved deduction and logical reasoning,' she complained. 'It's bad for my thinking powers to get knocked about like this.'

'Welcome to the real world,' said Eddon brusquely. 'Now, let's look at the problem. Consider all the facts so far. What're the possibilities?'

'Hey!' Beano spoke up suddenly. 'There's one more fact!'

'Yes?'

'The plants on this planet have been growing wrong. Jaralax told me. Like some sort of disease that attacks the crops.'

'In what way wrong?'

'Twisted, deformed . . . I'm not sure exactly. Maybe it's different in different places.'

'Ah, that's what I saw,' said Vail dolefully. 'Another thing I never even guessed.'

'What?'

'When I looked over that high wall. Outside East Lair. I thought it was just wild and overgrown. That must've been the plants growing wrong.'

'Yes,' said Beano. 'If a field goes wrong, they quarantine it. Close it off behind high walls.'

'When did this begin?' asked Eddon.

'About ten years ago,' answered Beano. 'Getting gradually worse ever since.'

'Same as the murders then?'

'Yes. Jaralax said they're down to seventy percent of their crop-growing land this summer. The harvests get smaller and smaller and there's no reserves of food.'

Eddon began pacing up and down the room.

'So! Now we're getting somewhere. Disease. What if this plant disease crosses over to human beings? Causing a special sort of brain disease — causing insanity! A murderous insanity!'

He turned to Vail. But Vail had her eyes half closed. She seemed to be hardly listening. Eddon continued pacing.

'Disease and homicidal mania! Could be!' He made a slicing gesture with his hand. 'Okay. Question now is: how could the disease be transmitted? Airborne, by spores or pollen? Or some sort of carrier, like flies or insects? Or —'

'Summer,' said Vail all of a sudden, opening her eyes and looking straight at Beano. 'What did you say about summer?'

'Summer?'

'You said something about this summer...'

'They're down to seventy percent of their crop-growing land this summer.'

Now Eddon made the connection. 'But it's not summer! Oaves told us it's winter.'

'No,' said Beano. 'It's the middle of summer.'

'Even though the nights are fifteen hours long?'

Beano nodded.

'Mmm.' Vail sucked at her teeth. 'Suits the killers, doesn't it? According to what ev Ghair said, the murders always take place at night or in the dark.'

'But why are the nights so long?' Eddon rounded on Beano. 'Is there some peculiarity in the tilt of the planet's axis? Or something to do with the Walder-J sun? Are the winter nights the same or shorter?'

Beano shrugged. 'I don't know.'

'You didn't think to ask Jaralax?'

'Er, no.'

'Don't blame Beano,' said Vail. 'He did a whole heap better than us.'

Eddon snorted.

'Happy to help,' said Beano.

'You did real well,' said Vail. 'We've been babes in the wood compared to you.'

'Whing-a-dooley!' Beano started to blush. 'I don't know about that.'

'When you two have finished,' said Eddon. 'Perhaps we can plan the next steps in this investigation.'

He held up his hand and began counting off his fingers.

'One. Take samples of blood and mucus for bio-chemical analysis from our killer here. Two. Gather samples of diseased plants, analyse them too. Three. Collect all data on past murders and murderers, see if there's any pattern of dissemination. Four. Collect all data on areas attacked by plant disease, check out possible significant correlations.'

He lowered his hand and looked around the room.

'Okay. This is the Filing and Records Room. So the official records are probably in these two filing cabinets. I'll start doing the data collection.'

Vail raised her eyebrows. 'Now?'

'Right now. What about you? Can you do the biochemical analysis?'

'Of course.'

'Regular experimental procedures?'

Vail scowled. 'Psychic science is founded upon the physical sciences. Every parapsych is an ordinary scientist too. We have to learn the ordinary stuff first.'

'You know how to test for all possible pathogens?'

'Micro-organism, virus, retro-virus. There are nine different tests. It'll take four days.'

'Too long. Do it in two.'

'I can't even begin until I've assembled the apparatus. I don't carry it in my bag.'

'Fine. Two days. Why don't you start by collecting the blood and mucus samples?' He gestured towards Graem on the table. 'While we've got him here.'

Vail shook her head. 'We can't all turn ourselves around as quickly as you. I need to think before I act. I need a lie down.'

'Tired are you?'

Vail yawned elegantly. 'What do you intend to do with him anyway?'

'This killer? Lock him up somewhere safe. I'll have to ask someone where's a safe place.'

Vail undraped herself from the filing cabinet and headed towards the door.

'If I see anyone, I'll tell them to come along.'

'Don't overexert yourself,' snapped Eddon sarcastically. 'In your tired condition.'

Vail swayed melodramatically at the knees and raised a languishing hand to her brow. Beano leaped forward to help.

'I'll take you back to your room? Shall I?'

'Why, sir!' exclaimed Vail. 'I feel fainter already.'

She hung an arm around Beano's waist.

'Take me to my bed,' she sighed swooningly.

They went out through the door side by side. Eddon thought of calling Beano to come back afterwards and help with the data collection. But he decided against it. He heard them talking as they went off down the corridor. The sound of Vail's drawl was somehow more irritating than ever.

He turned his back and went over to the nearest filing cabinet: the one that Vail had been leaning against. He caught the faint smell of perfume still lingering from her presence.

A memory sprang suddenly into his mind — a

memory of their very first night in the Big House, when Vail had psychosummoned him to her bedroom. He remembered her sexy tight-fitting sheathsuit and the overpowering smell of perfume in the air. She had psychosummoned him because of the intruder...but it wasn't for him that she was wearing the sheathsuit or the perfume. So who was it for?

He swung around and stared at the open door. Surely not Beano? Vail with Beano? Ridiculous! Or was it? Who else was there?

He clenched his teeth. If she was getting out of work just so that she could go back to her room and screw Beano...He pulled open the top drawer of the filing cabinet with a savage yank.

Bloody PPs, he said to himself. Was it possible? Vail with Beano? Amoral as cats, the whole lot of them!

He tried to feel cynical, but somehow he only felt angry. He began riffling through the files in the top drawer. There were barely a dozen of them, all unlabelled. He had to force himself to concentrate.

PART FOUR
Hypotheses

1

Vail awoke to the sound of a rat-tat-tat on her bedroom door, and a female voice calling out:

'Vail ev Vessintor? Argid ev Ghair wants to see you.'

Vail looked blearily towards the window.

'But it's not even dawn,' she protested.

Still she struggled up out of bed, and began to get dressed. A minute or two later another voice, a male voice, called out through the door:

'What's keeping you? Hurry up! Ev Ghair wants to see us!'

It was Eddon Brac. Vail swore quietly to herself. Half in a daze, she finished dressing.

Then she grabbed a few items from her make-up bag and went out into the corridor. Mairie ev Ghair stood there waiting patiently, along with Eddon, waiting very impatiently.

The Big House was quiet and swathed in sleep. Mairie turned and led the way. She turned on further lights as they passed along the corridor.

'What kept you so long?' asked Eddon sharply.

But Vail wasn't interested in conversation. She was drawing red and black shapes of kohl and lipstick on her face as she walked. Without a mirror, the effect was even more startling than usual.

Mairie led them across lobbies and through halls. After many twists and turns they came to a passage like an enclosed cloister. Along one side of the passage, a row of windows looked out onto a small courtyard.

Peering through the windows, Eddon and Vail could see Argid ev Ghair walking in the courtyard. He moved slowly, a tall sombre figure in the grey half-light of dawn. Mairie opened a door and ushered them out, then stepped back into the passage without a word.

They shivered in the cold fresh air. The same enclosed cloisters surrounded the courtyard on all sides, with numerous gilded pilasters set into the walls. The ground was marked out in squares of variously coloured stone.

Ev Ghair halted and turned to face them. Etched in the sharpness of dawn, his face looked drawn and haggard, with black pits of shadow around the eyes. Iron bangles glinted on his arms and he wore a vannamak draped loosely over his shoulders. He didn't seem to feel the cold.

'Yesterday,' he said, 'I treated you unjustly. I called you here in order to apologise.'

'That's okay,' said Eddon.

'Your frustrations spilled over,' said Vail. 'It wasn't really us you were shouting at.'

'Thank you. No, it wasn't you. It was myself, and my own helplessness.' He beckoned them forward with a courteous old-fashioned gesture. 'Will you walk with me?'

Eddon and Vail moved up to walk beside him, Eddon on the left and Vail on the right. They began to march slowly around the four sides of the yard. Ev Ghair's partially paralysed leg made a dragging sound on the ground, while his staff came down with a loud sharp rap.

'You know, you're under no obligation to stay on P-19,' he said. 'You were brought here under false pretences. You don't owe us anything. What's happening here is not your problem.'

Eddon shrugged. 'I'd still like to try and work it out.'

'The true detective instinct,' remarked Vail. 'There's no stopping him when he's on the trail.'

'On the trail?' Ev Ghair raised his eyebrows.

'I've got a hypothesis,' said Eddon.

'Ah, well. You're welcome to try, Inspector. No doubt my own scientific knowledge doesn't extend to the latest developments in forensics.' Ev Ghair smiled a slow sad smile. 'If there's anything you need...'

'A few things,' said Eddon at once. 'Access to communication facilities. I'll need to send messages and receive information from Central Police.'

'Our equipment is very slow, I'm afraid, only microdot transmission. But I'll tell our Messages

Officer you're authorised to use it. Just ask for Ailinh IV Ettray — she's in charge of the Messages Centre.'

'I'll need apparatus for conducting biochemical analyses,' said Vail. 'Reactor tabs, Heflin jars, four-way filters ...'

'I think you'll find most kinds of standard apparatus in my laboratory,' said ev Ghair. 'I no longer go there myself. The place is all yours if you want it.'

'And one last thing,' added Eddon. 'Do you have records kept on what's been happening over the last ten years?'

'Records?'

'I looked through the filing cabinets in your Filing and Records Room. There's very little information in the files. And nothing recent at all.'

'Those are the only records we have. We don't bother much about keeping records on P-19. I haven't had time to dictate anything over the past two months.'

'Dictate? You dictate the records?'

'Yes. Computer voice-transcription.'

'You remember everything that happens on P-19?'

'Yes.'

'That's phenomenal.'

'At least my powers of memory have not deserted me. What information do you need, Inspector?'

'All the killings so far. And all the murderers caught so far. And this plant disease too, the areas where it's spread, where and when.'

'Very well. And you'd like this information in written form?'

'If possible.'

'It's possible. Only it will have to wait until I have time to do the dictating. During the night, that means. I'll see if I can have a report ready for you by tomorrow morning.'

There was a long silence. Ev Ghair stared at the ground, seemingly lost in his own thoughts. Eddon and Vail hesitated to intrude. Around and around the courtyard they walked. Then at last ev Ghair fetched a deep sigh.

'Ah, I've loved this planet so much,' he said. 'Ever since I first arrived as a young visiting scientist, researching electro-magnetic fields. Right from the start I knew — this was my planet, my P-19. I fell in love with it even then.'

'Is that why you continued to fight with the rebels?' asked Vail. 'When you didn't change sides to the Hegemony like the other scientists.'

'Yes. But don't say rebels. Say, the permanent inhabitants, the real people of P-19.' He shook his head sadly. 'If only you could've known us at our best, before all this began. When we had hope and belief, when we were building a better world. You should've seen the festivals we used to have, and the pageants and dances. We were a true community then, working together, caring for each other. Not like your selfish-minded Hegemony. We were an example to the universe.'

His voice was calm, almost preternaturally

calm. But emotion radiated from him like a palpable heat.

'Do you know what it's like to watch a dream go wrong? To stand by helplessly while everything you've ever worked for crumbles away? Now we're no better than anywhere else. Fear and suspicion drive us apart. Now everyone thinks only of themselves, or their own separate families. You can't begin to imagine how much we've changed in the last ten years. No-one trusts anyone else any more.'

'That's what we found in Draive and East Lair,' said Eddon. 'People were suspicious, very guarded.'

'Don't judge us too harshly,' said ev Ghair. 'How can you trust your neighbour when you can't even trust yourself? Any society would break down under such conditions. We could've faced and fought an external threat. But this thing — this curse — saps our spirit from within.'

'Is that what you call it? A curse?'

'Do you have a better name? Plants growing wrong, people going wrong. Once we were lucky, and now we're cursed.'

No-one said anything further for a while. The only sound was the sound of their footsteps, and the faint mournful jangling of ev Ghair's iron bangles. The dawn crept slowly higher in the sky, and pale rays of light began to filter through the clouds. Around the courtyard the ornamentation on the pilasters stood out in clear relief, and shapes of silver tracery were visible on the roofs above the cloisters.

Suddenly ev Ghair came to a halt. Eddon and Vail walked on a couple of paces. Then they too stopped, and turned to face him. He stood with his hands folded over the top of his staff, looking at them. The eye on the withered left side of his face appeared somehow darker and larger than the eye on the right.

'It's getting rapidly worse, you know,' he said. 'The insanity and murders are multiplying day by day. Leave while you can. You've got your space-craft. You're under no obligation, there's nothing for you to do anyway. You may not be able to leave if you wait much longer.'

'Why?' asked Eddon. 'What do you think is going to happen?'

'I don't know. But I have a feeling that every-thing is accelerating and moving to a conclusion. Very soon now. You don't belong here, there's no reason for you to share our fate.'

Eddon looked at Vail.

'We'll stay,' he said.

Vail shrugged. 'Okay with me.'

Ev Ghair studied their faces gravely, intently.

'Well, thank you,' he said. 'You're being foolish, but thank you.' He turned away, gazing up at the light in the sky. 'I wonder how many more murders will have to be included by the time I dictate this report tonight?'

It was the end of the interview. Eddon and Vail mumbled a farewell and walked across to the door leading out of the courtyard. Ev Ghair continued to gaze up at the sky. His face was set like a statue, his profile as stern and severe as if it had been carved in bronze.

2

Vail sat in front of her bedroom mirror, while Eddon prowled around behind. She was improving her make-up, adding outlines and curlicues to the haphazard red and black marks she'd applied earlier.

'What caused the change of mind?' she asked.

'What?' Eddon was only half listening. He was looking for clues that would show whether Beano had stayed the night. Vail's clothing was strewn all over the floor. But there were no articles of male clothing or other tell-tale signs.

'You couldn't wait to get away from this planet. Now you want to stay.'

'Yeah, well, I don't like leaving unfinished business. I want to solve this serial killer thing.'

'By discovering some sort of disease pathogen?'

'Why not?'

'Too much left unexplained. How come these killers seem to know each other's experiences? You can't explain that biologically.'

Eddon stuck out his jaw. 'So you want to explain it psychically?'

'It has to be something less material.'

'Like what?'

'I don't know. There's a few possibilities.'

'Powers of darkness?' Eddon mocked. 'Agencies of evil?'

'Don't laugh.'

'I'm not. I'm showing contempt. Is this what you thought up in bed last night?'

Vail said nothing. She selected the thickest, blackest liner out of her make-up bag, and drew scowling black lines over her eyebrows. Eddon watched her reflection in the mirror.

'We're looking for a pathogen that crosses over between plants and human beings. I'll help you collect blood and mucus samples from the killer. Then you can start on your tests.'

'And you?'

'I'll go collect some samples of these diseased plants.'

'Where?'

'Wherever. I'll need some plastic gloves from you, and some bags to put samples in.'

'You're going on your own?'

'I'll take Flightman Berrit with me. And he can bring that Junior Leader friend of his.'

'Junior Leader Jaralax.'

'Yeah, Jaralax. He ought to know where's the nearest infected field.'

'I think I should come too.'

'Why?'

'You don't know what parts of the plants I need for analysis.'

'I'll dig them up whole.'

'I might observe something significant about the way they're growing.'

'I'll observe what's there to observe. I'll be making notes and diagrams. Next?'

'I'm curious.'

'Not good enough.'

'I'll be bored out of my skull here.'

'Nope.'

Eddon resumed his restless prowling. He couldn't stand still. Vail drew small, jaggedy points bristling up from the black of her eyebrows.

'Take Jaralax and leave Beano,' she said.

'No. Why Beano?'

'He can stay and talk to me.'

'Hnh!'

'Keep me amused while I conduct these tests.'

'Listen, ev Vessintor. These tests require your complete concentration.'

'No, they don't. I can do other things at the same time.'

'Hnh!'

'You said that before. What's "Hnh!" supposed to mean?'

'It means Flightman Berrit is coming with me. While you stay and conduct your tests. Every damn one of them. And carefully. Got it?'

Vail pulled a face.

'Oh, I'm really going to enjoy this,' she said to her reflection in the mirror. 'Like the good little housewife staying at home. The domestic. Treated like some sort of hack-worker. What a fun time this is going to be!'

She leaned forward with her liner and drew a sign on the glass. Eddon didn't know if it was a magical hieroglyph or an insulting obscenity.

3

According to Junior Leader Jaralax, they didn't need to go as far as the cropfields to find plants that were growing wrong. There was a park near the centre of Steyne-2 with a walled-off section of diseased flowers. Eddon carried a snap-bag containing items of protective clothing, while Beano brought along a trowel for digging up roots.

Jaralax led them down one of the streets running off from the square in front of the Big House, then along a broad avenue between grandly decorated houses. They crossed a bridge over a gloomy river and trudged uphill through a district of small lanes and coppery roofs. The sky was dark with low-lying streamers of cloud.

'Not many people around,' commented Eddon. 'Seems almost deserted.'

'Seems but isn't,' said Jaralax. 'More and more people are crowding into Steyne-2 all the time.'

'From the farming areas?'

'Yes. People are coming in to stay with their relatives, everyone who has relatives in town.'

'So where are they all?'

'Inside. Indoors. Busy setting up defences.'

The park was at the top of the hill, an island of striking greenery rising up out of the metallic colours of Steyne-2. It was like a chequerboard composed of different types of moss and grass and clover. There were wrought iron pergolas and wrought iron benches, and a great many bronze statues on pedestals.

'This is the War of Independence Memorial Park,' said Jaralax. 'In memory of our freedom fighters.'

'Where's the diseased section?'

Jaralax winced. 'This way,' he said. 'It's not exactly an ordinary disease, you know. Not something growing *on* the plants. More like the plants themselves turning mad and twisted.'

He led them over the brow of the hill. There on the other side was a high curving wall of moulded metal. Completely flat and featureless, it enclosed an area of about a hundred square metres. They could just glimpse a few spiky growths over the top of the wall.

'Why do you build walls around these areas?' asked Eddon. 'What's the purpose?'

'To close the madness in,' said Jaralax.

'To stop it from spreading?'

'No. It doesn't spread.'

'It doesn't spread?'

'It only affects the plants of a single species, only within a given area.'

'But it spreads from one plant to another?'

'Not as far as we can tell. It affects them all at the same time.'

'But then why the walls? If it doesn't spread?'

'So that we don't have to see it.'

'I don't understand.'

'You will when you go inside.'

They had come to a door in the wall. Set flush and made of the same dull grey metal, it seemed like a part of the wall itself. Only the thin crack of its outline gave it away. Jaralax fished in his pocket and pulled out a bunch of keys.

'This is one of the older walls,' he said. 'Three metres high. We can't build them so high nowadays. There's too many fields growing wrong. The people out in the cropfields are already spending half their time building walls.'

He fitted a key into the keyhole and unlocked the door.

'Wait a minute,' said Eddon.

He opened the snap-bag and drew out three gauze face-masks and a pack of plastic gloves. Jaralax watched with surprise.

'What's all that for?'

'Against infection,' explained Eddon. 'Airborne infection or infection by contact.'

'It's not that sort of disease,' said Jaralax. 'It doesn't work like that.'

'How does it work then?'

'Nobody knows.'

'Therefore. We take precautions until we find out otherwise.'

Eddon handed a face-mask and a pair of plastic gloves to Beano. Then he offered another face-mask and pair of gloves to Jaralax. But Jaralax lowered his eyes and shook his head vigorously.

'I'm not coming in with you,' he said.

Eddon gave him a long hard stare. Then he shrugged. 'Fine. There's no need.'

He and Beano donned their face-masks and pulled on their plastic gloves. Then he nodded to Jaralax to open the door. Jaralax pushed it a few inches ajar, almost reluctantly.

'I'll close it again after you've gone in,' he said. 'But it won't be locked.'

He had a hangdog shame-faced air, not at all like his usual self. His face was strangely pallid and the hollows around his eyes seemed darker than ever. Eddon stared at him curiously for a moment. Jaralax averted his gaze.

'I'm not *afraid* to go in, you know,' he muttered fiercely. 'I just hate these places. They give me the creeps.'

He swung the door suddenly wide. Eddon and Beano moved forward and passed through.

It was dark and still on the other side. Long spindly stalks and stems made a tangled thicket all around, dense but not impenetrable. Overhead, the same stalks and stems were like a net across the sky. There were few leaves but many flowers, tawny-red in colour, with soft flat petals.

The door clicked shut in the wall behind them.

'Further in,' said Eddon, whispering. He didn't mean to whisper, but somehow his voice came out muted, as if flattened under a weight. When Beano replied, he spoke in a whisper too.

'Right behind you.'

They pushed forward through the thicket. Eddon could see why Jaralax had described the disease as a madness. There was something somehow wrong about the way the stalks twisted and bent. The angles were too sharp, too sudden, too jagged. No natural growing plants ought to have angles like that.

They advanced a dozen or so paces and then stopped.

Eddon took a closer look at the flowers. They reminded him of Mellorian Poppies. Surely they *were* Mellorian Poppies. But whereas ordinary Mellorian Poppies grew only knee-high, these plants were putting out blossoms two metres above the ground.

There were other differences as well. Mellorian Poppies had only a single stem, not branching out in multiple offshoots like this. Nor did they have these long needle-like barbs on their stems. The barbs reminded him of something else.

'That style of ornamentation,' he whispered. 'Those houses with the webs and barbs. The Extravagant Style.'

But Beano didn't hear. He was looking vaguely around, tilting his head this way and that.

'What's wrong, Flightman?' said Eddon sharply.

Beano came out of his daze.

'It's all so *sad*,' he whispered.

It was true. There was something profoundly dreary and depressing about the plants — about the thinness of their stems, their few lonely leaves, the twisted tortured angles at which they grew. Even the bright colours of the flowers seemed like a mockery.

Eddon clicked his tongue. 'Okay. Let's get started. You've got the trowel. You dig up the samples.'

He handed across a number of plastic sample bags.

'Go for the smallest plants,' he said. 'We want some whole ones.'

'And you?'

'I'll do a sketch of the way they're growing.'

Beano chose an area of ground, squatted down and began digging. Eddon took out his pad and scriber, and tried to trace out the intricacies of a typical patch of vegetation.

They worked away in silence for several minutes. Tracing out the patterns of the growth, Eddon soon discovered that there were common stems feeding across from plant to plant. These Mellorian Poppies actually grew into one another. Beano discovered the same thing.

'I'll have to chop through the roots,' he said. 'They've all joined together like one huge plant.'

Eddon nodded and went on with his sketching. He was feeling more and more tired, as if oppressed by some great weight of sadness. All he wanted to do was to lie down and cry. He had to force himself to keep following the lines of the growth ...

But still he repeatedly lost track. His gaze kept wandering away, getting distracted, sliding off along distant lines and further connections of stems. Every time he turned his eyes from his sketch to the plants or back again, it was like a break in his thoughts, a discontinuity, a whole new world. He had to exert every ounce of his willpower to return to the same spot where he'd been looking, to recover the same place where he'd been drawing on the pad. Such an effort, such a struggle . . . For one whole moment he completely forgot what he was doing . . . or why . . . or who . . .

'Wheee-hup!' exclaimed Beano suddenly. 'Something strange here. Look at this, Inspector!'

Eddon shook his head to get rid of the cobwebs. He squatted down beside Beano. His mind seemed to come clear as soon as he was active and moving again.

Beano held out a tangled mass of stems and roots. He lifted up one stem from the tangle and showed Eddon the chopped-off end. From the interior of the stem oozed drops of a thick white creamy liquid.

'I didn't think anything about it at first,' said Beano. 'Just sap. But then . . !'

He lifted up a root that had also been cut through. There was the same thick white creamy liquid again.

'It's the same everywhere,' said Beano.

Eddon touched the cut root with the tip of one plastic-gloved finger. The white liquid was sticky and viscous. When he drew back his finger, a ropey strand stretched out between root and fingertip. Stretched out, hung down, sagged, and broke.

'The same stuff that was in the mouths of the killers,' he breathed in wonder.

'What does it mean?' asked Beano.

'It's what I suspected. Same disease in plants as in humans.' Eddon snapped his fingers soundlessly in the plastic gloves. 'Let's get these plants in the bags.'

There was already a large pile of plants on the ground. Beano held the sample bags open, while Eddon filled them up with stems and roots, whole handsful at a time.

'Mind the barbs, Inspector,' Beano advised.

Working rapidly, Eddon squeezed in as much as the bags would hold. He made sure to include plenty of tawny-red flowers. Beano sealed off each bag as it was filled.

'Right,' said Eddon. 'Now we're out of here.'

They rose and turned. For a moment it was as if they were lost: every direction looked exactly the same. But then they glimpsed the wall and the outline of the door. It was less than ten metres away.

'Over there!' cried Beano in relief.

They collected three bags each and made their way through the thicket of stems and stalks. They had to hold back from running. They couldn't get out quickly enough. And yet nothing moved. The network was as still and silent as ever. It was only the wrongness of the angles, the abnormalities, the deformities and distorted growths.

Beano was first to the door. He seized the handle and pulled it open. He rushed out into the wide open space of the park. Eddon rushed out behind him, gasping in great draughts of fresh air.

Jaralax was standing some distance away. They removed their gauze face-masks. It was like escaping from a nightmare.

In sudden jubilation, Beano held his three bags aloft.

'We've got a clue!' he cried. 'We've got a clue!'

Jaralax advanced towards them, coming to re-lock the door. Eddon punched the air with his fist.

'Breakthrough!' he exulted.

4

Compared to most of the rooms in the Big House, ev Ghair's laboratory was unusually well lit, with multiple groups of glowing lights extending on brackets from the walls. Two benches occupied the middle of the room, and more benches with basins ran around the sides. At one end of the room was a chaotic jumble of equipment, piled high from floor to ceiling. Other items of equipment were set out on the benches, interconnected by trailing wires and hoses.

Vail was in a foul mood. She was sitting on a stool in front of a computer printer, studying a sheet of results that had just been printed out.

Eddon threw open the door and marched in, closely followed by Beano.

'Whoo-hup!' cried Beano.

'It's all coming together!' announced Eddon.

'Whang-zang-a-dooley!' added Beano.

They deposited their plastic sample bags on one of the benches. Vail swivelled around and regarded them sourly.

'Just like I said. The disease in the plants crosses over into human beings. Hypothesis confirmed!' Eddon was triumphant. 'Come here and look.'

Vail rose slowly from her stool and walked across. She peered at the plants inside the bags.

'See the white liquid oozing out of the stalks?' Eddon pointed. 'Same stuff that comes out of the killers' mouths!'

'Could be,' she said grudgingly.

'Could be and is. Of course, it'll need testing.'

'Of course.' Vail slumped her shoulders. '*More* testing.'

'Total biochemical analysis, ev Vessintor.'

She pulled a face. 'Before or after I finish testing for pathogens?'

'Before. No, after. How much longer are you going to take?'

'I've completed the first three tests.'

Eddon punched the air with his fist.

'Three? Is that all? Out of nine? Speed it up!' He gazed around at the various clusters of equipment on the benches. 'So? Any positive results so far? Any pathogen?'

'No.'

'No? Well, keep looking. There will be. Speed it up, PP!'

Vail gritted her teeth and said nothing.

'You sure you know the proper way to carry out these tests?'

Vail whirled away angrily. She pointed to a cluster of devices on one particular bench-top. There was a centrifuge with a double rotor, linked to a battery of zinc cartridges and a spectroscanner.

'The Standard Burrs-Holding Analysis,' she said in a cold haughty voice. 'No signs of D- or E-type viruses.'

She pointed to an array of glass vessels and pipes, and a large tank containing stratified layers of sponge and membrane.

'The Berkeley Filtration Test. Failed to pick up on any significant strain of retro-virus.'

She pointed to a kind of frame with keys like a piano and a complex arrangement of brass wheels and shutters.

'The Eichendorff Procedure. Reveals the presence of bacteria. But there weren't any.'

Beano meanwhile had been peering at the jumble of equipment heaped up at the other end of the room.

'Er, what about this one?' he asked.

'That's not mine,' said Vail. 'That's some old experiment of ev Ghair's. Measuring electromagnetism. I just pushed it out of the way.'

She strode back across to the computer printer.

Beside the printer was a tray containing printout pages.

'My results so far,' she said. 'Negative. Negative. And negative.'

She held the pages up in front of Eddon's face. They were covered with rows of figures and complicated graphs. Some of the figures had been circled, and there were notes scribbled by hand in the margins.

Beano came across to look over Eddon's shoulder.

'Yeee-wow!' he breathed admiringly. 'How could anyone make sense of all that!'

Eddon reached out and took the pages from Vail's hands. She looked surprised. She was even more astonished when he tucked them under his arm.

'I wasn't *giving* them to you,' she said. 'What do *you* want them for?'

Now it was Eddon's turn to look surprised.

'Of course I want them. I'm sending them back to Central.'

'What for?'

'The forensic scientists at Central.'

'What for?'

'So they can analyse and interpret your results.'

'You don't trust me?'

'They're the experts.'

'No more than me.'

'That's your opinion.'

'Oh I see. They're the conventional scientists.

And I'm some sort of a witch. Is that what you mean?'

'Yeah.' Eddon raised his voice. 'If you want to know. That's exactly what I mean.'

'Phah!' Vail raised her voice too. 'What do you understand about anything!'

'I understand *your* motives.'

'*My* motives?'

'You don't want to believe it's a physical disease.'

'Hey! Don't put the blame on me! It's not my fault your stupid hypothesis is wrong!'

They stood glaring at each other, eyeball to eyeball. Beano gave an embarrassed cough.

'I think I'll be leaving,' he said. 'So long, everyone.'

'No, don't go,' said Vail.

'Yes,' growled Eddon.

'There's no need,' said Vail.

Eddon didn't even turn in Beano's direction. 'Out.'

Beano looked from Vail to Eddon and Eddon to Vail. Then he left the room without another word.

Vail set her jaw. Her make-up was unchanged from the morning: black scowling lines and spiky eyebrows.

'What've you got against Beano?'

'What do you care?'

'I don't like to see people throwing their weight around.'

'You don't have to like.'

'You treat him like a dog!'

'He's in charge when we're on the spacecraft. I'm in charge of this investigation.'

'And me?'

'You're in charge of nothing. You're a PP assistant. *My* assistant.'

'Oh, *yours*! You own me, do you? What am I supposed to do? Serve you? Service you?'

'You're supposed to act like a PP assistant.'

'What does that mean?'

'It means, being fully committed to the job I give you. Not slowing the investigation down.'

'I think it means, stop having any ideas of my own.'

'I'll listen to reasonable ideas. But not —'

'But not unless they're your own! You must think you're some kind of wonderful! What do you want? Do you want me to be in awe of you? Worship and adore the great detective?'

'Don't be ridiculous!'

'Oh yeah. I've heard about you CIs. You expect every new PP to go ga-ga over you.' She pulled a ga-ga face, all pop-eyed and droopy-mouthed. 'Serve you and idolise you and provide plenty of sex on the side. Isn't that how it goes?'

'Not with me, it isn't.'

Vail curled her lip. 'Oh, you're different? I don't believe you. Don't tell me you've never taken advantage! I bet you've had some nice juicy PPs in your time! I bet you think you have a natural right to it! I bet you expect your PPs to be just hanging out for it! Yes sir, no sir, open up my legs, sir?!'

Eddon clenched his fists. Red spots of anger burned on his cheeks. 'If I —'

'All body and no brains! That's what you want! But you don't get to screw this PP! Not Vail ev Vessintor! Sorry if I'm bad for your self-image!'

Eddon controlled himself. He turned away and headed towards the door. He drew out the sheaf of result-sheets from under his arm and placed them on the nearest bench-top.

'There's hardly enough to be worth sending off yet,' he said. 'I'll leave these until you've got the rest of the tests finished.'

He tried to maintain a level tone. But Vail was getting more and more carried away.

'The results will be the same! All negative!'

'Get them finished tomorrow.'

'Didn't you hear? I said, the results will be the same!'

'I'm not interested in what you said. You —'

'And I can't get them finished tomorrow! It'll take another two days!'

'I want them —'

'Waste of time!' Now she was shouting at the top of her voice. 'It can't be a physical disease! Your hypothesis is wrong!'

'If you —'

'Wrong!'

'If —'

'Wrong!'

Eddon lost control. He smashed his fist down on the bench-top.

'Shut up!' he roared. 'Listen! You do those tests! And if my hypothesis is wrong, then I'll become *your* bloody assistant.'

'Hah! And if your hypothesis is right, then — then —' Vail gestured wildly. 'Then you *can* bloody well screw me!'

'What?'

There was a long moment of silence. They were both gasping for breath. Vail realised what she'd said. But she wasn't going to back down.

'You heard me.'

'You better be careful what you say.'

'I don't have to be careful. If your hypothesis is right, you can screw me. But I know it's wrong.'

Eddon stared. Something like a blush spread over Vail's face. She looked away.

'Wrong,' she repeated. 'Don't get your hopes up.'

Eddon didn't trust himself to reply. He spun on his heel and marched out of the room. The door slammed violently behind him.

5

Next morning, as promised, Eddon received the information on previous murders and murderers from ev Ghair. There were about sixty pages of data. He established an office in his bedroom, borrowing a computer and an additional table. Then he set to work, searching for possible patterns of disease dissemination.

Vail went straight to her laboratory without seeing him. She set up the Mann-Winckler test and the Revised Viral Diffusion test. By lunchtime she was very bored and disgruntled.

She went along to the guests' kitchen and dining-room. Beano was already sitting at the table, tucking into a bowl of browny-grey soup. There was a plate of waferbread on the table too, and a dish of fruit jelly.

'Eddon not around?' she asked.

'No. He made himself a sandwich and took it back to his bedroom.'

'Good. What's that soup?'

'Sort of fish with dumpling. It's in a pot in the kitchen.'

Vail went through to the kitchen and found the pot still simmering on the stove. She ladled herself a full bowl of soup and carried it back. She sat down facing Beano across the table.

'Yuggh!' She sniffed and wrinkled her nose in disgust. 'Smells like slops.'

'We eat better than most P-19ers,' said Beano. 'Jaralax says there's hardly any food left in some of the outlying settlements.'

'Okay. Point taken.'

She began supping the browny-grey liquid, still making faces at every spoonful.

'Did you find anything yet?' asked Beano.

'You mean, a disease-causing pathogen? No.'

'You don't believe in Inspector Brac's hypothesis, do you?'

'No.'

'Have you got an alternative hypothesis?'

Vail nodded.

'You think it's something psychic?'

'Has to be.'

'Don't you think perhaps —?'

'What do you know about psychic phenomena, Beano?'

'Not much. I mean, I believe in them, of course.'

'Of course. Everyone believes in them nowadays. Even Eddon Brac. But you still prefer to think in physical terms, right?'

'I suppose.'

'Like most people. You imagine that psychic phenomena can be added on as an afterthought.'

'I never thought much about it.'

'Exactly. Like most people. People watch popularised versions on visi-text, and they think it's all some kind of magic. The old pre-scientific superstitious attitude. They don't realise that the boundaries of scientific understanding have expanded, that what was once superstition is now real knowledge.'

'I'd like to learn,' said Beano. 'If you can explain.'

'If I can explain. Hmm. Can you throw off your physicalist assumptions and do a total re-think?'

'I'll try.' Beano pushed aside his empty bowl. He ran his fingers through his sandy-coloured hair and leaned forward with an earnest expression.

'Okay.' Vail pushed her bowl aside too, though it was still half full of soup. 'There are three fundamental modes or levels of phenomena — you know that?'

'Matter, wave-energy, psychic propensity.'

'Good. When science was first developing, scientists believed only in matter. Mechanics, dynamics, mass, gravitational attraction. People knew about things like static electricity and lightning, but wave-energy phenomena seemed very rare and peripheral.'

'What about ray-tubes and wave-transmission and —?'

'Before all of them, Beano. They're all man-made phenomena.'

'Wow! Back in the prehistoric past then!'

'Yeah. Before space-travel and colonisation and everything. Anyway, after scientists eventually learnt how to explain wave-energy phenomena, they then discovered that wave-energy explanations were also relevant to matter. That sub-atomic matter involves wave behaviour as well as particle behaviour. But a balance of negative and positive polarities holds the potential wave-energy neutralised, locked up within the atom.'

'And the wave-energy is made to flow by unbalancing the polarities, creating differentials.'

'Exactly. And the pattern of the wave is simply the dynamic form of a previous static configuration within the atom. It's the science of transferred configurations that lies behind the ELP drive of your spaceship.'

'Zoot! I studied all of that!'

'So that's how matter and wave-energy have a kind of interreaction, even though they're in totally different modes. Similarly with the interreaction between wave-energy and psychic propensity.'

'Psychic propensity interreacts only with wave-energy, doesn't it?'

'Yeah. It can't affect matter directly, only by way of wave-energy. Psychic propensity is potentially present wherever there's wave-energy. But mostly it doesn't appear, it's in a balanced, neutralised state. It's only under special conditions that it becomes manifest.'

'As in the human brain.'

'Not only the human brain, Beano. Any site where wave-energy is doubled back upon itself. The self-reflexive form of a pyrax. It can happen anywhere. But the cyclical carbon organisation of organic life tends to make it happen far more often. Especially in the nervous system of animals. Supremely in the structure of the human brain.'

She pointed a dramatic finger at Beano's skull.

'The human brain is the most efficient known device for opening up psychic differentials. The chemistry of the brain is the material base for synaptic firing, and the patterns of synaptic firing generate patterns of waves in the brain. Very low-powered waves, but endlessly doubling back on one another. Which is the base for generating activity on the further level of pyschic propensity. Like a movement built on top of a movement. That's what we call the superordinate character of psychic propensity.'

Beano's brow was furrowed with concentration.

'Our parapsych techniques work by unlocking psychic propensity and extending it beyond the individual brain and body. We set up flows that catathesise with other brains and nervous systems, other pyractic sites of every kind. That's how . . .'

But Beano's eyes had started to glaze over. Vail paused.

'Are you following?'

'Whoo! I think I missed something along the way.'

'It's difficult to put this stuff into words. To grasp it properly you need paramathematics and Claussen geometry.'

'You understand paramathematics and Claussen geometry?'

'Yeah. The self-reflexive form of a pyrax can only be represented in terms of Claussen geometry.'

Beano shook his head. 'Too abstract for me.'

He reached out for a slice of waferbread from the plate on the table. He chewed on it for a few moments.

'I get the general idea, though,' he said, between mouthfuls. 'What does it mean for this case you're investigating? What's your alternative hypothesis?'

'My best guess at the moment is that someone on P-19 is sending out a SPEL.'

'A spell?'

'No, a SPEL. Capital S, capital P, capital E, capital L. It's an acronym for Sourced Pyractic Energy-Launch.'

'Oh, SPEL.'

'Psychic science has a lot of acronyms like that. For example, CHARM, standing for Coded Hyper-Affective Rule Manipulation. Or CURSE, standing for Continuous Un-Regulated Symbolic Emission.'

'I get it. And these acronyms have nothing to do with spells and charms and curses in the ordinary meaning? The magicky meaning?'

'Well, they have a related meaning. The acronyms embody a modern scientific understanding of phenomena that would once have been considered magical. A SPEL is a flow of psychic propensity which catathesises with other brains. In this case, if I'm right, the brains of people who turn into killers.'

'And the plants?'

'Same thing. There are pyractic sites in plants too. Like I said, the cyclical carbon organisation of organic life.'

'And this SPEL is being sent out by some parapsych?'

'No.'

'Not by a parapsych?'

'Parapsychs are only trained to use their talents affirmatively. This would have to be someone who can use psychic powers for evil and destruction. Also, someone much more powerful than any parapsych.'

'More powerful than you?'

Vail nodded. 'Much. The question is, who could possess such powers on P-19? The inhabitants are descended from simple settlers, workers and farmers. And the planet's been isolated for seventy years. So who could've been trained to use such powers?'

'No idea.' Beano shook his head. 'No-one.'

'I don't know. It needs thinking about. I might work something out if I didn't have to waste all this time doing senseless tests for CI God-bollocks Brac.'

'You're sure they're senseless?'

'Sure I'm sure. Eddon Brac's hypothesis is wrong. He's wrong and I'm right. And I'm going to prove it.'

Vail reached for a slice of waferbread. Beano reached for the dish of fruit jelly.

'I *have* to prove it now,' she added with a grin.

'Why?'

But Vail didn't reply.

6

Eddon was surrounded by pages of data: on the floor, on the bed, on the desk and bedside table. All morning and afternoon he had been feeding information into the computer and plotting locations on maps. His eyes were strained from working under the small glowing lights in his bedroom.

'Come in,' he said, in response to the knock on the door.

Vail walked in, tall and magnificent in black and red. Her eyebrows were purple, and gold-glitter sparkled on her cheekbones. She carried a stack of printout sheets almost ten centimetres thick. She swirled her cape and clicked her boot heels together.

'Humble servant wishes to present unworthy results of obedient day's work,' she said.

Eddon pointed to an empty space on the floor.

'You want me to prostrate myself on the floor?' asked Vail.

'The printout sheets on the floor,' said Eddon, wearily.

'You sound tired,' said Vail, dropping the stack of sheets on the floor. 'Not a successful day for you, CI?'

'What did you find in your tests?'

'Ah, a question answered by another question. This bodes ill.'

She moved forward and leaned over Eddon, sitting at his desk. She closed her eyes and made an exaggerated show of sniffing the air.

'Mmm. I detect an aura of failure here. An aura of not being able to prove a certain hypothesis. Mmm, definitely. A psychic vibration of not having discovered any patterns of disease-like dissemination.'

'Get your hair out of my face,' said Eddon. 'No, I haven't discovered any patterns of disease-like dissemination. This murdering insanity appears all over the place — north, south, east, west. Totally random. And it doesn't tie in with the fields that go wrong. They're all over the place too, but not the same places.'

'Therefore it's not from people eating diseased plants?'

'Not unless the plants get transported long distances between settlements.'

'Unlikely.'

'Yeah, unlikely.' Eddon snorted. 'What about your blood and mucus tests?'

Vail gestured towards the stack of sheets on the floor. 'Finished. All nine tests finished in two days.'

'And?'

'Slow down. Don't you want to know the names of the tests?'

'No. Get on with it.'

Vail took a deep breath and opened her eyes dramatically wide.

'No pathogens.'

'No pathogens?'

'No pathogens.'

'There must be.'

'Not a twinge, not a tweak, not a whisker.'

'Hnh. Maybe the forensic specialists at Central Police will spot something you missed.'

Vail smiled an artificially sweet smile. 'After all, who am I? Compared to the greatest police minds in the Hegemony?'

Eddon ignored the smile. 'I'll take your results over to the Messages Officer later this evening.'

'When?'

'Later.'

'Can I come too?'

'Why?'

'I've got my own message to send.'

'Why would you want to send a message back to Central Police?'

'Not Central Police. St Alda's Psychoseminary.'

'What sort of message?'

'Oh, er, just to say hello.' Vail waved her hands vaguely. 'Tell them how I'm doing.'

'No.'

'No?'

'This isn't a holiday, ev Vessintor. The communications facilities are for serious messages. Inquiries and reports directly related to the investigation.' He threw a sudden suspicious look at her. 'You're not trying to follow up some alternative hypothesis of your own, are you?'

'Who me?'

'I don't want you wasting time on the side. I need all your efforts concentrated on the main investigation.'

'Of course. Only now I've finished testing for pathogens.'

'So you can start on the full biochemical analysis of the white stuff in the plants.'

Vail groaned.

'And the white stuff in the killer's mouths. I want to know if they're the same.'

'They look the same.'

'I want to know for certain. No short cuts. Hard work is what I need from you, ev Vessintor.'

'Hard work is your speciality. I have other talents.'

'Not talents that I need.'

'And what about you? What hard work are you going to do?'

'I'm still sorting out this data, if you must know. Tomorrow I'll get someone to help me check back over the past history of each murderer. See whether there's any common thread. Any family connection or previous sickness or childhood episode — anything that could make them prone to a particular contagion.'

'Yeah, well, keep trying, CI,' said Vail sarcastically. 'Who knows, you may still get to win your prize.'

'What prize is that?'

'Ah. You know.'

'Do I?'

She flung one long leg up in the air and ran a hand along her thigh.

'Vail ev Vessintor is the prize! One night of sensational sex with Vail ev Vessintor. Don't you wish you were going to win it?!'

Eddon looked pointedly in the other direction.

'What makes you think I'd be interested?'

'Oh, you're interested. I don't have these legs for nothing, you know!'

Vail clasped her hands behind her neck and paraded across Eddon's bedroom with long slinky strides. Slowly, unwillingly, Eddon's eyes swung back towards her. She came to the side of the bed and performed a twirling catwalk rotation. Then she retraced her steps with even longer, slinkier strides.

When she came to the doorway, she stopped for a moment and posed, hands on hips.

'Keep hoping, CI,' she said mockingly. 'Work hard on your hypothesis!'

She threw back her head, sending her hair spraying out like a greeny-black waterfall. Then she strode out.

Eddon sat glowering. It was true, he hadn't really forgotten about the 'prize'. He hadn't stopped thinking about it all day. Or about Vail either. Was she using some kind of psychic influence over him? What was it that made her so infuriating?

He re-pictured her walk across his bedroom, the catwalk twirl and model pose. How could she have such an incredibly high opinion of herself? She seemed to believe she was the ultimate in sexiness. But there was nothing very amazing about her, except her legs. And perhaps her hair. But who knew what her face was like underneath all that make-up?

No, he didn't want to waste any more time thinking about her. The lazy, languorous manner, the slinking, boneless movements — she was everything he most detested. His complete antithesis in every respect.

He looked down at the pages of data on his desk, trying to remember what page he had been working on. There was a mystery to solve, a hypothesis to prove. And *not* for the sake of sex with Vail ev Vessintor.

7

The first group of refugees arrived the following morning, and another two groups later on in the day. 'They're from the outlying settlements,' Jaralax explained to Beano. 'Our Headman has given permission for them to stay in the Big House, in any rooms that aren't being used.'

There were people scurrying about everywhere, searching for rooms, shifting furniture, helping, questioning, calling out. Junior Leaders gave directions, Reeves carried cushions and mattresses, women brought bowls of hot soup. The Big House was a ferment of bustling activity.

The first group set up camp in half a dozen rooms not far from the Major Portal. They had brought with them an odd assortment of possessions: pots, pans, tools, boots, clothing, bedsheets, sleeping bags, along with such personal treasures as musical instruments, statuettes and rolled up wall-hangings. Everything was laid out on the floor, each family surrounded by its own small piles of jumble. Ornate stately ceilings looked down on an invading tide of human chaos.

Jaralax had made himself responsible for drawing up a list of each family's particular needs, the things they'd forgotten to bring. Beano teamed up with him. It was difficult to make themselves understood amidst all the noise and confusion. Many of the refugees seemed hardly able to think straight. They were edgy and jittery and distraught.

'This group is from Brassiter,' Jaralax explained to Beano. 'A settlement on the northern moss-moors.'

'Why did they leave?' Beano wanted to know.

'More and more killings,' answered Jaralax. 'Twenty in a single night.'

'But not just that,' said another voice, sharply.

Beano and Jaralax looked down at the speaker: an old grey-haired woman on the floor nearby. Beside her sat two young boys and another woman nursing a baby.

'Not just that?'

'My brother was slaughtered!' cried the nursing mother, before the older woman could reply. 'My brother and his wife and children! Why? Why? What's happening to us?'

She seemed on the verge of hysteria. The baby joined in with a fit of tears and howling.

'The bars on the window had been broke through!' cried one of the young boys.

'And another three houses too!' cried the second boy.

'Twenty-two bodies! All in the quarry!'

'In the quarry?'

'A quarry just outside of Brassiter,' the old woman explained in her calmer voice. 'Used for mining metal ores. We found the victims there this morning.'

'You couldn't tell who was who!' The younger woman was shaking and shuddering. 'The killers had smashed them with rocks! There was blood everywhere! Blood and pulp!'

'Wait a minute,' Jaralax interrupted. 'Am I getting the picture here? This was all done by killers working together? Cooperating?'

'Yes,' said the grey-haired woman. 'That's why we abandoned the settlement. That's what I meant when I said it wasn't just the number of murders. There must've been at least five killers all working together. We can't defend ourselves against that.'

Jaralax turned to Beano with a frown.

'This is something completely new,' he said.

Beano nodded. 'Sounds less and less like any serial killers I ever heard of. I always thought serial killers operated on their own.'

'It's the first time it's happened on P-19 too,' said Jaralax.

They went through all the rooms occupied by the refugees from Brassiter, and Jaralax finished drawing up his list of items lacking. Then they moved on to the next group: the refugees from Taranx. They had taken up residence in the library and nearby corridors.

Compared to the Brassiter refugees, this group had come better equipped, with their own bedding and packages of dried food. They had rigged up sheets across the corridors and between the book-racks, partitioning off separate areas for separate families. Most of the children were curled up asleep, and several adults too.

When Jaralax and Beano began asking questions, a whole crowd soon gathered around. The people from Taranx were eager to tell their story. They too had fled from a band of killers. Only they hadn't fled immediately.

'We stayed last night in the Community Hall.'

'It's the strongest building in Taranx.'

'Our own houses weren't safe any more.'

'We built huge barriers over the windows and doors. Solid plates of metal.'

'We hid inside after nightfall. All of us together. Then we saw them gathering.'

'A dozen of them.'

'More. Fifteen!'

'Twenty!'

'It was like an army.'

'They couldn't get in through the windows and doors, so they started trying to make a hole in the wall.'

Jaralax waved his arms to quieten the hubbub.

'And they were all cooperating? All working together?'

'Yes. They had a plan.'

'They'd collected metal bars and things.'

'They started scraping away at the back wall. Trying to make a hole.'

'We couldn't see them. Only hear them.'

'Scraping and scraping.'

'It went on for hours.'

'We couldn't do a thing.'

'It was only the daylight saved us. They went off when it began to get light.'

'We came out and looked around and there was this huge hollow in the back wall. A few more inches and they'd have been through.'

Again Jaralax waved his arms and raised his voice.

'You say they went off. Where?'

'They were heading across the moors.'

'Towards the steppes.'

'We think they're gathering together out there.'

'Some secret hiding place.'

'More and more of them.'

'Maybe out in the Eairy Mounds.'

There was no more definite information that they could give. The rest was all guesses and speculation. After a while, Jaralax went back to his list-making. The crowd drifted away and returned to their separate family areas.

Beano wanted to move on to the next group, to hear their story. But Jaralax insisted on going up and down between the bookstacks, noting down the particular needs of every single family. Only when he had completed his duty was he willing to move on.

They found the next group in the New Wing, where the Reeves' living quarters were. The Reeves had emptied out a number of rooms for the use of the refugees. Now they were arranging different families into different rooms. The refugees stood around clutching their possessions, waiting to be given directions. They seemed bewildered, almost stunned, as if unable to adjust to what was happening.

One of the Reeves passed by carrying a pile of quilts. He stopped for a moment in response to Jaralax's signal.

'This group's from the west,' he told them. 'From Slieve-a-Sterry. They only arrived an hour ago.'

'They seem half-dazed.'

'Not surprising after what they've been through.' The Reeve pointed to a heavily built man leaning against the wall. 'Ask him. He'll tell you.'

The heavily built man turned out to be a Warden, with a star-shaped badge pinned to the front of his vannamak. He moved away from the wall and drew himself up very straight.

'Yes, I can tell you,' he said. 'What do you want to know?'

'Everything. From beginning to end.'

'It began last night, when Grimmon IV MetHourn was murdered.'

'Just a single murder?'

'Yes, just a single murder,' said the Warden grimly. 'Not the first we've had in Slieve-a-Sterry. We had a young girl killed three weeks ago. And one of the very first murders, nine years ago.

'Anyway, old Grimmon must've been drinking. He saw this killer outside in the night, and went out with an iron bar to destroy him. Crazy old fool. He didn't stand a chance.

'We found him this morning, hanging upside down in his own porch. Disembowelled. His wife told us what'd happened. And something else too. She told us she'd recognised the killer.'

'She'd seen him?' asked Jaralax.

'Yes. It was Teague IV Terrick. Not from our settlement. He'd come from High Slieve, about four kilometres away.

'So in the morning we gathered up a party, a dozen of us, and went out there. We were going to reveal the killer so that the people of High Slieve could destroy him.

'When we got to High Slieve there was no-one

around. We knocked on doors but they all stayed shut. The door of the Terrick family house stayed shut too. So then we decided to do the job ourselves. Break into the Terrick family house, catch and destroy the killer if he was there.

'We were battering down the door when Teague IV Terrick opened the door from inside. Godalmighty! He just stood there in front of us, with his mouth open in a kind of snarl, and the white stuff dripping down out of it.

'I shouted "Let's finish him!" and we pulled out our weapons. But then we heard this screaming coming from behind us. Scream upon scream upon scream. It was the most bloodcurdling sound I ever heard in my life.'

The Warden paused in his story. There was sweat on his face and his eyes were wide.

'Killers,' he said at last. 'Killers coming out of the houses. God knows how many. Coming out of the same doors we'd been knocking on earlier. Snarling and screaming and moving towards us. We turned and ran.'

'Wheeeow!' exclaimed Beano. 'And they let you get away?'

'Yes. They followed us for about a kilometre. Then they stood and watched us go. It was daytime after all. They're different by daylight. But at night! We couldn't take the risk of another night, with those things living just four kilometres away. That's why we abandoned Slieve-a-Sterry, that's why we're here.'

Jaralax pulled thoughtfully at the ends of his

moustache. 'You believe they're actually *living* in High Slieve?'

'What else? There's no humans there any more. The killers have taken over.'

'But how can there be so many of them? Did the whole population turn suddenly mad?'

'No, it's not like that. They're not all from High Slieve. I recognised a couple of them myself, from families in Slieve-a-Sterry. One woman who said she was going to stay with friends in Steyne-2. And a boy who was supposed to be off doing metalcraft training with his uncle in Carnoss.'

Jaralax groaned and turned away.

'Worse and worse,' he muttered. 'It's becoming like a war.'

The Reeve who had talked to them before was passing by again. This time he was carrying a roll of matting. He stopped and clapped a hand on Jaralax's shoulder.

'Have you heard the latest rumour?' he said.

'There's more?'

'People are saying that the killers are hiding in the closed fields. They've been seen climbing in over the walls.'

'When?'

'At night. Twilight.'

'People are scared and panicking.'

'Maybe. I'm only telling you what I heard.'

'Next thing we'll have the cropfield settlements abandoned as well. Everyone'll be looking for refuge in Steyne-2.'

The Reeve shrugged and moved away. He carried the roll of matting through to another room.

'What fields did he mean?' asked Beano. 'Where the plants are growing wrong?'

'Yes.' Jaralax turned and looked Beano straight in the eyes. His own eyes were full of gloom and misery. 'You ought to fly off in your spacecraft before it gets any worse. Escape from this holocaust while you can.'

8

It took Vail most of the day to complete a full biochemical analysis on the white stuff in the plants and the white stuff in the killers' mouths. She strolled along to Eddon's bedroom to present her results. There was no answer when she knocked.

She opened the door and went in. The room was littered with more sheets of paper than ever. But no Eddon.

She shrugged. She deposited her stack of results on top of the computer. Then she found a scriber and an empty sheet of paper. She scribbled a note:

*Summary of Results for the Great Lord Brac:
The white liquid in the plants is identical to
the white liquid in the killers' mouths. In both
cases, the liquid is a mucus or defensive*

barrier formed by the organism itself in
response to some unknown invasive agent.

Yours scientifically,
Vail ev Vessintor

She signed off with a flourish and left the note propped up against the computer screen.

'Now for *my* hypothesis,' she murmured.

She took another empty sheet and composed a message to St Alda's Psychoseminary. It took her five minutes to write it out in her neatest handwriting. She had always been in trouble over her handwriting at the psychoseminary. She folded the sheet up small and tucked it into the pocket of her cloak.

Then she went in search of the Messages Centre. She had to ask directions several times. The Messages Centre was in the Main Power Room, she was told, over in the New Wing. She zigzagged from corridor to corridor across to the New Wing.

At last she came to the Main Power Room. She pushed through a strange rounded door like the door on a ship. Inside was a large factory-like space, poorly lit by a few dim lamps. Tall rectangular boxes and brooding black machines stood everywhere: rows upon rows of them, enclosed in wire cages. Some of the machines were cowled and hooded, others displayed their interior coils and wiring. Narrow gangways ran this way and that between the cages.

There was a continuous low hum in the room,

316

although nothing seemed to be moving or rotating. Vail stepped forward — then stopped. Above the hum she could hear two voices talking.

'How long is it since I sent your message off?'

That was a female voice. A male voice replied.

'About eighteen standard hours ago.'

Vail ducked down behind the nearest row of machinery. She recognised the male voice. It belonged to Eddon Brac.

'I checked earlier this afternoon, you know,' the female voice continued.

'I know. I'm probably wasting your time.'

There was an easy, pleasant laugh. 'Oh, I don't mind.'

Vail nodded to herself. She remembered that ev Ghair had spoken of the Messages Officer as a woman — Ailinh IV Ettray. The female voice must belong to the Messages Officer.

The conversation continued but Vail could no longer make out the words. Instead she heard the sound of a door opening. Then lights came on, shining out from the windows of a small cabin of corrugated iron. The cabin stood like a miniature house in the middle of the Main Power Room.

Vail advanced along the nearest gangway, between the rows of humming machinery. She turned left and right, heading in the direction of the cabin. The inscription MESSAGES CENTRE was stencilled on the cabin door.

She didn't approach the door but detoured around to the side. She came up towards one of the windows: a long narrow window with shutters but no glass. Pressing herself flat against the corrugated iron, she peeped in through the shutters.

The interior of the cabin was very snug. Shelves piled high with books and papers filled two walls from floor to ceiling. A third wall was occupied by a massive console with a three-tiered keyboard and a control panel of switches and red winking lights.

Eddon and the Messages Officer were standing in front of the console. Ailinh IV Ettray was a young woman in her twenties, with dark brown, short-cropped hair. She wore a bunch of keys on her belt and ornaments of heavy copper dangling from her ears. Like all P-19ers, she was short and strongly muscled. But she had a shapely old-fashioned kind of figure, with an hour-glass waist, wide hips and ample breasts.

'I guess you'll just have to wait a little longer,' she said.

'I guess.' Eddon spread his hands. 'I can't believe they're taking so long.'

'Why not? It takes six hours for our signal to travel to Central. And six hours for their signal coming back. Suppose your message reached them in the middle of the night?'

'Yeah. And Forensics probably won't send a reply until they've finished checking all the results. Could take a day or more. Especially if they have other priorities.'

'Therefore.'

'I know. You're right.'

Vail raised her eyebrows. Never before had she heard Eddon's voice sound so soft and agreeable.

Ailinh laughed. 'Must be a very important message. Or are you always this impatient?'

'I guess I'm always this impatient.' Eddon laughed too.

Vail's eyebrows went even higher. 'Glory be!' she murmured. 'I never knew he could!'

Vail studied the woman's body language, the way she moved and gestured towards Eddon. No doubt about it, she found him attractive. Vail grimaced.

'Well.' Eddon shrugged. 'Time to be getting back.'

Ailinh touched him on the sleeve, directing his attention towards the console.

'This is where the incoming messages are printed.' She indicated a feed-out slot. 'This green light goes on whenever a message is being received.'

Eddon bent forward over the console, standing beside her. They were standing very close together. Vail wondered if Eddon was attracted by large breasts and well-developed muscles.

'And here's the keyboard for sending off the outgoing messages.'

'All in microdot?'

'Yes.' She laughed. 'Very old-fashioned, isn't it?'

'Antique.'

'It's the old Governor's equipment from Steyne-1. It was shifted here when the Big House was built. Long before my time!'

Vail gritted her teeth, listening to the under-tones in the Message Officer's voice. She wasn't really talking about transmission equipment at all. The undertones in her voice were suggestive, caressing, conveying something entirely different. Surely Eddon could hear them?

Already the woman's shoulder was brushing his arm. Vail had the idea that he was about to turn and clasp her in a close embrace. Any moment now. Vail held her breath. She didn't want to see, but she couldn't look away either.

'*No. Don't.*' She willed the words in her mind. '*Don't do it.*'

'Well', said Eddon, straightening up. 'Time to be getting back.'

'You've got work to do?'

Eddon nodded. 'Thanks for your trouble.'

'No trouble. You only have to ask.'

There was an edge of disappointment in Ailinh's voice. You could have asked for much more, her tone seemed to say.

As they turned away from the console, Vail dropped her head below the level of the window. She heard them cross to the door, heard the door swing open. There was a sharp click as the lights went out.

She moved around to the side of the cabin to watch them go off. Ailinh's shapely hips were even more noticeable as she walked, accentuating her hour-glass figure. But Vail's attention was focussed on Eddon.

Only twenty-eight, she thought. Unusually

young to be a Central Inspector. Not her type personally, but she could understand why Ailinh was attracted to him. It wasn't just that he was good-looking. There was a kind of energy in everything he did. The air almost crackled around him.

Not her type, though. Too prickly and driving, too sharp-edged. She and Eddon were complete opposites. Still, it was a pity they'd fallen out. A pity he had to be so domineering.

She watched him striding along beside Ailinh. Always that springing step, always on the balls of his feet. She was pleased to observe half a metre separating the two of them as they walked.

She watched until they made a sudden turn and vanished behind the rows of machinery. Now only the very top of Eddon's head was visible. Vail heard them start talking again. It sounded like ordinary friendly conversation.

A few moments later they arrived at the door through which Vail had entered. The top of Eddon's head was briefly silhouetted in the rounded doorway. Then they went out, clanging the door shut behind them.

Vail stopped thinking about Eddon. She stepped round to the front of the cabin and entered the Messages Centre. She found the light-switch and turned on the lights.

She surveyed the console. The switches on the control panel were clearly labelled, along with most of the keys on the triple-tiered keyboard. Being so old-fashioned, it shouldn't be too difficult to work.

She located the feed-in slot just below the control panel. She drew out and unfolded her message to St. Alda's Psychoseminary, and fed it into the slot. Then she ran her fingers lightly over the keyboard, not pressing down on the keys.

She closed her eyes. She was using the same absorption interfacing technique that she had used when Eddon had given her the punchgun. She closed her eyes and waited to get a sense of what the different keys were for.

9

Beano awoke from a strange dream. There was a sort of colour. And things that had happened. But what was it that had happened? And why was it so fearful and sickening?

He rolled over cautiously in bed, not sure of his bearings in the dark. He was sweating like a pig. He reached out and found the switch of his bedside lamp. He switched it on.

The room flooded into existence. Pillow, quilt, bedside table. The humps under the bedspread made him jump for a moment, until he realised that it was only the shape of his own legs. He blinked and rubbed his eyes.

Carpet, curtains, mirror on the wall. He looked around, trying to remember everything as it had been last night, before he went to sleep. It was somehow very important to be sure that everything was still the same. So far as he could tell, there were no changes.

His head was pounding with a dull continuous throb. He rubbed his eyes again and squinted at the numerals on his time-band. 08.13. So it wasn't the middle of the night, as he'd assumed, but already morning. He'd even slept in longer than usual.

Still the dream hung and hovered in his mind. But he could no longer remember the whole of what had happened. There were only glimpses and details remaining. Glimpses and details, and a kind of vague atmosphere which still seemed to cast its shade over his perceptions and thoughts. He felt ashamed of having dreamed something so monstrous.

With an effort he forced himself to sit up in bed.

'Zow-ow-ow-ow-ow,' he muttered, holding his head in his hands.

He wished there was someone he could ask about the dream. What did it mean? But at the same time he knew he could never share it with anyone. He could never own up to anything so monstrous and horrific. It was shamefully private and secret. He shuddered to think what would be said about a person who could dream a dream like that.

The strange thing was that he couldn't remember what made it so monstrous. He tried to piece the details together again in his mind. But now even the details seemed to be disappearing. The more he tried to pin them down, the more they slipped away. There was a sort of colour and . . . and . . . But the dream was sinking, seeping out of his mind, back to wherever it was that dreams came from.

The dull throb behind his temples was like the start of a headache. Slowly, delicately, he got up out of bed and walked across to the mirror. His legs trembled under him, weak and debilitated. In fact his whole body seemed curiously awkward and hard to coordinate.

He stared at his face in the mirror. His own familiar face, clean-cut and square-jawed. Sandy-coloured eyebrows and hair quiffed up in a Spacer's peak. He felt somehow comforted and relieved.

For a moment he was tempted to go back to bed. But then he shook his head. If he fell asleep again, he might dream the same dream again. Better to get moving and doing.

He began his usual morning exercises. Ten arm-swingings, followed by ten toe-touchings, followed by ten sit-ups, followed by ten press-ups. At first he could hardly manage to flex and bend at all. Then gradually the strength flowed back into his muscles and he felt the pulse of returning vigour. The headache retreated to the back of his skull.

But still the after-effect of the dream lingered on. It was still there when he went along to the dining-room for breakfast, still there when he did the rounds of the refugees with Jaralax. A feeling without a cause, a memory of remembering. All through the day it returned in flashes, in moments of sudden heaviness.

He tried not to think about it. But he couldn't expel it completely out of his mind.

10

'Bapp! Bapp!'

There was a thunderous double knock on Vail's bedroom door.

'No!' she shouted.

She had been getting undressed for bed. She was wearing nothing but her panty-nix. As the door handle started to turn, she snatched up her cloak from the floor and flung it around her nakedness. The door flew open.

It was Eddon Brac. He stood there fuming with rage. He held two sheets of microdot paper, one in either hand. He brandished the right-hand sheet violently in the air.

'What's this?! Hey? What's this?!'

Vail held the cloak clasped over her breasts. It was long enough to cover her panty-nix, not long enough to cover her thighs. She felt exposed and vulnerable.

Eddon marched forward into the bedroom.

'I'll tell you what it is!' he shouted. 'It's for you! A message from St Alda's Psychoseminary!

Received at the Messages Centre just before my answer from Forensics! Well?'

Suddenly he seemed to notice her state of undress. He paused for a moment in his tirade.

Vail did a quick re-think. She had made a serious mistake. The Messages Officer must have handed her reply from St Alda's to Eddon, assuming that it was a part of *his* investigation.

'How dare you!' She adopted a tone of outrage. 'What gives you the right to come charging into my bedroom?'

'Don't change the subject! What gives you the right to go sending transmissions to St Alda's Psychoseminary? When I've *explicitly* forbidden it!'

'How do you know I contacted them first? They probably just wanted to keep in touch with me.'

'Oh yeah? *In answer to your query,* it says. Don't try to play me for a sucker!'

'So you make a habit of reading other people's messages, do you?'

'And don't give me that lah-de-dah voice! You've been going behind my back! Look at this!'

He waved the microdot paper under her nose. There were rows of esoteric symbols in amongst the text.

'Bloody mumbo-jumbo! Pentagrams! Witches' hieroglyphics!'

Vail reached out to grab at the paper. But Eddon pulled his hand away and she clutched on thin air. He held the paper behind his back.

Immediately Vail switched the direction of her

attack. She grabbed at the other sheet of microdot paper in his other hand. This time he was taken by surprise. Vail plucked the second paper clean out of his grasp.

'Give me that!' he snapped. 'That's *my* answer from Forensics.'

But Vail backed away.

'If you can read my messages I can read yours.' She scanned through line after line. 'It's about *my* results anyway.'

She continued to retreat around the room. Suddenly she gave a crow of triumph.

'Hah! *Negative results confirmed*, it says. *Experimental data shows no evidence of any form of pathogen.*'

She stopped backing away.

'So much for your hypothesis! Admit it, you were wrong!'

Eddon growled ominously.

'Remember what you said, Eddon Brac. If your hypothesis was wrong then you'd become *my* assistant!'

'Bullshit!'

'Yes, you have to become my assistant! I was right and you were wrong!'

'No, you were wrong too!' Eddon flourished the message from St Alda's Psychoseminary. 'Listen to this!'

He turned to the bottom of the paper and read:

'*In summary, a psychic SPEL can be directed towards only one specific objective at a time, whether a particular person or particular site. Cases of simultaneous mental breaching in widely separated locations are impossible under the General Theory of Sourced Pyraxes, as outlined above. It must be concluded that your hypothesis of a SPEL projected by a single originating mind is incompatible with the facts described.'*

Vail's face dropped at the first sentence. But she had managed to recover her poise by the time Eddon finished reading.

'A SPEL is not the only psychic explanation,' she sniffed.

Eddon glared at her. 'Yeah, well. You can forget about psychic explanations. That's the end of alternative investigations. Understand?'

'So then there's no investigation. Since your pathogens bombed out.'

'Pathogens aren't the only physical explanation.'

'No?'

'No. From now on, we start looking for toxins.'

Vail sniffed again. 'Love that "we",' she muttered.

'Toxins accumulating in the brain and causing insanity. Probably some toxic metallic element. All the food and water on this planet tastes of metal. Probably builds up over a long period of time, first in the plants, then human tissues, then the human brain.'

Vail gave a groan. 'Can't you tell when you're on a losing streak? Aren't detectives supposed to have hunches about these things?'

'Start testing tomorrow morning, PP. Plants and

tissues. You're looking for any unusual accumulation of metallic elements. Got it?'

'You like giving orders, don't you?'

'It's my job.'

'And don't you enjoy it!'

Hot angry points appeared on Eddon's cheeks. His chin stuck out aggressively.

'This is the real world, ev Vessintor! Not some protected little haven! Not like your precious little psychoseminary!'

'What do you know about psychoseminaries?'

'Enough.'

'What?'

'Phuhh! Poshy upper-class girls poncing around and playing smart-ass games.'

'That's really stupid! That's the most stupid prejudice!'

'Yeah, and you're confirming all my prejudices!'

'I suppose you think we screw around too? Isn't that the popular stereotype?'

'You said it.'

Vail flicked her hair contemptuously. 'It's impossible to talk to someone like you.'

'So what's the truth? If that's only the stereotype?'

'You wouldn't understand.'

'Oh, ootsy-woo! "You wouldn't understand!" How cute! Is that what they teach you at psychoseminary? How to get out of answering questions by acting superior?'

'What's your problem, Eddon Brac?'

'No problem, ev Vessintor. I just don't care for upper-class snobs who think they're better than ordinary people.'

'And you're ordinary people?'

'I wasn't born *ev Brac*.'

'Ah, right. So that entitles you to feel all salt-of-the-earth and sweat-of-the-brow and honest-working-class-ish?'

'I'm not ashamed of my working-class background.'

'Not ashamed? You're utterly proud of it!' "I worked my way up by my own honest toil, Ma!" The Central Inspector as working-class hero! "Started out as a humble Brac, and now look, I can even order ev Vessintors around!"'

'Except *ev Vessintors* don't take orders, do they?! Too bloody born-to-rule arrogant!'

'You don't —'

'Listen, ev Vessintor! Tomorrow you start testing for metallic elements! I want to see your results at the end of every day. And as for communicating with St Alda's Psychoseminary . . .'

He held up the sheet of microdot paper in his hand, and tore it neatly down the middle.

'Hey, stop!' cried Vail. 'That's mine!'

Eddon put the two halves together and prepared to tear the paper into quarters. Vail leaped forward to save it. Eddon lifted his arm high above his head. But Vail was taller, with a longer reach. She grabbed hold of the paper at one end. Still Eddon didn't relinquish his hold. Instead he brought his other hand across and gripped Vail's arm above the elbow. Then he started to squeeze.

'Let go my arm!'

'Let go the paper!'

'You're hurting me!'

'That's right. Let go the paper!'

Vail couldn't match Eddon's strength. She was still clasping the cloak with her left hand over her breasts. Their faces were inches apart, their bodies almost touching. Muscles straining, Vail struggled to free her right arm. But Eddon applied more and more pressure. Tears of pain appeared in her eyes.

She was desperate. Not for anything would she surrender! She let go of the cloak and swung her left arm in a circle. As the cloak fell to the floor, she brought her left arm down on top of Eddon's arm, breaking his grip.

His arm dropped to his side. He was pop-eyed and open-mouthed. Except for her panty-nix, Vail was completely naked. The cloak lay in a heap around her feet. Her bare belly was brushing his waist, her breasts brushing his chest. Her nipples stood out fierce and erect against him.

She glowered with anger. Her face coloured up a bright red.

'Back off, Brac!' she gasped.

She could have used her free arm to push him away. But she didn't. She was panting for breath.

A confused inarticulate sound came from Eddon's throat. They were both still holding on to the message from St Alda's Psychoseminary.

Then Eddon let go. He stepped back a pace, hot and staring. His face was as red as Vail's.

'Tomorrow,' he said thickly. 'You start. Metallic elements.'

Then he spun on his heel. He walked out through the door without a backward glance.

Vail stood there recovering her breath. She could hardly believe he'd gone so suddenly. She made no move to cover herself with the cloak.

Instead she crossed to the door and closed and locked it. Then, still naked, she came back to the bed and picked up the bolster. She whirled it round her head and flailed it against the nearest wall.

'Take that!' she muttered ferociously.

She hit the pillow with the side of her left hand, then she made a fist and pummelled it with her right. When it fell to the floor she kicked it half-way across the room.

'Take that, Eddon Brac! And that! And *that*!'

Refugees continued to flood into Steyne-2, into the Big House. Over the next three days they took up every spare corner of the building. They brought with them stories about killers gathering in gangs, roaming the moss-moors, attacking houses at night.

Ev Ghair's prediction of things accelerating towards an end seemed to be coming true. Many of the outlying settlements were no longer in communication with Steyne-2. There were more and more killings, more and more cropfields growing wrong. In the end, ev Ghair ordered the stricken cropfields to be burnt. People had neither the time nor the will to keep building walls around them.

The Big House was a-buzz with news and rumours from morning to night. Stories became blown-up until it was impossible to tell the real facts from the imagined fears. Everyone had their own versions of events.

Vail didn't try to keep up with the news and rumours. She was too busy performing the tests that Eddon had ordered, checking for the presence of metallic elements in plants and tissue samples. At the end of the day, she printed out her results and slipped them underneath his bedroom door. She didn't bother writing comments or summaries on them. Let him try and understand for himself!

But that wasn't the end of her work. She went back to the laboratory after dinner to do some thinking on her own ideas. There *were* other possible psychic explanations: the difficulty was to make them cover all the facts. Sometimes she worked through until the middle of the night. Her wastepaper bin was filled with sheets of discarded jottings.

Then Beano brought her some crucial new evidence. He came walking into the laboratory late one afternoon. There were dark heavy shadows under his eyes. But he was bursting with news.

Vail put down the glass pipette she was using.

'Long time no see, Beano.'

'Whoo-hup! I've found out something important for you. You know how dark this planet is?'

'Mmm-yeah.'

'Even though it's summer?'

'Seven hours of daylight and fifteen hours of night.'

'But there's something we didn't know. The darkness only started ten years ago.'

'Ten years ago? Same time as the murders and the plants?'

'Dead spot on! And it's been getting darker every year since then.'

'It's not the clouds getting thicker?'

'No, nothing like that.'

'So why?'

'Nobody knows. Jaralax was telling me about it. The light from the sun gets somehow blocked off. Even ev Ghair can't explain it.'

'Even ev Ghair...'

Vail turned her gaze towards the jumble of equipment heaped up at the far end of the laboratory: ev Ghair's old experiment. She'd pushed it aside without even considering it before. Now she pursed her lips thoughtfully.

'Hmm. I wonder.'

She rose and went across to the equipment. She began peering and probing, pulling at wires and tracing connections. Beano watched in respectful silence. For a few minutes she was totally absorbed. Then she turned back to Beano again.

'Ah, ev Ghair couldn't explain it. But I know what he was trying to prove.'

'So did I help?' asked Beano. 'Does it all fit in with your hypothesis?'

'My hypothesis?'

'About someone casting a SPEL?'

'A SPEL? No, no.' She wafted a hand. 'Didn't I tell you? I abandoned that hypothesis ages ago.'

She frowned and focussed a sudden intent look upon Beano. 'Why *is* it so long since I've seen you, Beano? Must be days and days. Have you been avoiding me?'

Beano lowered his eyes. He had a guilty, hang-dog air.

'I've been going around with Jaralax. You know, the refugees.'

'You don't look real good either. What are those dark circles under your eyes? You're starting to look like a P-19er.'

'Me?' Beano almost jumped.

'Is something the matter? Are you tired? Are you sleeping okay?'

'No. Yes. I mean, I'm sleeping plenty. Twelve hours a night. More than plenty.'

Vail came up close to him. Still he wouldn't look her in the eyes. She pulled up a stool.

'Relax,' she said. 'Take a seat.'

Beano sat down.

'I'm sleeping plenty,' he repeated.

'"More than plenty", you said. There's something you don't like about this sleep, isn't there?'

Beano stared at the floor and said nothing.

'Relax,' said Vail. Standing beside him, she rested a hand on his shoulder. 'What's wrong with this sleep? You can tell me.'

'I don't know.' Beano wriggled on the stool. He seemed to be engaged in some kind of internal struggle.

Vail extended her first two fingers and pressed against the nape of his neck, just above the collar. At first a gentle pressure, then gradually firmer and firmer.

'Tell me, Beano.'

The tension went out of Beano's body.

'I've been having bad dreams.'

'What about?'

'I don't know. Nightmares.'

'When did they start?'

'Four nights ago.'

'And you've had them every night since?'

'Yes.'

'What were they about?'

'I can't remember.'

'But you know they were bad?'

'Yes.'

'Were they frightening?'

'Sort of. Disgusting.'

'What were they about?'

'I can't remember.'

'Try.'

'I can't!'

Vail relaxed the pressure of her fingers. 'That's

okay, Beano. If you can't you can't. It doesn't matter.'

Beano leaned forward and put his face in his hands. 'I never meant to tell anyone,' he muttered.

'Why not?'

'I don't know. I feel ashamed. Wrong. I can't explain it.'

'There's nothing wrong about having nightmares. Unless...'

She clicked her tongue and nodded to herself. She came around to stand directly in front of Beano.

'Beano,' she said. 'I'd like to observe you asleep. When you're having these dreams.'

'What for?'

'It might be relevant.'

'To what?'

'My hypothesis.'

'My dreams are nothing to do with anyone else.'

'Nevertheless. I'd like to observe you. Tonight.'

'I don't want to be observed.'

'Of course you don't. I'd feel the same. But it could be important. For the sake everyone on P-19.'

'I don't want —'

'I can't force you. But I'm asking you. Please.'

'What will you do?'

'Sit beside you through the night. I'll have various kinds of equipment to monitor you with. Please.'

Beano looked unhappy, reluctant, almost hunted. But eventually he agreed. Vail gave him a cheering smile.

'Come and call on me when you're ready to go to bed. I'll stay here in the laboratory.'

'I go to bed about eight.'

'Good. I'll see you then.'

As soon as Beano had gone, Vail picked up a pad and a scriber. She sat on the stool and began scribbling down equations. Each equation was followed by a furious question mark.

She filled up three pages of the pad, then stopped. She tapped her teeth thoughtfully with the end of the scriber.

More information! She needed more information for her theory. And there was only one way to get it. She would *have* to send another message to St Alda's Psychoseminary. But this time she'd arrange for a coded reply. And this time she'd make sure to collect it herself.

It was a few minutes after eight that night when Eddon heard them coming along the corridor. Vail and Beano, whispering together. Why were they whispering?

He was working in his bedroom with the door closed. He turned and saw half a dozen sheets of paper slide in underneath the door. Vail's result sheets for the day.

Then the footsteps moved off down the

corridor. They stopped outside the door of Vail's bedroom. There was a sound like a smothered giggle. Then the squeak of a handle turning, a door opening. Then silence.

Eddon froze at his desk, straining to hear more. Had Beano gone into her bedroom? He must have. But maybe only to talk? If they hadn't closed the bedroom door...

He rose up from the desk and went across to his own closed door. There was a strange taut feeling in his chest. Vail and Beano. He had been wondering about them for days. Did they really have a sexual thing going on?

He knew it was stupid, but he had to find out. Very carefully he opened his bedroom door and stuck his head out into the corridor. The corridor was empty, Vail's bedroom door was still open. He stepped out to inspect further.

At that very moment, Vail and Beano re-emerged from Vail's bedroom. They turned and looked straight at him.

'Why, hullo Inspector!' said Vail. 'Popped out for a breath of fresh air, have you?'

Eddon was caught at a loss. He uttered the first phrase that came into his mind. 'None of your business,' he said.

Vail was carrying her bag. She came walking along the corridor with Beano following. They stopped outside the door of Beano's bedroom.

'No, this is *our* business,' said Vail sweetly, opening the door. 'We're going to spend the night together.'

'Hnnh.' Eddon snorted his most cynical snort.

'But we'll try to be quiet. Not to disturb your hard work.'

Beano was blushing to the roots of his gingery hair. He stood beside Vail in front of the bedroom door.

'It's not what you think, Inspector,' he muttered.

'It isn't?'

'No.'

'What is it then?'

'Er, I'd rather not say.'

'Don't worry about it, Flightman,' said Eddon. 'You can screw till your balls drop off, for all I care.'

'Mmm-yeah!' said Vail. 'What a drift!'

Beano couldn't cope with the situation any longer. He shook his head and disappeared into his bedroom. There was a brief silence between Eddon and Vail.

'I hope I haven't put him off his stride,' said Eddon. 'Still, I expect you'll soon bring him up to the mark again. A little witchcraft, a little hypnotism...' The cynical tone dropped momentarily. 'You can make him do any damn thing you want, can't you?'

Vail fluttered her long black artificial eyelashes.

'What's it to you?'

'Nothing. Except I feel sorry for him.'

'Why so?'

'He's too young to know the kind of witchy tricks you play.'

'I don't need witchy tricks.'

'Oh, sorry, I was forgetting. Your legs. You're the ultimate in sensational sex.'

'Hah!' There was a sudden fierce flash in her eyes. 'Lucky for me your hypotheses are all wrong. I don't think you'd be much of a lover. Far too uptight.'

She turned and vanished into Beano's bedroom. The door closed with a loud click of the lock.

Eddon was left standing there. Too late he thought of a particularly cutting retort. He went back to his own bedroom, slamming the door. He was trembling like a violin string. Emotions churned through him, strange irrational emotions.

Stop this, he told himself. Why get angry about it? Why should he care? After all, it was no more than he had always suspected.

But it was one thing to suspect, another to know for certain. Blood burned in his face. He stood in the centre of the room, clenching and unclenching his fists. Stop this! Stop! Stop! Stop!

Around midday of the following day, Eddon received a message from Central. He decided he had to see Vail about it. He didn't *want* to see her — but professional duty came first.

He went along to the laboratory. His mouth was

set in a hard firm line. He expected to find her working on the metallic toxin analysis. But she wasn't in the laboratory.

Still in bed with Beano? A vivid picture flashed through his mind, Vail lying naked with Beano beside her. But then he noticed that the laboratory lights were turned on. Cold reason told him she must have been in the laboratory and left.

There was a girl cleaning out the room next door. Eddon went and asked. Yes, answered the girl, she'd seen a tall, striking-looking young woman come out of the laboratory. About fifteen minutes ago. And carrying an electric torch.

Eddon scratched his head. Why a torch? Then he remembered the cell where Graem was being kept: a small lightless chamber hollowed out in the underlying bedrock below the Big House. He'd taken Vail there a week ago, to collect the blood and mucus samples from the killer.

He headed off in the direction of the cell. He didn't bother finding a torch for himself. He wondered why she was visiting Graem again. Collecting more samples on her own?

He strode through corridors and halls, and came to the top of the steps leading down to the cell. The steps were in darkness, winding around and around in a spiral. He descended slowly, feeling his way with his hands against the walls.

Towards the bottom of the spiral there was a gradual brightening ahead. He came around the last bend and saw the door of the cell wide open. Inside were the figures of Vail and the killer, illuminated in a weak yellowish light.

Vail glanced over her shoulder at the sound of Eddon's footsteps. When she saw who it was, she turned back without a word and continued what she was doing. She was taking pictures of Graem with her scan-camera.

The light came from a torch propped up on a table. Graem sat bolt upright on a high-backed chair in the centre of the cell. Solid iron hoops encircled his chest, and his legs were almost invisible under a mass of chains. Additional chains fastened the chair to rings in the floor.

He could move, but only a few inches in any direction. At present he seemed inactive, eyes closed and resting. Vail focussed her camera and snapped another shot of his head.

'What're you doing, PP?' Eddon kept his voice very cold and flat.

'Electrostatic imaging.'

'Head shots?'

'Mmm.'

'And this is relevant to the investigation of metallic toxins?'

Vail didn't answer immediately. She shifted around to take a shot from a different angle. The killer made tiny twitching movements, like a sleeping animal. Vail kept her distance, always at least a metre away.

'One thing that'll interest you,' she said. 'The

white liquid that comes out of his mouth. It's produced in the cranial cavity.'

She snapped her shot and lowered the camera. Then she beckoned Eddon across to the table where the torch was propped. There was a flat plastoplex developer also on the table, and a folder of photographic transparencies.

She lifted up one of the transparencies: an electrostatic image in shades of ghostly green.

'Interior section of Graem's skull,' she explained. 'See those lighter patches? There and there. And there. That's the mucus being produced.'

Eddon snapped his fingers. 'Fits with my hypothesis. Metallic toxins accumulating in the brain. Mucus as a defensive barrier against the toxins. That's exactly where it ought to be produced. Right?'

Vail made no reply. She put the transparency back in the folder. She seemed blithely indifferent to Eddon's deduction.

'Right?'

'Could be.'

'What else?'

'Oh, only if you want to consider a psychic hypothesis.'

'Supernatural stuff? Powers of darkness?'

He couldn't help jeering. He was getting more and more irritated by her nonchalant manner.

'But then you don't want to consider a psychic hypothesis, do you? So it'd be a waste of time telling you?'

Eddon's brows came down like a portcullis. 'Yeah. A total waste of time.'

Vail turned away with a shrug. She clicked a button on the side of her camera. There was a whirring sound and a small gold-coloured cartridge popped out. She took the cartridge and inserted it into the plastoplex developer.

Eddon fought down a wave of anger.

'What I came to tell you,' he said. 'I've received a message from Central, with information on the metallic elements known to cause forms of insanity. I'm going to talk to Argid ev Ghair about it this afternoon. As soon as I've correlated the information with my own data. Have you got anything to contribute?'

'Me?' She twiddled a dial on the developer and switched on the development process. 'No. I've given you my results.'

'Yeah. Several elements in unusually heavy concentrations. But you haven't nominated any element as particularly likely.'

'Likely? Likely to cause *this* form of insanity? I don't think so.' Vail glanced up from the developer. 'You don't want to hold off talking to ev Ghair maybe a little longer?'

'Why?'

'Oh, something might come up.'

Eddon gave her a dark look. He felt sure she was still pursuing alternative investigations. But he didn't want to get into an emotional argument.

'No. I'm talking to ev Ghair this afternoon.'
He ascended the winding steps in the darkness.

Vail's head was spinning with new possibilities. Now she had the electrostatic images of Graem's brainwaves to add to the recorded data on Beano's dreaming. So many implications! But she knew better than to grasp too soon for answers and conclusions.

She went back to the laboratory and picked herself a position on the floor by the wall. She sat down and leaned back, drawing her legs up under her chin and wrapping her arms around her legs. It was important to be in a completely relaxed posture.

Then she closed her eyes and began the ritual for inducing the kind of meditative state she wanted.

Navala-mas, she said in her mind.

> *Navala-mas*
> *Create an empty space*
> *Navala-mas*
> *Discard assumptions*
> *Discard the obvious*
> *Navala-mas*
> *Let the facts be free*
> *Let them float in the space*
> *Navala-mas*
> *Let them move and transpose*
> *Now widen the space*

Navala-mas
No forcing, no controlling
Shuffle, reshuffle
Shuffle, reshuffle
Navala-mas

For ten minutes she rotated the facts through her mind. The latest facts and the earliest facts: so many diverse things that had been happening on this planet. But all related, all connected...

There was a vacant blank expression on her face. Only the tiny flickerings of her eyelids showed that she wasn't asleep. For ten minutes she remained motionless.

Then a grin crept over the corners of her mouth. She opened her eyes. Her pulse was racing, she was breathing as fast as a cat. She blinked and jumped up from the floor.

She took three strides across to the bench where all her papers and jottings were scattered. She was in such a hurry that she almost tripped over her own feet. She riffled through the papers and pulled out half a dozen separate sheets.

She laid the sheets out side by side. Some were covered with equations, others with diagrams. She studied them intently. Then she snatched up a scriber and began drawing extra lines across the diagrams. Yes! A total conceptual revelation! Incredible!

She was trembling with excitement. At last the pieces of the puzzle were all falling into place. She was almost there. She was ready to start her final calculations.

Then she stopped. She couldn't begin her final calculations until she received the necessary information from St Alda's Psychoseminary. Damn! damn! damn! damn! damn!

How much longer would it take for the reply to arrive? She wiped a hand across her brow. She took a deep breath and told herself to quieten down. She gazed at the diagrams and equations in front of her.

Anyway, there was also another experiment to perform. She needed to measure the special characteristics of the electro-magnetic field on P-19. She had to have every possible particle of evidence. It was going to be hard enough to convince people as it was.

She went across to the jumble of equipment stowed away in a corner of the laboratory. The apparatus of ev Ghair's old experiment. He too had measured the characteristics of the electro-magnetic field on P-19. But now she knew things that he had never known. She knew how to fit the measurements into a far larger theory.

She hauled out the various bits of equipment and re-erected them on the nearest bench. Condensers and equalisers, five-pin valves and gyro-stands, an Elphick's bridge and tolerance-gauge, a wave-translator with a Demi board.

She was perfectly calm and unhurried once again. She adjusted the screen of the wave-translator, set the hammer-slides of the tolerance-gauge and waited for the expected patterns to appear on the Demi board.

She was confident that the results would conform to her predictions. All she needed were the exact figures for her calculations. It would take about an hour. And by then perhaps the reply from St Alda's Psychoseminary would have arrived? It must be sixteen hours since she'd sent off her request.

She nodded to herself. Okay. As soon as this experiment was finished, she'd go along and check at the Messages Centre.

15

'He's up there,' said Mairie. 'Just follow the steps.'

Eddon climbed the steep iron steps at the side of the gallery. There was a trapdoor at the top of the steps opening out onto the roofs. He came up through the trapdoor and found himself standing on a metal walkway with a handrail at the side.

He was surprised that the afternoon light was already so dim. It was only two-thirty, after all. And the light had a strangely yellowish quality, acid and ominous. Overhead stretched an unbroken mass of stormcloud, a great black base weighing down across the sky. The air was very still and windless.

He looked out over a choppy sea of roofs, the endlessly varied roofs of all the different rooms and wings of the Big House. There were sharp peaks and cambered ridges, carved crests and copper domes, oriels and turrets and pinnacles. Far away on one side he could recognise the line of spires marking the facade of the building, where it faced out towards the main square.

But where was Argid ev Ghair? Like a low-slung bridge, the walkway ran over the tops of the roofs, angling around the turrets and pinnacles, joining up with other walkways. Eddon set out across the roofs in search of the Headman. The open metal grid of the walkway reverberated under his feet.

He didn't have to walk very far. The Headman had been hidden behind an elevated dome. He was standing at the end of one particular walkway that led to the very edge of the roofs. Eddon changed direction and headed towards him.

Premonitory rumbles of thunder rolled around the circumference of the sky. There was lightning too: flickers of brightness cast intermittently upon the undersides of the clouds. But the thunder and lighting were very remote. Eddon pulled his vanna-mak more tightly around his shoulders.

Ev Ghair stood gripping the handrail, gazing off into the distance. He looked a mournful solitary figure. He had his back turned to Eddon's approach.

'Argid ev Ghair!' Eddon's voice carried piercingly in the still air.

Ev Ghair glanced around. The contrast between his white hair and the dark withered side of his face seemed more shocking than ever. He beckoned Eddon forward, then turned again and resumed his gazing.

He was gazing out over the settlement of Steyne-2. Coming up beside him, Eddon could see a wide spreading panorama of streets and rows of houses. The end of the walkway was like a viewing platform.

Eddon stood in silence at the handrail. There was the Golgass Market, all wires and spikes and angles. And the river . . . and the bridge where he, Beano and Jaralax had crossed on their way to the War of Independence Memorial Park. He traced their route and spotted the rounded green hill of the Park itself, away on the extreme left.

The view extended to the outskirts of the settlement and beyond. Eddon squinted, trying to pick out details in the fading light. The cropfields were a mere blur. But he could see the upright silvery tube of their own spacecraft, sitting on its tail in the centre of the spaceport. And further around to the right, a range of ghostly shadows, like tall ruined buildings in the distance. Must be the ruins of Steyne-1, he thought, the ruins of the Old Settlement.

'Great view,' he remarked.

'Yes.' Ev Ghair's voice was low and rumbling, like the thunder. 'I often watch from up here. Sometimes the whole night.' He turned to face Eddon. 'So what have you come for?'

'To tell you the state of the investigation.' Eddon fished in his pocket and produced a folded sheet of microdot paper. 'This is a message from Central Police. Let me read you this list.'

He unfolded the paper and read:

'*Lead. Mercury. Tin. Molybdenum. Lithium. Antimony. Boron. Vanadium.*'

He looked up. 'All of those metals would be present on P-19?'

'Yes.'

'Some more than others?'

'Especially lead and tin. And antimony. Why?'

'All of those metals enter the food chain. They absorb into the bloodstream and accumulate in the brain. Causing insanity.'

'Insanity? You mean, murdering?'

'Murderous impulses could be one consequence.'

'You don't sound very certain.'

'I'm not saying it's certain. But what other explanation is there?'

'And what about the plants?'

'The same. All of those metals can also cause abnormal growths in plants.'

'Well.' Ev Ghair seemed strangely unconcerned, almost uninvolved. 'And what do you advise?'

'What do I advise? I think you'll have to bring in uncontaminated food from off-planet. Get in touch with the Hegemony, ask for emergency assistance. They'll send in experts and food aid. That should solve your problem in the short term.'

'And in the long term?'

'Depends if the particular metals could be somehow filtered out of the soil. If not, then I guess P-19 would have to be evacuated. The Hegemony won't provide emergency assistance forever. Eventually they'll send ships to transport your settlers here to other planets. To start a new life on other planets.'

'We'd rather die first,' said ev Ghair.

'What?'

Ev Ghair raised his voice. 'We'd rather die first.' He looked coldly into Eddon's eyes. 'Do you think we'd go crawling back to the Hegemony? Do you think we'd let them decide our future ever again? We've chosen our own way. We're not just day-trippers here. This is our own planet, our home! We'll stay with it.'

'Even if it poisons you?'

'I don't believe in your metal toxins. I don't believe that our planet is killing us. I'd trust this planet sooner than I'd trust your Central Police. We'll stay whatever the consequences.'

'And everyone on P-19 feels the same way?'

'Ask them.'

Ev Ghair suddenly seemed to lose interest. He turned away and looked out over Steyne-2 again. Eddon shrugged and looked out too.

Already the twilight was much further advanced, and night was closing in fast. The out-skirts of the settlement had disappeared completely into the dark. Closer to the Big House, electric lights were being turned on in the houses. Tiny gleams and glimmers shone forth in rows along the streets. Most of the windows were heavily shuttered.

The stillness was uncanny, like a trance. No-one moved in the streets, no breath of wind stirred in the air. The faraway lightning and thunder seemed only to intensify the absolute immobility of the scene.

Then came a scream. Somewhere in the distance, a terrible high-pitched scream, a killer's scream. On and on it continued, for two whole minutes: then stopped. Ev Ghair shuddered.

'How long would it take to call in help?' he asked.

'From the Hegemony?'

'Yes.'

'About three weeks to bring in food from the nearest populated planets. About six, seven weeks for the experts to arrive.'

'So you see, it would be too late anyway. We don't have weeks.'

'Why not?'

'Something is about to happen. Any day now. Can't you feel it? How dark it is? Some terrible change is coming —'

Ev Ghair broke off as another killer's scream pierced the night. Closer this time, somewhere in the streets of Steyne-2. Insane and inhuman and chillingly cold. He stared in the direction of the sound, then spun around as yet another scream started up in a new direction.

'Why? Why us?' he muttered. His hands clenched on the handrail as if to crush the metal in his grasp. 'What have we done to deserve this? Why are *we* being punished?'

He turned to Eddon. His eyes were glittering and his face was working.

'What's happening to our world?' he demanded. 'We've been peaceful people on P-19. How can this violence come out of us? How can we be the ones to produce this murderousness? Simple farmers raising our crops — that's all we ever wanted. How did we lose control? What did we do wrong?'

He was starting to shout. Although he addressed Eddon, he seemed to be looking through him rather than at him. Eddon stood his ground.

'If metal toxins are the cause, nobody did anything wrong,' he said.

But ev Ghair was deaf and blind to everything except his own passion. His voice rose to a crescendo.

'Is there always something that goes wrong? Some depth of evil buried in the universe? No matter how much you strive to make a better society? Something always waiting to emerge and mock you? Is everyone deep down crazy and evil? Is that it? And the more contented and fortunate you are, the more viciously it takes revenge?'

He was beating with his fists on the handrail. There were tears running down his face. He turned and shouted out into the night, out into the yawning darkness.

'I won't accept it! Never! I don't understand and I won't understand! My planet, my P-19! Why are we cursed? Where's the sense? Where's the justice? Why are we cursed? Why?'

The last 'why?' turned into a kind of howl and trailed off into silence. In the silence another voice could be heard. It was a female voice, coming from somewhere over near the trapdoor.

'Argid? Where are you?'

Then a second female voice joined in.

'Is that Headman ev Ghair? Inspector Brac?'

The speakers were invisible in the darkness, but Eddon recognised the two voices. One belonged to Mairie ev Ghair, the other to Vail ev Vessintor.

'Yes, over here,' he called back.

In a moment they appeared, Mairie leading and Vail following. Vail was almost dancing with excitement, her usual languor completely cast aside.

'I've got the answer!' she cried. 'The problem is solved! I can explain everything!'

She addressed her words equally to Eddon and ev Ghair. But the Headman continued to stare out into the night. There were tears rolling down his cheeks, though his face was as fixed as a mask.

Mairie went across and placed her hand over his hand, over the withered hand gripping the rail. He put an arm around her shoulder.

'Don't stay out here,' she said. 'Let's go down.'

Ev Ghair allowed himself to be turned around and guided back towards the trapdoor.

'She says she's got the answer,' Mairie told him as they went. 'She says she knows the cause of what's been happening.'

Eddon and Vail followed the older pair along the walkway. Eddon spoke in a loud angry whisper.

'What does "got the answer" mean? I've already said it's most probably due to metal toxins.'

'No,' said Vail.

'What?'

'No.'

'How do you know?'

Vail grinned and flicked her hair triumphantly.

'All will be revealed! You'll see! It's the most amazing solution!'

They came up behind Mairie and ev Ghair at the top of the steps. Mairie was helping her husband down through the trapdoor.

Vail nodded towards ev Ghair. 'His idea was closer than yours,' she whispered. 'He was nearer the truth than he ever realised.'

But Eddon wasn't listening. He had suddenly noticed what Vail was carrying in her hand.

'Hey! What's that!?'

'This?' Vail waved the microdot paper casually in the air. 'Oh, a message for me. This was the last bit of evidence I needed. It just came through.'

'Where from?'

'St Alda's Psychoseminary.'

'What!!?'

Mairie and ev Ghair had reached the bottom of the steps. Vail took the opportunity to hurry down after them, disappearing through the trapdoor as Eddon prepared to explode.

Eddon started down after her. His loud whisper grew to a full-throated shout.

'Did you send another request for information? In spite of my explicit order! Did you?'

Vail kept descending the steps, not looking around. Eddon rushed down hot on her heels.

'Answer me!' he yelled over her shoulder. 'Who do you think you are?! What makes you think —!'

He became aware that Mairie and ev Ghair were looking at him. They were standing waiting at the bottom of the steps. Ev Ghair frowned imperiously.

'Not now', he said to Eddon flatly.

Vail moved to join the others. Eddon followed, fuming silently. Ev Ghair turned to address Vail.

'Well. You think you know the cause of the murdering?'

'Yes.'

'And it's not metal toxins accumulating in the brain?'

'No.'

'So what is it?'

'I need everyone gathered together first.'

'Tell me now.'

'I need everyone gathered together first.'

Ev Ghair stared at Vail. Vail stared back.

'There's a reason', she said.

'Who's "everyone"?'

'Everyone in the Big House.'

'That's a lot to ask. Why should I believe you've got the answer?'

'Why shouldn't you? You're desperate. This is your only hope. What have you got to lose?'

Ev Ghair opened his mouth in a sudden savage laugh.

'You're right. What have I got to lose?' He clapped his hands together. 'Very well. We'll gather everyone together in the Old Hall. What about the refugees?'

'Them too.'

Ev Ghair turned and spoke to his wife. 'The East Wing and all the guard rooms, Mairie. Can you look after that?'

Mairie nodded. Ev Ghair turned to Eddon.

'You know the New Wing? Where the Messages Centre and Reeves' quarters are?'

'Yes.'

'Go along the corridors. Knock on every door. Get the Reeves to help you.'

He turned to Vail. But Vail shook her head.

'Sorry,' she said, 'but I need to finalise my theory.' She flourished the message from St. Alda's. 'I only just received this. I still have to write out the final equations.'

Eddon snorted but said nothing.

'Very well,' said ev Ghair. 'I'll look after the rest myself. Everyone to be in the Old Hall, half an hour from now.'

17

The assembled people couldn't all fit into the Old Hall. There were about two hundred packed inside the Hall and another hundred milling around in the lobbies and corridors outside. The air was filled with a continuous murmur of voices and shuffling feet. Everyone was asking questions, telling rumours, exchanging hopes and fears.

Then Vail and ev Ghair appeared in view. They were climbing the wrought iron staircase, ascending the truncated pillar in the centre of the Old Hall. Vail carried a stack of folders under her arm. Sounds of hushing spread out across the Hall, and the murmur died gradually away.

They went up into the pulpit at the top of the pillar, about three metres above the central floor. The pulpit was like a small cup encircled by a balustrade of polished red and gold rock. On one side of the balustrade was a large visi-screen, set up in accordance with Vail's instructions.

Ev Ghair raised an arm, holding his staff high in the air. Tall and white-haired, he looked like a wizard waving a wand.

'This is Vail ev Vessintor,' he announced in his deep ringing voice. 'She thinks she can explain the cause of the murdering. Let us pray that she is right.'

Vail stood forward in the pulpit. She placed her folders on the ledge of the balustrade. Her eyebrows were two inverted golden moons, and an outline of black lipstick extended her mouth to enormous size.

'Yes, I can explain the murdering.' She spoke clearly and slowly, in her characteristic drawl. 'I can also explain the crops growing wrong. But what's really wrong is something much bigger. To understand my theory, you have to understand the total picture. So I'm going to start off with the lengthening nights and increasing darkness on planet P-19.'

She turned to ev Ghair. 'Please. Tell everyone what you were investigating as a cause of the darkness.'

Ev Ghair seemed surprised. He was even more surprised when Vail clicked on the visi-screen and cast up a set of mathematical equations.

'Yes. Mulholland's formula,' he said. 'For calculating what happens when electro-magnetic waves interfere with light waves. Under certain conditions it's possible for the light waves to be deflected and dispersed. I thought that the unusually strong electro-magnetic field of our planet might be somehow blocking off the light from our sun. But I could never get the formula to apply in the right way.'

'Because you didn't know about this.'

Vail switched the visi-screen on to another image: a black and white diagram of intricate superimposed spirals.

'This is a special way of mapping waves,' she explained. 'It's called Claussen geometry. It brings out the superordinate properties of the wave-pattern.'

Ev Ghair stared. 'Pyraxes,' he exclaimed.

'Exactly. The electro-magnetic field of the planet itself doesn't interfere with the light waves. But there's something configured on top of the field. A higher-level pattern on top of the basic electro-magnetic pattern. That's what's blocking off the light from the sun.'

She took a sheet of paper from one of her folders and passed it across to ev Ghair.

'You can check my equations if you like. They all work out.'

Ev Ghair barely glanced at the paper. 'But pyraxes? That's what psychic propensity is founded upon.'

'It is.'

'So how — where —?'

'Hold on. I'll come back to the pyraxes later.'

She switched off the visi-screen and looked out over the audience. She could see Eddon near the front, a clear head and shoulders above the surrounding P-19ers. Beano was standing a little further back.

'Now for the next part of my theory,' she announced. 'For the next part — I call on Flightman Zeno Berrit.'

She swung out an arm and pointed straight at Beano. Beano looked nonplussed.

'Me?'

'Tell everyone about the nightmares you've been having.'

Beano shrank visibly into himself.

'Er, don't. I mean, wow, not now.'

'Your nightmares,' Vail continued remorselessly. 'Don't be ashamed. How many times a night?'

'You know,' muttered Beano. 'You were there.'

'Yes. Five separate nightmares last night. I

recorded the signals in your brain each time. And each time you woke up sweating and shaking. Why?'

'I don't know. I can't remember exactly.'

'But you can remember that your dreams were somehow disgusting and sickening. Abnormal. Isn't that right?'

Beano was in an agony of embarrassment. He looked as though he wanted to disappear into a hole in the ground.

'Don't be ashamed.' Vail lowered her voice dramatically. 'Because everyone in this room is having the same nightmares.'

There was a moment of frozen silence. Ten seconds it lasted, twenty seconds, a minute. The Old Hall was so quiet that faint sounds of thunder could be heard, grumbling faraway in the distance.

'Look at each other!' cried Vail suddenly. 'You all know it already! Only you haven't admitted it! Look each other in the eyes!'

And slowly the P-19ers turned to face one another. Eyes met, heads nodded. There was an almost palpable sense of relaxing tension.

'Yes, it's true!' one voice called out.

'I've had them!'

'Me too!'

It was like a wave breaking. Soon there were voices calling out from every side. A hundred different forms of answer, but all saying the same thing.

'Yes!' Vail raised her voice above the clamour.

'You've all had them! But no-one can remember exactly what they were! Isn't that so?'

Again came the rising chorus of assent, like a second breaking wave.

'All you remember is the horror and abnormality,' said Vail. 'But don't feel guilty. The same nightmares come eventually to everyone on P-19. It's not your fault, you're not responsible.'

The mood in the Old Hall was changing. The P-19ers weren't exactly smiling, but the expression on their faces was no longer so haunted and haggard. They stared up at Vail, eager to hear what she was going to say next.

'Now! Are you ready to hear about the killers?' Vail threw out her arms in a grandiose gesture. She seemed to be enjoying herself.

'Okay. You know how the killers hide their insanity during the day and only reveal themselves at night. You know about the screaming and the white mucus that comes out of their mouths. But do you know about this?'

She clicked an image onto the visi-screen. It was an electrostatic image in shades of ghostly green. She clicked again for another image, then another, then another. They were all very similar, green lines and blotches.

'These are interior head shots of Graem V Craill. A killer we captured in East Lair. The photoscans show the patterns of electrical impulses in his brain, passing through his brain in a typical four-minute period. Now look at these.'

She clicked a new sequence of images onto the visi-screen. The green colour was less intense and the blotches were differently shaped. But there was something undeniably similar about the pattern of the lines.

'You see the similarity? But these are not pho-toscans of a killer. These are interior head shots of Beano Berrit, taken last night in the times when he was having nightmares.'

A gasp ran around the Old Hall. Vail waited to let the idea sink in, then continued.

'Periods of dreaming are REM sleep, when the brain waves take on a distinctive REM pattern. But the patterns here are something entirely different. And it's the same for every one of you — *in the times when you're dreaming those nightmares.*'

Ev Ghair was staring intently at the last image on the visi-screen.

'What about the superordinate level?' he demanded. 'What does it look like in Claussen geometry?'

'Hah!' Vail grinned. 'Got it in one! Here's what the waves in Beano's dreaming brain look like in Claussen geometry.'

She clicked on to another image, all intricate superimposed spirals.

'And here's what the *killer's* brain waves look like in Claussen geometry.'

She clicked on to a further image.

'And, just to remind you, here's the Claussen mapping of the planet's electro-magnetic field.'

She double clicked and returned to the same black and white diagram she'd shown earlier.

Ev Ghair gave a sort of growl and thumped his staff on the floor of the pulpit. There was a rising excitement in his eyes.

'Yes.' Vail nodded. 'The same kind of pyraxes in every case. You can see it just by looking. In the killer's brain, in Beano's dreaming brain, in the planet's electro-magnetic field. Algorithmically they're identical. And what's more —'

She held up her hand for complete attention. 'What's more, these forms all belong to a particular category of pyractic phenomena recognised in psychic science. Let me read a few things out to you.'

She fumbled in one of her folders and drew forth a sheet of microdot paper. It was the message from St Alda's Psychoseminary, the same message she'd been carrying half an hour ago.

'I won't bother you with the mathematical details,' she said. She ran her finger down over the page and began:

'Such continuous symbolic emissions are configured in the form of a polysemous or "wild" pyrax. As higher-order codes they are matched to standard organic codes, but are also able to influence and override them...'

She mumbled and skimmed several lines. Then she nodded and read out another passage:

'The transition from influence to overriding action depends upon constant reinforcement over a long period of time. The effect of an emission is

cumulative and incremental, and may take years before manifesting itself in noticeable symptoms.'

She broke off momentarily and looked up. 'You see how it relates to P-19?'

She skimmed another half page. 'And here's the most important bit. *Being unregulated, a continuous symbolic emission differs from a SPEL or CHARM in that it requires no controlling mental agency. Once the text has been fixed and planted in physical form, it may disseminate its influence without further direction from its originator.'*

She turned to ev Ghair. 'So you see! You were on the right track without ever realising. When you said that this planet was cursed.'

Ev Ghair looked perplexed. 'I said "cursed" because —'

'I know, in the ordinary sense of "cursed". But now I'm telling you that this planet is cursed in a very specific and scientific sense. That is, it's under the influence of a Continuous Un-Regulated Symbolic Emission. C — U — R — S — E. Which spells CURSE.'

The audience gazed up at her, goggling. Ev Ghair knitted his brows, waiting for further explanation.

'And the important thing about *this* kind of CURSE,' said Vail, 'is that it's not something mysterious. It can be understood through the equations of psychic science.'

She clicked and projected an array of equations onto the visi-screen. Strange esoteric hieroglyphs mingled in amongst the ordinary algebraic symbols.

'Let me put it all together and explain it in

simple terms,' she said. 'What we're facing is a prop-agating code that rides on the back of the planet's electro-magnetic field. It has the capacity to over-ride organic codes everywhere on the entire planet. With plants, that means the chemical codes deter-mining patterns of growth. The most vulnerable are the flowers and vegetables and plants with com-plex growth patterns. Lower species like mosses and lichens are too simple to be affected yet. The com-plex plants would be even worse affected except they have a temporary defence mechanism. Cells with warped chemical codes are enveloped in a sticky white liquid that blocks out their distorting messages. But when the warping goes beyond a certain point — well, you all know about plants growing wrong.

'Human beings are more complicated. With us, the distortion of messages doesn't influence growth so much as behaviour. And since all the body's messages are processed through the central nervous system, that's where the attack is focussed. Above all, the code tries to propagate its distorting messages onto the patterns in the brain. And because the brain is mental as well as physical, there's a psychological dimension involved too. The distorting messages have meanings just as the pat-terns in the brain have meanings. In one way, that makes us especially vulnerable.

'However, we have an additional defence mech-anism. On the biological level, we can produce the same white mucus as the plants, we can quarantine brain cells that are going wrong chemically. But on the psychological level, we also have the Unconscious. And that's like a reservoir, a safety tank for holding what the conscious mind can't cope with. Unacceptable and destructive meanings are automatically siphoned off and sent into the Unconscious. It's a sort of quarantining on another level.

'That's why you've all been having nightmares — because the meanings quarantined in the Unconscious rise temporarily to the surface in dream. But the storage tank can only hold so much. Beyond a certain point, the unacceptable meanings break out and overthrow the balance of the mind. What was in the Unconscious takes over. And then those nightmares which you merely glimpse when dreaming turn into the whole world, the only world. The killers are actually living their waking lives inside those nightmares.'

Vail leaned forward against the balustrade of the pulpit, and made a sweeping gesture with her hands.

'So the killers and nightmares and white liquid are all the effects of a CURSE. Incredibly widespread effects from an incredibly powerful CURSE. In fact, I've never heard of a CURSE as powerful as this. There are some features I still don't understand. But I understand enough for what we need.

'A CURSE *must* have a physical source. It works by transmitting signals from an electronically stored program or text. So there must be at least a transmitter containing a text. And the transmitter must have been planted in some specific location.'

She paused for one dramatic moment. Then:

'Find the location. Destroy the transmitter. And the effects of the CURSE will just fade away.'

18

A hubbub of excited discussion filled the Old Hall. Everyone began talking at once.

'What do you think?'

'It sounds so strange.'

'Do you believe her?'

Eddon stared at the equations on the visi-screen. With one half of his mind he wanted to reject Vail's theory. He still hadn't forgiven her for the messages to St Alda's Psychoseminary. And he still hated unintelligible esoteric hieroglyphs. But facts were facts, regardless of personal feelings. He had to admit it: her theory could explain so many things simultaneously. His own hypotheses had fallen a long way short. Some gut instinct told him she was right.

Others were coming to the same conclusion.

'It makes sense.'

'Everything started at the same time.'

'It has to be all connected.'

'Maybe she's right.'

Eddon raised his voice above the hubbub.

'Of course she's right! Let's get on with it! Of course she's right! New start, new problem!'

His vehemence was like a kind of anger. He swivelled to face Vail in the pulpit. She was looking down at him, goggling in amazement.

'Okay, ev Vessintor. So we're searching for a transmitter. How do we find it? Tell us what it looks like!'

The discussion died down all around. Everyone was turning their attention back to Vail. She stopped goggling.

'I don't know exactly,' she said. 'There are so many different ways of storing and transmitting a text. Maybe linked chips, maybe micro-loom, maybe softwiring — some form of network.'

Eddon snapped his fingers. 'How big?'

'I don't see how it could be smaller than, say, a large suitcase. Whatever the technology. The text would have to be incredibly complex for a CURSE as powerful as this.'

'Where should we start looking then?'

'Ah.' Vail pulled a wry face. 'All I know is, the transmitter must be located within the electro-magnetic field in order to superimpose signals on top of it.'

'Meaning, anywhere at all on planet P-19?'

'Yes.'

'But there must be a way of homing in on the transmitter? Can't we use some kind of direction finder?'

Vail shook her head. 'Not possible. The transmitter isn't beaming out any form of wave-energy. It's only re-patterning what already exists in the field.'

371

'But it has to be electrically powered itself, hey? That would give off some traceable effect?'

'I assume it's electrically powered. But remember it works with information. It doesn't need large amounts of electrical power. Just a very low and constant power working away over years and years. I doubt it would give off anything we could trace.'

Eddon snorted. 'So we have to physically search the entire planet for something the size of a large suitcase!'

The P-19ers, so exuberant a minute ago, fell silent as they realised the magnitude of the task. There were downcast looks all around, and grim shakings of the head.

'I'm sorry,' said Vail. 'I'm only an expert in the theory. I don't know how to solve the practical problem.'

'Ah, you don't!' Ev Ghair's staff rapped suddenly on the pulpit floor. 'But I do!'

The Headman stepped to the front of the pulpit. He seemed somehow taller and charged with energy. He scanned the assembled crowd, looking directly into face after face.

'Think about it from the other end!' His voice filled the Old Hall. 'Think about motive! Who would *want* to ruin us with a CURSE?'

It took the P-19ers only a moment. The reply came simultaneously from two dozen throats.

'The Hegemony!'

Ev Ghair swung his staff and brought it down with a crash on the ledge of the balustrade.

'It has to be! The Hegemony! Taking revenge on Independent P-19!'

Ev Ghair turned suddenly to Vail.

'You say this CURSE could have been planted a long time ago?'

'Must've been.'

'Long before the darkening and murders and plants growing wrong?'

Vail shrugged. 'You heard what I read out. About the effect being cumulative over many years, before any symptoms would start to appear.'

'So!' Ev Ghair whirled around to face the audience again. 'It's obvious! We all know the history of our planet! How we humbled the mighty Hegemony! They could never forgive us for that!'

Eddon tried to speak out. 'But wait a minute! That's not right! The Hegemony wants you to come back and rejoin the rest of the galaxy!'

But his voice was swept aside. Ev Ghair was smiling a strange smile, not happy but glittering and exultant.

'Ah, you should have seen them at the end. The Proctor-General and the representatives from the Hegemony. When we met to sign the final Treaty of Accord and Recognisance. How they gritted their teeth to remain polite! The humiliation smouldering inside them! The hatred in their eyes! They'd have done anything to get back at us then!'

Eddon tried again.

'But that's all been forgotten long ago. Why else were we sent to help you? If the Hegemony

373

planned to create serial killers, why would it send us to stop them?'

Ev Ghair pointed at Eddon with his staff.

'And was it likely that you'd be able to help?' he demanded. 'Could anyone have foreseen that you'd be able to solve this mystery?'

'No,' Eddon admitted. 'No, I guess no-one could've known I had some sort of scientific wonderwoman for an assistant.'

'Therefore.' Ev Ghair raised his voice. 'I believe that this CURSE was planted by the forces of the Hegemony before they finally withdrew from our planet. They left something behind that would work by itself, slowly spreading its poison through our world. Well?'

Eddon felt the intensity of his stare almost like a physical blow.

'I suppose it's possible,' he nodded.

Ev Ghair turned towards Vail. 'Well?'

'Mmm-yeah. I can't think who else would have the technical knowhow to construct such a CURSE.'

'The Hegemony!' cried ev Ghair. 'And that tells us where to direct our search! Because if they left this transmitter before making their final withdrawal, there's only one place they could've left it!'

He paused, and one of the P-19ers immediately called out:

'The Old Settlement!'

'Yes! The Old Settlement! Steyne-1! Where we had them besieged at the end of the War of Independence. Eighteen months they were trapped in there. That's when they knew they were beaten. That's when they had time to construct this thing. We don't need to search the whole planet! This thing could only have been left in one place! We search the ruins of Steyne-1!'

A surge of excitement ran through the assembled crowd. People who had been standing outside in the lobbies and corridors pushed forward in through the doors. The Old Hall was packed almost too tight to breathe.

'We need a search party! A huge search party!' Ev Ghair brandished his fist. 'Who'll be in it?'

Every head nodded, every voice responded. There was a roar of assent like a gathering tide.

'The more the better!' cried ev Ghair.

'Independent P-19!' yelled someone at the back of the crowd. The cry was taken up on all sides.

'Independent! Independent! Independent P-19!'

Now everyone was brandishing their fists, repeating the chant. The noise was deafening. But still ev Ghair managed to make himself heard above it all.

'We'll search every inch!' he thundered. 'Take every wall apart! We'll find it! *We'll find it*! WE'LL FIND IT!'

The chant turned into a cheer and the cheer turned into a stamping of feet. Hundreds of feet drummed and pounded on the floor of the Old Hall.

Ev Ghair lifted both arms in the air. Standing just behind him in the pulpit, Vail could feel the immense strength of purpose radiating out of his body. He didn't need the trappings of power, he *was* power. She could understand why the population followed him. She remembered what Beano had said, about how he'd appeared to the rebel forces and given them new belief in themselves, belief in the certainty of ultimate victory. It was more than mere charisma. It was a sort of grand simplicity, an absolute singleness of purpose. She had the feeling that, now he'd found out what to do, there was no force in the universe that could ever deflect him from it.

He lowered his arms. He willed the crowd to silence and the crowd became silent.

'I want all Senior and Junior Leaders to come with me to the Map Room,' he said. 'We'll start the planning immediately. Everyone else, get some rest if you can. The search starts tomorrow morning at dawn. I'll divide you into separate groups, each with a separate area of the ruins to comb. You all know the kind of thing we're looking for.'

Once more he smiled his glittering exultant smile.

'This is our old enemy in a new form! Seventy years ago we beat the Hegemony's troops! Now we'll destroy their CURSE!'

The P-19ers broke into another cheer. Again they began chanting:

'Independent! Independent! Independent P-19!'

PART FIVE
The Old Ruins

1

There was no dawn. By eight-thirty the P-19ers had gathered in their allotted groups, in different parts of the Big House. They stood around talking, peering out into the night, waiting for day to come. But the outside world stayed dark.

There were eleven groups of twenty to twenty-five people, each led by a Senior or Junior Leader. Many people had brought along tools to help in the search: poles, crowbars, cutters and hand-diggers. Each Leader had been given a map marked with the particular area for his or her group to search.

Nine o'clock passed, and nine-thirty, and ten. But still there was no sign of daylight.

People sat cross-legged on the floor or leaned with their backs against the walls. In some groups, they closed their eyes and tried to rest; in others, they studied the map of their own particular search-area; in others again, they shared and ate the scraps of food that they'd brought along in their pockets. Everyone was becoming tense and edgy. There was nothing to say or do.

Vail was in Jaralax's group, along with Beano. Also in the group were Jaralax's younger brother Tulaic, and the two Reeves who'd carried Jaith's body on a stretcher, Clon IV Quidder and Ewart IV Paig. Nine men and eight women made up the rest of the group. They had assembled in a small refectory. Anxiously they gazed out through the one window at the end of the room.

'How could it get so much worse so suddenly?' asked Beano.

'It looks like thundercloud over the sky,' said Tulaic. 'The same as yesterday.'

'There's no wind out there,' put in one of the women. 'The air is absolutely motionless.'

'I wish it would break like an ordinary storm,' said one of the men. 'Pour down and get it over with.'

'Perhaps it isn't an ordinary storm,' said Jaralax.

'It's the static electricity that worries me,' said Vail. 'The air is so highly charged. I don't like the thought of how it might impact on the electro-magnetic field.'

They stared out into the darkness, watching and waiting. Far off in the distance, the lightning cast its intermittent glimmer over the underbelly of the clouds. The thunder grumbled on and on, a little louder than the previous day.

Then around ten-thirty a kind of light showed through. It was a filtered yellowish half-light, coming in at a low angle, casting long shadows. Not so much a daybreak as a dim and eerie twilight.

Eddon was watching from a position just inside the Major Portal. He had been included in the Headman's group, along with twenty-two young men in their twenties. The members of this group carried special tools: heavy vibration-drills, cross-hoists and two-metre-long extractors.

The door of the Major Portal was partly open. Eddon peered out. The feeble light revealed the buildings around the main square in a sort of ghastly yellow.

'There's something very strange about this light,' he said. 'It's almost like thin bands of dark-ness in the air.'

'I can't see anything,' said someone behind him.

'Squint your eyes. It comes and goes. Like hori-zontal shutters.'

'It could be an effect of the interference pat-tern,' commented ev Ghair.

He ordered the house lights switched off inside. Everyone stared out through the open door, pray-ing and hoping for the light to improve. But there was no further improvement.

Instead a faint but unmistakable sound came to their ears.

'Listen!'

It was the distant sound of a killer screaming. Ev Ghair ground his teeth together.

'This is what happens when there's no proper daylight,' he muttered. 'The killers are still active. It's the same as night-time to them.'

Eddon clicked his tongue. 'Then the groups in the search party could come under attack?'

'Yes.' Ev Ghair put his hand to his brow, pondering. 'But how much longer can we wait? This may be all the light we're going to get.'

No-one spoke. Ev Ghair dropped his hand.

'Very well. We'll have to break open the armoury.' He singled out two members of his group. 'Torrey III Peggar and Grion IV Bras. Issue T-guns and pommelguns with full ammunition. There'll be enough T-guns to give out three or four to every group. And share out all the pommelguns we've got.'

Torrey and Grion nodded and hurried off towards the armoury.

It took fifteen minutes to distribute all the guns and ammunition. The search was turning into a military operation. There were grim looks on every face, grim but determined. Everyone understood the implications. If the killers attacked, they wouldn't be driven off easily, even with guns. Eddon remembered Jaith, and the mortal number of wounds he'd managed to survive.

At ten-fifty ev Ghair made the decision to start. The light was not improving, and would probably fade again in another three or four hours. The order to move out was passed around.

One by one the various groups left their places of assembly and marched along the corridors towards the Major Portal. The Big House resounded to the tramp of many feet, and the clanking of tools and guns.

Ev Ghair's group lined up in the lobby by the door. They would be the last to go, travelling by M-rail to the old ruins. For the other ten groups, the three kilometre journey would have to be made on foot.

Words of cheer and encouragement were exchanged as the first group passed through the lobby.

'Independent! Independent! Independent P-19!'

'We'll find this thing! We'll destroy this CURSE!'

There was a brandishing of fists and a waving of tools and guns. The first group marched proudly out through the door, forth into the yellowish half-light. The group's Senior Leader hung back for a moment. He held his hand out to ev Ghair.

It was a repetition of the ritual that Eddon and Vail had observed long ago in the Old Hall. Ev Ghair took the hand between his own two hands and held it clamped for a full thirty seconds.

'That's for luck,' explained one of the young men, in response to Eddon's whispered query. 'I think we're going to need it.'

2

The ten groups marched through the streets of Steyne-2, one following another at about fifty paces' distance. Eyes adjusted rapidly to the half-light, and the houses and buildings were clearly visible. But the impression of thin bands of darkness remained elusive, coming and going like a trick of the retina. The air was still cool from the night.

They passed by the Golgass Market and through a district known as the Uinnards. Here there were many small metalwork shops, and mossy squares with memorial statues. The streets were deserted, but voices called out from windows along the way:

'What's happening?'

'Where are you going?'

When the purpose of the search was explained, several people came out of their houses, carrying tools and offering to help. The offer was willingly accepted, and the new volunteers were distributed in equal numbers among the ten groups.

Beyond the Uinnards, the search party began to encounter barricades across the streets. Strange jumbles of furniture and household objects had been welded into solid walls, sometimes over two metres high. It seemed that whole rows of houses had tried to turn themselves into fortresses. In some places, roads had been dug up to produce huge gaping pits, and massive sheets of metal covered every window and door.

The search party had to wind an erratic course along streets that were not blocked off. There were no voices calling out here. The fear in the air was almost palpable.

Almost unconsciously, the groups fell into military formation, marching in regular ranks with guns pointing outwards. The stillness was oppressive. The rumble of distant thunder no longer seemed so distant. It had become a continuous roll, trundling around and around like the wheels of some mighty machine.

Jaralax's group marched along in ninth position, last but one of the ten groups. Jaralax, Tulaic, Vail and Beano led the way, four abreast at the front of the group. Jaralax and Tulaic carried T-guns and Beano a pommelgun. Vail preferred to rely on the punchgun that Eddon had given her.

By now they were passing through the outskirts of Steyne-2. The houses were starting to thin out and they could glimpse open country ahead. There were fewer and fewer metalled streets, more and more allotment-like fields growing vegetables and root-crops.

Beano sniffed the air. 'What's that smoky smell?'

Vail sniffed too. 'It's everywhere. What's burning?'

'Probably fields that have been set fire to,' said Jaralax. 'Our Headman gave the order to burn any field where the plants are growing wrong.'

His guess proved correct. As they came out from amongst the last rows of houses, they could see scattered plumes of smoke rising up above the cropfields, left and right. Half a dozen separate plumes, half a dozen patches of blackened ground. The smoke formed perfect verticals in the motionless air.

They marched on. The road under their feet changed to loose gravel. It cut across the cropfields, with small paths joining in at the sides. Away to the left, the track of an M-rail ran along the top of an embankment.

By and by the road led them past one of the burning fields. The smell of the smoke grew thicker, catching in their throats and making their eyes water. The field was mostly charred stalks and ash, with just a few spots still smouldering.

Vail stared curiously. It was impossible to tell what plants had originally grown there, but a pattern in the ash seemed to indicate the forms into which they had been distorted. A greyish-black pattern on a greyish-white background, enormously intricate in an odd angular way. Jaralax and Beano kept their eyes averted.

'I wonder if the burning really helps,' murmured Vail.

'The same warped plants will soon re-grow,' said Tulaic.

'The soil's useless,' added Jaralax. 'No-one will ever lay spade to it again.'

They left the burning field behind. They seemed to be marching more quickly, along with all the other groups. The pace had never been slow, but now there was a sort of nervous hurry about it.

'Do you get the feeling of being watched?' asked Beano.

'I do,' said Ewart. He was right behind Beano in the second row.

'I keep thinking I see movements,' said someone else.

'Hard to tell in this light.'

'There's been no screams though. Not since we started out.'

'Doesn't mean they're not there.'

'Maybe they're holding back and waiting.'

They stared suspiciously at the buildings and walled enclosures, standing block-like and solitary amidst the level cropfields. Many of the buildings were sheds or storage barns, with few if any windows. Everything seemed ominous in the yellowish half-light.

The sense of being watched became more and more oppressive. One young man suddenly hoisted his gun to his shoulder and took aim. But he didn't fire.

'I thought I saw someone over there in that drainage ditch,' he said. 'The top of someone's head.'

The same thing happened several times again as they continued along the road. People lifted their guns to shoot, then lowered them without firing.

'It's all in our imagination,' said Jaralax. 'Because of the rumours.'

'It's not just rumour,' objected one of the women. 'The killers are gathering in secret places — that's a fact.'

'Out on the moss-moors, yes.'

'Closer. There's been definite sightings in the cropfields.'

'Okay. But still not this close to Steyne-2.'

'How do you know how far they've come? They're getting closer all the time. When's the last you heard?'

Jaralax shrugged and turned to Vail. 'What do you think?'

'I don't know. I doubt they'd be gathering this close yet. How much further do we have to go?'

'Not much.' Jaralax pointed ahead. 'There! You can just see the ruins now.'

Everyone looked where he pointed. The impression of obscuring bands of darkness was stronger than ever. They rubbed their eyes and saw vague looming outlines ahead.

'That's the central cluster of towers,' said Jaralax. 'The rest of Steyne-1 has mostly collapsed. Even the central towers are only empty shells of the original buildings.'

'Tall, aren't they?' remarked Beano. 'For P-19, I mean.'

'Because they're Hegemony buildings,' explained Jaralax. 'They insisted on constructing everything up high in those days.'

The towers came gradually clearer as they approached. Though badly ruined, with yawning holes and fallen bits of wall, they still showed the typical stepped-crown effect of Hegemony architecture. Also visible were the rows of diamond-shaped windows interspersed with diamond-shaped panels of microplastic. There were even patches of pastel colour remaining on the microplastic — bright pinks and blues.

Vail grimaced. So slick and superficial! She had forgotten how much she disliked the Hegemony style of architecture. She far preferred the heavy moulded metal and rich sombre hues of the P-19ers' own style. Hegemony buildings looked completely out of place on this planet.

Jaralax was studying his map.

'Our area to search is on the left,' he announced. 'What used to be the workers' dormitory area.'

A little further on, the cropfields came to an end. The ground around the ruins was covered in a thick carpet of moss. The road altered too, suddenly broader and surfaced with interlocking blocks of carbon compound. This was a road in the Hegemony manner, but so worn by time and weather that the blocks were buckled and gaping with cracks.

Up ahead, the separate groups of the search party had started to veer off towards their own particular search-areas. Jaralax consulted his map again, and called out over his shoulder:

'This is where we turn off to the left!'

He led them off the road and across the moss. There was no track to follow. They marched along parallel to the line of the central towers. Now other, lower ruins came into view: broken shafts and bits of machinery and crumbled remains of walls.

'Looks like the perfect place to plant a CURSE,' commented Vail. 'No-one ever normally comes here, right?'

'That's right,' said Jaralax. 'No-one visits the old ruins. Even children keep away. There could be something the size of fifty suitcases hidden here, and no-one would ever have found it.'

He pulled fiercely at his moustache. 'But we're sure as hell going to find it now!'

Vail nodded and said nothing.

Ev Ghair's group came towards Steyne-1 from the opposite side, dismounting from the M-rail where it made its nearest approach to the ruins. This group had no area of their own to search. It would be their task to move around and tackle the most difficult lifting and shifting jobs for the other groups.

They walked along, almost staggering under the weight of their special tools. Eddon carried one end of a massive cross-hoist. Ev Ghair led the way, leaning on his staff.

'Steyne-1 was built in the standard radiating Hegemony pattern,' he told them. 'Administration in the centre, workshops to the east, workers' quarters south, scientists' quarters and laboratories west, storage and warehouses north. Completely planned and completely regular. Everyone told where to go and what to do.'

'Doesn't look very regular now,' commented the man on the other end of Eddon's cross-hoist.

'Standard settlements were designed to be

compact and self-contained,' ev Ghair went on. 'The total ground area of Steyne-1 is only half of one square kilometre. Living in here you hardly even knew you were on a strange planet. Especially since all the materials were shipped in from other parts of the Hegemony.'

He pointed contemptuously with his staff. 'Look at it! Microplastic. Orio-glass. Fibre steel. Even the metals they brought in from outside!'

He led them towards the area that had once been the scientists' living quarters.

'We'll work round in order,' he said. 'Starting with Group One.'

Nothing of the scientists' living quarters remained standing. There was only a deep litter of broken glass, shattered microplastic and small chunks of concrete. Here and there odd shapes protruded: a chromium coil, the plastic hood of an auto-server, a curve of white-alloy that might have been a bedhead.

Still it was possible to distinguish the rectangles of different rooms, marked by the sealing lines of long-disintegrated walls. Ev Ghair stooped and studied them as he walked.

'Ah! This used to be the canteen!' he exclaimed. 'The canteen here and the buzz-lounge straight ahead. And over to the right —' He waved his staff at a more distant stretch of rubble. 'Over to the right, the Van Hass Units. Used to be seven storeys high, would you believe!'

He laughed a brief humourless laugh.

'That's where I lived when I first came to Steyne-1. Twenty-one years old. Seventy-four years ago. I thought it was so luxurious, six rooms to myself, all the latest appliances. And it *was* luxurious, compared to the workers' quarters. But nothing compared to the Governor's own rooms, of course.'

They walked on over the litter, picking their way carefully, balancing and teetering with the heavy tools in their arms. Glass and plastic crunched and popped under their feet.

The men and women of Group One were spread out in a line, three metres apart from one another. They were advancing systematically across the ground, probing down through the debris with long poles and bars. They kept right on working as ev Ghair and his group approached. But the group's Senior Leader broke away and came across.

'Well, Jervis?'

'Nothing so far.'

'You're checking below the surface?'

'Of course. We'll need help with a few concrete slabs though.'

Jervis led ev Ghair and his group around the site. He indicated three huge slabs of concrete half-buried in the ground.

'Could be a hiding-place underneath.'

Ev Ghair's group divided into three teams. First they used vibration-drills to crack the concrete into smaller segments, then extractors to hollow out the surrounding ground, then cross-hoists to lever the segments aside.

After about ten minutes there was a sudden shout.

'Something here!'

Everyone hurried up to look. It was a rounded black box, nearly a metre square, marked with red lettering and warning signs.

But ev Ghair shook his head. 'I don't think so. That's a sensi-feel projector. Break it open.'

Three vibration-drills set to work. After a few minutes the upper side of the box caved in. Inside was a mass of tiny silvery-iridescent hemispheres.

'And there are the sensi-feel discs,' said ev Ghair. 'Just a form of relaxation for bored Hegemony colonists.'

People shrugged off their disappointment and went back to their own jobs. There were no further discoveries. Ev Ghair's group finished digging out the three concrete slabs. Then they shouldered their special tools and moved on to the next area.

Group Two were searching through what had once been the settlement's workshops and manufacturing plant. Here stumps of metal pylons still rose up from the ground. Sheets of duralumin roofing lay scattered about, interspersed with fallen twisted girders of every shape and size. There were even various recognisable items of machinery: a length of conveyor belt with rollers, a set of liquid hydrogen cylinders, a scattering of cogs and wheels from a gearing system.

Ev Ghair's party had to duck and weave their

way over and around numerous obstacles. Eddon was surprised at the sheer extent of the plant.

'What sort of manufacturing went on here?' he asked.

'Military,' said ev Ghair. 'You know the old Governor was planning to attack the Anti-Human?'

'Yeah.'

'This is where his attack fleet was being prepared. Thirteen spacecraft. God knows how he got hold of them. Wheeling and dealing with other planets probably. He acquired them as ordinary transport craft, then had them fitted out here with military hardware and weaponry. I don't think even the Hegemony realised half of what he was up to.'

'But they must've known he planned to attack the Anti-Human.'

'Maybe. But the Anti-Human wasn't a big thing in those days. No-one understood much about it, no-one took it so seriously. The patch beyond Walder-J was one of the first discovered.'

'But still. How did he expect to overcome it?'

'Atomics and firepower. The usual way.' Ev Ghair gave a sort of growl. 'It must've seemed like the answer to his prayers. He was a professional soldier through and through. Never cut out to be the Governor of a peaceful planet like P-19. Military action was his life. The discovery of the Anti-Human gave him what he always wanted — an enemy to fight. He became completely obsessed by it.'

The men and women of Group Two were busy lifting girders and dragging aside sheets of duralumin.

A female Junior Leader was in charge. She took ev Ghair across to a collection of objects that the group had already unearthed. There were bulb-headed tanks, moulded metal blocks, solid-state cabinets with trailing wires and filaments. All larger than a large suitcase.

'This is what we've found,' she said. 'Could anything here be the source of the CURSE?'

Ev Ghair went along from object to object, tapping each one with his staff.

'No ... no ... only an axle-drum ... only a hot-presser ... no ... no. These are all bits of industrial machinery.'

'Just wanted to be sure. All right, the search continues.'

She indicated a number of jobs where assistance was needed. Ev Ghair's group set to work with their vibration-drills, cross-hoists and extractors. Some of the girders were so massive that only the entire group working as a single team could lift them. Others were bolted together and had to be cut apart before they could be moved.

This time it took the group over forty minutes to accomplish all their tasks. Then they proceeded on to Group Three. Group Three's search-area was in the central administration zone, covering four of the eight towers.

'The Michel Tower,' said ev Ghair, pointing. 'The Andervise Tower. The Illerman Tower. The Tower of Ness.'

Viewed close up, the gutted hollow state of the

towers was plain to see. There was nothing but sky behind their gaping windows. Not one building had all its walls intact; some revealed themselves as mere two-dimensional facades. It was only the strength of their tensed alloy frames that kept them upright.

'The Tower of Ness is where we met and negotiated with the Proctor-General,' said ev Ghair. 'After the old Governor had been deposed.'

'Who's "we"?' asked Eddon.

'The scientists and researchers. Not the ordinary settlers, they weren't included. You see that set of rainbow-glass windows? Three storeys up?'

Eddon nodded.

'The Oblong Room. That's the room where the negotiations took place. That's where we agreed to change sides and swap over to the Hegemony.'

'*You* agreed? Yourself?'

'Not me individually, no. I tried to insist on proper terms. But the others weren't interested. There was no fight in them. They just wanted a quiet life. They didn't care about P-19, once their own demands had been met.'

'They sold us out!' cried one of the men in the group angrily.

'The traitors!' cried someone else.

'Ah, the rational scientific spirit betrayed you,' said ev Ghair. 'They didn't understand the importance of what was happening here. No feelings. No vision. They never understood the special destiny of P-19.'

'Independent P-19!'

'We drove the lot of them out!'

They came up to the walls of the Tower of Ness, and passed in through a jagged hole like an archway. Inside, the shadows were longer and darker, and every sound magnified by a thousand echoes. The walls seemed taller too, looming high overhead as if leaning inwards and already starting to topple. Looking up, one could see the stumps and roots of collapsed floors rising level by level like horizontal scars. A section of staircase hung and dangled by a metal thread thirty metres above the ground.

The men and women of Group Three were digging away in the foundations. The group's Junior Leader shook his head in response to ev Ghair's query.

'No, nothing yet. We've finished going through the Andervise Tower and we're half way through here.'

He pointed up at the broken walls.

'Do you want us to check *inside* the walls? They're mostly no more than twenty centimetres thick. Is that enough to hide this thing we're looking for?'

'Probably not.' Ev Ghair looked thoughtful. 'It wouldn't have been hidden high up anyway. They'd've known the walls would fall down sooner or later. Maybe if you check around at the base. Tap on the walls low down and listen for any hollowness.'

'Okay.'

'You're sure you haven't missed anything in the foundations?'

'Totally sure. It's all either polypore honeycomb or solid alloy. We've been slicing though the honeycomb, down to the underlying rock.'

Group Three needed no helping out with special tools, so ev Ghair and his band moved on to Group Four. Group Four was searching the other towers in the other half of the central administration zone. Ev Ghair and his band met up with them in the ruined Tower of Arx.

The Leader of the group was full of excitement. The group had just unearthed two huge canisters covered with dials and switches. But when ev Ghair inspected them, he recognised them immediately.

'No, those are old-fashioned optonomic registers,' he said.

The Leader's face fell. 'We'll have finished searching everywhere in about another hour.'

'Then start from the beginning again,' said ev Ghair grimly.

So it continued. Ev Ghair's group passed on to Group Five, then on to Group Six, Group Seven and Group Eight. Some of the groups needed little assistance, others needed a great deal. It took almost an hour to clear away the fallen concrete pillars that littered Group Seven's search-area. But none of the groups had found anything that might have been a transmitter — none of the groups had found the source of the CURSE.

It was three hours after the start of the search

when ev Ghair's group came around to Jaralax's group, Group Nine. That was when the mysterious sounds began.

4

'Did you hear anything?' asked Vail.

'No,' said Ernish III Stoer. 'What sort of thing?'

'I don't know. There it goes again!'

'I hear it!' cried Ernish's wife, Guenna.

They were down on their knees in a powder of pulverised concrete, asbestos and glass. In the workers' dormitory area, only the walls were still standing. The pulverised material lay spread like drifted sand between the walls. The whole area was a maze of roofless rooms and gaping doorways.

There were five people altogether in this particular room. They were sifting with their hands through the pulverised material. The other eighteen members of Group Nine were spread out through similar rooms nearby.

Vail and Guenna rose to their feet. A light wind was starting to blow. Sudden small flurries whisked hither and thither. It was like the forewarning of a storm.

'Maybe we're imagining sounds in the wind?' Guenna suggested.

Vail shook her head. 'What do you hear?'

'A sort of dull moaning.'

'Same here. And a sort of singing, like bass voices in a choir?'

'Yes.'

Then Ernish got up off his knees. 'Now I can hear it too!' he exclaimed. 'Who's doing it?'

'It's not close.'

'Where is it?'

'I think it's up there!' cried Guenna, raising her arm. 'Up in the sky!'

Now everyone was on their feet. They stared upwards, straining to hear. The sounds were growing louder all the time.

'Where?'

'There!'

'No, over there!'

'There's more than one!'

'Dozens!'

'They're moving across the sky! They're moving through the air!'

Fingers pointed this way and that. The disembodied sounds were criss-crossing in every direction. They seemed to be coming from a height just below the base of the overhanging thundercloud.

'There's a sort of deep breathing!'

'And a hammer beating!'

'Do you hear a tolling of bells?'

'I can hear a sound like heavy wheels!'

There was an edge of panic in their shouting. Vail lifted her voice to be heard:

'Listen! This is what we thought was thunder! It sounded like thunder when it was in the distance!

Now it's directly on top of us!'

But no-one was paying attention. Every face was turned up to the sky. Eyes flicked from side to side as they followed the sounds passing over.

Vail pulled a face. What could she say anyway? She didn't understand what was happening either.

She walked away from the shouting and gesturing. She wanted to listen to the sounds without distraction. She focussed on the disembodied singing, the deep bass choir. Like all the sounds, it was somehow unpleasant and disturbing. There seemed to be words in it — but not proper words, not proper language. The more she focussed, the more she heard only an inarticulate parody of language. Mere garbled, mangled syllables.

She walked slowly to the far end of the room and came to a gaping doorway in the wall. She leaned in the doorway, pondering possibilities.

These disembodied sounds had no place in her theory. And yet she was sure they must be related to the CURSE. But how? This wasn't like any ordinary CURSE. Perhaps...

Meanwhile Ernish and Guenna and the two others had come to a decision.

'We can't keep searching now!'

'Let's get back with the rest of the group!'

'Let's find Jaralax!'

Vail looked up and realised that they were heading off in the other direction. Her train of thought was broken. She shrugged and decided she might as well go and talk to Jaralax herself.

But even as she turned to follow, she caught a sudden flash of movement out of the corner of her eye. Someone behind her! She spun round. There was a woman running across the empty room on the other side of the doorway.

'Hey!'

But already the woman was vanishing through a further exit. Vail's cry seemed to have no effect upon her.

Vail frowned. Although she'd caught only a glimpse from behind, the woman reminded her of someone in Group Nine, a woman called Arriga IV Isgort. But what was she doing? Why was she running through the empty rooms?

Vail plunged through the doorway and gave chase.

'Hey!' she shouted again.

She came to the further exit just in time to see the woman take a turn to the left. Vail followed her into a kind of roofless corridor. Then a turn to the right. Now they were zigzagging through a maze of cubicles.

Vail couldn't catch up. The woman was always disappearing around corners ahead of her. Vail came out of the cubicles and into a wide circular space with numerous doorways. Too late. The woman had disappeared altogether. There was no telling by which doorway she'd left.

Vail slowed to a halt. What was she chasing for anyway? She was about to turn back when she caught sight someone moving in a room to the left.

Not one but *two* women. Arriga IV Isgort and another, much older woman. Arriga carried a cutter under her arm, the older woman carried a long pole.

They were standing motionless in the centre of the room. But they swung around when Vail entered.

There was a moment of silence. The sounds in the sky seemed louder than ever: singings, groanings, thuddings, and now also a kind of gurgling.

'What're you doing here?' Vail demanded.

The two women looked at the ground and said nothing. Vail turned to Arriga.

'Why were you running?'

The answer came in a dull flat voice. 'Because of the sounds.'

'You were running away from the sounds? You panicked?'

But even as she spoke, Vail had the feeling that that wasn't the reason. She turned to the older woman.

'What about you?'

'Trisla II Hullion.'

'Are you with the search party?'

'Group Five.'

The two women moved apart, Trisla to the left and Arriga to the right. They began coming around closer to Vail.

'Do *you* know what the sounds are?' Trisla asked. Her voice was similarly dull and flat.

'Perhaps. I think —'

'Listen!' said Arriga, interrupting.

Now there was a sound of roaring on top of all the other sounds. The wind was rising. Fierce gusts of air blew across the tops of the walls. Overhead, the dark base of the thundercloud was churning and boiling with extraordinary violence.

'The storm is coming,' said Arriga.

The two women had circled around until they were facing Vail from opposite sides. Vail had to keep turning her head to keep them both in view.

She was beginning to have a bad feeling in the pit of her stomach. She put her hand in the pocket of her vannamak and took a grip on her punchgun. She checked with her finger that the setting was on lethal.

'You ought to go back to your groups,' she said. 'If there's a storm, ev Ghair may order a retreat.'

Arriga suddenly swung her cutter up high in the air.

'The storm is coming,' she repeated.

She advanced upon Vail, waving the cutter over her head like a sword. Vail was momentarily frozen. The cutter was raised and ready to come down —

'Stop!' cried Vail, and simultaneously pulled the trigger. Without aiming, without taking the gun from her pocket, she fired a single shot through the material of her vannamak. The projectile hit Arriga in the neck.

The cutter dropped to the ground. Arriga rolled her eyes and fell forward. She hit the ground with a loud thump.

Vail drew the punchgun out of her pocket and spun around to face Trisla.

But the older woman hadn't moved. There was nothing aggressive about her stance or the way she carried her pole. She stared at Vail.

'What have you done?'

Arriga lay motionless, face down on the ground. A cloud of powdery dust settled slowly around her.

A dreadful doubt flooded Vail's mind.

'I thought...'

'You've killed her.'

'I thought she'd turned.'

'Turned?'

'You know. Gone insane. I thought she'd become a killer.'

'Arriga become a killer?'

Vail bit her lip. 'That's what I thought.'

Trisla pointed her arm accusingly. 'You are the only killer around here!'

'Then why did she lift the cutter up over her head?'

'You shot her because of that?'

'It was an instant reaction.'

'Did you see white stuff coming out of her mouth? Did she scream? Did you see any evidence?'

Vail shook her head unhappily.

'Maybe she's not dead,' she said. 'There are special forms of healing I can do.'

She knelt down beside the sprawled-out body.

There was a gaping exit-hole at the back of the young woman's neck.

Trisla came padding across. Vail put down her punchgun and took hold of Arriga's wrist. She felt for a pulse.

'Ah, I think I can feel something,' she said.

Trisla's pole whirled and struck Vail a smashing blow across the head. In the same moment, Arriga twisted over and sprang up from the ground. She seized the punchgun with one hand and Vail's left arm with the other.

Now the white stuff came pouring out of their mouths, spilling down over their chins. They were both snarling.

5

Ev Ghair and Jaralax were in deep discussion at one side of the room. Everyone else stood around waiting: the members of Group Nine and the members of ev Ghair's 'special tools' group. No-one was even pretending to work any more. They talked together in low nervous voices, glancing repeatedly up at the sky.

Eddon stood with Torrey III Peggar and Grion IV Bras. Beano went across to speak to them.

'Do you think he'll call off the search?' he asked, nodding towards ev Ghair.

'Not until he has to,' said Eddon.

'Have you nearly finished here?' asked Torrey.

'Long ago,' said Beano. 'We're just going back through some of the rooms we've done once already.'

'Same story everywhere,' commented Eddon. 'There's nothing going to be found now.'

'The search is as good as over,' said Grion.

They looked up as a particularly strange sound passed across the sky: an ominous throbbing chant. They followed it across with their eyes. Another sound like a rattle passed across in the opposite direction.

'I wonder if Vail could explain it?' said Beano.

Eddon scowled. 'Where is she? Isn't she with this group?'

'She was working in one of the rooms through there.' Beano turned and pointed. 'Through that doorway there.'

'Hnh. I'll go find her. I want to hear how she explains *this*.'

Eddon had to raise his voice as the roar of the wind intensified. It was turning into a gale. People clutched at their flapping vannamaks, pulled their hoods up over their streaming hair.

'Not the first room, the next room beyond,' shouted Beano.

Eddon nodded and strode off.

He passed through the doorway and into the first room. The room was empty.

A sense of alarm registered at the back of his mind. Obviously most of Group Nine was already congregated in the room with Jaralax . . .

He hurried through the second doorway. The next room was also empty. Where the hell was she?

'Ev Vessintor!' He cupped his hands and called. 'Vail ev Vessintor!'

There were so many sounds flying around in the air, he couldn't be sure if he'd heard a reply. But he was suddenly very certain that she was in trouble. He set off running.

'Vail?' he called out. 'Where are you?'

He ran through the doorway at the far end of the room and entered a kind of roofless corridor. He couldn't have said what guided his choice of direction. He turned to the right and came to a maze of cubicles.

'Mmm-aaaaagh!'

It was a long drawn-out choking cry.

He raced through the cubicles and emerged into a wide circular space with numerous doorways. The choking cry turned into a moan of agony. Eddon cursed and pulled out his punchgun.

The moan was coming from one particular room. He swung in through the doorway, then halted, hardly able to believe his eyes.

Vail was stretched out horizontal, in mid-air. Two women were tugging at her in opposite directions. An older woman gripped her by the ankles, a younger one had hold of her wrists. They seemed to be trying to pull her apart.

Eddon aimed and fired. The first projectile ripped through the old woman's cheek. The second caught the young woman in the back of the skull.

They dropped their victim and turned to face him. The look in their eyes was completely inhuman.

The old woman snarled and advanced to attack. Eddon backed away, loosing off shot after shot. The projectiles shattered her forehead and smashed through her eyes.

Still she tottered forward. But she could no longer see. She lifted her arms blindly in front of her face. Eddon eluded her with two quick side-wards steps.

'Look out!' came a gasping cry from Vail.

Eddon whirled around, saw the danger. The young woman had moved across to pick up Vail's punchgun, which had been lying on the ground. Now she had it in her hand, now she was pointing it at him.

He flung himself to one side as she fired. The projectile whizzed harmlessly past. He landed full length on the soft powdery ground.

But already she was taking fresh aim. There was no time to regain his feet. He rolled over, dodging another projectile. The doorway through which he had entered was behind him. He did a backflip that carried him right out of the room.

The young woman didn't attempt to follow. She stood in the centre of the room with the punchgun in her hand. She looked at Vail, spreadeagled on her back.

Vail struggled to move but her limbs wouldn't respond. Where had Eddon got to?

A great slobber of viscous liquid disgorged from

the young woman's mouth. Dripping a white trail, she bent down towards her victim.

Then Eddon re-appeared. He had circled around to a different doorway on the opposite side of the room. First, the snout of his punchgun poked out around the side of the wall; then his left eye, taking careful aim. The young woman bending over Vail had her back to him.

There was a single shot followed by a sharp metallic ping. The projectile struck the punchgun in the young woman's hand, sending it spinning through the air. Eddon darted instantly into the room. He ran and swooped and plucked up the gun almost before it touched the ground.

Then he turned on the young woman, firing with both guns. She lunged across the room towards him. But the sheer number of projectiles brought her down. Chips of bone and strips of flesh flew from her head in all directions. Her forward rush petered out, and she sank down onto her knees.

'You okay?' Eddon called out to Vail, without taking his eyes from the killer.

Vail made an okay-sounding noise.

Eddon stood over the killer and poured in another dozen shots, destroying the skull completely. He prodded the young woman with the toe of his boot and she keeled over like a slowly toppling tower. All that remained of her head was a red mass of pulp.

Then he spotted the cutter lying nearby on the ground. He pocketed the two punchguns and picked up the cutter. He set the cutter-blades whirring and applied them to the side of the young woman's neck. She twitched and writhed as he sawed clean through the top of her spinal column. Then the twitching stopped.

He turned and went across to where the old woman was still perambulating blindly around. She was rotating in circles like a clockwork toy. He swung the cutter and felled her to ground with a single blow.

Then he repeated the operation with the cutter-blades. It took less than a minute. He wiped the spattered blood from his boots and went over to Vail in the centre of the room.

She hadn't moved from her position on the ground. There was something odd and twisted about the way she was lying. He squatted down on his heels beside her.

'What's wrong with you?'

But Vail was staring fixedly up at the sky.

'I think the storm's about to break,' she said.

6

The storm broke simultaneously all across the sky. It was as if some kind of charge had built up to bursting point. Lines of colour sluiced down towards the ground.

There were shouts of warning and cries of dismay.

The members of Group Nine and the 'special tools' group held their hands up over their heads.

It wasn't rain and it wasn't lightning. It was colour — slanting vertical lines of colour. It was like watching the air open up in thin seams, unzipping all the way from the sky to the ground. And in the seams — strange lurid colours, coiling shapes of blood-red, purple, yellowy-green. But only for a moment: then the seams sealed over again.

At first there were just a few, then dozens, then hundreds. More and more colours, pouring down out of the sky. Now bluey-blacks appeared, and mottled browns, and greys streaked with white. An infinite variety of colours — but always lurid, glistening, somehow disgusting. It was like looking into the depths of a wound, like a momentary glimpse of entrails.

'Yiii!'

'What are they?'

'Keep down!'

'Come over here!'

The men and women in the workers' dormitory area ducked and jumped and jinked as though being shot at. Many ran for the walls, flattening themselves into corners, crouching and cowering. But the walls offered little protection when the lines of colour came slanting down in different directions.

More and more colours: violet, orange and rust, livid lime green. People yelled and shrieked with horror as the colours touched them.

'Aghhh!'

'Watch out!'

'I can't —'

'No!'

Beano jinked and jumped like everyone else. Even Jaralax was hopping from side to side. Only ev Ghair didn't move. His white hair blew in the wind like an aureole round his head.

'Stay calm!' he thundered.

He dropped his staff and reached out for the two men nearest him. He clamped a hand over their shoulders and held them immobile.

'Don't lose control!'

But the seams of colour were too terrifying. His words couldn't quell the rising hysteria. He released the shoulders of the two men and strode to the centre of the room.

'WATCH THIS!' he called out.

He held both arms high in the air. The veins stood out on his forehead. There was an air of tremendous determination about him. He commanded attention in spite of the panic.

A seam of colour struck him, passed through him. He didn't flinch. A line of clotted red and black opened up through his body, vertically from head to toe. There was a gasp from every throat.

Then the seam was gone. Ev Ghair still stood there, unharmed.

'You see?' he shouted.

Another seam came down through his right arm and shoulder. For a moment it looked as though he was splitting apart, in a haemorrhage of yellows and browns. Then the seam passed, and his body returned to normal.

'Nothing to fear! These things can't hurt us!'

He lowered his arms. There were beads of sweat on his face.

Jaralax was the first to step up and stand beside him. Then Beano. They stood steady and upright, refusing to duck or dodge. A seam of colour passed down the side of Jaralax's body, but he didn't move a muscle.

Tulaic joined them, then Torrey and Grion. The mood of hysteria was starting to subside. People moved out from the shelter of the walls, stopped holding their hands over their heads.

'Come and stand with me!' called ev Ghair. 'Everyone. Gather around!'

Gradually everyone congregated in the centre of the room. There was an occasional gasp when someone was struck by a seam of colour. But there was no wavering. On every face was a look of grim determination.

'The search is finished!' ev Ghair announced. 'We can't continue in this. We return to Steyne-2.'

Heads nodded. Someone picked up ev Ghair's staff and handed it to him.

'Now. I need nine volunteers to carry that message to the other groups. Who —'

There was an immediate raising of hands. Everyone was willing.

'Good. Okay. Grion — to Group Ten. Ernish — to

414

Group Eight. Wandel — to Group Seven..!

One by one he detailed messengers for each of the other nine groups.

'All groups to rendezvous on the old roadway outside the ruins. Tell them we'll be there and waiting.'

The nine messengers hurried off. Ev Ghair pointed his staff in the direction of the old roadway.

'We retreat,' he declared. 'But we retreat in good order.'

Eddon and Vail watched in awe as the seams of colour poured endlessly down. Vail was still on her back, Eddon still squatting beside her.

From the very beginning the seams had struck and passed through them. They knew there was no actual physical effect. But the livid glistening colours made them shudder and feel sick.

'What the hell are they?' asked Eddon.

'I can only guess.'

'So guess.'

'Psychic manifestations.'

'Manifestations?'

'Like the sounds in the sky. I think they're both manifestations of the same thing.'

'What thing?'

'A nightmare.'

'Come again?'

'The visual and auditory manifestations of a nightmare. Or many nightmares.'

'I don't understand.'

'Do you remember what I said about nightmares in the Old Hall?'

'Everyone was having them. People become killers when the nightmares take over.'

'Correct. And the nightmares are generated by signals transmitted on top of the planet's own electro-magnetic field.'

'A code, you said.'

'Yeah, well now it's become something more than a code. Now the signals are realising themselves objectively, in images and sounds. The nightmares are being actually displayed in mid-air.'

'Like a holo-film projection!'

'Something like. But you can only glimpse them in compressed form.'

'Yeah. The colours are sort of coiled up. You can't look at them properly.'

'And the sounds are folded up so you can't hear them properly.'

Eddon stared as a seam of colour passed down through Vail's left foot, turning it momentarily black and brown.

'You never said this was going to happen.'

'I never knew it was going to happen. The CURSE has built up to something totally new. These effects don't equate with any psychic phenomena I ever heard of.'

'But it's still part of the CURSE?'

Vail frowned. 'I must've missed something. I don't know what.'

'Will it last long?'

Vail gave a shrug, lying on her back. The movement made her wince.

Eddon looked at her with sudden concern.

'What's wrong with you?'

'My back is wrenched out of joint. Those killers were pulling me apart.'

'Do you think you can walk?'

'I can't do anything. I can't even sit up.'

'Hmm.'

They fell silent for a while. Eddon gazed at the descending colours of the nightmare. Vail pondered with half-closed eyes.

The wind continued to surge and swirl and roar. It drove erratically in every direction, like the sounds criss-crossing erratically in the air. Now it was starting to beat up particles of loose powder from the ground.

Eddon sneezed. He rose to his feet.

'I'll have to go find help,' he said. 'See if there's anyone still around.'

Vail opened her eyes. 'I doubt it.'

'I won't be long. You —' He stopped in mid-sentence, hearing a new noise. Even above the sounds in the air, even above the roaring of the wind. 'What's that?'

'What's what?'

'That. Screaming!'

They froze. It was like a tidal wave of scream-ing. A wave that spread all the way from side to side ...

'Killers!'

'Hundreds and hundreds of them!'

'Hordes!'

'Like a battlefront! Advancing in a line!'

'Must be a kilometre wide!'

Eddon clenched his fists. 'We can't fight them.'

'I can't move.'

'I'll support you.'

'Impossible.'

'We've got to get out of here!'

'You go. Leave me my punchgun.'

'Don't be stupid.' Eddon looked around in des-peration. 'We'll have to hide.'

'How? Where?'

Eddon snapped his fingers. 'I'll bury you. Cover you up with powder.'

'And you?'

'The same.'

He stood listening for a moment. The line of killers had already entered the ruins of Steyne-1.

'We'll do it in that corner over there.'

The wind was now whipping up long streamers of white dust from the ground. The air was thick with murk. Eddon ran to the corner and dropped on his knees. Frantically he began digging, scooping out handfuls of pulverised material. He made two hollows in the soft sifted ground.

The tidal wave of screaming came steadily

closer. The killers seemed to be combing through every part of the ruins.

Eddon returned to Vail. He seized hold of her feet and dragged her across to the corner. Her face went rigid as she struggled to shut out the pain. He manoeuvred her into her hollow. Then he began heaping powder and debris on top of her.

Still the wind intensified, obscuring everything in a white duststorm. Fiercer and fiercer it blew, as if in sympathy with the approaching killers. But Eddon smiled grimly to himself. The obscurity was to their own advantage. It would help to screen them from the killers' eyes.

He finished covering Vail up. She lay outstretched and motionless, with just her eyes and nose showing above the level of the ground. Then he threw himself into his own hollow.

He piled granulated concrete and asbestos over his feet and legs. Lying flat on his back, he pulled more debris over his chest. It was like being sealed in a tomb.

The killers were almost upon them. Now he could hear individual screams — the screams of the killers in the nearest part of the battlefront. He wondered how many of them would pass through this particular room.

He wriggled his arms and head and shoulders deeper down into the loose ground. Only his face remained out in the open. He rolled his eyes towards the opening at the far end of the room.

Suddenly there they were. One by one they

entered, looming grey silhouettes in the opaque duststorm. They looked strangely bowed as they pushed forward against the wind.

He counted: one, two, three, four, five, six of them. They spread out in a line and advanced methodically across the room. Their screaming was a paean of hate and triumph.

Eddon followed them with his eyes. He didn't dare shift the position of his head in the ground. They turned and scanned from side to side as they advanced. They looked into the corner where Eddon and Vail were hiding — but saw nothing.

They saw something else however. In the middle of the line, one of the killers suddenly halted and knelt down. Eddon cursed to himself. Of course! The decapitated corpse of the young woman! All six killers stopped screaming.

A moment later the body of the old woman was also discovered. This time it was the killer over by the opposite wall who halted and knelt down.

Eddon shifted his buried arm and felt for the punchgun in his pocket. What would they think had happened? Would they assume that the decapitators had fled? Or would they begin a thorough search of the room? He tensed his muscles, ready to spring up and start shooting.

The two kneeling killers rose to their feet and moved on. As if at the press of a switch, the other four killers moved on too. Now they were all screaming again: scream after scream after scream. Without even gathering to inspect the bodies, they continued their advance. They converged towards the single doorway at the other end of the room. Then they were gone.

Eddon relaxed. Everything seemed suddenly quieter. The battlefront had passed simultaneously through the nearby rooms. Now the screams were receding further and further away.

He lifted his head slightly and turned towards Vail. She looked at him out of the corner of her eye and blinked in response. For several more minutes he lay unmoving, wary of any stragglers following the main battlefront.

Then he heaved himself up out of the ground. Debris streamed from him in cataracts. He shook himself like a dog, throwing off clouds of powder in all directions.

'I think they're about out of the ruins now,' he said, listening to the retreating wave of sound.

Vail spat dust and powder from her mouth.

'You look like a ghost!' she laughed.

The wind had already eased off. Even the lines of colour seemed to be falling less frequently. But the murk was as thick as ever.

'I guess you helped save my life again,' said Vail. 'How many times is it now? Why does it always have to be you?'

Eddon grinned. 'Murphy's Law.'

He took off his vannamak and gave it a vigorous shaking. Then he began digging for Vail's feet.

'Be gentle with me!' she said. 'As the space maiden said to the rocket captain.'

He grasped her by the ankles and tugged her out of her hollow. He hauled her up onto the surface of the ground.

'Ouch! Oh! Oooooh!'

She was completely coated with white powder. Her face was like a mask. Flakes and fragments clung to her hair and clothes. She moved one hand and wiped the powder from her face. But she still couldn't move her legs or hips.

Eddon pursed his lips. 'It's real bad, isn't it?'

'Yeah. Completely out of joint. But there's one way to heal it.'

'How?'

'A form of parapsychic healing. It'll take a long time.'

'That's okay.'

'And I'll need your help.'

Eddon frowned, then shrugged. 'What do I do?'

Vail managed an ironic grin. 'Well, first, you can roll me over and lift up my clothes.'

Eddon dug down into the soft debris and took hold of Vail around the thighs and waist. Very carefully he rolled her over from her back onto her side, and from her side onto her front.

She lay outstretched like a floppy rag-doll. She brought her left arm up under her chin for a pillow.

'Now what?'

'Slow down, slow down. This can't be done in a rush. Next I have to locate the damage. Lift up my clothes at the back.'

'Your vannamak?'

'Vannamak and topvest and undersilk. We're talking naked skin here. Don't you know how to undress a lady?'

Eddon lifted the vannamak up around her shoulders. Then he pulled up the topvest and undersilk. He had to raise her slightly in order to roll the topvest up over her stomach. The undersilk was looser and slid upwards without difficulty.

'What do you do with your amorous PPs?' asked Vail. 'Do you expect them to undress themselves?'

Eddon didn't lower himself to reply.

'Okay.' Vail laughed. 'So now you're looking at a well-modelled — even classical — back. Not as spectacular as my legs, but then what is? Your next job is to run your hand very gently over my spine.'

Eddon ran the palm of his hand over her spine, from top to bottom and bottom to top. Her skin was very smooth and perfect.

Vail made faint wincing noises.

'Does that hurt?'

'Not yet. Not enough. Try at the base of the spinal column.'

Eddon ran his hand down to the waistband of her soft-hose.

'Eee-ow!'

'Is that it?'

'Nearly. Go lower again. Not too far.'

Eddon leaned forward and slid his hand in under the waistband. He felt down to the hollowest part of her back, where the soft convexities of her buttocks began to rise on either side. He touched the tightly stretched top of her panti-nix.

'YOW-OW-OW!!' yelled Vail suddenly.

Eddon withdrew his hand as if bitten. It took Vail a few moments to recover her breath.

'Sorry if I made you jump.' she said. 'You must've been getting carried away.'

Eddon gave a snort, slightly muffled.

'The dislocation is in the first and second joints of the lumbar back. Shouldn't be too hard to realign. If you can do your bit.'

Eddon nodded.

'You see, parapsychic healing works by mind over matter. The vertebrae have to be clicked back into place and the damage to the cartilage repaired. So I have to impose a guiding image over my own nervous system.'

'An image?'

'An image of how my first and second joints *ought* to be aligned. And you have to supply it.'

'Me? Why me?'

'Because I can't imagine it for myself. I'm not an osteopath. I can't form an exact mental picture of how the joints should look. So I need a model. I have to draw the image from someone else.'

'I don't know how the joints should look either.'

'You don't have to know consciously. The model

is there in you, in your own spine. What you have to do is let it pass over.'

'Sounds easy enough.'

'Not that easy. Normally I'd only do this with another parapsych. You have to be extremely gentle and patient. Can you manage that?'

'Of course.'

'Hmm. *Extremely* gentle and patient. Start by relaxing. I suggest a sitting position, cross-legged.'

Eddon moved into a cross-legged sitting position.

'Now. You have to put your hand over the base of my spine again. Pressing firmly this time.'

'You'll cry out again.'

'Probably. It'll hurt like crazy. But don't take your hand away. You might hear a couple of clicks after ten, twenty minutes. That'll be the vertebrae shifting.'

'Got it.'

'Okay. Start pressing.'

Once more Eddon slipped his hand in under the waistband of Vail's soft-hose. He felt with his fingers down her back, down to the bumps at the base of her spine. Again his fingertips touched the tightly stretched top of her panti-nix.

He pressed down firmly. She quivered and shuddered and gasped. But this time she didn't cry out.

Eddon bit his lip. There was a long silence. Then Vail spoke up, in a slightly unsteady voice.

'Right. Stay there. Now, you have to make yourself into a channel.'

'A channel?'

'So that the image can pass over. You have to bend your thoughts towards me, flow towards me. Focus away from yourself and towards me. Can you do that?'

'I can try.'

'Yeah, try. And try to persuade yourself that it's really going to happen. The image is really going to cross from your body into mine. It's more likely to work if you believe in it. Try to set aside your negative anti-parapsych attitudes.'

'Don't ask much, do you?'

'And your negative attitudes towards me. Think nurturing helping healing thoughts. Positive feelings.'

'Is that all?'

'I'm serious.'

'I'm doing my best.'

But his feelings kept taking a different turn. Not hostile but sexual. He couldn't help being aroused by the touch of Vail's skin, the soft valley at the base of her spine. He couldn't help being aware of the rising curves of her buttocks, of the triangle of open space between her buttocks and the top of her panti-nix . . .

'Sexual feelings are fine,' said Vail, as if she'd read his mind. 'As long as they're positive. And as long as you don't move your hand. You've got good hands'

Eddon didn't move his hand. He was starting to feel almost faint. The blood pounded behind his eyes and throbbed through his temples.

'Close your eyes,' said Vail.

'I don't know . . . I'm getting sort of dizzy.'

'You'll be all right. The healing process will put us both in a state of semi-consciousness. Could even send us to sleep. Does that bother you?'

'No. Yes.'

'I know, you don't like to lose control. But trust me. Think how far I'm trusting you.'

Eddon nodded and closed his eyes.

'Accept the dizziness,' said Vail. 'Think of the channel. Like a passage, like a tunnel. Be in it. Come across in it. Keep your thoughts flowing towards me . . .'

Eddon didn't know whether her voice was fading, or merely his hearing of it. He was no longer aware of the walls, of the ground, of his own sitting position on the ground. There was only the passage, the tunnel, the channel. Even the sensuous touch of Vail's skin seemed to dissolve and become a channel. Only the channel . . . and two pulses, two rhythms coming gradually closer and closer together, converging to synchronicity . . .

When Eddon awoke , he was lying curled on his side on the ground. He must have fallen asleep, he realised — fallen asleep and toppled over. Vail was lying beside him, no longer on her front but facing upwards.

'Ah-hah!' she exclaimed. 'Awake at last!'

Eddon stretched and yawned.

'You were *very* relaxed in the end,' she said.

'Mmm. How long have you been awake?'

'Oh, a couple of hours.'

Eddon blinked. 'What time is it now?'

'Mid-morning.'

'You mean, I slept through the whole night?'

'You did.'

'Hey, why didn't you wake me up? We haven't got time —'

'I needed the time. For the cartilage to repair. I've been resting and recovering.'

'Hmm. And you're okay now?'

'I think so. I'll test it out in a minute. Look at the sky.'

Eddon rolled over to look upwards.

'The thundercloud has gone,' he said in surprise.

'And the wind and duststorm and the colours raining down,' said Vail. 'Only the nightmare sounds are still there.'

For the first time since they had arrived on P-19, they could see right up into the sky. Even the planet's usual cloud-cover had blown away. All that was left were a few cloudy tatters and rags, very wispy and remote. The vault of the sky seemed suddenly high and spacious.

It was a twilight sky, with a raw, scoured, windswept look. The horizontal shuttering effect was more noticeable than ever. Both stars and sun were visible, but the stars were dimmed and the sun was a dull orange ball. The face of the sun appeared as if trapped behind thin horizontal bars.

'It's darker than yesterday,' said Eddon, after a

while. 'The light's more orangey than yellowy.'

'Yeah. Colder too.' Vail shivered. 'You want to help me up now?'

Eddon rose to his feet. He took a grip on Vail's uplifted hand and pulled her slowly upright. She stood there teetering and tentative, like a new-born foal. She was still covered with white powder and debris.

Then she began experimenting with small movements, flexings and straightenings. A smile spread over her face.

'It worked,' she said.

'No pain?'

'Nothing. Back to normal.'

'Incredible.'

She flung out a leg, kicking high in the air.

'Yes, I admit it. I'm incr-r-r-edible. You're not so bad yourself.'

'Hmmm.'

'Who'd ever have guessed you could be so gentle?'

She beat at her clothes, sending out clouds of powder. Then she began plucking fragments of debris from her hair. Eddon watched impatiently for a couple of minutes.

'Are you ready?' he asked at last.

Vail laughed. 'I guess you've got over your relaxation.'

'Let's go.'

'Zap! Blam! Powee! Lead the way, Inspector.'

They set off walking. Vail strode along as though she had never been injured. Eddon took her punch-gun out of his pocket and handed it back to her.

'You've got potential, you know,' said Vail. 'Psychic sensitivity. With proper training, you could become a full-time parapsych.'

'You reckon I did all right?'

'For a first attempt, I give you nine points out of ten.'

'Only nine? Where did I lose a point?'

'Impure thoughts. But it's understandable.'

They passed cautiously from room to room, peering around every doorway before entering. In some places the loose powder had been blown into great drifts against the walls.

The rooms were all empty. But back in the room where ev Ghair's group had joined Jaralax's group, they found two cross-hoists and half a dozen vibration-drills lying on the ground.

'Those are from my group,' said Eddon. 'They abandoned the heaviest tools.'

'But not the lighter ones?'

'No, they couldn't have been completely desperate. And there's no signs of fighting. They probably got out before the killers came through.'

They proceeded on through further rooms, making their way out of the ruins. Overhead, the moanings and singings and tollings and thuddings continued across the sky, neither louder nor softer than before.

'I suppose none of the other groups found anything?' asked Vail. 'No transmitter?'

'No, nothing. The search was as good as finished anyway.'

'Mmmm. That's our best possibility knocked on the head then.'

'Unless we didn't search hard enough. Unless the transmitter was too well hidden.'

'Do you believe that?'

'No.'

'Nor me.'

'So we've come to a dead end? Do you have any ideas for what to do next?'

'No. I need some new leads.' She sucked at her cheeks thoughtfully. 'There's one thing I *could* do.'

'What's that?'

'Something very, very dangerous.'

'Go on.'

Vail shook her head. 'I don't want to talk about it right now. I don't want to even think about it. Anyway, we have to get back to the Big House first.'

They walked on until they came to the edge of the ruins. There was a final wall and a doorway leading out onto open mossy ground. They stood in the doorway and surveyed the scene.

It was a strange and terrible sight. Everything looked ominous and baleful under the high scoured sky and filtered orangey light. Like a murdering tide, the killers had left death and destruction everywhere in their wake. It was like an image of Armageddon.

Not one building remained intact. Eddon and Vail could see out over the cropfields almost as far as Steyne-2. There were barns smashed open and houses with their roofs staved in. Even the contents of the buildings had been strewn around as if in childish rage. Farming equipment, furniture, chests, casks, bags, rugs, curtains — everything lay scattered on the ground.

There were also corpses scattered on the ground, around the houses and in the fields. Like small huddled heaps they lay, surrounded by dark pools of blood. Many of the victims had been disembowelled or hacked apart.

'Listen!' said Eddon, holding up his hand.

Far off in the distance came the sound of shooting: not a disembodied sound in the sky, but real gunfire. It came from the direction of Steyne-2.

'I guess the P-19ers retreated and the killers went after them,' said Eddon. 'Sounds like they're all in Steyne-2 now.'

'Might be difficult getting back into the Big House.'

Eddon pointed. 'That's our best route, I reckon. Where the M-rail heads in towards Steyne-2. We'll be more hidden if we keep close to the side of the embankment.'

'Blam! Zap! Powee!' Vail pulled a face. 'Let's do it!'

They made their way from the ruins to the M-rail, taking a straight line across the cropfields. The fields were littered with broken bits of plant and foliage. The wind had snapped off flowers and twigs and stalks, scattering them far and wide. But not ordinary flowers and twigs and stalks.

'They're all diseased,' said Eddon, staring. 'It's only the warped plants that have been scattered.'

'They'll spread like wildfire then,' said Vail. 'Many of these bits are capable of growing new roots.'

When they reached the M-rail, they turned and walked along at the bottom of the embankment. They moved warily, scanning constantly in every direction. In several places drainage channels blocked their way, filled with deep water. Many of the channels were narrow enough to jump, but sometimes they had to detour along the banks until they could cross by a bridge. The water had a dull reddish tinge, with leaves and twigs floating on the surface.

They passed a mutilated corpse in a ditch and a broken-backed killer crawling in circles in a field of rye. In one place they came upon a derailed M-rail car that lay tumbled over at the bottom of the embankment. Its four passengers had been agonisingly impaled on the four poles that had once supported its fabric roof. The poles had been driven between their legs and up through the entire length of their bodies.

They saw only one gang of killers. They were some way off in the distance, gathered at the side of an unroofed house. They had clubs or batons in their hands, and they were battering something red and shapeless on the ground. Vail shuddered.

'We can't help,' said Eddon. 'Too late anyway.'

'I know,' said Vail.

They advanced for a while in a sort of half-crouch, until they were safely out of the killers' sight.

With all their caution and detouring, it took them fifty minutes to reach the outskirts of Steyne-2. Gradually the houses became more frequent: at first, single houses among the fields; then houses gathered together in clusters; finally rows of houses arranged along proper metalled streets.

They turned aside from the M-rail and began to make their way through the streets. Many of the houses had obviously been broken into, displaying shattered walls and gaping doors and windows. Others appeared intact but deserted.

'Occupants must've fled before the killers arrived,' commented Eddon.

They crept along in the shadow of the walls. The sickly-sweet smell of blood lay heavy in the air. They chose small lanes and backstreets wherever possible. But they couldn't entirely avoid the larger streets.

In one larger street they came suddenly upon a fortified area under siege. Emerging from a side-lane, they saw a gang of half a dozen killers attacking a row of houses.

They pulled back into the lane.

'We'll take another route,' said Eddon.

'Wait a minute,' said Vail. 'Just let me watch for a minute.'

Cautiously she advanced her head around the corner. Eddon groaned, but took a look too.

The houses were defended with massive sheets of iron and steel fastened over their doors and windows. There had been a barrier of wire constructed across the street, but the killers had broken through and trampled it down. Now they were hurling chunks of rock at the people on the roofs.

The people on the roofs brandished long staves and spear-like weapons. They carried shields that looked as though they had been made from table-tops and cupboard doors. The shields gave only limited protection against the flying chunks of rock. Every now and then came a cry as someone was hit, answered by a harsh inhuman screech of triumph from the killers.

'Seen enough?' asked Eddon.

Vail shook her head. 'There's something about these killers. We knew they were cooperating together. But the *way* they cooperate.'

'What about it?'

'They never talk to each other. Never even look at each other. No signals, nothing. So how are they able to cooperate so well?'

Eddon could see what she meant. One of the killers down the street was prising up slabs of paving, another was breaking the slabs and making a pile of smaller chunks. The other four were collecting chunks from the pile and throwing them. They moved in a continuous cycle, almost like a conveyor belt.

'It's a clue,' muttered Vail. 'This CURSE isn't just incredibly complex. It works on a different level —'

She was about to say more. But there was a sudden shout from one of the people on the roofs.

'Help!'

The shout was directed at Eddon and Vail. Without realising, they had stuck their heads further and further forward around the corner. Now a keen-eyed young woman on the roofs had spotted them.

'Help! Help!'

The killers looked round to see who was being shouted at. At the same time, other people on the roofs also began calling out to Eddon and Vail:

'We need help!'

'Bring help!'

Catching sight of Eddon and Vail, the killers opened their mouths and snarled. They turned in a line and came racing down the street. There was white creamy stuff all over the front of their clothes. Many of them still held rocks in their hands.

'See!' said Vail, pointing. 'They don't have to talk to synchronise what they're doing.'

Eddon dragged her back away from the corner.

'What they're doing is coming after us!' he yelled. 'Run for your life!'

'Run?'

'RUN!!'

He grabbed her by the hand and pulled her along after him. Vail came out of her state of contemplation, and started to accelerate. They ran back down the side-lane. There was a turning off to the left.

'This way!' yelled Eddon.

They turned out of the lane at exactly the same moment when the killers entered. A volley of rocks came flying through the air, missing them by inches, crashing against the walls behind them.

Vail reclaimed her hand and ran side by side with Eddon. They ran along a winding street littered with wreckage and broken glass. Heating pipes had been wrenched from their stanchions and wrought silver metalwork stripped from the porches and windows.

'I don't know how long I can keep this up,' gasped Vail.

Eddon looked back over his shoulder.

'You better,' he puffed. 'They're still after us.'

They turned corners to left and to right, zigzagging wildly from street to street. But the killers were always close enough to tell which way they turned. Eddon and Vail could hear the sound of footsteps pounding along thirty metres behind.

They ran down main streets and through alleys and across moss-carpeted squares. In one square was a strange cluster of flowers spreading over the moss.

'They're deformed!' shouted Eddon. 'Turn away!'

They veered to the side. The plants resembled yellow avineas, but with oversized sickly-rich heads and stems that ran like vines across the ground. For a moment, Eddon felt overwhelmed by a sense of heaviness and dark depression — the same feeling he had experienced in the War of Independence Memorial Park. Vail felt it too. But only for a moment. Then they ran out of it as if out of a shadow. They left the square by the nearest exit.

On and on they ran. Often there were wire fences and welded metal walls constructed across the streets. If any fence or wall had remained intact, Eddon and Vail would have been trapped. But fortunately every barricade had been already breached. There was always at least a gap to slip through.

Then they ran into another gang of killers. They entered a wide main street and found another siege going on. Four killers were attacking the door and windows of a fortified house. Two were bashing at the metal coverings over the door, two were using metal bars to lever off the metal coverings over the windows. Knives on sticks flashed out at the sides of the windows, slicing at the arms that held the metal bars.

It was too late to turn back. They swerved across to the far side of the street and put on a desperate spurt of extra speed.

But the killers saw what was happening. Screaming, they turned away from the fortified house and lunged across the street to cut them off.

'Use your gun!' shouted Eddon. He pulled out his own punchgun.

The foremost killer had a huge open cleft in his skull. Already he was almost upon them. For a second, Eddon and Vail stared into the eyes of utter insanity.

Then Eddon started shooting. He loosed off a rapid succession of projectiles. Vail pulled out her punchgun and started shooting too.

The projectiles couldn't halt the killers, but they

were enough to slow them down. The killer with the cleft skull staggered momentarily, another killer dropped his metal bar. Eddon and Vail raced past mere inches away from their reaching hands.

By the time the killers had re-oriented themselves, Eddon and Vail were fifteen metres ahead. But now there were twice as many in pursuit, the new gang of killers as well as the old.

Street after street, alley after alley. Vail had got her second wind and was running more easily. But they couldn't seem to increase their lead. They had long since lost all sense of direction.

There were streams of blood in the gutters and bloodstains smeared on the walls. In one place they passed a dozen pale naked bodies strung up by the ankles like meat in an abattoir. In another place they had to dodge around severed limbs and internal organs scattered over the paving. Vail put her foot in a grey paste of human brains.

'Yikes!' She skidded violently.

'Hold up!' Eddon clutched her by the elbow. He yanked her upright as she slewed over towards him. They kept right on running, not missing a stride.

There was a hubbub of noise growing louder ahead. Still Eddon and Vail ran on. Too late they realised what they were running into. They swung around a bend in the street and stared at a massed crowd of killers directly in front of them. The street was blocked from side to side.

There was something else too. Beyond the crowd rose the glittering mirror-glass walls of the Big

House. They had arrived at their destination by sheer accident. The street they were in led straight up to it.

They skidded to a halt. Luckily the crowd was all looking the other way, towards the Big House. There was a small courtyard off to one side of the street. Eddon and Vail raced into it.

But it was a courtyard with no exit.

'Here!' Eddon darted towards a projecting porch decorated with wrought ironwork. 'Onto the roofs! Climb!'

Vail leaped and scrabbled up the ironwork. Eddon caught her from behind and boosted her upwards. Then clambered up after her.

There were plenty of hand-holds and toe-holds in the fretted metal. They hauled themselves up onto the roof of the porch, then onto the main roof of the building. Flat on their bellies, they wriggled up the slope towards the roof-ridge.

Vail was still in the lead. There was a bronze metal crest at the top of the ridge. She grasped hold of the crest and swung herself sideways along the roof.

'Other way!' Eddon called out.

But Vail didn't hear. She moved with a loping, crouching gait, hand over hand along the crest. It was too late to change direction. The pounding feet of their pursuers were entering the small courtyard, closing in behind. Eddon grasped hold of the crest and followed after her.

They were heading towards the Big House. The roofs formed a continuous chain all the way to the end of the street. Eddon and Vail progressed easily from rooftop to rooftop.

But not unnoticed. There was a sudden scream from the small courtyard. One of the pursuing killers was staring straight up at them, looking up over the edge of the roofs.

They tried to move even faster, taking risks, running without handholds. They crossed over a roof embossed with gold and a roof ornamented with sculptured figurines. One roof in the Extravagant Style slowed them down with an intricate network of spiky masts and wires. They had to crawl through the wires as if through an obstacle course.

Behind them, the pursuing killers had already climbed up onto the roofs. They were still half a dozen houses away. But they were starting to close the gap. They came forward at a reckless pace, with unnatural leaping agility.

Eddon and Vail kept going. The Big House glinted and glittered up ahead. But it was separate from the row of houses. They couldn't reach it by way of the rooftops.

They passed above the crowd of killers in the street below. There was a similar crowd in the street on the other side. The crowds were massed behind impromptu barriers of furniture and wreckage erected across the ends of the streets.

Eddon and Vail would have been surely visible if any of them had looked up. But the crowds' attention was wholly focussed upon the Big House. Several killers held up human bodies or parts of bodies mounted on poles. They waved their trophies high in the air, jeering at the defenders.

'I think they've got the place surrounded,' Vail called back over her shoulder to Eddon.

Roof by roof they advanced, until they came to the very last house in the row. Vail made her way along the ridge until she could go no further. Dead end. The ridge terminated in a tall silver pinnacle. The Big House was twenty metres away.

Eddon came up beside her. They stood leaning against the pinnacle, trying to work out their next move.

Below them was a wide road that ran in a loop around this side of the Big House. It seemed to form a kind of no-man's-land between the besiegers and the besieged. Several objects like misshapen red and white balls lay scattered on the road: human heads, which the killers had evidently been using as missiles.

Eddon looked down and considered the five metre drop to the ground. Then he looked round and considered the killers advancing over the rooftops. Now they were only three houses away.

'We jump,' he said grimly. 'That door over there!'

He pointed to a small door in the side of the Big House. A solid metal door: but two vertical slots had been cut into it at shoulder height. The tips of two guns protruded menacingly from the slots.

'Go! You first!'

Vail swung herself off the edge of the roof. She

clasped her hands around the base of the pinnacle, dangled for a moment in mid-air — then dropped. The impact knocked all the breath out of her.

As she struggled back onto her feet, Eddon landed heavily beside her.

'Move!' he gasped.

They flung themselves forward, raced for the door. Would anyone in the Big House realise what was happening? At least they weren't getting shot at by their own side.

They reached the walls of the Big House and flattened themselves against the door, one on either side of the slots.

'Who's that?' came a voice from within.

'Answer or we shoot!' cried a second voice.

The tips of the two guns angled menacingly towards them.

'Inspector Brac and Vail ev Vessintor,' Vail called urgently. 'Let us in.'

'Hurry!' shouted Eddon.

'The Hegemony people?'

'Yes. Let us in!'

'What're you doing out there?'

'We got left behind by the search party.'

'How do we know you're —'

'Please!' Vail pressed her mouth right up against the nearest slot. 'Let us in! Please!!'

There were mumbles and whispers behind the door.

Eddon stood facing the other way, punchgun drawn and ready. The crowds in the streets seemed hardly to have noticed them; or if they had, they were taking a long time to respond.

But then the pursuing killers on the roofs appeared. They stood silhouetted against the dark orangey sky: two, three, half a dozen of them. They were screaming a pure white stream of sound.

Their screaming seemed to arouse the crowds in the streets. Suddenly a great many figures began swarming over the heaped-up barriers of wreckage and furniture. At the same time the killers on the roofs jumped down to the ground.

Eddon started shooting. The killers from the roofs were the most immediate threat. He hit the first two with several projectiles as they landed. They slipped and stumbled and got in the way of the next two, who landed on top of them.

From behind the door came the noise of bolts being drawn and bars slid back.

'Hurry!' Vail willed them on. 'Hurry! Hurry! Hurry!'

But now the other killers had cleared the barriers. From all sides they were rushing across the roadway, converging towards Eddon and Vail.

There was the well-oiled click of a lock unlocked. The door swung open — a few inches only.

Vail pushed forward with both hands, Eddon pushed back with his shoulders. The people on the other side tried to resist. But Eddon and Vail were desperate. They hurled themselves bodily through the door. They fell in a heap and slid along the floor.

'What's going on?' shouted a loud commanding voice. 'Shut that door immediately!'

PART SIX
The Last Defence

1

The door was slammed shut and the lock clicked back into place. Just in time. There was a tremendous rattling and pounding as the killers attacked from outside.

A man and a woman stood by the door, sliding home the bolts and bars. A second man strode forward to help, the man with the loud commanding voice. It was Jaralax IV Fallender.

The rattling and pounding stopped almost as quickly as it had started.

Jaralax drew back, leaving the other two to finish the job. He stared down at Eddon and Vail. Vail lay sprawled on the floor, with Eddon sprawled on top of her. A smile of recognition appeared on Jaralax's face.

'So you survived,' he said. 'Amazing.'

'We survived,' said Vail. She spoke into the ear that was one inch in front of her face. 'You can climb off me now, Inspector Brac.'

'Sorry, PP.'

'Such lack of manners.'

Eddon grinned. He rose to his feet and started dusting himself down. Vail straightened her clothing and stood up too.

Jaralax was peering out through one of the slots in the door.

'They've given up,' he announced. 'Not a major attack.' He turned to Eddon and Vail. 'So. What happened to you two?'

'Long story,' said Eddon. 'Can you take us to ev Ghair?'

'Okay. I'm not sure where he is. But I'll find him.'

'We can tell you the story as we go.'

Jaralax nodded and set off at a quick marching pace. Eddon and Vail hurried along at his side.

'So what happened?'

Eddon explained how they'd been left behind by the search party, and how they'd been chased through the streets and across the roofs. Vail described what they'd seen on the way back. Jaralax was particularly interested to hear that there were still some fortified houses holding out against the killers.

'Maybe there could be some settlements holding out too,' he commented.

They turned from one corridor into another. The corridors were empty, but many of the rooms on either side were full of people.

'What about you?' asked Eddon. 'What happened to the search party?'

Jaralax tugged at the ends of his moustache. He told them about the decision to retreat and about the gathering of all the groups outside the old ruins.

'We were on the way back to Steyne-2 when the killers attacked us,' he said.

'But you held them off?'

'It was touch and go. Ev Ghair formed us up into squares to concentrate our firepower. The killers couldn't pick us off individually.'

'Smart tactics.'

'We lost only thirty-nine people from the entire search party,' said Jaralax with some pride.

They walked through a long gallery and entered a curving corridor. Two women came towards them from the other end of the corridor.

'Megges! Pammeda!' Jaralax called out. 'Do you know where our Headman is?'

'Try the Map Room.' One of the women jerked a thumb back over her shoulder. 'That's where he was heading ten minutes ago.'

The two groups crossed in mid-corridor and continued their separate ways. Megges and Pammeda never slowed their stride. They seemed to be on some urgent errand.

Jaralax, Eddon and Vail walked on in silence for a while. They passed more rooms crammed full of people. Eddon peered curiously in through the open doors.

'Why are there so many people in the rooms and no-one in the corridors?' he asked at last.

'Ev Ghair's orders. The corridors are to be kept clear at all times. So there's no obstruction to rapid communication and bringing up reinforcements. We've got a whole lot more people in the Big House now.'

'More refugees?'

Jaralax nodded. 'Mostly from Steyne-2. They fled from their homes and took refuge in the Big House. My own family included. The Fallenders of Strone. They managed to get out before the killers came through.'

'So how many people altogether?'

'About three thousand.'

'Phew!' Eddon whistled. 'Three thousand packed in here!'

'People have been divided into three categories,' said Jaralax. 'Ev Ghair organised it. One: the non-combatants, the old people and children and such. They've been put into rooms well away from the outward-facing parts of the building. Two: the front-line sentinels with guns, on guard at the windows and up on the roofs. We've got as many sentinels as we've got guns — about two hundred. The third category are the reserves.'

'Who don't have guns?'

'That's right. They have knives, clubs, whatever makeshift weapons they've been able to get their hands on. They won't be used until the big attack begins. Then they'll be moved forward as they're needed, anywhere the killers look like breaking through.'

'You're sure there's going to be a big attack?' asked Eddon. 'You're sure the killers will try to storm the Big House?'

'Yes. Sooner or later. I hope it's not too much later.'

'You hope?' Eddon and Vail were mystified.

'Better than the alternative,' said Jaralax. 'Think about it. One by one people will start turning into killers *inside* the Big House. If we don't die fighting the killers from outside, we'll die in the end from killing each other.'

'Ah. Mmm.'

Eddon and Vail were still thinking about it as they turned into the final corridor leading to the Map Room. Simultaneously, the doors of the Map Room swung open and a group of men and women stepped out into the corridor. At the head of the group was Argid ev Ghair.

Most of the men and women wore the triangular badges of Senior Leaders. There were ten of them altogether. They were engaged in animated discussion, centring around ev Ghair. They carried maps and diagrams under their arms.

It was ev Ghair himself who looked up and recognised Eddon and Vail.

'Eddon Brac! Vail ev Vessintor!' he exclaimed. 'I knew you'd come back to us somehow!'

His eyes lit up. He held out his hands, one to each of them. Vail found herself taking hold of the withered left hand. It felt cold and dry and wrinkled, but not unpleasant. Not dead, but very much alive.

'Walk along with us,' said ev Ghair. 'We're on our way to the Old Hall. We're setting up the Old Hall as the command centre for the defence.'

He seemed almost blazing with energy. He led the way along the corridor with his bangles jingling. The partially paralysed side of his body didn't appear to slow him down at all.

The group turned from the corridor into an open lobby. Suddenly an old man emerged from a side-passage. He scurried up to ev Ghair.

'Maive V Millijon! She — we —'

His voice quavered and broke down. Ev Ghair put a hand on his shoulder.

'Be calm, Tuir. You've had someone turn, is that it? Someone turned killer?'

'Maive V Millijon. She murdered Shayise. Her own mother.'

'Ah.' Ev Ghair sighed. 'And you destroyed the killer?'

'Yes.'

'You did well.'

'But what if someone else —?'

Ev Ghair looked thoughtful. 'You're in the Main Power Room, aren't you?'

'Two hundred of us. Non-combatants.'

'We'll make a small detour,' said ev Ghair. 'I'll come and talk to you.'

The Main Power Room was only a couple of corridors away. It was the same room where Eddon and Vail had gone to send their messages from the Messages Centre. But this time they entered by way of a different door.

The wide open space was dim and humming. Eddon and Vail saw again the rows upon rows of tall rectangular boxes and black machines in wire cages, the storage batteries and condensers and generators. But whereas before the gangways had been empty, now they were everywhere submerged under a sea of humanity. Old men, old women, children, mothers with babies, the wounded and injured — two hundred people squeezed in elbow to elbow. The air was stale and heavy with sweat.

A murmur ran round the room when ev Ghair entered. All eyes turned towards him, wide eyes staring out of dark hollows.

'Over here,' said Tuir, leading the way. 'The bodies are over here.'

There was an open space between two rows of cages. The bodies lay locked in death, the young girl's hands still clenched around her mother's throat. Ev Ghair stepped forward to inspect.

The girl had been run through by a long pole, spearing her torso. But it was the blows to the back of the head that had destroyed her. Half of her skull was completely missing. Splashes of grey matter lay spilled from her brainpan, mingled with splashes of white creamy liquid.

People began explaining what had happened.

'There was no warning. She sprang on Shayise from behind.'

'Completely silent!'

'She broke her neck.'

Ev Ghair prodded with his boot at the killer's body. 'Poor Shayise,' he said. 'And poor Maive.'

'She broke her neck and then started chewing through her throat!'

'She didn't stop chewing even when we struck her down!'

'That's how we destroyed her so easily!'

There were gaping holes in the victim's throat, where great chunks of flesh had been torn away. It looked like the attack of a wild animal.

'But what if it happens again?' The question was almost a shriek, uttered by a young woman with a child in her arms.

'It mightn't be so easy next time!'

'How can we know?'

'How can we stop it?'

There was a note of nervous hysteria in their voices. Babies had started crying, and children were whimpering.

'You can't know and you can't stop it,' said ev Ghair.

He raised his arms in the air and stared around the room, taking in every frightened face, gazing into every pair of eyes.

'Look at me. Listen to me. Be calm.' His voice was quiet but authoritative. 'Let me tell you a story,' he said.

Gradually the crying and whimpering died down. He allowed a long moment of silence. Then:

'This is a true story. From the time of the Break-away.' He turned and singled out the young woman with the child in her arms. 'Involving your own grandmother, Choira III Eyr.'

The whole room was listening. Now even the wounded held back their sighs of pain.

'It was the day I joined up with the so-called rebel forces in the Eigessy Basin. The so-called rebels, the true inhabitants of P-19. Do you know, they were a riffraff of an army! I remember them coming out of their tents, so thin and wasted with hunger. Seven hundred skeletons they were!'

He nodded to a boy about ten years old. 'Your great uncle was there, Daim V Kaigh.' He pointed to a girl, a couple of years younger. 'And your great-great-grandmother, Phair V Augarder!

'Their guns were antiquated and their military equipment was a joke. What hope did they have against the Hegemony's finest trained troops? But then I came closer and I saw something else. Let me tell you! I saw the look in their eyes. That look of a people fighting for their home — for a planet of their own. What a look! Unswervable! Unconquer-able! I compared it to the Hegemony troops, and the look in *their* eyes. And then I knew they couldn't beat us. With that look I knew we couldn't fail!

'And yes, it was your grandmother who spoke the truest words that day, Choira III Eyr. When we swore the oath to keep fighting for a million years, she cried "We outnumber them now!" And when we laughed, she said, yes, because we've got seven hundred whole hearts — whereas they've got two thousand bodies, but there's only half-hearts and quarter-hearts and little bits of hearts in them.'

He raised his voice, booming out to every corner of the room.

'Whole hearts! That's where you come from! That's whose children and grandchildren and great-grandchildren you are! That's the spirit that you inherit!'

He lowered his voice, suddenly very soft and intense.

'Maive V Millijon is not the only one amongst you who will turn and become a killer. It'll happen again, sooner or later, while you wait here. And there's no telling who it'll happen to. But you must deal with it, as you dealt with Maive. You must deal with it without blame and without panic. However many times it happens.'

He surveyed the room, nodded grimly.

'Yours is the hardest task,' he said. 'Much easier to guard the walls or prepare for the fighting. Much easier to be active and doing things. But you are the ones with the time to think and fear. Yours is the hardest task, of waiting and enduring and lasting out.

'But we need your determination and your courage! Believe me, we need it! Panic is contagious. If you panicked here, it would spread and influence the whole defence. But courage spreads too. Your courage and determination here goes out to all of us. We rely on you!

'Remember who you are! The descendants of those who won the impossible victory! Inheritors of the true spirit of P-19! I can see it in *your* eyes, I can see it right now! There's nothing we can't do! We can perform miracles!'

The mood had changed completely. A voice called out from the crowd:

'Yes! Yes! We can perform miracles!'

'All of us together,' said ev Ghair. 'Supporting each other! A community once again!'

'All of us together!' echoed a dozen voices.

'Independent P-19!' cried ev Ghair.

'Independent P-19!'

The words came simultaneously from two hundred throats. It was not so much an acclamation, more like a heartfelt prayer.

The old man, Tuir, stepped forward and held out his hand, palm upwards.

'For all of us,' he said.

Ev Ghair took Tuir's hand between his own two hands and held it tightly pressed. It was the 'luck' ritual. Ev Ghair looked into the old man's face without a word. There was a kind of shining in both of their eyes.

Then ev Ghair turned and walked to the door. The crowd watched him go, needing no further demonstration. A calm firm resolution was visible on every face.

Eddon and Vail followed ev Ghair out of the Main Power Room, along with the ten members of ev Ghair's party. He led them back in the direction of the Old Hall. They strode purposefully along the corridors with a new firmness of step. Even Eddon was touched by the changed mood.

'My assistant and I both have punchguns,' he told ev Ghair. 'We'd like to be a part of the defence. We could do sentinel duty.'

'Accepted,' said ev Ghair with a smile. 'We need all the help we can get. In fact I was going to ask you to be a part of the command centre.'

'Fine, we can do that. But don't you need sentinels too?'

'We do, yes. We can give you sentinel duty until you're needed at the command centre, if you like.' He turned to one of the Senior Leaders. 'Alguis?'

'Their punchguns would be most useful up on the roofs,' said Senior Leader Alguis. 'I'll arrange it.'

'Hang on a minute,' said Vail. 'I haven't volunteered.'

There was a long moment of silence.

'Haven't volunteered for what?' asked ev Ghair. 'Sentinel duty or the command centre?'

'Both. Neither.'

She could feel the hostile glances directed upon her. But she went on regardless.

'You say you need all the help you can get. But you can't win by fighting anyway. More and more people will turn into killers. In the end there'll be no defence left to defend.'

Ev Ghair made a rumbling, growling noise in his throat.

'No, we can't win in the end,' he said at last. 'But we can fight off these killers around the Big House. We can perform miracles of defence against them. We'll show how P-19ers can fight! We'll make a defence to remember!'

'But what's the difference? If you can't win in the end?'

'You want to abandon hope and give in?'

'No, I want to continue my investigations.'

'Investigating what?'

'This CURSE.'

'But we found nothing. Our searching is finished. I can't send out more search parties. There are too many killers against us now.'

Vail gritted her teeth. She couldn't help the sense that she was in the wrong and letting everyone down.

'I'd still like to continue my investigations.'

'You'd rather think than fight?'

'Because thinking's what I'm good at.'

Ev Ghair turned and looked straight at her. Of all the inhabitants of P-19, he alone was tall enough to meet her on level terms. His left eye glittered out of the withered, blasted skin on the left-hand side of his face.

'We need your help,' he said simply.

Vail shook her head. She could feel the power of his appeal almost like a physical force. It was the same raw power of personality, the same sheer strength of character that she had recognised long ago.

Then suddenly he turned away. There was a grim smile on his face.

'Well, I won't force anyone to join us. It has to be by your own free choice. You must do as you will.'

Vail drew forth her punchgun, and held it out by the barrel.

'This can be for someone else to use,' she said.

'Thank you,' said ev Ghair, but made no move to take it.

In the end, Vail handed the gun across to Senior Leader Alguis.

'I'll be on my way then,' she said. 'If someone can give me directions to the laboratory.'

Alguis stopped for a moment to give her directions. The rest of the group walked on towards the Old Hall.

3

Eddon was given a sentinel duty for the night. His position was immediately above the Major Portal, overlooking the main square. He lay stretched out in a V-shaped gutter between two sloping roofs.

The killers were on the other side of the main square, half-hidden behind their barriers. All through the night they whooped and danced. Eddon could see the flickering glow of fires they had lit in the streets. He had the impression of something unspeakable going on, something involving the bodies of their victims. He was glad they were too far away to see clearly.

Overhead, the sounds in the sky grew gradually louder. Vile garbled voices, all the more suggestive for being incomprehensible. Eddon had to keep reminding himself that none of it had any power to harm.

It was around six o'clock when someone came walking towards him over the roofs.

'Sentinel Brac!' a female voice called out from the darkness. 'Just paying a visit! They said you were here.'

It was Vail. She approached along the channel of the gutter.

'Whew!' she whistled. 'Those sounds in the sky are getting worse.'

'Maybe there's something building up to happen.'

'Maybe the all-out attack,' agreed Vail.

She sat down crosswise across the hollow of the gutter, her feet on one roof and her bottom on the other. Her legs formed a bridge over the top of Eddon's legs.

'Do *you* think I ought to be helping in the defence?' she asked.

'No, I guess not. Not if you think you can solve the mystery of this CURSE.'

'I've been re-examining my equations all night.'

'And?'

'Maybe I relied too much on information from the psychoseminary. I didn't question the standard principles of CURSE theory.'

Eddon snorted to express his opinion of the psychoseminary.

'There's something else,' said Vail. 'You know when ev Ghair was describing how he joined up with the P-19ers in the Eigessy Basin? That started me thinking. There are things that puzzle me.'

'Like what?'

'Puzzling things.'

'Oh, excuse me. Is this an ev Vessintor hunch?'

Vail laughed. 'Yeah. I want to know more about the history of this planet. Who do you think I could ask?'

'About the history of the planet? Ask Argid ev Ghair. He's the one who lived through it.'

'Mmm. I don't think I'm in favour with him at the moment.'

'So-o. What about Mairie ev Ghair?'

'You think she could help?'

'When I was working on my disease hypothesis, looking into past family histories. It was Mairie who gave me all the information.'

'Ah, I remember. Your unsuccessful disease hypothesis.'

'Don't rub it in.'

'And such a great prize to encourage you too!'

'Prize?'

Vail laughed again. 'The one you didn't win.'

'Shame,' said Eddon. He became suddenly serious. 'What about that other thing you said you could do?'

Vail stopped laughing.

462

'When we were in the ruins,' Eddon pursued. 'You said there was something else you could do, but you didn't want to think about it.'

'I've been thinking about it.'

'But you haven't done it?'

'I'm still trying to build up courage.'

'As dangerous as that?'

Vail nodded.

'You'd be risking your life?'

'More than my life,' said Vail.

Eddon raised his eyebrows.

'I'm thinking of going into the mind of a killer.'

'Into the mind of a killer? Why?'

'To understand how their state of mind works. Maybe find out what causes it.'

'How?'

'By memoscopy.'

'Like you did in Draive?'

'Yes. I could use that killer we captured — what was his name? Graem V Craill. I expect he's still chained up down below.'

'But he's not dead.'

'Doesn't need to be. As long as his conscious mind isn't working. I just knock him out with an injection.'

'But you can't go into a mind like that! He's totally inhuman.'

'I know, it won't be easy. But I think I can do it. The only thing is...'

'Is what?'

'I'm not sure about being able to cross back again afterwards.'

'You'd become a killer yourself?'

'Yeah. That's what I mean about risking more than my life. I don't know how strong their state of mind is, I don't know if I'd be strong enough to counteract it.'

'I'd say you're very strong.'

Vail smiled. 'Thanks. I'll do it if I have to.'

Overhead, the nightmare sounds continued their singing and chanting, gurgling and gibbering. They seemed to be coming closer as well as growing louder.

Vail gave an exaggerated shiver. 'Brrr! It's so cold.'

'No real sun for two days,' commented Eddon. 'And a completely open sky.'

'Looks warmer where you are,' said Vail. 'Move over. I'm coming down alongside.'

She twisted around from her awkward sitting position. She knelt beside Eddon and lowered herself full length into the channel of the gutter.

'There. Now you can't accuse me of class snobbery.'

'Eh?'

'Because I'm down in the gutter with you.'

They lay side by side, pressed together by the camber of the channel. For a long time neither of them spoke. Then Vail said:

'You know that night I went into Beano's bedroom? Did you ever work it out? What we were doing?'

Eddon went very stiff. 'Not my business.'

'We were together all night. But we weren't screwing. Can't you guess?'

'You weren't —?'

'No.'

Eddon considered. Then his brows suddenly lifted.

'Of course! You were recording his dreams. That was when you took those electrostatic images of his head.'

Vail grinned. 'See? And all this time you thought we were having a night of sensational sex.'

'Not that sensational.'

'Why not?'

'I'd've heard you.'

There was another long period of silence. Over on the other side of the main square, the killers' fires had died down. They seemed to have finished whatever they were doing to the bodies of their victims. Now they were massed behind the barriers, staring ominously towards the Big House.

'So your stereotype was wrong,' said Vail. 'Admit it.'

'What stereotype?'

'About psychoseminary students.'

'You mean, upper class girls prancing around acting superior?'

'And.'

'And screwing everything in sight?'

'Yeah.'

'Amoral as cats?'

'Yeah.'

'Jumping into bed with —?'

'Enough! Take your hand off my waist.'

Eddon grinned and unwrapped his arm from Vail's waist.

'You didn't win, remember!' she said. 'No consolation prizes!'

They remained pressed up together in the channel of the gutter. Then Vail took a look at the timeband on her wrist.

'6.42,' she said. 'Getting up time. I'd better go call on Mairie ev Ghair. She'll probably be awake by now.'

She stretched lazily, cat-like, and rose to her feet.

'See ya,' she said.

Mairie ev Ghair wasn't up and dressed, but she wasn't asleep either. When she opened the door in response to Vail's knock, she was wearing only her undersilk.

'Oh, come in,' she said. 'No, you didn't wake me. I've been lying in bed wide awake all night.'

The room was very simple, with three chairs, a desk and a large double bed. Clothes were hung up on hooks on the walls. Vail recognised ev Ghair's dark tunics and Mairie's silver jewellery. The only sign of luxury was an elaborate bronze carving of intertwining plants on the ceiling.

'Were you looking for my husband or me? He's in the Old Hall, you know.'

'I know. I wanted to talk to you.'

Mairie pointed Vail to a chair and closed the door behind her. Vail sat down and Mairie sat on the edge of the bed facing her.

'What did you want to talk about?' Mairie's manner was as quiet and gracious as ever. Sleepless night or not, her clear grey eyes had the same calm look of serenity.

'I want to learn about the past history of P-19.'

'What, everything?' Humorous wrinkles appeared at the corners of Mairie's eyes.

'Particularly the early part of the Breakaway. When the scientists joined in the P-19ers' rebellion against the old Governor. And then when the old Governor was displaced and the scientists changed over to the side of the Hegemony.'

'All except my husband.'

'Except your husband. Who left the scientists in Steyne-1 and came across to the rebel army in the Eigessy Basin.'

'He came walking in from the east with the sun rising behind him.' Mairie smiled. 'That's one of the best-loved of all the stories about the Breakaway.'

'Must be a famous day in the history of the planet?'

'Yes, the 24th of the 4th, 588. We've celebrated the 24th of the 4th every year since Independence. It's our most important celebration after Independence Day itself.'

Vail nodded. 'Tell me about what happened before that date.'

Mairie gave a small shrug. 'Most of our stories come from later.'

'I thought you might know more than the usual stories.'

'Me? No. The Breakaway was over before I was born. I was an Independence baby. Born one week after the signing of the final Treaty.'

'I thought maybe your husband would've told you more?'

Mairie shook her head. 'You have to remember, it was eighteen years after the Breakaway before we even met. Twenty years before we were married. It was all far in the past by then. Especially Argid's time as a Hegemony research scientist. I think that was almost like a different lifetime to him.'

'Mmm.' Vail sat musing for a moment. 'It must have been strange, getting married to a living legend.'

'It was. It still is.' Mairie smiled. 'I believe I've been very lucky.'

'You admire him, don't you?'

'Yes. I admit it. Even after fifty years of living together, there's still a part of me that marvels at him, the same as when I was a girl. He really *is* a legend, you know. Not just outwardly, not just in public acts — but through and through.'

Vail raised her eyebrows. Mairie leaned forward on the bed.

'Ah, my dear, I know him so well, so many private things that no-one else knows. I know how gentle and caring and loving he can be — more than you might imagine. But there's always a sort of nobility about him. He's not like other people. He never learnt to play a role or put on a mask. He has so much strength and sureness inside himself, he's never had to be anything other than what he is. He's the same all through. Can you understand that?'

'I think so.'

Mairie nodded. She looked radiant, almost like the girl she had described, the girl of fifty years ago. Vail could hardly bear to gaze into her eyes.

There was a long silence. It was Mairie who eventually broke it.

'But this isn't helping you with the history of P-19, is it?' She clapped her hands together. 'I know who you need to talk to! Of course! Carreck I Fallender!'

'Fallender? Is this a relative of Jaralax's?'

'Their great-grandfather. He's in the Big House now. He's the only man still living who fought with Argid in the great battles of the Breakaway.'

'Would he remember the early part of the Breakaway too?'

'I expect he'd remember even back to the time when the old Governor ruled. He's ninety-three years old.'

'Where is he?'

'In the Blue Chamber. He arrived with the last lot of refugees from Steyne-2. Just ahead of the killers.'

'The Blue Chamber? I think I know where that is.'

'There's a hundred non-combatants packed in there. I can take you if you want to wait while I get dressed.'

'No need.' Vail rose up from her chair and turned towards the door. 'I can find it. Thanks a lot.'

'Just ask for Carreck I Fallender.'

5

Beano was on sentinel duty all morning. It was dark when he arrived at his post at seven-thirty, and it was still dark at ten-thirty.

'Zikes! It's even worse than yesterday!' he said to Derrad IV Gasker. Derrad stood on guard at the same window.

'Not even a half-dawn,' said Derrad. 'Not even that orangey light.'

Their post was in the male shower room at the back of the West Wing. Behind them ran a row of shower cubicles, fronted with stainless steel doors. The floor was a mosaic of green and gold tiles.

There was only the one window in the room. It had been blocked off with five heavy metal plates, and the glass knocked out behind. Beano and Derrad stood side by side, with the nozzles of their pommelguns poking out through the slots between the plates.

Here at the back of the West Wing the killers were about twenty metres away. The road around the Big House widened out into a triangular area, beyond which the ground sloped steeply downhill. The buildings at the top of the slope were blank-walled like warehouses, separated by narrow stepped lanes. The killers were gathered in the entrances of the lanes.

Beano and Derrad kept watch on them, straining their eyes to peer through the darkness. The killers were leaping and jigging around as if galvanised. Sometimes it seemed as if they were moving in time to the singings and tollings and thuddings in the sky. Strangely though, they made no sounds of their own.

'I don't like it,' said Derrad.

'Doesn't look good,' said Beano.

They kept their guns trained on the killers. They could easily have scored a few hits. But they were under orders not to fire until attacked. These killers couldn't be seriously incapacitated by a single shot from a lightweight pommelgun.

Eleven o'clock came and went, and still there was no sign of dawn. Nor by eleven-thirty, nor twelve.

At twelve-thirty, the killers attacked.

Beano blinked. One moment they were leaping and jigging around, the next they were rushing towards the walls of the Big House. It was as though a wave of movement had swept through them all simultaneously. From every entrance of every lane, the killers came surging forward.

Beano and Derrad began shooting. They tried to concentrate their fire, aiming for the ones in front, aiming for the eyes. The only certain way of disabling a killer was to destroy both eyes. But they were coming so fast, so many of them!

Countless shots rang out from all along the West Wing. The killers opened their mouths and screamed: a terrible cold deluge of sound. Some fell, blinded or injured, tripping and tangling those in their wake. But the rest were unstoppable. In no time at all they were up to the walls.

A dozen or more attacked the window of the male shower room. They rushed up and grabbed the protruding nozzles of the pommelguns. Beano and Derrad kept on firing, shot after shot. But the killers held on regardless.

It was impossible to break their grip. Beano and Derrad struggled to pull the guns back in through the slots. Desperately wrenching and twisting... until finally the guns came free. The two sentinels fell back away from the window.

Immediately fingers began reaching in through the slots, clutching and seeking. But the slots were too narrow for whole hands to follow. At the same time there was a screech of tortured metal. It was the sound of a metal plate being prised away from the wall.

Beano and Derrad exchanged glances. They moved up close to the window again. There at the bottom left-hand corner, one of the plates was bending slowly outwards. The fingertips of two pairs of hands were hooked in under the edge of the metal.

Derrad angled his gun and aimed down towards the bottom left-hand corner of the window. At point blank range, he began shooting off fingertips.

Meanwhile Beano reversed his own gun, holding it by the barrel. He started hammering with the butt, hammering down on the fingers in the slots.

At first, nothing seemed to have any effect. Beano smashed fingers to a bloody pulp, yet still they kept on reaching in through the slots. Derrad shot off one fingertip after another, yet still the metal plate kept bending further and further away from the wall.

Frantically, they redoubled their efforts.

And then at last the two pairs of hands hooked under the plate began to weaken. They didn't withdraw; but all of a sudden they lost their grip. The plate sprang back with a resounding clang. A moment later, and the fingers in the slots vanished too.

'Whoo-za-whooop!' crowed Beano.

They wiped their eyes. The air was filled with the acrid chemical smell of X-Z-T, the propellant used in the pommelguns. Derrad in particular was almost blinded by painful stinging tears.

Beano looked out through one of the slots. There was a single dark figure nearby on the ground, and another shambling about in the roadway. The rest of the killers seemed to have gone.

But then a loud thudding sound reverberated through the West Wing. It came from somewhere to their left. Beano swivelled to look in the direction.

'There's a crowd of them over to the left!' he exclaimed. 'They're all gathering there!'

'Where? How far?' Derrad was still rubbing his tears.

'About twenty metres.'

'That's the laundry. There's an outside door. Maybe they've broken in!'

Without another word they turned and ran for the laundry. Out through the shower room door, pounding along the corridor, pommelguns cradled in their arms.

Everywhere there was calling and shouting, everywhere the acrid smell of X-Z-T. The thudding sound grew louder and louder.

Other sentinels emerged from other doors, also heading for the laundry. But Beano and Derrad were the first to arrive.

The door of the laundry was wide open. Just inside lay the dead body of a young woman. Beano was about to rush straight in, leaping over the body. But Derrad clamped a hand over his shoulder and dragged him down to the ground.

'No!' he cried. 'Look!'

Beano looked. There was a small round hole in the young woman's chest. It was obvious that she had been shot.

'They must've captured some of our guns,' muttered Derrad. 'Probably during the retreat yesterday.'

He held up a warning hand. As the other sentinels arrived, they halted and crouched down, on either side of the door.

Then Derrad advanced his head and peered cautiously into the room. Beano followed suit. There were another two bodies lying sprawled on the floor. It seemed that all the laundry room sentries had been shot and killed.

But the killers hadn't yet managed to break in. The thudding sound came from the repeated blows of some heavy object which was being used as a battering ram against the outside door. The door was bulging and its hinges were threatening to burst. But they hadn't burst yet.

Two guns were poking in through a window to the right of the door. It was a barricaded window with narrow slots in the metal, exactly like the window in the shower room. The two guns swept from side to side, covering the area of the laundry.

'They'll be through the door in a minute!' gasped Beano. 'What can we do?'

Derrad surveyed the room. He looked at the boiling vats and flatboards and racks of clothing hanging from the ceiling. He studied the clothes-presses and tumble-washers, the hot water tanks and stainless steel benches. And then his eye lit on three tall drying cabinets, against the wall on the far side of the room.

'They're on wheels', he said, pointing. 'If we can push one of them up against the window —'

'We can block off the slots'. Beano completed the thought. 'Which one?'

'The one at the back'.

'Looks heavy'.

'Both of us pushing . . .'

'How do we get across?'

'Run like crazy and pray like mad. Ready?'

Beano nodded. They rose up on toes and fingers like runners in the starting blocks.

'GO!'

They burst in through the door and raced down the aisle between a row of benches and a row of washers. For one precious second, there was no response. Then the firing began.

A barrage of shots blasted across the room, smashing into metal surfaces, ricocheting and zinging through the air around them. They swung to the right past a massive vat. The racket was deafening.

They threw themselves forward, skidded across the floor, and landed up against the wall behind the drying cabinet. Derrad scrambled instantly to his feet.

'Start pushing!' he cried.

They put their shoulders against the cabinet and pushed. But the cabinet was made of solid metal, nearly two metres tall, and full of drying clothes. It didn't budge.

'Harder!' cried Derrad. 'One of those guns is a T-gun! They can bounce projectiles at us off the walls, if they know how!'

Again they heaved. This time the cabinet rolled forward a few inches, then banged up against the corner of the cabinet in front.

'Over to the left!'

They joggled and manoeuvred their cabinet around the other cabinet. The thudding of the battering ram on the outside door was growing louder, and they could hear the sound of rivets popping.

'Don't think about it!' shouted Derrad.

They trundled their cabinet into an aisle and steered it in the direction of the window. The cabinet shook and juddered as shots from the killers' guns slammed into it from in front. But now they were starting to build up momentum.

Faster and faster they moved. The cabinet careened through half a dozen clothes presses, knocking them out of the way.

'On target!'

'Whang-a-zang!'

There was a bone-jarring crash as the cabinet fetched up against the window. Derrad and Beano wedged their feet behind the wheels to stop it from being rolled back. The slots were blocked.

Derrad waved an arm towards the sentinels in the corridor.

'Quick!' he yelled. 'Before the door bursts!'

The sentinels poured into the room — and not only the sentinels. There was a whole crowd of men and women, carrying clubs and tools and all kinds of implements. The reserves had arrived!

They swung into action like a well-oiled machine. Half a dozen secured the door, leaning into it with their backs, bracing their legs against the floor. When the battering ram struck again, a human wall absorbed the impact. Instead of a booming thud, there was only a dull impotent sound.

Other men and women scattered across the laundry, gathering flatboards and stainless steel benchtops. They collapsed the frames of the flatboards and yanked the benchtops off the benches.

'Drills! Screws!' shouted a voice.

Two women stepped up carrying hand-drills. At the same time one of the benchtops was brought forward and held across the top of the door.

The two women drilled holes through the steel of the benchtop and into the wall behind. Then they screwed in huge twenty-centimetre screws. In no time at all the benchtop was firmly fixed into place.

Then a flatboard was brought forward and the work began again. The flatboard was slid in behind the legs of the human wall and positioned across the bottom of the door.

'We'll reinforce that door until it's thicker than the walls themselves,' said one of the reserves, winking at Beano and Derrad.

Beano and Derrad looked around and found a couple of broken legs from a clothes-press. They wedged them in under the wheels of the cabinet. Then they stood back to watch the work.

But they didn't get long to relax. Suddenly a young boy appeared in the corridor. Panting and breathless, he stuck his head in through the doorway.

'Emergency in the East Wing!' he gasped. 'Guns

needed! They've broken in! Anyone with guns to go to the wardrooms in the East Wing!'

Beano and Derrad looked at each other and set off running.

6

Vail stepped out of the laboratory and looked up and down the corridor. She could hear faint sounds from distant parts of the Big House, sounds of shooting and shouting and fighting.

A girl came running along the corridor. She was about thirteen years old. Her black hair streamed out wildly all around her face.

Vail stood in the middle of the corridor, spreading her arms.

'Stop! Is this the big attack?'

'Yes!' The girl kept running. She veered to go around Vail at the side. 'Can't stop! I'm a messenger!'

Vail moved promptly out of the way, and the girl ran past.

'Have you seen Inspector Brac?' Vail called out after her. 'You know, the Inspector from Central Police?'

The girl looked back over her shoulder. 'In the Old Hall! Where I just came from . . !'

Her voice faded away down the corridor. In another moment she had turned a corner and was gone.

Vail clicked her tongue and went back into the laboratory. When she re-emerged a few moments later, she was carrying her bag in one hand and a thick sheaf of papers in the other. She set off in the direction of the Old Hall.

The distant sounds continued like an ominous approaching tide. But Vail was no longer listening. She was checking over the top sheet on her sheaf of papers. She muttered aloud as she strode along.

'If $C->\int^2$ is greater than $\Omega 10.1$, then the pyractic index transforms into $^a(mn \geq {}_tv\infty i)(^\copyright\approx)$. A *configuratio syntagmatica*.' She nodded to herself. 'Has to be. In which case, the deflectional uptake for the total transmission . . .'

She took a turn to the left and entered the Long Gallery. At the end of the Long Gallery, she turned right into another corridor.

'So apply the Claussen conversion. Given that ß defers μ and μ defers $\triangle$, then the index $-(mn \geq {}_tv\infty i)(^\copyright\approx)$ necessarily falls under the Field Identity Principle. So if the text has the form . . .'

She glanced up, suddenly aware of a thunder of tramping feet. A horde of men and women were bearing down upon her. Four abreast, they filled the corridor from wall to wall. They waved clubs and knives in their hands as they ran. Evidently a group of reserves, moving up to join the fighting.

A Junior Leader at the front gestured Vail to get out of the way. She looked and saw an opening to her left, a passage leading off at the side.

Three quick steps carried her out of the main corridor and away from the horde. She stood waiting in the passage as the reserves pounded past.

The passage was comparatively dark, lit only indirectly from the lighting in the main corridor. It was a cul-de-sac about five metres long, with numerous closed doors on either side. Signs on the doors announced that these were store-rooms for LINEN, MATTRESSES and so on.

The last of the group went by. As the thunder of their feet receded into the distance, Vail took a step back towards the corridor. Then stopped. She could hear whispering.

The whispering came from behind a door at the darkest end of the cul-de-sac. BLANKETS, announced the sign on the door. Why would anyone be whispering in there?

She tiptoed closer. The door was shut but there was a keyhole below the handle. An empty key-less keyhole. Vail bent down and applied her eye.

The room inside was tiny. It was lit by a dim light like the glow of a torch. There were stacks of folded blankets piled up against the walls, all the way from the floor to the ceiling. One grey blanket had been opened out across the floor like a picnic rug.

In her restricted field of vision, Vail could see an assortment of personal possessions set out on the blanket: a container of drink, a towel, a small portabag. But she couldn't see the source of the whispers. The people in the room must be sitting all to one side, out of sight.

She was becoming more and more curious. What sort of people would want to hide away like this? Why weren't they helping in the defence? Were they afraid of the fighting?

She listened to the whispers, trying to make out the words. But only the intonations were distinguishable. There were two older voices, one male and one female. And a number of children's voices, perhaps two or three.

Vail had the idea that the older male voice sounded familiar — even in the unfamiliar form of a whisper. Where had she heard that voice before?

She didn't have to remain wondering for long. The owner of the voice came suddenly into view. He was leaning forward, reaching for the container of drink. Vail almost whistled with surprise.

For only a moment his face was visible. Then he picked up the container and leaned back out of sight once more. But there could be no possible mistake. The face fitted the whisper.

Vail grinned to herself. She abandoned the keyhole and stood upright. She was tempted to throw open the door and burst in upon them. But she resisted the temptation. The revelation could wait. Right now there were more important things to think about.

Still grinning, she turned and tiptoed away. Back down the passage, out into the main corridor. She resumed her march towards the Old Hall.

Headman ev Ghair stabbed a finger at the map.

'Half of the Library reserves to move forward.'

'Only half?'

'What if the killers break through in the main kitchens?'

'They won't break through.' Ev Ghair spoke with complete certainty. 'If we commit our forces too heavily now, there'll be nothing to draw on later. We mustn't lose our nerve. This is only the beginning of the attack, remember.'

He looked around for agreement. Kneeling around the map were six Senior Leaders, two Reeves, two Junior Leaders, and Eddon Brac. There was a general nodding of heads.

The command centre had been set up at the edge of the Old Hall, on the uppermost outermost ring of steps. The skylight windows were dark overhead, but there were small glowing lights in the walls.

The map they were studying was one of several spread out on the ground. It was a general plan of the Big House, showing every room and every doorway. Small labelled markers were arranged to represent the forces of the killers and the forces of the P-19ers.

Ev Ghair called towards the messengers who were waiting in the nearest doorway. A young boy stepped forward.

'Now, Vorl. Go to Yougen in the Outer South Lobby and tell him we're sending up another forty reserves. They'll be approaching via the Training Rooms and the Nursery. Got that?'

The boy's lips moved as he ran through the message in his mind. He nodded.

'Go then.'

The boy flew off.

'I think we'd better send someone in charge of those reserves,' said ev Ghair. 'I want the South Outer Lobby defended at all costs.'

'I'll go,' put in Eddon promptly.

Ev Ghair smiled. 'You want to be involved in the fighting, Inspector Brac? No, I don't think so. Are you the best man for the job? Do you know how to get to the Outer South Lobby by way of the Nursery?'

He looked Eddon straight in the eyes. Eddon could have said that the reserves would show him the way. But somehow the words remained unspoken.

'I know how you feel.' The Headman lowered his voice. In spite of the Leaders and Reeves gathered around, it was as though he were talking to Eddon alone. 'Do you think I don't want to be there in the fighting myself? Don't worry. We'll both be involved soon enough. Believe me, things will get much more desperate than this.'

Eddon nodded. The appeal was irresistible. Under the simple necessities of defence and survival, ev Ghair had recovered his own overpowering simplicity. He was like some hero from an earlier Age of the Hegemony.

'Jerrol?' Ev Ghair turned his gaze upon one of the Junior Leaders. The young man rose to his feet immediately.

'The Outer South Lobby,' murmured Jerrol. 'At all costs.'

In a moment he was gone. The others turned back to the map.

'So. Let's have a look at the situation now,' said ev Ghair.

One of the Reeves had just finished re-labelling a marker. Ev Ghair placed it in position on the map, over an area marked 'Outer South Lobby'.

'Still the same three break-ins,' he said. 'But we're already driving them back from the Pillar Room. We'll clear them out of the Big House completely there. As for the Outer South Lobby —'

'We'll hold on to it now,' said one of the Senior Leaders.

'Yes. And as long as we hold on to it, the killers can't advance further forward into the Big House. All passages go by way of the Lobby, there's no other route. So it's a holding operation. We can't drive them out, but they can't advance. Which leaves the East Wing as the greatest threat.'

Everyone studied the area of the East Wing on the map. Half a dozen green markers represented the forces of the P-19ers, ranged in a concave battlefront; a larger number of red markers represented the forces of the killers.

Ev Ghair ran his finger slowly across the map.

'Here I believe we'll have to proceed to our

extreme option. Explosives. Flatten every room beyond this line. Agreed?'

There was a general nodding of heads.

'Cut off the outer part from the rest of the Big House,' said one of the Senior Leaders,

'Create a barrier of rubble,' added another.

'Maybe destroy a whole force of killers,' added a third. 'If we can catch them in the blast.'

Ev Ghair smiled grimly. 'Destroy a few of them perhaps, Huisin. Set them back for a while. Can you supervise the explosives team?'

'The whole team?'

'No, take half and leave the rest. You'll find them in the Tiled Courtyard.'

'Can you show me the placement again?'

Again ev Ghair ran his finger across the map. He indicated rooms and explained where the explosives were to be placed.

Eddon rose to his feet and stretched. He looked around. Vail had just entered the Old Hall, by a doorway on the opposite side.

She held her bag in one hand and a sheaf of papers in the other. She waved the papers to attract his attention.

Eddon signalled her to wait where she was. He circled around the upper steps to join her.

'I'm getting there,' she said as he approached. 'I've been making major modifications to my theory. I know what I left out before.'

'How about Mairie?' Eddon also spoke in a whisper. 'You talked to her?'

'Better. Someone better than Mairie.'

'Who?'

'I'll tell you later. Right now I need your help.'

Eddon shrugged. 'I'm involved here. The command centre —'

Vail was looking at him with a strange intensity. He stopped in mid-sentence. 'Sure I'll help. What help do you want?'

'You remember what I said I might have to do?'

She didn't need to spell it out. It was there in the grimness of her manner, the heaviness of her voice, the shadow in her eyes.

'You're going to go into that killer's mind.'

'It's the only way I can be sure.'

'Sure of what?'

'I can't say.'

'You know but you can't say?'

'Because it's so unbelievable. I have to be sure.'

'Hmm. So where are you going to do it? In his cell?'

'Yes.'

'And there's some equipment you want me to operate?'

'No, I can do that myself. I need you for afterwards.'

'I don't understand.'

'Afterwards, if I turn into a killer myself. You know. If I get trapped in his mental state.'

'I can bring you back?'

'No. You can destroy me.'

For a moment Eddon couldn't take it in. 'But

how do you —? There must be something...isn't there a way?'

'No, there isn't.' Vail was very quiet and serious. 'I don't want to live on in that state, Eddon Brac. You have to destroy me, like any other killer.'

Eddon swallowed. There was a long silence.

'You'd ask the same from me if it was the other way round,' said Vail. 'You know you would.'

Still Eddon didn't reply.

'Well? Do you promise?'

Eddon cleared his throat. 'I promise,' he said.

Vail leaned suddenly forward and kissed him on the left eyebrow. He jumped back, startled.

'It's agreed then.' She smiled a lopsided sort of grin. 'Now. There's something else I need your help with.'

She put her bag down on the ground and unzipped it. She rummaged inside and pulled out her scan-camera. She handed it across to Eddon.

Eddon stared. 'You want me to take pictures?'

'Electrostatic images.'

'Why can't you —?'

'I'm going down to the killer's cell to set up the memoscopy. It'll take a while. You'll be able to do this while I'm setting up.'

'I think I should come down to the cell with you.'

'You can come later. *Please.* We don't have much time.'

She glanced across at the group around ev Ghair. A new messenger had come in and there was an animated discussion going on. They were talking about 'more explosives', 'kit-bombs', 'additional reserves'.

'I'll show you how the camera works,' she said, picking up her bag. 'Let's just move a bit further away first...'

Beano half supported and half carried Derrad back from the front line. Derrad hobbled along on his one good leg with his arm wrapped over Beano's shoulder. His other leg was gashed above the knee, all the way through to the bone. It had happened during the last attack on their position in the East Wing. The wounded leg was bound around with a tourniquet made from the torn-off sleeve of Beano's vannamak.

The rooms through which they passed were all rigged up with explosives. The furniture had been pushed back from the walls, and kit-bombs and wastemakers had been attached to key points about ten centimetres up from the floor.

In the East Wing Refectory they came upon two members of the explosives team. Both women, they wore loose multi-pocketed jackets bulging with dozens of bombs. They were stooping down low behind the furniture.

One of the women rose to stare at Beano and

Derrad. She had dark-brown short-cropped hair, and a striking hour-glass figure which even her bulging jacket couldn't disguise. She gave Beano an appraising look.

'Where's the medical station?' asked Beano.

'Through that doorway into the Main Lobby. Turn left into the Round Parlour.'

Beano followed her pointing finger. They went through the doorway and across the lobby. Derrad was breathing heavily and his face was grey. He had lost a lot of blood. Beano took a firmer grip on his waist and propelled him into the Round Parlour.

The Round Parlour was literally round in shape, with mirrors set into the walls. A dozen easy-chairs had been assembled in pairs to make sick-beds for the injured. Other bleeding bodies lay sprawled on the floor, reddening the carpet. There was a smell of powerful antiseptics.

Three women moved amongst the injured, administering drugs and fixing dressings. One of the women was Mairie ev Ghair. Her medical satchel was opened out on the carpet, displaying bottles and phials and bandages.

She glanced up and gave Beano a nod of recognition.

'Leave him there,' she said, pointing to a space on the floor. 'I'll be across in a second.'

Beano lowered Derrad gently to the floor. He took off what remained of his vannamak and rolled it up for a pillow. Derrad grunted approval as the pillow slid in under his head.

Then Mairie came across, bringing an elastic tourniquet, a bottle and a swab. She tore the clothing away from Derrad's leg and made a quick inspection.

'Just shock and loss of blood,' she said. 'I'll need you to apply pressure above the wound.'

Beano knelt down and pressed on the main artery in the thigh, where Mairie indicated. Mairie poured antiseptic onto the swab and applied it to the gash.

Derrad jerked once, twice, then lay still. Mairie calmly continued cleaning the wound.

'What's the situation at the front line?' she asked.

'Not good,' Beano admitted. 'The killers have built up shields for themselves. We can't get to shoot them at a distance any more.'

'The attacks are becoming more difficult to fight off?'

'Yeah. I think we're going to be making a withdrawal very soon. The explosives are already in place. I think we're going to pull back our line and blow up a section of the East Wing.'

Mairie finished swabbing. She fastened the elastic tourniquet around Derrad's leg and hauled on the strap to make it tight.

'That'll do,' she said. 'Thank you for your help.'

Beano rose to his feet. 'Bye, Derrad,' he said.

Mairie smiled, also rising. 'He'll be conscious again in a few minutes.'

She moved away to tend someone else on the

other side of the room. Beano turned and headed back the way he'd come.

In the Refectory the two women had finished fixing explosives to the walls. They stood together, talking quietly. Seeing Beano, the woman with the short-cropped hair held up her hand.

'Wait,' she said.

'Why? I've got to get back to my position in the front line.'

'No point. The order will be coming through any moment now.'

Even as she spoke an authoritative voice boomed out:

'FALL BACK! FALL BACK! ALL FORCES TO RETIRE TO FALL-BACK POSITION!'

It was the voice of one of the Senior Leaders, coming from somewhere up near the front line. The order was taken up and re-echoed from voice to voice all along the line.

'FALL BACK! FALL BACK! ALL FORCES TO RETIRE TO FALL-BACK POSITION!'

The two women started running towards the door.

'Back!' they shouted at Beano. 'Clear the way!'

Beano retreated with the two women at his heels. They took up positions on either side of the doorway. Beano was on the same side as the woman with the short-cropped hair.

'This will be the new front line,' she explained. 'When the rooms in front are flattened.'

There was a thunder of pounding feet as the

492

old front line fell back all across the East Wing. People poured through the Refectory, through the doorway and into the Main Lobby. Beano watched them stream past.

Everyone was running, but without panic or shouting. There were sentinels carrying guns and reserves with clubs and knives. There were two young messengers and a Senior Leader — Grion IV Bras. Once in the lobby they began forming up in their groups again. When the lobby became too crowded they moved on into further rooms.

Beano kept a lookout for the men to whom he'd entrusted both his own and Derrad's pommelgun. He felt vulnerable without a weapon. But the two men must have fallen back in another direction.

The woman with the short-cropped hair reached into her jacket pocket and brought out a small control unit with an aerial.

'What's that?' asked Beano.

'Detonator.' She turned to look at him. She had to tilt her head back to meet him eye to eye. 'You're one of the Hegemony people, aren't you? You came with the Inspector and that tall parapsych woman?'

'I'm Flightman Zeno Berrit.'

'I'm the Messages Officer. Ailinh IV Ettray.' She laughed. 'You're all so tall, you Hegemony people. I wish I could be so tall.'

'I think you look fine,' said Beano, and blushed.

Ailinh was about to reply when suddenly another sound arose. It was a wave of screaming, icy-cold and inhuman. The killers were advancing through the now-deserted outer rooms of the East Wing.

Ailinh and Beano peered out around the corner of the door. There was no-one in the Refectory. The P-19ers had all passed through and the killers hadn't yet appeared. The wave of screaming grew louder and louder.

'Any moment now,' whispered Ailinh. 'Cover your head.'

Everywhere in the lobby people were wrapping their arms over their heads. Beano did the same. Ailinh protected her head with one arm: with the other she held out the detonator. She pointed its aerial into the Refectory.

Then the killers appeared. One, two, three of them charged in through the door at the far end of the Refectory. Their mouths were wide open, screaming, streaming strings of thick mucus. They sprang across the room with a horrible bounding energy.

Ailinh squeezed a button on the detonator.

There was a burst of purple-white radiance and an ear-shattering blast of sound. Explosions went off in the Refectory, in rooms beyond the Refectory, in rooms all across the East Wing.

Beano closed his eyes against the light streaming through the open doorway. A moment later, and the light was followed by a blast of fiery hot air.

Then came the rumble of collapsing walls and roofs. All across the East Wing, great sections of building were falling to the ground.

Overhead in the Main Lobby the ceiling shook

but didn't fall. Beano felt flakes and fragments raining down on his arms and hands.

'Perfect!' muttered Ailinh with satisfaction.

Beano opened his eyes and gazed out through the doorway.

There was no Refectory any more — just a wide open expanse of rubble. Twisted chunks of metal, slabs of roofing, fallen iron spires, the shattered dome of a cupola. It was a scene of waste and devastation.

The killers were there too. Caught in the explosions, they had been burnt as if in an oven. Beano could see three of them half buried amid the rubble. One was motionless, the other two moved feeble blackened limbs.

A cheer arose from the P-19ers in the lobby. Now everyone was looking out though the doorway. They cheered and flourished their weapons triumphantly.

'Okay, okay! Don't get carried away!' It was the voice of Senior Leader Grion IV Bras. 'They're only halted for a while! We've got to move fast before they start attacking again!'

The cheering quietened.

'I need a dozen people to go and finish off those killers in the rubble. Everyone else to start work on the new defences. Reinforce the walls, barricade the —'

He stopped in mid-sentence. Cries and shouting came from the Round Parlour next door. And mingled with the human cries, a sound of snarling which was not human.

For one second the people in the Main Lobby froze, listening. Then they rushed towards the doorway. There was a momentary log-jam as a dozen bodies tried to squeeze through simultaneously.

'There he is!'

'Get him!'

Shots were fired as the crowd poured through into the Round Parlour. Everyone was yelling at the tops of their voices.

Beano and Ailinh were at the back of the rush. By the time they squeezed through, the action was almost over.

There was a wild mêlée going on at one side of the room. From the centre of the mêlée came a frenzied snarling. Clubs and knives rose and fell, rose and fell, striking down repeatedly. Then the snarling ceased.

Beano's first thought was for Derrad. He was still lying where he'd been left, with the tourniquet round his leg. He was sprinkled all over with fragments of shattered mirror glass.

Beano crouched down beside him. Derrad winked his eyes and gave a faint grin. Beano breathed a sigh of relief.

'What happened here?' he asked.

'One of the killers. Mairie threw a bottle of antiseptic in his eyes. I guess they've got him now, have they?'

Beano looked across to the side of the room. The knives and clubs were no longer rising and falling.

'I guess they have,' he said.

Derrad was still very weak. He spoke in barely a whisper. 'He must've survived the explosions. It happened so fast, it was like a blur. He came through where the wall collapsed. You can see, over there.'

Beano followed the direction of Derrad's gaze and saw where the wall of the Round Parlour had fallen away. There was a jagged V-shaped gap about a metre wide at the top, narrowing down towards the floor.

Ailinh saw it too. She frowned disapprovingly and went across to inspect. But half-way across she halted.

'Come over here!' she called out. Her voice was low and unsteady, directed towards Beano.

She was standing beside one of the easy-chairs, looking down at something on the floor.

Beano rose and went across. He could see a foot sticking out around the corner of the chair. A terrible foreboding seized hold of him as he approached.

There was a woman lying behind the chair. She lay limp as a rag doll, covered in blood, face flat to the floor.

Beano bent down slowly. He took hold of the body and rolled it over. He hardly needed to see the face to know who it was. But he rolled the body over anyway. The head flopped loosely on the broken neck, the eyes stared up blank and dead.

It was the body of Mairie ev Ghair.

Vail descended the spiral steps to Graem's cell. She opened the door and shone the light of her torch in his face. He looked at her with an indecipherable expression. He was still bound by iron hoops and chains, still sitting upright in his chair.

Down here in the cell it was perfectly quiet and calm. The noise of the fighting failed to penetrate.

Vail strode across and dumped her bag on the table at the side. She took out a syringe and filled it with 20 millilitres of ethobirynol. A massive triple dose: but she needed to render him completely comatose — even catatonic.

The thick white liquid was starting to dribble from his lips as she turned towards him. He followed her with his mad inhuman eyes. When she came up close, he opened his mouth and started to scream. She plunged the needle into the exposed skin at the back of his neck. He didn't try to fight the needle — but just kept on screaming. On and on and on, at an incredibly high pitch. Vail winced and blocked out the sound.

The drug acted quickly. After thirty seconds he stopped screaming; another thirty seconds and his eyes closed over; another thirty seconds again and his whole body hung like a corpse in the chains.

Vail felt for his pulse. It had slowed down to the barest life-supporting minimum.

She began her preparations for the memoscopy, working carefully and methodically. There was no immediate hurry. It would take several minutes for the drug's traumatic toxicity to clear from the system. Until then the electro-chemical traces in the brain would be uninterpretable.

She took the equipment out of her bag: the brain-reading device and the black ergalite box. She opened the spindly brass legs of the device and screwed it into place over the killer's temples. Then she connected up the wires between the device and the box.

She wondered about the memories in his brain. What would she find? She felt sure that she'd be able to re-live his experience empathetically. The only question was afterwards, whether . . .

She shook her head, not wanting to think about it. She averted her eyes from the killer. Better to keep busy as long as possible.

She sat down cross-legged on the floor, with the box beside her. She connected up another set of wires, the wires with the four silvery discs at the ends. She attached the discs to her own head. Then she fiddled with the controls on the box, adjusting the input for a live subject. She couldn't stop her hand from trembling. She fiddled and fiddled, waiting for the minutes to pass. Then she looked at her time-band.

Time to begin. She began to compose herself. She breathed very slowly: in-out, in-out, in-out. The trembling ceased. Still she continued: in-out, in-out, in-out. Slower and slower, calmer and calmer.

Then she touched the switch on the box with one finger. She closed her eyes. She pushed the switch and prepared to enter the mind of a killer.

Now.

At first there was only a chaos of shapes and outlines. Ghostly red shapes, thin black outlines. Nothing fitted together. A million separate shapes and outlines, receding in a dimension of seemingly endless depth. Vail felt as if she were falling, helplessly, with nothing to cling on to.

But she steadied herself. No need to panic. Everything would fit together if she could only find the right vantage-point. She was still too close to her ordinary mode of experience. She had to discover a new position from which to look.

She relaxed and emptied her mind. She used every de-centring technique she knew. She called up her most ingrained assumptions, her data-organising principles, her sense of her own body — she called them up and then cancelled and excluded them. Further and further out she moved, forgetting, dissolving, leaving her own centre behind.

And then it started. The elements began to click together. Outline with shape and shape with outline. Reducing, cohering, simplifying.

She held her consciousness out there in the new position. It was all unbelievably strange and remote. A tautness arose in her throat, a sort of stretching. She cancelled and excluded the sensation.

The elements clicked together to form a room.

A small room, without windows. There was a table at one side and a door straight in front. She saw it in shades of red, light red or dark red, with sheer outlines of black.

Most amazing of all was the clarity. As element after element fell into place, she knew that never before had she seen with such sharpness or purity. Everything appeared in a state of heightened three-dimensionality. The edges of the door and table, the angles and corners of the room were absolutely *structural*, like a diagram. Looking at the outlines was almost like drawing them herself.

For one long minute nothing happened. She studied the room with a sense of complete control. So clear, so clean, so cool. It was a world without affect, perfectly objective and perfectly comprehensible.

It was totally different to anything she had ever known. And yet one part of her mind could interpret it — the Vail ev Vessintor part of her mind. From her own residual point of view, she knew that she was seeing the cell as Graem had been seeing it. In spite of the unrecognisable red shading, the diagrammatic quality, the heightened three-dimensionality, it was the very same room with the same table and door.

But of course it wasn't the room as it existed now, in the present. Graem in his coma was experiencing nothing in the present. The room was in his memories, as he had experienced it in the recent past. But how far back in the past?

Still nothing happened. She wished she could fast-forward to some significant occurrence. But she could only re-live the experience as Graem had experienced it.

Then she heard sounds. Mere elements of sound at first, chaotic and incoherent. She adjusted her mental position, seeking the exact listening point. But this time it was only a small additional adjustment. The sounds soon fell into place, becoming unified and locatable.

The sounds came from outside the room. They had been descending: now they stopped on the other side of the door. Simultaneously a light showed through the cracks around the door.

She experienced a surge of revulsion. There was something on the other side of the door, something associated with feelings of disgust. Sudden emotion soiled the cool clear vision. The structural world was about to be invaded.

Then the door swung open. A creature stood in the doorway: tumescent, moist, organic. The warmth and smell of it tainted the air. It was monstrous! An abomination!

It shone the light directly onto her face. But she could see through the light. She watched the swelling of its flesh, the throbbing of its organs, the pumping of its fluids. It was all touch, texture, inwardness! How could such a creature exist? How could this horror live?

But the other, residual part of her mind already knew the answer. If it was the same room and table and door, if the memories were recent, before the ethobirynol, then —

The shining light was from her own torch!

It had to be. The memories she was re-living went back to only a few minutes ago. When she had come down the steps and entered the cell. In which case —

She herself was the creature, the monster, the abomination!

She wanted to be sick. She wanted to reach out and turn off the switch on the black box. But she had no idea where the black box was, or even where her own hand was. The experience of the killer's memories completely drowned out any sensory awareness of her present location.

She felt as though she were being pulled in two. One part of her mind knew that the image of herself in the red room was the product of a warped nightmare, an insanity. But the other part of her mind saw how disgusting and hideous the creature was — saw it with the force of an overwhelming revelation. Both visions were complete and undeniable. But the experience of disgust was more immediate.

She watched as the creature walked across the room and deposited something on the table. It had its back turned towards her.

How could she think of that *thing* as herself? That filth, that slime, that body? It was so alien, so utterly *other.* It was impossible that she could ever have had anything to do with it!

If only she could move — attack — destroy! The creature was an offence, a blasphemy. It was abnormal and unacceptable, it was *wrong*. It could not be allowed to exist! The feeling of revulsion turned into an ice-cold rage.

She could see very clearly what needed to be done. The thing had to be erased and obliterated. She wanted to rend and pound and pulverise it, to reduce it to absolute nothingness. The world had to be cleansed of its presence. But she couldn't move.

Instead the creature moved: swung round and advanced towards her. Its flesh heaved, its organs slopped, its skin slithered. Thick soft flesh and fatty skin and wet lumpish organs. It was unspeakably palpable!

It lifted one hand. There was something made of glass in its hand.

My syringe! The thought came through suddenly from the residual part of her mind. That's *my syringe* I'm looking at!

Its syringe, the nightmare insisted. The creature is holding *its* syringe in *its* hand.

Closer and closer the creature came. It was going to touch. Its hand was going to touch! As if in close-up she saw the wriggling veins and pulsing blood in its hand. Every loathsome liquid cell stirring and flexing, preparing for contact.

And still the residual part of her mind struggled against the vision. My hand — its hand — closer and closer — approaching — the thing — me — the *thing* —

The oscillations grew more and more extreme. Her mind was flying apart.

Closer and closer, the horror and filth. Its rotten breath, the sickening warmth of its tissues —

A scream burst forth from her throat. A scream of pure disgust and horror. Screaming, screaming, screaming, screaming!

And at the same time, further in the distance, were the sounds of other screams. Other minds responding. Her own scream echoed and re-echoed, resonated out across a whole network...

10

Eddon came hurrying down the winding steps. Under his arm he held what looked like a bundled-up vannamak. The door of the cell stood open.

'I got the photoscans!' he called out. 'You haven't started, have you?'

He swung in through the door and halted abruptly. The cell was lit by the light from Vail's torch, next to her bag on the table. Graem sat slumped in his chair with the spindly brass device fixed over his temples. And Vail —

Eddon's heart missed a beat. Vail lay on her side in a semi-foetal position on the floor. Completely motionless. She had her arms crooked in front of her and her hands up over her face. He stared at the four wires leading to the four silvery discs on her head.

He uttered a sort of strangled sound. He dropped the bundle he had been carrying and flung himself down on his knees. One by one he ripped the discs away from her head.

'What? What have you done?' He hardly knew what he was saying. 'Why the hell did you start without me?'

Still motionless. He pulled her hands away from her face. Her make-up was a smudgy mess, with red-black smears all over her cheeks.

He held his fingers in front of her mouth and nostrils, feeling for any faint stirring of breath.

'Nothing,' he muttered. 'Oh damn you! You fool! You shit! You stupid bloody —'

'Phoo!' said Vail. 'Swearing won't bring me back.'

Eddon goggled at her with a foolish uncertain expression. She opened one eye and looked up at him.

'Hullo! Take your smelly hand away from my face.'

Eddon seemed incapable of understanding the words. Vail reached up and pushed his hand away.

'Why?' he demanded at last. 'Why were you like that?'

'I was meditating. Working out my final conclusions.'

'Goddamn you! I thought you were dead!'

'No.'

'Then what the —?'

'It's no good getting angry, Eddon Brac.' Vail grinned. 'I can see the wetness around your eyes.'

506

'Like hell you can.'

'Okay, have it your own way. I was never going to *die*. Did you forget? The danger was I'd become a killer myself.'

'Hnh.' Eddon was half-scowling, half-smiling.

'I nearly did. If I hadn't managed to turn the switch off...' She pointed towards the black ergalite box. 'I nearly lost connection with myself completely.'

She rolled over and sat up.

'Hah! My greatest feat ever! No other parapsych in the entire galaxy could've gone in and come back from there!' She preened her long greeny-black hair. 'Sheer natural talent! God, I'm good!'

Eddon snorted and rose to his feet. 'And you got what you wanted?'

'Sure did! The final confirmation. Now all I need are those photoscans you took.'

Eddon gathered up the bundle he'd dropped before. He unrolled the vannamak. There inside was Vail's scan-camera.

Vail stretched and stood up. Eddon handed her the camera. She clicked a button and ejected the photoscan cartridge. Then she delved into her bag and brought out her plastoplex developer. She inserted the cartridge and twiddled a dial on the developer. Finally she put the developer back in her bag.

'It'll be ready in five minutes,' she said. 'Let's go.'

'Go where?'

'To the Old Hall. With one important stop on the way.'

'Don't you want to see what's on the photo-scans first?'

'I *know* what's on the photoscans.'

'You've got everything totally worked out?'

'Totally, absolutely, completely!'

'So what's the answer? What's your solution?'

Vail grinned. 'I'll explain it as we go! Come on!'

She picked up her bag and torch. Graem still hung slack and inert in his chains. On the floor lay the discarded memoscopy equipment.

She walked towards the open door, shining the light of the torch ahead. Eddon followed behind.

'Tell me,' she said, as they began to climb the spiral steps. 'Were you really upset when you saw me there on the floor?'

Beano and Ailinh entered the Old Hall carrying the body of Mairie ev Ghair. Mairie's arms hung down at the sides and her steely-grey hair trailed almost to the floor. Beano held the body under the shoulders while Ailinh supported the feet.

The men and women of the central command group were kneeling in a circle around the operations map. But one by one they looked up and saw the grim sight approaching. One by one they fell silent. Argid ev Ghair was the last to realise. He turned around only when Beano and Ailinh came to a halt behind him.

Then he rose to his feet, very slowly. Everyone else was deathly still, frozen in mid-movement. It was as though they were bracing themselves for a storm.

'She's —' began Beano.

'I can see for myself what she is!' Ev Ghair's voice was not loud but it came out with extraordinary force. 'You don't have to tell me what she is!'

He stood looking down at the broken, bloodstained body. He reached forward and touched her hair very softly. Then he stooped and caught hold of her hand. He lifted and gripped it with a sudden fierce intensity.

He was taut and trembling like stretched elastic. He stared at her sightless eyes as if trying to read some message in them. One minute, two minutes went past.

'Shall we put her down?' asked Ailinh at last.

Ev Ghair let the hand fall.

'Yes. Put her down.'

He turned to the men and women of the command centre.

'Continue organising the defence. Create another reserve for the East Wing. Work out how to do it. I rely on you.'

He spoke firmly and sternly. The furrowed patch on the side of his face was as white as a scar. He turned to Beano and Ailinh, who had now lowered Mairie to the ground.

'Cover her up,' he ordered.

Then back again to the command centre:

'Hand me my staff.'

Someone handed him his black staff. He took it in his withered left hand and moved off down the steps. He moved like an old man, all of ninety-five years old. His left shoulder was tilted at a crooked angle, his left foot dragged heavily over the edge of each step.

Everyone watched him go. He was heading down towards the pulpit, towards the massive pillar in the centre of the amphitheatre. A dozen times he seemed about to slip and fall. But he didn't.

He reached the bottom level and shuffled across to the pulpit. A sound came from him like a deep wrenching sob. He stood at the foot of the iron staircase which spiralled up around the pillar. With a sudden lurch he sat down on the lowest step of the stairs.

Immediately the men and women of the command centre turned back to the business of organising the defence. They discussed ways of reinforcing the sentinels on the roof of the South Facade, they summoned a messenger to carry instructions. But there was something forced and unnatural about the manner of their discussion. It was obvious that their minds were only half focussed on the task.

Ailinh looked at the body of Mairie ev Ghair.

'How do we cover her up?' she whispered.

Beano shrugged. They couldn't cover the body with Ailinh's jacket, which still bulged with several unused explosives in the pockets. And Beano's own vannamak had been left as a pillow for Derrad . . .

But it was a problem they didn't have to solve. Suddenly they realised that ev Ghair was signalling to them, beckoning them to come down.

'Does he mean us?'

'Must be.'

'He wants us to go down?'

'I think so.'

They descended the steps to the centre of the Old Hall. As they approached they could see that ev Ghair's face was streaming with tears.

'Tell me how she died,' he said.

Beano and Ailinh stood side by side in front of him. They explained how the killer had broken through into the Round Parlour, how Mairie had thrown antiseptic into his eyes, how they had discovered her lying dead behind the chair. Ev Ghair listened with his head lowered.

'It would have been a quick and painless death,' Beano concluded lamely.

'It was an *honourable* death,' said ev Ghair, looking up. 'She died as she lived. She was the most *honourable* person I have ever known.'

He spoke in a strong, steady voice, even while the tears streamed faster and faster down his face. He was like two different personalities in the same body. He stared at the black metal staff held horizontally over his knee.

'Ah, there's no-one like her, not any more. There never was, not even fifty years ago. Mairie, my Mairie.'

Beano and Ailinh said nothing. There was nothing to say.

'Do you know, when I first met her, I was the Headman and leader of the planet, I was the hero of the Breakaway.' He said it as a simple statement of fact, with no hint of boasting. 'And she was a young girl just eighteen years old. But she looked me straight in the eye, so calmly, so serenely, with such dignity. I shall always remember it, that amazing natural dignity. Fifty years ago.'

He was pressing down on the staff across his knee, pressing down so hard that the staff began to bend. He was not even aware of doing it. A muffled sort of sob rose up out of him, out of his chest.

'If only she could have been with me at the end. I know we're all doomed, I know we can't hold out against the killers forever. But I wish she could have been with me, I wish I could have said to her . . .'

Suddenly he realised what he was doing to his staff. He had bent it almost into a right angle. He shook his head as if rousing himself.

The voices of the men and women of the command centre drifted down from the upper steps of the Old Hall. Again ev Ghair shook his head.

'And now I don't even have time to grieve for her. I shall have to go back up to the command centre.'

'Give yourself time,' said Ailinh gently. 'No-one expects you to go back up straight away. Don't force yourself.'

'No, no-one expects it,' said ev Ghair, glancing up towards the command centre. 'But they need it. They're distracted by me being down here. They need me to give them focus and belief, to keep their spirits up.'

'You can't take responsibility for everything,' said Ailinh. 'You can't do the impossible.'

'Ah, but I can. It's what I've always done.' Ev Ghair turned a piercing look upon her. 'You don't understand, do you?'

Ailinh didn't know how to respond. Ev Ghair's mouth curved in a strange sorrowful smile.

'It's not easy to explain. You see, I'm not an ordinary person.' Again he uttered it as a simple statement of fact. 'There's nothing, absolutely nothing I can't make myself do. If I decide that the impossible has to be done, then I do it. I have a power of will in me that's capable of overriding every instinct, every fear or feeling. My body and nerves might be screaming to stop — it makes no difference. I'm unstoppable. I feel *in myself* that I'm unstoppable. You've heard the stories about the battles in the Breakaway?'

Ailinh nodded, and Beano too.

'I gained a reputation then, a reputation for superhuman bravery. But believe me, it might've been superhuman but it wasn't bravery. It never felt like courage to me. It was like a power to override my fear of dying. I knew what had to be done, and I willed myself into doing it. It was a matter of priorities.'

'Jaralax said you led some of the attacks without even a weapon,' Beano put in.

'Because it was needed. We had to have a

symbol, a symbol to announce that we could achieve the impossible. I decided to become that symbol.'

'That's why everyone followed you,' said Ailinh. 'I still think it's a kind of courage.'

'Is it? Or is it only a kind of abnormality? A twisted state of the brain? I don't think you'd want too many people like me around. It's a dangerous power, to be able to wield yourself like a blade. Having so much will and control. I've sometimes thought, with this power I could have been a conqueror, a tyrant, a monster. I could have been as mad as those killers we're fighting. I could have been a terrible force for evil.'

Again the strange sorrowful smile flickered over his face.

'But I'm not. I'm a P-19er. And we don't think like that on planet P-19.'

He rotated the staff over his knee and gripped hold of it with both hands. He applied more and more pressure, slowly bending it back to its original shape. He kept on pressing until the angle was completely straightened out.

'And now I must go back up to the command centre,' he said.

He grasped the pommel of his staff and rose from his seat on the metal staircase. Beano and Ailinh turned to follow.

But even as they prepared to re-ascend the steps, there was a sudden commotion above. It was Vail, striding dramatically into the Old Hall, calling out at the top of her voice.

'Where's ev Ghair? I've got the solution for him! The total solution!'

Ev Ghair rapped loudly with his staff on the floor. 'Here I am.'

Vail came down the steps swinging her bag. Her make-up looked like the aftermath of a long night on the town.

The men and women of the command centre had stopped talking about strategy. They rose from their maps and stood listening. Further behind stood half a dozen young messengers who had crept in from the doorway. They too wanted to hear the revelation.

Vail reached the bottom level of the amphitheatre. She dumped her bag on the ground in front of ev Ghair.

'So what have you got for us?' he growled. 'A new theory about this CURSE?'

'Mmm-yeah.' Vail gave a slinky mysterious look.

She bent down over her bag. Her hair fell forward in a long greeny-black cascade. She unzipped the bag and took out a sheaf of papers.

'Exhibit Number One,' she announced.

She passed the topmost sheet from the sheaf across to ev Ghair. He held it in his hand, not looking at it.

'I was mostly right before,' she said. 'The code for

this CURSE *is* carried on the planet's electro-magnetic field waves, it *has* accumulated over many many years, and it *does* work by overruling natural organic codes in plants and human beings. But what I didn't do was follow through on the exact pyractic configurations of the code. I established equivalences between configurations, but I didn't notice the oddity in the configurations themselves.'

She jabbed a finger at a line of figures on the paper that ev Ghair was holding. Ev Ghair frowned and looked down.

'That's the crucial bit. The pyractic index is actually a *configuratio syntagmatica*. Therefore it falls under the Field Identity Principle. But if it falls under the Field Identity Principle, it clearly contradicts the Fourth Equation of Psychic Instantiation.'

'That's impossible,' said ev Ghair.

'Yes. Two alternative states of existence at the same time.'

'So what does it mean?'

'It means I underestimated this CURSE. I knew that it was incredibly complex and powerful. But I never guessed it was so totally new and different. It seems to be a sort of living CURSE.'

'Living?'

'I believe the codes are in some sense *thinking themselves.* They're not just transmissions — there's a kind of qualitative consciousness involved. That's why we hear those nightmare sounds in the air. And why we saw those colours coming down from the sky. I believe the patterns in the code are

516

realising themselves as objective ideas, as nightmares outside of any one individual mind.'

'Hmm.' Ev Ghair was now scrutinising the figures on the paper very closely. 'You haven't proved that here.'

'No, it's only a belief. I can't prove it because there's no known form of mathematics to explain what happens when the Field Identity Principle is in contradiction with the Fourth Equation of Psychic Instantiation. The paradox goes beyond our mathematical understanding. But I believe that's what's happening.'

'If we can't understand it, how does that help us?'

'The very fact that it goes beyond our mathematical understanding is a sort of clue in itself.'

'Is it? Then what do we do about it? Are we still looking for a transmitter that someone has planted? Do we still destroy the CURSE by destroying the transmitter?'

'Yes.'

'And your new theory can locate this transmitter?'

'No.'

'No?' Ev Ghair's voice turned into a low threatening rumble. 'Then what...'

'The new theory can't locate it,' said Vail airily. 'But I can.'

'You can? Where?'

'Wait. You see, I have other clues to go on too.'

She looked up towards one of the four doorways of the Old Hall, on the opposite side to the command centre.

'Bring forward Exhibit Number Two!' she called out.

Everyone stared. Two figures appeared in the doorway. One was Eddon Brac. The other was a P-19er, a middle-aged man with bangles on his arms and the triangular badge of a Senior Leader on his chest. He held his head down low, hiding his face. But he couldn't avoid recognition for long.

'It's Masilin!'

'Masilin III Crouth!'

'The runaway!'

'I thought he was out on the steppes!'

Masilin's wrists were tied behind his back with a length of whipperwire. Eddon propelled him forward with a hand on his shoulder.

Ev Ghair turned to Vail. 'Where did you find him?'

'In the blankets storeroom near the Long Gallery. The whole family was hiding there. They must've joined in with the refugees and slipped back into the Big House without being noticed.'

'You didn't find Wyvis and Oaves?'

'Just Masilin and family.' She gestured to Eddon. 'Bring him down!' she called out.

Eddon pushed Masilin forward down the steps.

'He's one of your clues?' asked ev Ghair.

Vail nodded. 'What we're looking for is the traitor within.'

'A traitor? Masilin? But he only tried to steal a spacecraft and escape from the planet. Are you saying he's an agent for the Hegemony?'

'We'll see. I want to interrogate him under hypnosis.'

From the opposite side of the Old Hall, the men and women of the command centre began to descend the steps. Behind them, trying not to be noticed, came the young messengers. Everyone wanted to see the unmasking of Masilin.

'Are you saying Masilin is the one who planted the transmitter?' ev Ghair demanded. 'When? Why? How could he have obtained the transmitter? I hope you've got very strong evidence for this!'

Vail said nothing. She bent down over her bag and began to dig out various items of equipment.

Eddon and Masilin arrived at the lowest level of the Old Hall. Masilin kept his eyes sullenly on the floor, refusing to meet ev Ghair's piercing gaze.

Ev Ghair shook his head. 'I don't believe it. I won't believe it. What could they have offered you, Masilin? How could they have made contact you? Tell me it's not true.'

'Don't question him please,' said Vail, over her shoulder. 'Everything will come out under hypnosis.'

By now there was a crowd of twenty people gathered in a circle at the bottom of the steps. Vail set out her globe-like luminator and the control-box for regulating the luminator. She wired them up and plugged them in.

Then she turned to Eddon. 'Okay. Sit him down in a relaxed position.'

Eddon directed Masilin forward to the pulpit. He moved sluggishly but without resistance. Eddon made him sit on the ground with his back leaning against the side of the pulpit.

'Good.' Vail nodded. 'Now, everyone has to be very quiet and very still. I'm going to start chanting to begin the hypnosis.'

She stood in front of Masilin with the control-box in her hand. She flipped a switch and ripples of light pulsed out around the luminator. On-off, on-off, on-off.

'It would help if I had someone else chanting along with me,' she said. She turned to ev Ghair. 'You've got the right sort of voice.'

Ev Ghair frowned. 'What do I have to do?'

'Come and stand beside me. Repeat the syllables of the chant exactly as I say them. At exactly the same speed. Concentrate your thoughts and let the syllables of the chant become the only thing in your mind. Focus your eyes on one single spot. The badge on his chest, for example.'

'Very well.' Ev Ghair shifted across to stand beside her.

She touched a knob on the control-box and the ripples of light altered their rhythm. She began to chant in a drawling monotone, very slow and eerie.

'Munnnn. Daaaaa.

Immm. Vaaaaa.

Munnnn. Daaaaaa.

Immm. Vaaaaa.'

Ev Ghair joined in with his deep bass voice.

'Munnnn. Daaaaaa.

Immm. Vaaaaa.

Munnnn. Daaaaa.
Immm. Vaaaaa.'

Over and over they repeated the chant, more and more slowly. Vail adjusted the knob on the control-box and slowed down the pulsing of the luminator. There was no sound other than the syllables of the chant, no movement other than the moving ripples of light.

'*Munnnn. Daaaaa.*
Immm. Vaaaaa.'

Slower and slower, until time itself seemed to have come to a stop. Masilin's eyelids drooped and his head tipped sideways.

But still Vail continued the chant, endlessly insistent. Now even ev Ghair was faltering. His voice faded away as if into some remote distance.

Beano craned forward and eyed Masilin closely.

'It's okay,' he whispered. 'He's completely under.'

But someone else was completely under, too. There was a soft swishing sound as ev Ghair crumpled suddenly at the knees and collapsed.

Eddon caught him from behind and lowered him carefully to the floor.

There were cries of surprise.

'You've gone and hypnotised our Headman too!'
'Wake him up!'

'Is he okay?'

'Shh!' Vail put her finger to her lips. 'He's just the way I want him.'

Eddon held ev Ghair in a sitting position, supporting him from behind.

'This isn't a mistake,' he explained to the crowd of puzzled faces. 'Argid ev Ghair is the one we want to question under hypnosis.'

'Not Masilin?'

'No. Masilin has nothing to do with the CURSE.'

There were shocked looks and shakings of heads all around. But Vail paid no attention. She sat down on the floor, cross-legged. She took up a position just to the left of ev Ghair. His eyes were closed.

'Argid ev Ghair,' she began in her slow drawling voice. 'Listen to my words. Exclude everything except the sound of my words.'

The mutterings of the crowd died away. Their curiosity was stronger than their disapproval. And it was somehow very difficult to speak over the top of Vail's soft drawl.

'Now my words are in your mind. They are taking you back in time. Back, back, back. They are going to reawaken memories long forgotten. Memories that have almost disappeared.'

The light from the luminator continued to pulse at a constant rate: on-off, on-off, on-off.

'Back to the time when you were twenty-three years old. Back to the 10th of the 4th, 588. The day when the scientists negotiated with the Proctor-

General. You were one of those scientists, Argid ev Ghair. Remember the negotiations in Steyne-1, after the old Governor had been replaced. Do you remember?'

'Yes.' Ev Ghair's voice sounded hollow, almost sepulchral.

'There are many memories for that day. I want you to overleap the time of the negotiations. Come to the evening of the same day. Think of that evening, Argid ev Ghair. What images appear? What are you doing?'

There was a long silence. Ev Ghair's eyes were still closed, his face as expressionless as a mask.

'Walking,' he murmured at last.

'Walking where?'

'Past the Illerman Tower. It is dark and drizzling with rain. The lights from the towers shine on the walkways.'

'What are your thoughts? What are your feelings?'

'I feel anger. Intense anger.'

'Why?'

'I don't know.'

'Is it because the other scientists have negotiated an agreement with the Hegemony?'

'Yes. That is why. I shouted at them before I walked out. They betrayed the cause. They gave up on the rebellion. The P-19ers have been left to fight on alone.'

He paused, then resumed in the same hollow tone.

'I look back up at the Van Hass Units. Noises and music. They are celebrating the peace agreement. I make a vow.'

'What vow? That you'll never abandon the cause of the rebellion?'

'Yes. Never abandon. Never. I pass by the storage depot and the warehouses. There's no-one around in the rain. I come out from amongst the buildings and start walking along the road.'

'Where are you walking?'

'Away from Steyne-1.'

'Where to?'

'To the spaceport.'

'Why?'

'I don't know.'

'You have a plan?'

'Yes.'

'What is it?'

'I don't know.'

A kind of wincing shiver ran across his face as he spoke. His eyelids fluttered.

'Relax,' said Vail, making her voice even more slow and soothing. 'Concentrate on my words. Relax and be calm, Argid ev Ghair. Let's go on a little further. A little later. What do you see now? Where are you?'

Ev Ghair's eyelids stopped fluttering.

'Dials,' he murmured. 'Red and green lights. Control panels. Flight cabin.'

'The flight cabin of a spacecraft.'

'Yes.'

'What spacecraft?'

'On the spaceport. One of the old Governor's first wave attack fleet. Five of them still sitting on the spaceport.'

'And you're preparing to take off?'

'Keys inserted. Screens on. Systems checked. Leave ignition to the last possible moment.'

'You know how to fly this spacecraft?'

'Any spacecraft. Scientific training.'

'How did you get hold of the keys?'

'From the flightman's room in the control tower. I knew where.'

'What about the navigation beams? Are they set?'

'I turned them on in the control tower. Already set. I'm ready to blast off.'

'Where?'

'Away from planet P-19.'

'In what direction?'

'I don't remember.'

'But you have a plan. What are you planning to do?'

'I don't know. I don't remember.'

Again the wincing shudder, like a stab of pain. Again the fluttering of the eyelids.

'My words are penetrating deeper into your mind. Think deeper, Argid ev Ghair. Think into the depths of this memory.'

Another shudder. Ev Ghair's breathing became more shallow and more rapid.

'Where are you going, Argid ev Ghair? What are you planning —?'

But before she could say another word there was a sudden violent interruption. Junior Leader Jaralax rushed into the Old Hall waving his arms and yelling at the top of his voice:

'Killers on the roofs! Killers on the roofs!'

He came to a bewildered halt at the top of the steps. He stared down at the crowd at the bottom of the amphitheatre.

'Where's the command centre? What are you doing down there? Didn't you hear? The killers have climbed onto the roofs! The defence is breaking down!!!'

Ev Ghair's breathing changed again. He opened his eyes and blinked.

14

Jaralax came running down the steps. The circle parted to let him in. When he saw ev Ghair he was even more bewildered.

'What is it? Is he sick?'

Ev Ghair frowned and focussed his eyes.

'Of course I'm not sick, Jaralax IV Fallender. I heard you shouting. What were you shouting about?'

'The killers have climbed up onto the roofs. They're above the East Wing, advancing towards the centre. Our line can't hold them back. I came myself to get reinforcements. It's desperate.'

Ev Ghair didn't waste a second.

'Duisha. Heiska. Garvie.' He pointed to three of the young messengers. 'Run to the West Wing. The South Facade. All along the Storerooms. Everyone with any kind of gun is to move up onto the roofs. We want fifty extra guns reinforcing that line. Go!'

He clapped his hands. Duisha, Heiska and Garvie spun on their heels and ran off.

'The worst possible development.' Ev Ghair shook his head. 'We have to have guns on the roofs. No other weapons would be any use. But we'll need to make up for the loss of guns on the ground. This may take the last of our reserves.' He looked around. 'Where's the map?'

No-one answered. He looked around again, and a slow realisation dawned over his face.

'What are we doing down here? Why am I sitting on the floor like this?'

Vail stood up. She switched off the luminator. 'You were telling us about some things that happened in the past,' she said.

'I was?'

'About a time during the Breakaway. The day when the scientists negotiated to switch sides and join the Hegemony. And the evening of the same day, when you slipped away and stole a spacecraft from the spaceport.'

'Slipped away and stole a spacecraft . . . So I did. Yes, I remember now.' Ev Ghair knitted his brows. 'But why was I telling you that?'

'You were hypnotised!' one of the Senior Leaders burst out. 'She hypnotised you!'

'WHA-A-A-T??'

'I needed to find out some information from you,' said Vail.

Ev Ghair's roar turned into a question.

'Find out what?'

'I didn't exactly find it out.'

The Headman's face darkened, his muscles clenched. He was in a state of fury. But with a visible effort of will he brought himself under control.

'If I had time . . .' he growled. 'But the defence is more urgent. You've wasted enough of my time already.'

He rose to his feet. Someone handed him his staff. He fixed Vail with his eyes and crashed the point of his staff on the ground.

'Keep out of my sight! I don't want to see you again! Understood?'

Vail blanched and took a pace backwards. She couldn't help it.

Ev Ghair turned to the circle of faces gathered around.

'Messengers — back to your positions! Command centre — back to the maps! AT ONCE!'

Leaning heavily on his staff, he led the way back up the steps. The men and women of the command centre fell in behind him.

'Stop!' cried Vail, recovering her voice. 'Ev Ghair, you did reveal one piece of information under hypnosis!'

The men and women of the command centre faltered momentarily. But ev Ghair never paused.

Vail summoned up all her psychic power, focussed with all her skill and training. Rigid with intensity, she addressed ev Ghair's retreating back.

'STOP!' she ordered.

Ev Ghair stopped. He turned and glared. Vail pointed an accusing finger at him.

'You told us that you took off in the spacecraft on the evening after the negotiations between the scientists and the Proctor-General. No delay. The evening of the very same day.'

'Well?' His voice was like low threatening thunder.

'The day of the negotiations was 10–4–588.'

'Well?'

'And the day you joined the P-19er forces in the Eigessy Basin was 24–4–588. The day still cele-brated every year on this planet: the 24th of the 4th. There's a gap of two weeks!'

There was a murmur from the people on the steps as the significance of Vail's words sank in.

'Argid ev Ghair, what happened in the two weeks between the time you took off and the time you joined the P-19ers in the Eigessy Basin?'

The look on ev Ghair's face had changed dra-matically. He pursed his lips. Now he appeared troubled and thoughtful.

Vail lowered her finger and continued.

'When you walked into the Eigessy Basin, the dawn was behind you. Therefore you approached from the east. From the uninhabited lands further east. That was where your spacecraft had landed, wasn't it?'

Ev Ghair nodded slowly. He seemed to be having difficulty remembering.

'How far to the east?'

'I'm not sure.'

'A long way?'

'I don't think so. I think I'd been walking for a few hours.'

'I don't think so either. Say an overnight walk. That still leaves thirteen whole days unaccounted for.'

'I must have been in the spacecraft all that time.'

'Just flying around in space?'

'I didn't land anywhere. I don't have any memory of landing anywhere.'

'But something happened to you in that time. Carreck I Fallender told me. Jaralax's great-grandfather. He remembered you as a young scientist before the rebellion ever began. And he remembered how you'd changed when you walked into the P-19er camp in the Eigessy Basin. You know what I mean, don't you?'

Ev Ghair reached up with his withered left hand and touched the patch of withered skin on the side of his face. 'You mean this. This — paralysis.'

'Yes. Your paralysis. How did it happen?'

'I don't know. But you're right about the time. I must've suffered some kind of a stroke. Perhaps I blanked out, perhaps I was unconscious for most of those thirteen days, just circling round and round the planet. That would explain why I don't seem to remember anything.'

'Except that it wasn't a stroke.'

'It wasn't?'

'I'll show you. Time for Exhibit Number Three!'

She delved into her bag and drew out a roll of photographic transparencies. There were six of them: green-tinted, fifteen by twenty centimetres. She unfurled and smoothed them out.

'These are electrostatic images, Argid ev Ghair. Interior photoscans of your cerebral cortex.'

'I took them,' put in Eddon. 'I stood right behind you when you were bending over the map. I had the camera hidden inside a vannamak.'

Ev Ghair came back down the steps to the lowest level of the Old Hall. The men and women of the command centre followed. Vail handed one transparency to ev Ghair and distributed the remainder to other eager hands.

'Hold them up against the light,' she advised.

Everyone tried to squeeze in for a look. Those with the transparencies angled them up against the light, squinting at the green-tinted images.

'There's a dark spot on one side,' said ev Ghair. 'What is it?'

'That,' said Vail, 'is the traitor within. The traitor within and the source of your paralysis.'

'I don't understand.'

'That part of your brain has been taken out of ordinary action. The dark spot is blocking off the neurones governing your left hand and leg and the left side of your face. It's like a stroke that destroys a part of the brain — except that it isn't a stroke.'

'Then what is it?'

'An implant.'

'You mean some sort of solid object?'

'Not exactly. What's been implanted is a pattern. Using the natural organo-chemistry of the cerebrum, but removing it from ordinary functioning.'

'Hmm. And why is it so dark?'

'Because the pattern is incredibly dense. Ordinary synaptic connections in the brain use only a fraction of the brain's potential. This pattern is a million times more complex.'

There was a long silence.

'I think I'm beginning to get the idea,' ev Ghair said slowly. 'This incredibly complex pattern — this is what you've been talking about all along?'

'Yes.'

'This is the text? This is the transmitter?'

'Yes.'

There were sounds of sharply indrawn breath from a dozen throats.

'Yes,' repeated Vail. 'We went out searching for it, while you were carrying it around in your skull all the time.'

'But I thought . . . ?' It was Beano who expressed the general amazement. 'I mean, we were searching for something so big!'

'My mistake,' admitted Vail. 'I said it couldn't be smaller than a large suitcase because I was thinking in terms of manufactured components. I never thought of the synaptic potential of the human brain. Even the most highly inscribed silicon chip can't begin to match the information-carrying capacity of the human brain.'

'And the brain's own tiny electrical differentials are enough to transmit the code.' Ev Ghair nodded to himself. 'Because the code only has to be imprinted on top of existing electro-magnetic field-waves.'

'Exactly.'

'But what known technology could do such implanting?'

'No technology that *we* know,' said Vail.

Ev Ghair stared hard at her. Then a momentary spasm of pain ran across his face.

'I think I can guess,' he said.

Vail shook her head. 'We need more than that. We need the definite truth. I'd like to hypnotise you again. With your full cooperation this time.'

'My cooperation makes a difference?'

'Yes. If you can make yourself willing. Then we can get down to the deepest buried memories in your unconscious.'

'This missing thirteen days?'

'Yes.'

'So be it. I shall make myself willing.'

Once again the luminator was turned on and adjusted. Masilin was moved from his position leaning against the pulpit and ev Ghair took his place. Vail sat down alongside and began chanting.

Distant sounds of fighting could be heard outside: gunfire and shooting and feet running on the roofs. There were nervous looks on several faces. But everyone kept their attention focussed upon ev Ghair.

Vail continued her chanting longer than ever before. Ev Ghair went limp after barely a minute. But still she continued, on and on. His chin sank forward onto his chest.

'Argid ev Ghair,' she said at last. 'Relax and be calm. Listen to my words. We're going to return to the memory you were remembering before. Do you know the memory I mean?'

'In the spacecraft.' Ev Ghair seemed to speak almost without opening his mouth. 'Taking off from the spaceport.'

'Yes. And you do take off, don't you? Off and away from planet P-19?'

'Yes. Out into empty space.'

'Tell me what you see, out in empty space. Look around and describe it.'

Ev Ghair's head rotated slowly. He seemed to be staring first one way and then the other. But his eyes remained shut all the time.

'Quiet and dark in the flight cabin,' he murmured. 'The sunshield covers the view-screens on one side. Cutting out the radiation from the Walder-J sun. On the other side I can see stars. Millions and millions of stars.'

'And straight in front?'

There was no response.

'Look straight in front of you, Argid ev Ghair. Look where you're heading towards. How many stars?'

'No stars. There's a patch straight in front without any stars.'

'What is that patch, Argid ev Ghair? Where are you heading towards?'

A sudden spasm ran down the side of his body. 'Towards the Anti-Human,' he said.

Vail nodded. 'And why are you heading towards the Anti-Human?'

'To make an alliance. Get help for the rebel forces.'

'You believe the Anti-Human will be on your side?'

'The old Governor was preparing an attack on the Anti-Human. We stopped the attack by our uprising. I thought if I told them...'

'They'll help you against the Hegemony?'

'Yes. It's the only hope.'

'You must be very desperate?'

'Yes.'

'So you travel on and on. The light from the Walder-J sun fades away. The dark patch grows larger in the sky. Look at it, Argid ev Ghair. What does it look like now?'

'A web.'

'What sort of web?'

'Strange angles. Strung out across millions of miles of space. Like wires, like lines of darkness.'

'And this would be about three days after taking off?'

'I don't know. I feel very heavy, very weary. There's something wrong about the angles of the web. Out of true. Impossible Sharp.'

'Causing your feeling of heaviness and weariness?'

'It's like a weight, a pressure. Pushing me down in my seat. I feel as though I'll never be able to move or get up ever again. It's so sad and depressing. Everywhere I look is this terrible weight of intricate meanings. And I can't make sense of any of them.'

'Do you think about turning back?'

'It's too late. I don't know what else to do. I'm starting to pass in amongst the lines. Lines behind lines behind lines. Crisscrossing over and above the spacecraft.'

'Can you see what they are now?'

'No. They're not anything. Shadows. Huge dark things. Falling this way and that. Endlessly long. So dreary and dismal, so solemn . . .'

'So you just keep on going?'

'I don't seem to hit them. I can't avoid them but I don't seem to hit them. My mind feels very strange. I don't know if I'm asleep or awake. Drifting and drowsing.'

'Then what happens?'

'Nothing.'

'Nothing?'

'There's no-one to make contact with. No place to land. Only these crisscross shadow things. I keep on flying until I turn around and come back out again.'

'You reverse the direction of the spacecraft?'

'I don't remember. I just come back out and I'm on the way home to P-19.'

'But your journey through open space would take no more than three and a half days. Seven days there and back. What happened during the other six days?'

A muscle in ev Ghair's forehead began to twitch. He spoke lopsidedly, with his mouth askew:

'Nothing happened. Drifting and drowsing.'

'But there's something else,' Vail insisted. 'Perhaps it doesn't seem like a true memory. Perhaps it's in a different compartment of your mind, like something that never really happened. But it's associated with this period. It's connected to what you've just been remembering.'

She reached out a hand and took a grip over his shoulder. She pressed two fingers against the nape of his neck. Sweat was running down her face, leaving tracks of black and purple make-up.

'Listen to my words, Argid ev Ghair. My words are drawing you on, like a thin silvery strand. They're leading you across the association. We're crossing over towards the other memory, the one that seems as if it never happened. My words have found it, haven't they? Can you feel them touching its surfaces? Penetrating through its surfaces? And now starting to open it out? What do you see opening out?'

'I dreamed it spoke to me,' said ev Ghair.

'It?'

'The Anti-Human.'

'When?'

'The spacecraft has stopped. Suspended in space in the web.'

'Go on.'

'Something came to me. I dreamed it in my seat in the flight cabin. My eyes are closed all the time.'

'Do you hear voices in the dream?'

'Not voices, no. Meanings in my head. As though I've already heard and understood. It's the thinking of the Anti-Human. Totally different. Laid out spatially, knowing everything all at once. I think my own thinking back in reply.'

'In reply to what?'

'A deal. An exchange being offered.'

'Go on.'

'They show me what will happen if I agree. The Hegemony troops being driven back in chaos, because we've disrupted their Distance Control Telearchics. The Proctor-General forced to sign the final peace and withdraw his forces from the planet. Independent P-19: a true community. Building a better world, an example to the entire galaxy.'

'You *see* all this?'

'Not in images. Like a diagram. Everything is crystal clear. Infallible.'

'Ah, they must have been working from the information in your mind,' murmured Vail. 'Communicating with you and drawing information from you at the same time.'

538

'The Anti-Human will give me the power to defeat the Hegemony. The P-19 cause will triumph with their assistance.'

'And the other side of the deal?'

Ev Ghair made no response.

'Argid ev Ghair. This is a deal, an exchange. They give something to you. What do they get in return?'

'I don't know. It's nothing important.'

'Something for nothing?'

'I can't remember. It's not clear.'

'Even though everything is crystal clear?'

'Yes. No. It's clear and not clear. I can't...'

Vail lifted her fingers away from the nape of his neck.

'It doesn't matter,' she said. 'You've told us enough. I think we can work out the rest.'

She rose to her feet. She moved across to the control-box and switched off the luminator.

'Argid ev Ghair,' she addressed him again. 'I'm going to wake you up. When you wake up, you will remember every detail of what you've told us. The memories you had forgotten will be transferred and incorporated into your conscious mind. You will remember what happened and you will remember it as really happening. Do you understand?'

'Yes.'

'I shall count slowly back from 10. When I reach the number 1 you will be fully awake and returned to normal consciousness.

'10 . . . 9 . . . 8 . . . My words are withdrawing

from your mind, retreating outside, no longer inside your head.

'7 ... 6 ... 5 ... You hear me speak to you as a separate person. You are in the Old Hall leaning against the side of the pulpit.

'4 ... 3 ... 2 ... Sensations return to your arms and legs. You are about to wake up.

'1.'

Ev Ghair opened his eyes. He stared at everyone standing in a circle around him. He blinked.

Then he clutched convulsively at his skull and a cry of agony burst from his lips.

The cry sank back to a moan, burst forth in another harrowing cry, then subsided to a moan again. Jaralax and Beano stepped forward to help, but Vail shook her head. Ev Ghair squeezed and kneaded at his skull.

Jaralax turned to Vail.

'But he couldn't have agreed,' he protested. 'If he'd made the deal, why didn't the Anti-Human send any assistance? There was no assistance. We won the war by ourselves.'

'They sent Argid ev Ghair,' said Vail. 'They put the power to win in *him*.'

'In him?'

'In his mind. They reconfigured and improved his mind. They gave him an invincible will to win.

His resolution, his courage, his cunning, his strategy, his inventiveness — all his abilities heightened and improved by the technology of the Anti-Human. That was what they gave him.'

'Oh.' Jaralax chewed thoughtfully at his moustache. 'And what did he give them?'

'He gave them access to his mind. So that they could carry out their improvements. Almost nothing — no price to pay at all. But while they were there, they did something else as well.'

'The implant.'

'Yes. During those six days, while his spacecraft hung motionless in the web. They improved his mental powers by altering his brain, just as they'd promised. But at the same time they inserted a thing of their own. An implant that was unknown to his mind even though it was a part of his brain.'

One of the Senior Leaders stepped forward. 'You're certain about this?'

'Yes. I'll show you. Where are those photoscans again?'

The six transparencies had circulated around the crowd. Now they were mostly in the hands of the young messengers. At Vail's request, all six were promptly held out towards her. She bent over the nearest transparency, steadied it, and pointed with one finger.

'Look very closely at the dark spot in the brain. Look at it around the edges. Can you see those strange sharp angles? The darkness actually has the form of a very tightly woven web.'

Everyone clustered around the transparencies, craning and squinting, trying to get a look.

'I see it!'

'Horrible!'

'What does it mean?'

'It means,' said Vail, 'that the implant itself is in the form of the Anti-Human.'

'Ah-aaahh!' Another tortured cry burst from ev Ghair. His left eye was now completely closed over. He seemed to be trying to hold himself very still, as though even the tiniest movement would worsen the agony.

'Why does it hurt?' he whispered. 'Why this pain now?'

'Because you've become conscious of the foreign element in your brain,' said Vail softly. 'When your mind didn't know it was there, there was no clash. But now your consciousness has located the place and recognised the alien signals being sent out.'

'I can feel the exact place,' whispered ev Ghair. 'Just behind my left eye.'

'That's where it is, yes. But there are no sensory receptors in the brain. What you feel is by way of your mind, psychically.'

Ev Ghair shuddered and ground his teeth.

Vail watched in pity. 'Your mind can't stop struggling to exclude the foreign element. That's the cause of the pain — your conscious mind's own urge to nullify and quarantine the alien signals. It's like an electrical war going on inside your brain.'

Again and again ev Ghair shuddered, as pang

after pang passed through him. He leaned his head forward between his knees, pressing clenched fists against his skull. He seemed to be trying to burrow away from the pain.

Beano shook his head. 'Why do they want to do this?'

'What? Who?'

'The Anti-Human. What have they got against P-19ers? Don't they know that the P-19ers never wanted to attack them?'

Vail shrugged. 'They don't need a particular reason. It's a much deeper antagonism than that. They hate *all* human beings. They hate the very nature and existence of human beings.'

'Why?'

'Because we disgust and horrify them. Our bodies are utterly repulsive to them.'

'Repulsive?'

'You can't imagine how repulsive. Believe me, I know. I've experienced it myself.'

Everyone stared at her. Vail flicked her hair.

'I had to be sure where the killers' state of mind comes from. I had to be sure it was something more than *human* madness. So I entered the mind of Graem V Craill. One of the killers, that we've got chained up down below.'

She shivered at the memory.

'Try to understand. When someone turns into a killer, it's because they've been taken over by an alien way of thinking and seeing. The killers are still in their own human bodies, but they're not aware of their own human bodies. And when they look at *other* human bodies, they see them exactly the same as the Anti-Human would see them.'

She paused and checked herself.

'Okay, maybe not exactly the same. I suppose the Anti-Human must have something different to our five senses. But human sense-data get translated into Anti-Human terms in the killers' minds. So they see organic flesh as red wet slop, slimy organs, blood, fattiness — I can't explain it. To them, living human bodies are an abomination. Sickening mess and filth.'

'Which explains why the killers typically smash or slice or mutilate their victims,' put in Eddon. 'They don't just want to kill human beings, they want to destroy the very flesh of them.'

'Also it explains their screaming,' said Vail. 'Because the mere sight of our bodies is so loathsome to them. They frighten us, but we're like monsters to them. They scream out of sheer horror.'

'But what about the Anti-Human?' demanded Jaralax. 'Are you saying they don't have bodies?'

'Exactly. Their form of consciousness has no biological basis. They're grounded on pure structure. Argid ev Ghair didn't meet anyone out there because there was no-one — in our sense — to meet. But he saw the physical manifestation of the Anti-Human.'

'The web?'

'Yes. The web itself. That's the only kind of body they have.'

The P-19ers stared wide-eyed. They were having difficulty taking it all in.

'It's an unbelievably different mode of existence,' continued Vail. 'I shouldn't even be talking about "they" and "them" in the plural. Did you notice how ev Ghair sometimes used the singular? "I dreamed it spoke to me" he said.'

'So there's only one of them?'

'Not that either. They exist both as many minds and as a single mind. Our notion of separate centres of consciousness housed in separate bodies doesn't apply to them. They share a sort of common consciousness — singular and plural at the same time. I've experienced that, too.'

The P-19ers waited to be told. They were beyond asking questions.

'I experienced it in Graem V Craill's state of mind. Just for a moment. I had a sense of echoes reaching out across mind after mind after mind, making contact with all the other killers on this planet. Like a resonating network, a common consciousness. I cut off in a hurry when it started to happen.'

'So that's how the killers can share one another's experiences,' said Eddon, nodding. 'That's why Graem seemed to remember committing murders he hadn't really committed at all.'

'Yeah. And that's why they can act together without ever having to speak to each other. There's a sort of super-mind existing not *in* but *between* their individual minds.'

'Like you said before,' murmured Beano. 'Ideas

thinking themselves outside of anyone's mind. A living CURSE.'

'You've got it. My original concept of the CURSE was inadequate because I was thinking in terms of human psychic propensities. My information from the psychoseminary was in terms of individual human minds. But the contradiction in the mathematics — where the pyractic index falls simultaneously under the Field Identity Principle and the Fourth Equation of Psychic Instantiation — that contradiction points to something beyond our human-based standards. In Anti-Human terms, it *is* possible to be in two alternative states of existence — to be both *one* and *many* at the same time. But it would take an Anti-Human mathematics to work it out.'

Ev Ghair lifted his head from between his knees. He seemed to want to say something. But a spasm of pain distorted his face and mouth. All that came out was a slurring twisted groan.

'But if there's an Anti-Human kind of mind building up on P-19 . . . ?' Beano looked puzzled.

'The Anti-Human are trying to spread their kind of mind,' said Vail 'That's what it implies. We have to re-think our reading of the situation. The fact that the killers kill ordinary human beings is only a side-effect. Colonisation is the primary goal in the Anti-Human plan.'

'It's —' Again ev Ghair was trying to speak, fighting against the pain. He whispered out of the corner of his mouth. 'My fault.'

'Yes.' Vail looked at him very gravely. 'You let them in. You opened the way.'

Ev Ghair stiffened and clenched his jaw. The veins stood out on his forehead. Slowly he struggled to push himself up from the floor. Slowly, very slowly, sliding his back up against the side of the pulpit.

Everyone watched in horrified silence. His mouth was drawn back around his teeth like a wild animal. Tears of pain ran down from his open right eye. But finally he stood upright, leaning against the pulpit. He held himself very still and rigid.

'And this thing in my mind,' he whispered. 'This is the source and centre of it all?'

'Yes. The hub of their common consciousness.'

Ev Ghair was staggering under successive spasms of pain. But he spoke on regardless. 'How I've been fooled! What a joke! What a mockery!'

His whisper rose to a sort of gasping cry.

'I thought I was helping to build our Independent P-19! I thought I was doing so much good! And all the time I was undermining us, destroying us, helping to conquer us! I was working to someone else's plan all the time!'

'Yes,' Vail agreed. 'Even your remarkable achievements were due to the powers they gave you. Everything you did for this planet was because of the improvements they made in your mind.'

Ev Ghair's cry turned into an outright howl.

'Everything was them! Them! Them! Them! I was nothing!'

He was trembling, twitching like a puppet as the

spasms of pain jerked him this way and that. Only the pulpit behind his back kept him from falling.

But even as he howled, there came a sudden succession of sounds directly overhead, directly above the Old Hall. First shouting and snarling and pounding feet. Then cries and blows and the dull thump of something hitting the metal roof. Then a sound of crunching and scrunching, repeated half a dozen times.

Everyone looked up at the ceiling of the Old Hall. The shouting had stopped but the snarling continued. The snarling of two separate voices — two killers on the roof.

Then the footsteps started to move again, more slowly now. They were heading across the roof towards the skylight windows. Every head in the Old Hall turned to follow their passage, every eye stared in the direction of the skylight windows.

There was a sudden smash. Glass shattered and fell inwards, cascading in slow motion through the air. Two faces appeared in a hole in the glass.

Two killers. Their mouths hung wide open, drooling long strings of creamy-white mucus. An inhuman intensity shone in their eyes.

Seeing the group of men and women down below, they began to scream. Scream after scream poured out of them like water, terrible and cold and unearthly.

Ev Ghair stepped forward from the pulpit, swaying unsteadily on his feet. Something about their screaming seemed to drive him into a rage. He clasped his head in both hands and bellowed wordlessly at the top of his voice.

The P-19ers turned to one another in despair. They shouted to make themselves heard above the din.

'The defence has collapsed!'

'They've overrun the roofs!'

'There's no stopping them now!'

Ev Ghair stopped bellowing. 'I can stop them!!' he cried.

He wheeled around and struck his head violently against the side of the pulpit.

'Destroy the transmitter and destroy the CURSE!' He looked towards Vail. 'That's what you said? ISN'T THAT WHAT YOU SAID?'

'Yes. It still applies.'

Ev Ghair lined himself up against the pulpit and swung his head forward with all his might. There was another sickening smash as flesh and bone met solid stone. His head rebounded from the impact.

He took a grip on the back of his skull and drove it forward as if propelling a ball. Again and again: smash and rebound, smash and rebound.

And yet, incredibly, he was still standing, still conscious. His white hair was red with blood, streaming down where the skin had burst.

'I can do it!' he thundered. 'I will do it!'

He backed off for another lunge.

'Stop!' cried Vail. 'Wait!'

Ev Ghair paused.

She pointed. 'Look at them!'

The faces of the killers were still visible, looking down through the broken skylight. But they were no longer screaming. Their mouths were closed and their eyes had gone blank and glassy. They seemed to be gazing vacantly off into space.

Jaralax was the first to speak. 'What's happened to them? Has he shattered the implant?'

'No.' Vail was very definite. 'The implant can't be so easily destroyed. Remember, it's woven in the living texture of the brain.'

Ev Ghair stared up at the killers. There was a strange expression on his face, part agony, part triumph. His mouth was twisted and racked with agony — and yet it seemed that he was smiling.

'I'm in control!!' he exulted. 'I'm nullifying it!!'

He uttered a half-demented sound, somewhere between a laugh and a wail. He spun around to face Vail.

'You said my conscious mind was trying to nullify the alien signals! That's what I'm doing! I can feel it! I'm holding it in!'

Vail shook her head incredulously.

'Hrrahhh!!' He threw back his head and roared. 'So I'm not so mere and weak as they thought! I'm not their creature after all!'

'Is it possible?' asked Eddon, turning to Vail.

550

'I don't know.' Vail looked again at the killers, then back at ev Ghair. 'I can't think of any other explanation. Perhaps the sheer force of his rage . . !'

'Because I'm accepting this pain!' cried ev Ghair. 'I'm willing it! Not avoiding it! I *want* this pain!'

Vail shrugged and muttered to herself. 'If the brainwaves from the conscious mind can temporarily override the alien signals . . '

'My conscious mind is fighting — that's what the pain means! My conscious mind is winning!'

Vail frowned.

'Only temporarily,' she told him. 'There's a limit to how long you'll be able to maintain control.'

'Long enough!' he said in a quieter voice. 'Long enough for what I'm going to do.'

Again he smiled his twisted grimacing smile. On the left side of his face, the patch of furrowed skin had turned ominously dark.

'The Anti-Human improved my mind and strengthened my will. But my mind is still me, my will is still my own. I'm in charge of these powers! And I choose to turn them against the Anti-Human!'

His body was quivering, almost vibrating, as if on a leash. But there were no more spasms. He raised his gaze to the broken skylight and shook his fist. The killers hadn't moved. They seemed to have fallen asleep with their eyes open.

'I defy the Anti-Human! As once I defied the Hegemony — so now I defy the Anti-Human! I've been used, I've been a tool — no more! I'll prove what a human being can do! I know the way to show them! Let them see what *we* can do!'

'But the thing in your brain,' said Vail. 'The implant has to be destroyed.'

'Therefore I have to be destroyed!' cried ev Ghair. 'I know, I understand that. But I'm not going to die like a dog in a corner!'

He looked around the encircling crowd of faces, one by one. He stared at Jaralax, at the Senior Leaders, at the young messengers.

'Seventy years ago,' he said, 'I made myself into a symbol. You all know the stories — how I went into battle with no weapon, completely unarmed. I was the living proof of our unconquerable faith in ourselves. To show everyone that we could never be defeated — not even by the mighty Hegemony. So now I'm going to make myself into a symbol again.'

He fixed his stare on Beano.

'Flightman Zeno Berrit. I shall need your spacecraft for my last journey. And Ailinh IV Ettray.' He focussed on Ailinh. 'I see you still have some explosives in that jacket of yours?'

'Four kit-bombs and a wastemaker,' answered Ailinh, patting her bulging pockets.

Ev Ghair turned to Vail. 'I think that should be enough, don't you?'

Vail nodded.

'Why?' Ailinh knitted her brows. 'You're going to blow yourself up?'

'Of course. You heard what she said. I have to

be destroyed. Take off your jacket and fasten it around my neck.'

Ailinh looked unhappy, but she took off her jacket. She pulled the small control-unit with the aerial out of one of the pockets. She extended the aerial and handed it across to him.

'There's the detonator,' she said.

'Thank you.'

She moved around behind him and looped the jacket over his shoulders, so that the bulging pockets sat up high on his chest and the sleeves wrapped round at the back of his neck. There were tears in her eyes. She began tying the sleeves together.

'Why my spacecraft?' demanded Beano. 'What final journey where?'

Ev Ghair laughed a wild, humourless laugh.

'Back to the web! Where else? Back to the Anti-Human! I'm going to return this implant to those who sent it! And when I get there —'

He pointed the aerial of the detonator towards himself.

'When I get there, I'm going to blow their little present to kingdom come!'

Vail looked thoughtful.

'You'll have to stay awake,' she said. 'Three and a half days. If you fall asleep, the alien signals will be able to escape your controlling consciousness.'

'With this much pain,' said ev Ghair, 'staying awake will not be difficult.'

Ailinh stepped back. She had finished tying the

sleeves. Ev Ghair turned his one good eye upon Beano.

'I shall need you to come out to the spaceport with me,' he said. 'So that you can set the navigation beams. And tell me anything I don't know about the instrumentation in your spacecraft.'

Jaralax bristled. 'What about the rest of us?'

'No. No-one else to come.'

'But you'll need an armed force to guard you. To get you past the killers.'

'I don't think so. Listen.'

They listened. A strange silence reigned. It was not only the two killers in the skylight who had stopped their screaming. Even in the distance, there were no screams anywhere.

Vail clapped her hands.

'Yes. He's right. The centre has been taken out of their common consciousness. Nullifying the alien signals has disoriented them.'

'They won't attack,' said ev Ghair. 'I can feel it.'

He propelled himself forward. It was as though he had to fight against his own limbs to make them work. His left leg was rigid and unbending like solid wood, his left foot dragging behind him over the floor.

The circle of P-19ers parted to let him through. Someone picked up his staff and held it out to him. But he didn't even notice.

Slowly, clumsily, he began to ascend the steps. Beano followed and caught him up.

'Lean on me,' said Beano.

Ev Ghair nodded and hooked his left arm over Beano's shoulder. For a moment Beano almost staggered under the weight. Then he recovered and bore up. Side by side they continued to ascend the steps.

As if in a spell, the P-19ers watched their progress from below. There were red stains down the back of ev Ghair's tunic, caused by the bleeding from his head. He still gripped the detonator in his right hand.

At the top of the steps was the broken body of Mairie ev Ghair. She lay where Beano and Ailinh had left her, like a small forgotten bundle of clothing on the ground. Ev Ghair knelt down beside her.

He murmured as if speaking, but there were no clear words. He bent forward and kissed her very gently on the forehead, three times. Then he rose again to his feet. Beano had to help to haul him upright.

They moved on towards the doorway. But just before the doorway ev Ghair halted and turned around.

His face was hardly recognisable, so terribly had pain distorted his features. The patch of furrowed skin was now almost black.

He stood there, visibly struggling with every ounce of his willpower. With a superhuman effort he forced his closed left eye to open up again. He looked down at the people in the centre of the Old Hall.

'I shall send a message to the Anti-Human!' he cried. 'A message from all of us!'

Then he turned once more, swinging Beano back around with him. They went out through the doorway.

18

Their footsteps faded away down the corridor, always with the sound of one foot dragging along behind. Still no-one said a word. It was Eddon who finally broke the silence.

'Will it be okay?' he asked Vail. 'Do you believe he can do it?'

'He can do it,' said Vail. 'Do you think I'd let him walk off with that thing in his brain if I wasn't totally sure? He'll remain in control for three and a half days, then he'll explode the bombs. I'm as sure as if I had my own finger on the detonator.'

The P-19ers turned to one another and began discussing what had happened. There was an air of numbed shock in their voices. They seemed too stunned to rejoice in their deliverance.

After a while a young messenger came rushing into the Old Hall.

'The fighting's stopped on the East Wing!' he announced. 'The killers have gone drowsy and dopey! They aren't attacking any more!'

In the next five minutes another three messengers came bearing similar news.

Then a fifth messenger arrived, a young girl

with a frizz of black curls. She called down from the top of the steps:

'We've just seen our Headman walking out across the main square! Him and another man. They were heading towards the M-rail. Junior Leader Joram says to ask what to do?'

'Nothing,' said Vail. 'Did the killers leave them alone?'

'The killers aren't around any more. Not on the main square. Junior Leader Joram says they must have shifted their direction of attack.'

There was a whoop and a laugh from the centre of the Old Hall. The P-19ers looked at one another with a sudden new hope in their eyes. Now the mood was beginning to change. They really had been reprieved! It was true! They *could* believe it!

'How long by M-rail to the spaceport?' asked Vail. 'About ten minutes?'

'Yes.'

'And then another five or ten minutes to set the navigation beams,' added Eddon.

'Let's go and watch the take-off!' someone called out.

'Let's go up on the roofs,' said Vail.

'The roofs! The roofs!' cried several voices at once. The excitement was catching on. Most excited of all were the group of young messengers who'd been present in the Old Hall throughout.

Everyone seemed to expect Eddon and Vail to lead the way. They walked in front, with the others following behind.

They left the Old Hall by the southern doorway and marched along a long curving corridor. Then they cut through the Library and along another corridor. Everywhere the same stillness and quiet. They went past the Music Room and entered the gallery.

Vail pointed to the iron staircase at the end of the gallery.

'You remember coming here once before?' she asked Eddon. 'When you were up on the roofs with ev Ghair? And I came along afterwards with Mairie?'

'Yeah.' Eddon pulled a face. 'I remember explaining to ev Ghair how people were going insane because of metal toxins in their food and drink.'

Vail flashed him a brilliant pearly-toothed smile.

They went up the iron staircase and came to the trapdoor leading out onto the roofs. Eddon and Vail unbolted the trapdoor and heaved it open.

'Listen!' said Vail.

'I don't hear anything.'

'Exactly.'

'No sounds in the sky!'

It was true. There were no disembodied singings or moanings, no tollings or chantings, no thuddings or gurglings.

'Those sounds were manifestations of the super-mind,' said Vail. 'The killers' common consciousness. Ev Ghair nullified the super-mind when he nullified its centre in his brain.'

'It's still dark though.'

Vail nodded. 'That's more of a physical effect. It'll be a while before the sunlight gets back to normal.'

They came up through the trapdoor like a gaggle of gawping tourists. It was colder than ever outside. They zipped up zippers and turned up collars and hoods. Gazing all around they walked out onto the walkways.

The killers were not immediately visible in the darkness. But they were still there — only not standing upright. They lay scattered in the concavities of the roofs, slumped in the shadows. They moved their limbs unceasingly in slow, vague writhing movements. They looked like beached fish floundering out of water.

Two sentinels approached from a nearby walkway.

'What's going on?' they shouted. 'What's happened to the killers?'

'They're finished!' answered Vail. 'The CURSE is over!'

'Should we still shoot them?'

'Not necessary.' Vail shook her head. 'They might even recover eventually.'

'What? Become normal again?'

'It's a possibility. I don't know.'

Eddon and Vail headed in the direction of the lookout where they had once stood with Argid ev Ghair. They zigzagged from walkway to walkway, swerving around turrets and domes and pinnacles. The two sentinels joined in and followed along.

Eddon and Vail stopped and leaned against the handrail at the end of the final walkway. They gazed out from the edge of the roofs. The P-19ers squeezed in behind, all pressing forward for a look.

It was too dark to see very far. They looked down upon the nearby streets: smashed houses, litter and wreckage, broken roofs.

'So much destruction,' lamented one voice.

'We'll rebuild!' said Jaralax fiercely. 'Better than ever!'

The spaceport was shrouded in darkness, as were all the outer areas of Steyne-2. But Vail stared in the direction of the spaceport, where she remembered it from before.

'They're probably there by now,' she said. 'Won't be much longer.'

The gathering at the lookout had been observed by other sentinels on the roofs. One by one they came across to talk and question. The story of what had happened was repeated to each newcomer, over and over again.

Eddon turned to Vail. 'This message that ev Ghair thinks he's sending. What do you reckon? Will it have any effect on the Anti-Human?'

Vail shrugged. 'It might. It might make them think twice.'

'But it won't stop them?'

'No. They'll always want to destroy us. I have the feeling that this is only the start.'

'The start of a war?'

'A psychic war. Across the entire Galaxy.'

Eddon sucked his breath in through his teeth. 'God help us.'

'Mmm-yeah. How many patches are there now? Of the Anti-Human?'

'Thirty-two the last I heard. And more appearing all the time. The galaxy is totally encircled. And if they all have these incredible powers and superior technologies — how can we hope to defeat them?'

'Maybe that's what ev Ghair's message was about. Not to them but to us.'

'True.' Eddon grinned. 'And we defeated them this time, didn't we?' He grinned again. 'Or at least, *you* defeated them. I guess you're going to be a very important person when we get back to Central. All the top people will be wanting you to explain your theories and —'

He broke off. Far away a small flare of bright purple light had appeared in the darkness. There was a gasp from the crowd.

The violet light radiated outwards. Now the spacecraft itself was illuminated, tall and silvery and tubular, poised on its nest of fire.

Sound too: a distant rising whine. The metal grid on which the spacecraft stood was starting to glow an incandescent red. Plumes of white steam rose up all around. The whine intensified.

For a moment the spacecraft was once more hidden, submerged in a cloud of steam. But only for a moment. Then its front probe emerged above the cloud, sliding slowly upwards.

Higher and higher it rose. Now the full length of the fuselage was visible. Faster and faster, lifting away. The flare from the tail had changed from violet to white, pouring down in a long thin beam.

'He's off!'

'He's done it!'

The crowd broke into ragged cheering.

'Three and a half days,' said Vail. 'Then he destroys himself. Himself, his brain, and the thing in his brain.'

The cheering died away, to be replaced by a kind of solemn awe.

They watched as the spacecraft climbed through the sky on its pencil beam of light. Soon only the beam was visible, dwindling into the darkness overhead. Tinier and tinier, more and more remote.

They continued staring at the place long after the last pinprick of light had vanished.

Vail looked at Eddon, leaning on the handrail beside her. She leaned a fraction closer.

'You realise we don't have a spacecraft now? It'll be ages before we can get back to Central.'

'We'll have to send a message,' said Eddon. 'Ask for another spacecraft to come and collect us.'

'It'll take two months just to get here.'

'Yeah. Two months.'

'Long time. Could be boring. We'll have to find ways to keep amused.'

Eddon grinned. 'Got anything in mind?'

'Oh, I don't know.' She rested her elbows on the

handrail and her chin on her hands. 'Pity you were wrong in your hypotheses. Such a great prize I offered.'

'What was it again? One night of sensational sex with Vail ev Vessintor?'

'Mmm. But you didn't win it.'

'Yeah, I was wrong. But *you* were right.'

'Meaning?'

'I reckon there has to be a prize for you too.'

'Ah. A prize for me. Don't tell me. Could it be ... one night of sex with Inspector Brac?'

Eddon snapped his fingers. '*Sex*? What happened to the word "sensational"?'

'Huh!' Vail sniffed loudly. 'First prize — one night of sex with Inspector Brac. Second prize — two nights of sex with Inspector Brac.'

'Huh!' Eddon sniffed back even more loudly. 'You should be so lucky. No, I can't award you first or second prize. You got several things wrong on your first attempt.'

'I was still more right than you.'

'Yeah? Well, maybe you just about qualify for third prize.'

'Third prize?'

'Maybe.'

'Don't tell me,' said Vail laughing. 'Let me try and guess.'

Eddon and Vail's adventure continues . . .

As Eddon and Vail return to the Centre with information about the Anti-Human, their spacecraft is hijacked by a gang of brutal marauders. While Eddon is trapped in frozen cryo-sleep, Vail must try to fight off their ferocious lusts.

But something worse than brutal is stalking the marauders themselves; some cold ritualistic murderer is killing them one by one. So Vail makes a deal: she'll use her special skills to discover the murderer if they'll promise to guarantee her safety.

But what kind of a murderer is she dealing with? Will the marauders keep their promise? And what is it they are planning to do with Eddon?

COMING SOON FROM PAN MACMILLAN